BECOMING ISRAELIS

BECOMING ISRAELIS

Political Resocialization of
Soviet and American Immigrants

Zvi Gitelman

PRAEGER SPECIAL STUDIES • PRAEGER SCIENTIFIC

Library of Congress Cataloging in Publication Data
Gitelman, Zvi Y.
        Becoming Israelis.

        Includes bibilographical references and
index.
        1. Jews, Russian—Israel.   2. Jews,
American—Israel.   3. Israel—Emigration and
immigration.   I. Title.
DS113.8.R87G57   304.8'47'05694   82-634
ISBN 0-03-061374-4   AACR2

Published in 1982 by Praeger Publishers
CBS Educational and Professional Publishing
a Division of CBS Inc.
521 Fifth Avenue, New York, New York 10175 U.S.A.

© 1982 by Praeger Publishers

23456789 052 987654321

Printed in the United States of America

TO MARLENE

And I scattered them among the nations, and they were dispersed through the countries. . . . But I had pity for my holy name, which the house of Israel had profaned among the nations where they had gone. Therefore . . . I do this not for your sake, O house of Israel, but for my holy name. . . . I will sanctify my great name. . . . And will take you from among the nations and bring you to your own land. And I will sprinkle pure water on you and you shall be cleansed from all your uncleanliness and all your idols. . . . And I shall give you a new heart and a new spirit, and I shall remove the heart of stone from your flesh and shall give you a heart of flesh. And I will put my spirit among you . . . and you shall dwell in the land I gave to your fathers.

Ezekiel, Chapter 36

Caelum, non animum, mutant qui trans mare corrunt. (Those who run across the seas change the skies, but not the soul.)

Horace, quoted by Alan Richardson, "A Theory and a Method for the Psychological Study of Assimilation," *International Migration Review* 2, no. 1 (Fall 1967).

One main factor in the upward trend of animal life has been the power of wandering. . . . Animals wander into new conditions. They have to adapt themselves or die. . . . When man ceases to wander, he will cease to ascend in the scale of being. . . . A diversification among human communities is essential for the provision of the incentive and material for the Odyssey of the human spirit.

Alfred North Whitehead, quoted in Donald Taft and Richard Robbins, *International Migrations* (New York: Ronald Press, 1955).

I think it is fitting to answer those who address inquiries to me because they wish to live in the Holy Land. For it is necessary to know, and to give information, as to what this land is really like.

Many, many vicissitudes, experiences, and fates befall every single man who comes to this land, until he adjust to it, has joy in its stones, and loves its dust, until the ruins in the Land of Israel are dearer to him than a palace abroad, and dry bread in that place dearer than all delicacies elsewhere. But this does not happen in one day nor in two, not in a month, and not in a year. Many a year passes before the days of his initiation are over, his initiation into the true life. . . . Everyone who desires to go to the Land of Holiness must be born anew, requires a new infancy, childhood, and youth until he beholds the land face to face, until his soul is bound up with that of the land.

And that is how it is. He who comes and brings with him his knowledge, whatever he has attained according to his degree — does not adjust in the beginning. His mind is bewildered, he is cast hither and yon without finding repose or security, he climbs up to very heaven and sinks into abysses, like a ship that is tossed about on the seas, and he troubles others with his concerns and actions. . . . Until God shows him the face of the land, and then he will arrive at rest and peace.

This is something that cannot be definitely gauged: the length of time, how much, and when — with each individual, all these matters depend on his affairs, actions, capacity, and attitude. Therefore let everyone who ardently wishes to enter the Holy Land consider all these things, and examine himself as to whether he has the strength to surmount everything, lest he lose even what he had up to this time. . . . If a person makes himself good and ready, he will overcome everything, doing what he ought to do and following the advice of those who know.

Rabbi Abraham of Kaliska, Report from Tiberias, 1790s, transl. in *Forum* (Jerusalem), no. 2 (1976).

ACKNOWLEDGMENTS

Writing this book entailed several transoceanic relocations, library and field research in several languages, and some complicated logistic and bureaucratic arrangements. These were made successfully only because of the very generous cooperation of many individuals and institutions. Grants and financial assistance were received from the American Council of Learned Societies; the Social Science Faculty Research Fund and the Russian and East European Research Centre of Tel Aviv University; the Horace Rackham Graduate School and the Center for Russian and East European Studies of the University of Michigan. Israeli government officials, especially Dr. Eli Leshem of the Ministry for Immigrant Absorption, were very generous of their time and some data available to them. Officers and employees of Israeli political parties, trade unions, and immigrant associations were equally forthcoming. The Department of Political Science and the Russian and East European Research Centre at Tel Aviv University provided research facilities and a friendly atmosphere. Professors Asher Arian, Leon Boim, Michel Confino, Aaron Klieman, Yaacov Ro'i, and Ephraim Torgovnik gave me useful advice and assistance. Arian also read an earlier version of the manuscript, as did Professors Judith Shuval of the Hebrew University (Jerusalem) and my Michigan colleagues Kent Jennings and William Zimmerman. Dr. Tomas Hammar of Stockholm University and his colleagues gave me the opportunity to present my findings to their research group and to learn from their experience. I wish to express my deep appreciation to all of these colleagues and at the same time absolve them of any responsibility for what is said in these pages.

Exemplary research assistance was rendered by Lina Volkova-Yakobson and Avi Lavski in Israel, and by Drs. Valerie Bunce, Charles Hauss, Michael-John Morgan, and Gretchen Sandles at the University of Michigan. Several versions of the manuscript were typed with skill and unfailing good humor by Darlene Breitner and Jo Thomas of the Center for Russian and East European Studies.

This book's appearance is due in no small measure to my wife Marlene's fortitude, strength, skill, and support in closing and opening households three times, enabling me to do the research and writing. The dedication of this book to her is a small and inadequate token of my appreciation.

CONTENTS

LIST OF TABLES

BECOMING ISRAELIS

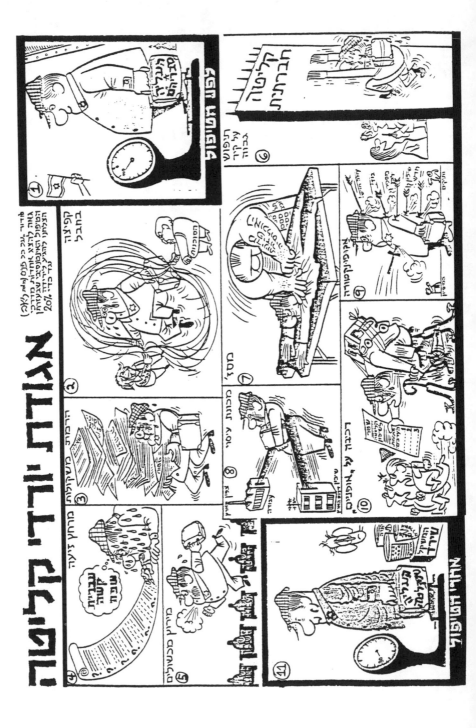

IMMIGRATION LOSS CLUB*

1. Before the treatment (suitcase says "Soviet immigration")

2. Jump-rope (Jewish Agency and Ministry for Immigrant Absorption hold the rope)

3. Weight-lifting

4. Sauna ("Hebrew hard language")

5. Obstacle Course (each desk is different government ministry)

6. Scaling a high wall (the wall reads "social integration")

7. Massage (policy of population dispersal)

8. Massage belt (workplace is in the north, residence in the south)

9. Acupuncture (derisive cries of "new immigrant," "new apartment," etc.)

10. Exercycle (immigrant is after cosigners to guarantee his housing loan)

11. After the treatment (suitcase says "Immigrants who were absorbed"; behind the immigrant is "the lost weight," labeled "Australia, Canada, United States")

*Translation for above cartoon
Source: Zeev, in *Ha'aretz*, October 11, 1974.

1

INTRODUCTION

Immigrants from Soviet Central Asia arriving at Ben-Gurion Airport. Courtesy United Jewish Appeal.

On a rainy night in January 1972 at Lod (now Ben-Gurion) Airport I witnessed the arrival of Soviet immigrants from the transit camp in Vienna. The first plane landed at two in the morning, but there was a class of senior high school students there to greet them, along with customs and immigration officials. As the immigrants entered the arrivals lounge — some young, some old, some Europeans and some Asians — the teenage students started to sing "Heveinu shalom aleikhem," a traditional greeting song, followed by "Am Yisrael khai" (the Jewish people lives). Though the welcoming ceremony had been obviously prepared in advance, the excited

1

response of the immigrants spurred even the porters washing the floors to join in the singing. The immigrants walked slowly into the hall, in a kind of studied dignity, most of them wearing heavy winter clothes and fur hats, strangely out of place in the Mediterranean version of winter. Minister for Immigrant Absorption Natan Peled made an appearance, mingling with the new arrivals and speaking to them in Russian. The high school students and the immigrants, who had been staring at each other in mutual curiosity, began to converse haltingly in fragmentary bits of Hebrew, English, and Yiddish. Some of the immigrants were crying, the older ones out of emotion, the very youngest ones out of weariness and perhaps fear. The Moroccan-born policeman, who had seen all of this many times before, tried as gently as he could to guide the newcomers to the registration desks, where they were first met by elderly Israelis speaking Russian in the accents of prerevolutionary days, and by more aggressive younger ones, representing the Union of Soviet Immigrants. Looking for friendly faces and Russian speakers, the immigrants were eager to strike up conversations and to inquire anxiously about the many things that were obviously on their minds.

I spoke to a young man from Chernovtsy in the Ukraine. A worker in a button factory, he declared he was ready to "take any job they give me," but he was hopeful of being located near his sister in Holon. He had spent two sleepless days at the border crossing in Chop, four days in Vienna, and was most anxious to find a place to live. He was impressed by the friendly reception in Vienna, by the literature he had gotten (in Russian), and said he thought "everything will be all right." Engaging another arrival in a political conversation, I was told that he knew about the "Vilner and Mikunis parties" (two Communist parties in Israel) but did not think he would join either, since he had not been a Communist in the USSR, and "because I have relatives abroad."

Bringing up the rear of the file of immigrants was an obviously ancient woman, bent practically double, aided on one side by a magnificently carved walking stick and on the other by a large and hefty man who looked to be in his fifties. The man spoke heavily accented Russian and explained that he and his grandmother were from the Caucasus. "How old is your babushka?" "Oh, she is 128 years old, God bless her."

The second plane arrived an hour later. As the students took up "Am Yisrael khai" once again, an old man suddenly burst into tears

and shouted in Hebrew "gam anakhnu khaim" (we too are alive) —
even the policeman shed a tear. The students shuffled about, a bit
embarrassed and more moved than they cared to admit. Short men
with stubby fingers and stubby wives. "What is your profession?"
A house painter, a wife who is a hairdresser, a barber, a photog-
rapher. The children were given bags of candy and were quickly
dragged into a circle of high school students dancing the hora. They
were joined enthusiastically by some Australian fund raisers for
Israel. One Australian woman turned to her daughter: "You see,
Valerie, I told you it would be worth waiting for."

A heavy set woman sat quietly, surrounded by six other family
members. She spoke in Russian, but after being introduced, she
switched to Midwestern American English. She smiled at my incre-
dulity. "Oh, I lived in Chicago a long time ago." Reluctantly, she
told how "37 years ago my husband and I went back to Russia where
we were both born. My husband is dead now, but four of my children are engineers," she said proudly. None of them spoke English,
however. One son, a chemical engineer, had begun writing a book
on Maimonides in Moscow 12 years ago, and he clutched the manuscript to his body. "I would like to study Jewish history here and
perhaps publish my book here. You understand that I could not
dream of this when I was living there." What made him decide to
leave? "After the Leningrad trials it was obvious that Jews have no
place in the Soviet Union. We all applied to leave and within two
months we had our exit visas."

Hearing our conversation, a short Georgian surrounded by five
children approached, took me aside, and asked if I lived in Israel.
He wanted some advice about what he should tell the immigration
authorities. He wanted to live in either Lod or Ashkelon, but he
wanted to make sure that he was sent to a "cultured" city. "I need a
place with culture, music, art, a choir." He was himself an artist,
perhaps? No, in a small town in Georgia he had worked in a store,
selling cheese. But he wanted a cultured city, and, moreover, he
had to make sure that there was a religious school there for his
children. "We heard over there that they will turn us into *goyim* —
can you be religious in Lod or Ashkelon?" Having been assured on
all counts, he took his place in line and anxiously accepted the offer
of a package, distributed by an official of the Ministry of Religions,
containing a prayerbook, phylacteries, a prayer shawl, an embroi-
dered cover for *khallah* (Sabbath bread), and a skullcap.

Sipping juice and tea, keeping a watchful eye on children and on suitcases (most of them bulging and held together with rope), the immigrants waited their turn. They filled out forms, anxiously looking at each official, nervously twisting their caps. One man, holding a violin case, was being offered a loan of IL2,500* by an official. He was discussing it unhappily with his family. "We'll have to work a whole year in order to pay it back. I'm afraid." Reassured by the official, he hesitantly signed the necessary form. The officials exchanged forms, scrutinized lists, and assigned the newcomers to the buses and taxis waiting outside to take them to immigrant hostels, to their relatives, or their apartments. By five in the morning everyone was gone — the high school students, the immigrants, the officials. The policeman had nothing to do but watch the two porters who were left, slowly mopping up.

A month later I was again at the airport, this time in the afternoon. An El Al flight from New York was bringing some American immigrants. Both the immigrants and their reception were in some contrast to the scene I had witnessed earlier. This time the faces were all European, but there was quite a variety of them. An elderly couple, with anxious looks on their faces, were eager to follow directions and get in the right lines. "Things are so bad in New York, you can't go out in the street any more, so I figured we might as well come here where our social security will go a lot further than it does in the States. We've been here many times before and we think everything will be all right. Of course, there are the children and the grandchildren back home, but there comes a time when you have to think of yourself too." A pale, bearded man was struggling with several items of hand luggage while his wife tried to pacify the infant in her arms. They were both natives of Chicago but had decided "to fulfill the *mitzvah* of *yishuv eretz yisroel* (the commandment of settling the land of Israel)." And what about *parnoseh* (making a living)? The young man had a degree in education and had "some leads" for an administrative job in a yeshiva. Of course, he wanted to live in Jerusalem and had already settled on a neighborhood, where, with the help of his father-in-law, he hoped to buy an apartment. He had spent a year studying in a Jerusalem yeshiva some years back, and he appeared to know the lay of the land, or at least part of it. As if coming from another country, nearby a family of

---

*The equivalent of $595 at that time.

four was camped next to an impressive pile of matched and obviously expensive luggage. The husband's sideburns were of a different type from those of the yeshiva graduate — carefully trimmed, graying a bit, and blending nicely with his "dry look" hair. The checked pants, casual loafers, and maroon blazer bespoke suburbia, two cars, the local temple, UJA "missions," and a rather comfortable existence. The Puma sneakers and aluminum tennis rackets of the two children, smiling through their braces — no doubt the work of a local orthodontist who would look much the same as the father — helped round out the picture, completed by their mother in a chic pants suit, carrying a fashionable tote bag from which she took out a sheaf of papers. "Our *shaliakh* (Jewish Agency representative) promised that with these, we should have no trouble, but we've heard all about the bureaucracy here and we have had some dealings with it, so we're prepared for anything." She told me confidentially that they did know some Hebrew, but "it's best to speak English to them and play dumb, unless they try to send us to the Nazareth hostel or some other distant place like that." Her husband was an electrical engineer, and though most of his letters to potential employers had gone unanswered, he remained confident of finding a job. He didn't think he would take a housing loan, as he wanted "to keep my dealings with the bureaucracy to a minimum." Besides, he hadn't sold his house in the States, "just in case," but when he found a "nice little villa" and was well settled in, he would sell it and use the money to pay for his new one "which I know will be a lot more modest." He was sure that Israel would be "good for the kids, and I won't have to worry about the drug scene or their marrying out," and besides, he said with a smile, "my friends all consider me a Zionist — though some of them think I'm nuts." It was hard to tell the immigrants from the tourists, until the former were led off to the building reserved for immigrant processing, thence to go through the same procedures as the Soviet immigrants. From there a few departed by cars or taxis ordered by the immigration officials, others went with Israeli relatives, and still others, after haggling with taxi drivers, some of them recent Georgian immigrants themselves, went on their own to their hostels, rented apartments, or other accommodations.

When the songs of the enthusiastic teenagers are no more than an echo, and the events of the first day in Israel fade into memories, the immigrants encounter the joys and the anguish of settling in a new country and culture. This book is about the process of resettling in Israel and, especially, its political aspects.

ISRAEL AND THE STUDY OF IMMIGRATION

Although several nation-states in modern times have been created by large-scale immigration, Israel is perhaps the most recent and most rapidly developed of these. Unlike most of the other countries of this sort — the United States, Canada, and Australia, for example — Israel continues to encourage immigration of people from all over the world. The very existence of the Jewish state, its security, economic well being, and future prospects are said by Israelis to depend heavily on Jewish immigration from the diaspora. Indeed, the very raison d'être of the state is to restore the political independence and viability of the Jewish people, exiled from their homeland over 1,900 years ago, and to "gather in the dispersed," wherever the vicissitudes of world history may have cast them. Immigration, then, lies at the core of Israel's meaning to its own citizens and to the Jewish people around the world.

Because immigration is a process of rapid and dramatic change, however, it has also attracted the attention of social scientists, historians, and linguists who are intrigued by the impacts of environmental change on individuals and groups. It is quite natural, therefore, that Israel has become a laboratory for students of social change and of migration. It has been said that "Jews are like everyone else — only a bit more so." Israel's brief history includes many experiences that have been shared by other peoples — economic ups and downs, wars, whirlwind social change, great triumphs, and dramatic defeats — but the Israeli experience seems to have been more compressed, more intense. It is as if the human condition were outlined more sharply in this tiny country than in far larger and more powerful ones. This feature, too, makes Israel attractive to those who would like to understand various aspects of collective human behavior.

This book also is an Israeli case study. It is a study of international migration and its relationship to politics. It deals with the three major areas of the political analysis of migration: migration policies, the political outlooks and behavior of migrants, and the political resocialization of immigrants. More narrowly, it is a study of Soviet and American Jews who have immigrated to Israel in the last decade, of the political decisions that caused or permitted this immigration, and of its political impact on the immigrants themselves and on the host society. Curiously, two large bodies of literature relevant to our concerns generally ignore the relationship of international migration to politics: The enormous literature on migration concentrates on cultural, economic, and social aspects, while the more recent literature on political change pays some attention to internal migration but generally ignores the international movement of peoples.[1] This, despite the fact that international migration has determined the political character of whole continents. Australia and North America are "Anglo-Saxon democracies" only because the original migrants to these continents were mostly Anglo-Saxons, some of them with high political consciousness. They established political systems compatible with the political cultures that had shaped them, preempting later immigrations from different kinds of systems. Latin America is a third continent whose political nature was formed by immigrants in modern times, and countries such as South Africa, Pakistan, and Israel have been molded politically by mass influxes of people in the late nineteenth and early twentieth centuries, who brought with them political values, ideas, and patterns of behavior acquired in other settings. With all that has been written on the causes and consequences of political change, scant attention has been paid to one of the largest of these causes, the international movement of peoples, and hence of ideas and of whole cultures.

In our century untold millions of people have moved back and forth among the continents and within them. Some of these movements have been voluntary, and many have not. Some have been the results of political changes, and others have been its causes. Voluntary international migrations include immigrants who seek political, economic, or social change, reunification of families, or simply a change of scenery or adventure, as well as migrant workers "temporarily" working abroad for economic reasons.[2] Involuntary migrants would include refugees and political expellees. (Population exchanges, such as those in the Balkans after both World Wars, are an intermediate category.)

Millions of refugees and expellees (such as Germans from Poland and Czechoslovakia) have played a significant role in twentieth-century international relations. The Palestinian refugee issue is but one illustration of this. Sometimes, refugees or expellees have acted as internal lobbies, advocating policies that stem from their experiences. Thus, in the 1950s and early 1960s, Germans in the Federal Republic (FRG) who had been "transferred" from the Sudetenland, Pomerania, or Silesia successfully influenced the policy of the FRG and delayed the "normalization" of relations with Czechoslovakia and Poland, thereby influencing all of Western policy toward the socialist countries of Eastern Europe and helping to delay the final settlement of World War II in Europe.

Some figures on international population movements should convince us that they must be a major source of changes of all kinds, including political ones. About 45 million persons emigrated from Europe to North America between the seventeenth century and the outbreak of World War II, with another 20 million going to South and Central America. About 17 million other Europeans went to Africa and Oceania at the same time. The slave trade involved about 20 million Africans from the sixteenth to the mid-nineteenth centuries; at least 10 million Chinese were living abroad by the time of the Communist revolution; nearly 4 million East Indians were living abroad.[3] The migration of Europeans alone meant that "when this redistribution was over, one-eleventh of the population of the world were people of European origin living outside Europe."[4]

World War II displaced over 30 million persons in Europe, and decolonization and revolution elsewhere added to these numbers. In the decade following the war (1945-55) about 45 million political refugees were found in all parts of the world. "The number of people expelled from one country to another in *the decade* after World War II was equal to the entire oversea [sic] emigration from Europe in *the century* ending in 1913."[5] In all, in the last 150 years there have been well over 70 million people who have "crossed international boundaries either expecting to reside abroad permanently or as part of a more or less regularized but not fully permanent labor supply."[6]

For a variety of reasons, certain peoples — Armenians, Chinese, Germans, Jews, Hungarians, Irish, Italians — have tended to migrate more than others. In Christian mythology the "wandering Jew" is the best-known symbol of migration, and the events of the last century have given new, and often tragic, meanings to this myth. At the beginning of the nineteenth century there were probably less than 4 million Jews in the world; by the end of that century, a period marked by great Jewish population expansion, there were nearly 4 million Jews from Europe alone who migrated to other countries. Of the 65 million people who emigrated from Europe in the years 1800-1940, about 6 percent were Jews, but if one considers their proportion in the total European population — never more than 2 percent —

> the intensity of Jewish emigration was . . . three to four times as great as that of the general emigration from Europe. If we consider only those sections of Europe from which Jews emigrated, i.e., middle, eastern and southern Europe, the intensity of Jewish emigration is not three to four times, but six to seven times as great as that of the general emigration.[7]

Over 70 percent of the Jewish migrants came to the United States, and 10 percent went to Palestine, though, because of U.S. restrictions on immigration after 1924, the American proportion fell and the Palestinian proportion rose.[8] Of course, the holocaust of 1939-45 further displaced the remnant of European Jewry, as whole countries were emptied of their Jewish populations: Instead of 3 million Jews in Poland, there were only about 300,000 in 1945, and by 1981 that number had shrunk to approximately 5,000; instead of 800,000 Romanian Jews, in 1945 there remained half that number, and by 1981 no more than 35,000 remained. In short, nearly two out of every three European Jews were exterminated by the Nazis and their allies. Most of those who remained alive could not or would not return to their original homes, and so a mass migration of "displaced persons" began. For Israel, the major recipient of these persons, this meant the doubling of its population in the short period from May 1948 to the end of 1951.

Just a few years after the war, as a result of political developments in the Middle East, a second mass migration, this time of North African and Asian Jews, began. Because of dispossessions and persecutions by Arab majorities, the so-called Oriental Jews found it necessary to flee their native lands, with several hundred thousand immigrating to Israel and thousands of others going to France, North America, and elsewhere. In all, nearly 700,000 Afro-Asian Jews immigrated to Israel in the late 1940s and 1950s.

There have been four major waves of immigration to Israel since the establishment of the state: from 1948 to 1951, when European refugees and thousands from Iraq, Yemen, and Libya entered the country; between 1955 and 1957, when North African and Polish Jews constituted the bulk of the immigration; between 1961 and 1964, when nearly 250,000 came, largely from North Africa and Romania; and between 1967 and 1973, when the immigrants arrived mostly from the Americas, Western Europe, and, for the first time since the 1920s, from the USSR. A detailed picture of the immigration can be obtained from Table 1.1.

Several things can be seen from this table. First, immigration has been an uneven process in quantitative terms (as shall be seen later, it has varied just as much in "qualitative" terms). Second, the ebb and flow of immigration depends on, among other things, international military and political events. Thus, immediately after the establishment of the state, the Suez War of 1956, and the Six Day War of 1967 there were surges in immigration, and after the 1973 War there was a decline. Of course, internal developments as well affect migration to Israel. Thus, the recession years of 1966 and 1967 were also years of very low immigration, as was the economically difficult period 1952-54. Finally, it can be observed that as the population has grown in size and immigration has diminished, the impact of immigration on society has lessened, at least quantitatively. In 1949, the peak year, one of every two Jews in Israel had arrived only that year, but in 1973, one of every 50 persons in Israel had settled in that year, still an astonishingly high ratio of immigrants to "veterans." These data take on more meaning when placed in comparative context. Looking at four other countries of immigration (in Table 1.2), we find that only rarely did immigration rates approach those experienced by Israel.

Thus, even when compared to other "classic" countries of immigration, Israel stands out as a state wherein immigration plays an enormous role in social, economic, and political life. Unlike in most other countries of immigration, it also plays an important ideological role in Israel as the very raison d'être of the state. The essence of Zionist ideology is the return of Jews to their ancestral homeland and a commitment to promote actively that particular form of migration. In 1950 the state enacted the "Law of Return," which guaranteed entry to all Jews who desired it, and nearly automatic citizenship thereupon.

In light of the dimensions of immigration, gargantuan when placed against the host population, the stability of the Israeli political and partisan systems is astounding. After all, it would seem that

TABLE 1.1
Immigration to Israel, 1948-80

Year	Number of Immigrants	Rate[a]
1948[b]	101,828	229
1949	239,576	266
1950	170,249	154
1951	175,095	132
1952	24,369	17
1953	11,326	8
1954	18,370	12
1955	37,478	24
1956	56,234	35
1957	71,224	41
1958	27,082	15
1959	23,895	13
1960	24,510	13
1961	47,638	25
1962	61,328	30
1963	64,364	30
1964	54,716	25
1965	30,736	14
1966	15,730	7
1967	14,327	6
1968	20,544	8
1969	37,804	15
1970	36,750	14
1971	41,930	16
1972	55,888	21
1973	54,886	20
1974	31,979	11
1975	20,028	7
1976	19,754	7
1977	21,429	7
1978	26,394	8
1979	37,222	12
1980	20,428	5
Total	1,647,413	

[a]Number of immigrants (including tourists settling) per 1,000 Jews in the population.

[b]As from May 15, 1948.

Sources: Statistical Abstract of Israel, nos. 30 and 31, 1979, 1980 (Jerusalem: Central Bureau of Statistics, 1980 and 1981); *Monthly Bulletin of Statistics* 32, no. 5 (Jerusalem: May 1981).

11

TABLE 1.2
Number of Immigrants per 1,000 Residents

Years	United States	Canada	Argentina	Brazil
1851-60	9.3	9.9	3.9	—
1861-70	6.5	8.3	9.9	—
1871-80	5.5	5.5	11.7	2.0
1881-90	8.6	7.3	22.2	4.1
1891-1900	5.3	4.9	16.4	7.2
1901-10	10.2	16.8	29.2	3.4
1913	12.1	38.4	38.3	7.7
1921-24	3.3	9.4	15.2	2.0

Source: I. Ferenczi, *International Migration,* as quoted in Moshe Sicron, *Immigration to Israel, 1948-1953* (Jerusalem: Falk Project for Economic Research and Central Bureau of Statistics, 1957), p. 37.

such a dynamic movement of people would be accompanied by movement and change in the political system. With immigrants coming from about 77 countries, from political cultures as different as Yemen and Czechoslovakia, Morocco and Poland, or Libya and the United States, the political system might have been in constant turmoil as the result of the various political cultures infused into it. Parties might gain and lose strength, depending on what kind of immigration happened to be prominent at the time and what attraction each party held for it. Yet, in contrast to many other developing countries, the Israeli political system has been remarkably stable — some critics would say stagnant. Until the election of May 1977, Israel had a "dominant party system," with the various incarnations of the Labor party holding power from 1948 — and, indeed, well before that date. Moreover, the proportion of the vote that each party received during the course of 25 years and eight national elections remained very much the same. How could this be in a dynamic country experiencing enormous population growth and social change, involved in dramatic wars and a rapidly changing international arena? It is not that the immigrants remained outside the political system — there has been a consistent turnout of about 80 percent for all the national elections. Nor have the parties ignored the immigrants. As we shall see, there has always been fierce competition for the loyalties and votes of the newcomers. Did the Israelis somehow evolve a system of perfect partisan resocialization, wherein the parties managed to reproduce themselves within every wave of immigration, no matter its origin, social composition, or political cultures? One aim of this study is to analyze the processes by which the political system has managed to assimilate the immigrants and maintain its stability in the face of potentially destabilizing waves of newcomers, who came, after all, not as political *tabulae rasae*, but as individuals whose political views and behavior patterns had been formed by particular political cultures.

Admittedly, the immigrant populations that we are concerned with in this study are not typical of most of the other waves of immigrants to Israel. Soviet and American immigrants come not as refugees but of their own free will from the higher strata of highly developed societies. They are, for the most part, educated and skilled, and they have come from the two most powerful countries in the world. However, by studying Soviet and American immigration we can discover much about the process whereby people make the transition from one state to another, from one political culture and system to a new one. When we study former Soviet citizens and former residents of the United States (who in almost all cases retain their American citizenship), we are looking at immigrants coming from different political "directions" to a common ground. The Soviet immigrants come from a system that calls itself socialist and is also authoritarian; the Americans come from a basically capitalist system, which is also democratic. The two groups of immigrants enter a system often described as socialist, though in a different way from the Soviet one, and generally acknowledged to be democratic. In a rough way the Israeli system may be seen as an amalgam of the Soviet and American patterns. Israel's Western political ideology and orientation and its East European political-cultural heritage are an unusual blend. Our question is how newcomers from the two sources react to the blend, and vice versa. We may conceive of this in the way represented in Figure 1.1.

FIGURE 1.1

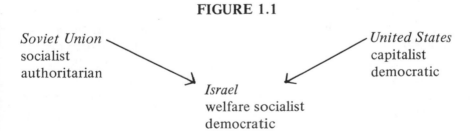

Soviet Union
socialist
authoritarian

United States
capitalist
democratic

Israel
welfare socialist
democratic

RESOCIALIZING IMMIGRANTS

Our main premise is that the transition represented by the arrows is a process of resocialization, specifically, adult political resocialization. This process shall be described and analyzed from two complementary perspectives: that of the socializing and absorbing political culture and system, and that of the individuals and groups presumably being socialized. Essentially, we are posing five general questions:

How does the Israeli political system attempt to involve and assimilate immigrants? In Chapter 2 we look at how the system absorbed the pre-1967 immigrations and in Chapters 3 and 4 we see how the system changed to accommodate the Soviet and American immigrations.

Are the immigrants, in fact, resocialized, or do they remain outside the political system and culture except in the most formal sense? Conceptual aspects of this question are discussed in Chapter 5, while it is dealt with empirically in Chapters 6 and 7.

If the immigrants are resocialized, by whom are they resocialized? This is the subject of Chapter 7.

If they are resocialized, how extensive is this process? Does only their external political behavior change, or are there deeper changes, such as attitudinal ones, or even changes in political values and in "primitive beliefs?" These questions and those posed in the next paragraph are discussed in Chapter 8.

Does the resocialization process result in partial or total change? If it is the former, what aspects of the immigrants' antecedent political culture are abandoned, transformed, or maintained? What aspects of the new political culture are most easily and rapidly acquired, and which least so?

While these are the main concerns of this analysis, it may also shed some light, however faint, on two other areas. One is adult political socialization, about which we know relatively little, and of which immigration is perhaps a special case. The other is the political values, attitudes, and behavior of those socialized in the Soviet political system, one that does not permit free and unbiased inquiry into these matters. Although our concern is not that of the Harvard Refugee Project of the 1940s, which tried to reconstruct the Soviet political world on the basis of emigré interviews, we may, nevertheless, learn about that world from this, the "third Soviet emigration." In addition, because the Soviet authorities have never given a full explanation of their emigration policies, by examining the outcomes of those policies — the numbers of immigrants, their geographic origins, occupational and educational composition, age structure, and the like — one can deduce what are the principles and guidelines of Soviet emigration policy.

METHODS

In this book a variety of complementary methods have been used. After reviewing the general literature on immigration and on political socialization, published and unpublished material on immigration to Israel was examined in detail. An effort was made to examine all the empirical studies made of immigrants in the 1960s and 1970s and to gather all relevant data on Soviet and American immigrants in particular. During 1971-72, and to a lesser extent in 1975, the Russian-language immigrant press — the dailies *Nasha strana* and *Tribuna* — was read regularly. Russian-language journals, including those published by political parties in Israel, were also surveyed, as were publications of the Union of Soviet Immigrants and of the Association of Americans and Canadians in Israel. Officials and members of these organizations were interviewed. The Jerusalem *Post*, Israel's English-language daily, was read because it pays special attention to immigrants from English-speaking countries ("Anglo-Saxons" in Israeli parlance). Two Hebrew-language dailies, *Haaretz* and *Maariv*, were surveyed intensively. Other newspapers were sampled as well, especially for material dealing with the administration of immigrant absorption and the competition among parties for the allegiance of the newly arrived Israelis.

Interviews were conducted with a former deputy minister of the Ministry for Immigrant Absorption, with several former directors-general of that ministry, as well as with officials of the Jewish Agency and of the Central Statistical Bureau. The directors of "immigrant absorption" departments of political parties were interviewed in order to ascertain what strategies and efforts were being pursued by the parties among the Soviet and American immigrants in particular. In all, nine party officials were interviewed, ranging from Communists to Gahal (now Likud). The director of the Histadrut's (General Confederation of Labor) immigrant absorption department was also interviewed.

These methods were used to understand the resocialization process from the perspective of the system and the socializing agencies, but more attention was paid to the perspectives of those being socialized. Somewhat unwittingly at first, and more consciously later on, I became a kind of participant observer in the immigrant absorption process. I did not have immigrant status, but my living conditions and social contacts were very similar to those of immigrants. Several close family members and good friends were actually recent immigrants – from both the USSR and, especially, the United States – and this gave me entree to their social circles so that I could observe their outlooks, fears, hopes, expectations, accomplishments, and disappointments. Many were the evenings or Saturday afternoons spent trading tales of Israeli bureaucratic horrors in a kind of "Can-you-top-this?" game, but just as many were the times when satisfied immigrants would urge me earnestly to make the same move they had. At the same time, I discussed immigrants and immigration with a great variety of Israeli veterans (*vatikim*) and learned their perceptions of the newer Israelis and their problems. I tried to maximize the angles from which the process could be viewed. This took me to the airport in the early morning hours to greet a newly arrived group of Soviets, as well as to several immigrant absorption hostels or centers (*meonai klitah*), to social events sponsored by immigrant associations, as well as to a senior high school class in Tel Aviv that was discussing immigrant absorption (*klitah*), their views – and those of their parents – of *klitah* and of the immigrants.

The immigrants themselves were more systematically interviewed. As shall be described in detail, two groups of "matched" American and Soviet immigrants were interviewed in depth in the spring and early summer of 1972, and were reinterviewed three years later, in the spring of 1975. These were personal interviews, conducted in the native languages of the respondents, by native speakers of those languages, generally in the homes of the respondents. The reason for the reinterviews is that absorption of immigrants, and certainly resocialization, are dynamic processes extending over time, and that static methods of studying the process are unsatisfactory. I am well aware of the limitations and shortcomings of the present study, but I hope that it will at least open a window on to a hitherto unexplored, but large, colorful, and interesting world — that of the politics of people in transition from one political system and culture to another. If dissatisfaction with the present study prompts others more capable than I to improve and expand it, to explore the same kinds of questions in this or other contexts, then the study will have achieved its purpose.

NOTES

1. For the literature on migration, see, for example, Edwin Driver, *World Population Policy: An Annotated Bibliography* (Lexington, Mass.: Lexington Books, 1972), and J. J. Mangalam, *Human Migration: A Guide to Migration Literature in English* (Lexington: University of Kentucky Press, 1968). A leading student of migration and politics notes that "the political aspects of international migration have thus far been almost completely neglected. This is astonishing, as the size, the direction, and the conditions of this migration is [sic] regulated by political decision." Tomas Hammar, "Migration and Politics: Delimitation and Organization of a Research Field," paper presented to the Workshop on International Migration and Politics, European Consortium for Political Research, Grenoble, France, April 1978, p. 2.

2. My colleague William Zimmerman is studying the political consequences for Yugoslavia of workers' migration abroad. See his "National-International Linkages in Yugoslavia: The Political Consequences of Openness," in *Political Development in Eastern Europe*, ed. Jan Triska and Paul Cocks (New York: Praeger Publishers, 1977).

3. Donald R. Taft and Richard Robbins, *International Migrations* (New York: Ronald Press, 1955), p. 31.

4. Brinley Thomas, "Migration: Economic Aspects," in *International Encyclopedia of Social Sciences*, ed. David Sills (New York: Macmillan, 1968), Vol. 10, p. 293.

5. Ibid. For details, see Joseph B. Schechtman, *Postwar Population Transfers in Europe, 1945-1955* (Philadelphia: University of Pennsylvania Press, 1962).

6. Taft and Robbins, p. 40.

7. Jacob Lestschinsky, "Jewish Migrations, 1840-1946," in *The Jews*, ed. Louis Finkelstein (Philadelphia: Jewish Publication Society, 1949), Vol. 4, p. 1200.

8. Ibid., p. 1217.

2

THE POLITICS OF IMMIGRATION AND IMMIGRANT ABSORPTION IN ISRAEL

At the airport, trying to see what lies ahead. Courtesy United Jewish Appeal.

How has Israel managed to absorb so many different kinds of immigrants into its political system? Starting from the perspective of the host society and its socializing agencies, we trace here the development of immigrant political resocialization in Israel and its contemporary institutional forms. We also examine the general attitude of the population to immigration and immigrants. The process of resocialization will account for the political outcome mentioned earlier, the remarkable stability not only of the political system but of the party system.

IMMIGRATION AND ABSORPTION
BEFORE THE SIX-DAY WAR

Though the State of Israel was established in 1948, its political institutions were formed long before that, during the period of the British Mandatory government. The willingness and ability of the Jewish population to develop authoritative institutions, even while sovereignty had not been achieved, contrasted strongly with that of the Arab population of Palestine and gave the Jews great political and organizational advantages, not only in the decisive confrontations of 1947-49 but for many years thereafter.[1] The Jewish Agency acted as a protogovernment for 20 years prior to independence, and the political parties had well-established programs, organizations, and even leaders. Thus, in contrast to many other newly independent states at the time, on the very morrow of independence Israel had a functioning government and administration and an established party system. Immigrants came, therefore, to a *state* that was in formation, but, in effect, to a *political system* with about one-quarter century's experience and standing. They came not to political chaos or even fluidity, but to established facts — institutions, behavioral patterns, values, and leaders.

Two ideological factors and two situational-historical ones explain this unusual phenomenon. The most important ideological factor was the evolving Zionist belief that the supreme goal was the establishment of an independent state for the Jewish people, and the pre-1948 period was one of concrete preparations for such a state. Since the immigration to Palestine was motivated for the most part by Zionist beliefs and convictions — aside from religion, there was little else to attract Jews to this small, impoverished land — the great majority of the population shared this aspiration. As S. N. Eisenstadt observes,

> the *Yishuv* [the pre-1948 Jewish population of Palestine] — with the exception of oriental Jews and some refugee immigrants — was largely free from many of the symptoms of social disintegration and tension specific to immigrant countries. Particularist identification did not develop, nor were there any institutional impediments to the attainment of fully recognized social status on the part of any group of immigrants.[2]

This may be an overly idealized picture — there were, after all, pronounced hostilities among adherents of different political movements and there was a definite ethnic pecking order — but it is true that the common bond of Zionism and the aspiration for national independence and the "ingathering of the exiles" provided a cohesive force absent in most other countries of immigration.

The second ideological influence was the "negation of the diaspora" (*shlilat hagalut*), a viewpoint shared by most Zionists. The diaspora was rejected, not only because it posed physical and spiritual dangers to the Jews living in it, but because it had, in the Zionist view, crippled the development of Jewish culture, and "diaspora culture" was to be rejected. For many, this meant throwing over religion, changing one's mode of dress, changing one's occupation — generally to farming or other forms of physical labor — changing one's language from Yiddish to Hebrew, and even cutting ties with family and friends who did not share these views. The diaspora was portrayed as an inferior form of Jewish existence that should be forgotten as soon as possible. This implied also an obliteration of the ethnic-cultural differences that had "accidently" and unfortunately developed following the exile of the Jews from their homeland. In other words, Zionism evolved a kind of "melting pot" ideology, whereby linguistic and cultural differences that had "artificially" differentiated Jews in the diaspora were to be eliminated. For this reason there were campaigns against speaking any language other than Hebrew, and those who continued to use their native languages were regarded with opprobrium, almost as if this were an act of national betrayal. One political consequence of this was that parties were not to be organized along ethnic lines and that associational groups and political activity based on common ethnicity were discouraged and regarded as part of the despised "diaspora mentality." Thus, rather than being influenced by immigrants, the Palestinian Jewish population was deferred to and regarded as those who should "set the tone" in social, political, and cultural life. Simply by virtue of living in Palestine, and thereby fulfilling the Zionist ideal, they achieved superior status and were deserving of deference.

> That the Jewish community in Palestine could absorb large-scale immigration without losing its identity was . . . due to its close links with the Zionist movement all over the world. . . . Those who had settled in Palestine were given greater authority and superior status within the movement. To live up to the standards they had set was the ambition of the would-be immigrant. It is easy to see that this created a

climate highly conducive to the rapid integration of the newcomers.
. . . They were expected to adapt themselves to the prevailing pattern
of life and they were prepared to do so.[3]

Eisenstadt observed of the immigrants that

> there is not much inter-ethnic organization based on *common* symbols
> of identification which differentiate them from the old *Yishuv*. What-
> ever the internal cohesion of any group and its symbols of particularist
> identification, these extend but seldom beyond the "in-group" to
> include other immigrant groups. The main areas of formal organi-
> zation are those provided by the absorbing society — local political
> parties, parents' associations, etc. Whatever the extent of negative
> identification and complaint on the part of different groups of immi-
> grants, they rarely give rise to common organized activity against the
> absorbing society.[4]

This sharing of values and commitments was made possible by
the system of immigrant administration established by the British
Mandatory power. The Mandate recognized the Jewish Agency for
Palestine as the authorized representative of the *yishuv* and it became
the dominant Jewish national institution in Palestine. The Agency
was a highly politicized body in which the political parties of the
yishuv enjoyed both formal and informal representation. This representation was granted in direct proportion to their strength within
the population, as determined by various elections held in Palestine.
Immigration and settlement of newcomers was the main business of
the Agency. Within quotas established by the British, the Agency was
given the power to allocate immigration certificates to potential
immigrants. "This control implied the possibility of selecting those
potential immigrants who suited the political and colonizing criteria
which guided the policy of the leadership."[5] In other words, most
certificates were granted not to individuals, but to party organizations abroad that were affiliated with the Palestinian party in
question. A labor-Zionist party in Poland, for example, might receive
100 immigration certificates. It would then select the certificate
recipients from a list of its adherents who were ready to settle in
Palestine. Since "there existed an unadmitted, unofficial, and yet
very real, agreement within the Jewish Agency on the proportionate
division of new settlers between the . . . different parties,"[6] the
partisan sympathies of entering immigrants were generally in rough

proportion to the strength of those parties within the *yishuv*. With immigration certificates divided according to the "party key," it is little wonder that the parties managed to perpetuate themselves and their relative strengths.

This brings us to the last determinant of the preindependence evolution of the political system, the party system. The politicization of the immigrants did not end with the receipt of certificates, but continued in Palestine through parties that fulfilled quasi-governmental functions. They provided public and welfare services, in addition to serving as the main broker between the immigrant and the national institutions. Jobs, housing, schooling, social contacts, and even sports clubs all were proffered to the immigrant by the political parties. Thus, a person might well work in a place where almost all employees shared his political views, go home to a housing project built by his party's construction firm and largely populated by party sympathizers, send his children to the educational "track" that was close to his party, and spend his leisure hours at a lecture organized by the party or playing soccer for the team identified with that party. The antecedent partisan socialization of the movement in the diaspora was reinforced many times over in the new country, where, of course, the immigrant's dependence on others was great and where party-provided services were essential to the immigrant's very survival.

The competition among the parties for the immigrants continued even in the emergency conditions of the holocaust and its aftermath. Veteran Zionist Meyer Weisgall, who, perhaps because of his American background, was put off by the partisan aspects of Zionism, describes a scene in 1944 in a refugee reception camp in northern Israel. Children who had miraculously escaped from Europe had been brought to Palestine and were now to be assigned to various agricultural settlements, boarding schools, and the like.

> There were about 300 or 400 children among the 900 people in the camp. All of them passed through a room where there were representatives of the ultra-orthodox "Agudat Yisrael," the religious "Mizrakhi," the General Zionists, the representatives of the labor parties. . . . After I had watched the procedure for about an hour, I began calling this the "inquisition room." Each child, irrespective of age, was asked: "What did your father do first thing in the morning? Did he put on *tefilin* [phylacteries]? Did he eat kosher food? Was he a member of a socialist party? What newspaper did he read? . . ." The children were

frightened. They had passed through hell, and had been in the Land of Israel only a day or two. They couldn't know this was not the Gestapo, that these people were simply trying to help them, to . . . decide whether to send them to a religious school or to a secular kibbutz. . . . I left, quietly remarking on the tribal culture being created among the Jews of Eretz Yisrael. Six hundred thousand had succeeded in creating five school systems. The children of the aristocratic labor parties would never mix with those of the despised bourgeoisie.[7]

Ada Sereni, widow of an Italian-Jewish Zionist who had left Palestine to jump behind enemy lines in Europe in an attempt to rescue Jews, was in Italy at the end of the war when Jews were trying to get around the British ban on immigration to Palestine. She saw Palestinian Jewish soldiers stationed in Italy trying to recruit immigrants to their respective parties. When a ship was to sail from Bari, representatives of the parties met to decide how the 35 places were to be allocated, what the real strengths of the parties were, and, finally, who among the party members would get the first priority.

In all this excitement those refugees who were not registered with any party were afraid they would never set sail. They decided to get in touch with the organized groups. A bitter struggle ensued among the party representatives over the registration of these immigrants in their respective parties. Everyone promised the refugees that his party would enable them to set sail, and to do so speedily.[8]

In sum, the absorption of immigrants in the *yishuv* period was characterized by partisanship, paternalism, and the dependence of the immigrants on the political powerholders of the society. It did produce a relatively homogeneous, politically organized community that was well prepared to meet the challenges of independence and self-administration. Eisenstadt's characterization of the results of the process is an apt one. He lists six outcomes: (1) "strong neutralization of the immigrants' cultural and social background; (2) almost complete dispersal of different waves of immigrants among the various strata of the differentiated institutional structure"; (3) no development of particularist identification by any immigrant group; (4) total transformation of leadership "according to the institutional demands of the country"; (5) absorption took place not only in formal institutions but also in primary groups open to different groups of immigrants and strongly linked to the formal, institutionalized "frameworks" of absorption; (6) rapid absorption of immigrants into institutions "and a relatively high extent of social activity and orientation to its central values."[9] Such a process precluded the development of politics based largely on ethnicity, though, as we shall see, ethnicity was by no means irrelevant nor is it today. In fact, it may well have been the decisive cleavage in the 1981 Israeli election campaign when the non-European Jews supported the victorious Likud party very strongly. But the pre-1948 system of immigrant absorption made it unlikely that the political culture, deriving from Eastern Europe in the late nineteenth and early twentieth centuries, would be much affected in the short run by the waves of immigration, especially when so many were coming from very similar cultures and even from the very same political movements.

In the years immediately following independence the nature of the immigrants changed radically, but the political system did not. Whereas the pre-1948 immigrants were mostly Zionists, with definite political ideas and commitments, those who came after 1948 were generally of two types. European refugees came to Israel because no other country would admit them, because surviving relatives were there, or because some had been Zionists before the war. Some came after their wartime experiences had convinced them that Zionism was the only solution to what was called the "Jewish problem." The second type were refugees from Islamic lands, where the creation of Israel brought declarations of *jihad* (holy war) and persecution of local Jews. The great majority of these Afro-Asian Jews had not been exposed to the ideas of modern political Zionism, though many adhered to messianic Zionist visions embedded in Judaism. Among the urban groups of Iraqi, Moroccan, and Tunisian Jews there were Zionist organizations linked to the parties in what was now Israel, but they were a minority. Therefore, the tremendous waves of immigrants that engulfed the newborn state did not come already socialized into the political and partisan systems. Yet the system that had existed since the 1920s hardly changed, despite the fact that the immigrants became citizens almost immediately.

What explains this stability in the face of great dynamism and pressure? The answer is to be found in the process whereby the immigrants were brought into the system. Despite the fact that a state now existed, and could presumably provide jobs, housing, and so on, the parties continued to play their traditional roles. Although the various military units that reflected different political ideologies were welded, not without difficulty, into a single Israel Defence Force, three school systems continued a parallel existence. Not until 1955 were the labor exchanges formally depoliticized and "nationalized," and not until 1968 did the government create a Ministry for Immigrant Absorption, and even then it shared responsibilities with the nongovernmental Jewish Agency. The Agency itself, the protogovernment of the *yishuv*, did not go out of business with the creation of the state, but like many organizations whose goal has been achieved, it was able to redefine and expand its raison d'être and thereby insure its organizational survival. To this very day the several health plans and polyclinic networks are linked, however tenuously, to political parties, and though there has been much talk of a national health care system, nothing has come of it. In short, the "neo-feudal" system[10] of the *yishuv* period was only modified after 1948, not eliminated.

In the distribution of immigrants to various settlements and of material resources for the absorption of immigrants, the "party key" continued to operate. Because they came with nothing, the immigrants were even more dependent on their hosts than their predecessors of the prewar era. Because they were regarded as people in need of help — as holocaust survivors or as those from cultures considered "primitive" or "backward" — paternalism became even more pronounced. Dependence and paternalism complement each other very well. This had obvious political implications.

> Frequently, the immigrants were subjected to political pressure, especially on the local level, by the officials of those very bodies on whom they were so dependent. This political-manipulative relationship of Israeli groups and parties to many of the new immigrants was intensified by the fact that many of the administrative organs working in absorption were very closely linked to the various centers of political power. . . . [While the official line emphasized equality, brotherhood, and cooperation] it also assumed that the existing groups and parties were sufficient for the desires, needs, and aspirations of the immigrants.[11]

Upon arrival, immigrants were given three months' free membership in the Histadrut (General Confederation of Labor) and its affiliated employment and health services. Here they were exposed to the parties, though the right-wing parties were generally not included. "The personnel manning the Histadrut labour exchanges . . . were chosen according to a party key. In theory employment was decided on a first come first serve basis, but in practice party criteria were widely employed. Housing, too, was often allocated in this manner."[12] Since the immigrant was dependent on official agencies to solve the most basic problems of life in a new country, his contacts with officials were frequent and often intense.

> In the agencies dealing with the problem of immigrant absorption, immigrants came into contact with officials who were party men, playing the dual roles of official and party recruiter, indoctrinator and socialiser. Although most parties shared in this division, Mapai, the majority party, had the greatest number of officials, and occupied the controlling and decisive positions at all points of recruitment.[13]

Party premises were used for official business and the parties undertook the "burden of educating the immigrants" in the ways of a parliamentary democracy. Mapai, the dominant labor party, tried to get immigrants into the Histadrut, which it controlled, created special departments in its headquarters based on countries of origin, and tried — successfully, in many instances — to control the immigrant associations. "Overall they constituted a party-organized and financed social-welfare agency which guided, instructed, educated and personally intervened on behalf of ethnic clients."[14]

In the rural areas and development towns, to which many immigrants were assigned, political recruitment was even more direct. The main agent of socialization in the agricultural cooperatives was the "instructor" or "emissary" (*shaliakh*) assigned by the Jewish Agency to instruct the immigrants, most of whom had never been farmers, in agricultural techniques, modern hygiene, and so on.

> The emissary played many roles: he was the director of the employment office, secretary of the health service, director of the *ma'abara* [immigrant tent city], coordinator of the crew which set it up, secretary of the labor council, or head of the local government. This . . . served mainly the Mapai approach of integrating immigrants into the political network. Israeli parties did not wait for independent political forces to arise among the immigrants or for spontaneous processes to reveal themselves. . . . They were satisfied generally with developing a complex instrumental system of benefits, but usually put some veteran at the head of the system.[15]

There were, in name or in fact, ethnic sections within the parties, and they served as much to transmit party messages to the immigrants as they did to bring immigrant concerns to the parties. The parties gave special courses to potential leaders, and it was widely understood that attendance at such courses was a prerequisite to advance to leadership positions.

In development towns the offices that dealt with housing, employment, credits, and licenses were staffed partly by new immigrants themselves, of course on the "party key" basis. According to Lissak, "this created an incentive for immigrants with an inclination to political activity to join parties with strong positions. This . . . was particularly significant with regard to immigrants with a traditional social background, as those from Yemen and from North Africa."[16] Because they were organized in extended families, manipulation of large groups of people became possible, since only the allegiance of the head of the clan need be won in order to insure the votes and support of the rest.

Lissak argues that these recruitment strategies in fact did change some aspects of the Israeli system. First, the parties shifted from an emphasis on ideology to instrumental benefits as the major attraction of parties to immigrants. Second, charismatic personalities – David Ben-Gurion, Menachem Begin – displaced ideology as the primary appeal to the voters. Third, as a result of these tactical changes, some parties became generally more pragmatic and less ideologic in their styles.

A clear picture of the political recruitment of immigrants in development towns, and of the interplay of ethnicity and politics, is given in three studies of politics in development towns, two from the 1950s and one from the 1965 election campaign. In the 1965 study, anthropologist Shlomo Deshen describes how it was the Mapai party that actually initiated the founding of ethnic associations and provided premises and funds for staff and maintenance. The party also organized "language cells," wherein party business was discussed in languages other than Hebrew. Leaders of these cells and ethnic associations were cultivated. "For instance, the head of the North African Association attained considerable power and prestige from his appointment as a sort of 'gate keeper,' having the power to decide if any particular immigrant from Morocco seeking a personal audience with the mayor warranted the latter's time and attention."[17]

While in the 1959 election campaign in the town candidates were chosen largely because of their positions as leaders of ethnic groups, by 1965

> the process of acculturation and disintegration of immigrant groups had become such that the local Maarak(h) [Labor Alignment] branch felt it sufficient to campaign with a list of candidates who were ethnic representatives in a purely formal sense. . . . These candidates are people who are assumed to have the general interests of the town most at heart and who place specific ethnic interests second.[18]

Still, great care was taken to present the kind of "balanced ticket" familiar to observers of politics, say, in New York. "The first candidate had to be a veteran European, the second an oriental (preferrably Moroccan), and the remaining certain candidates [those sure to be elected] had to include a Rumanian, an additional oriental (preferrably Tunisian) and another veteran."[19]

Beersheba in the late 1950s was considered a development town and was populated largely by immigrants from Iraq, Poland, Romania, and Morocco. The local Mapai party had seven ethnic associations identified with it and "all the party's institutions are set up according to the ethnic key."[20] Mapai attracted the leaders of the ethnic groups who saw it as most likely to be able to "deliver the goods" to their respective communities. "While in the labor exchanges and absorption department there is an explicit policy of rejecting partisan and ethnic pressures, this aim is not developed in the welfare office (*lishkat hasaad*). It is therefore clear that the officials will make all efforts to help people who are directed to them by their own party or ethnic group."[21]

Differences in the political styles of the ethnic groups stemmed from their different political traditions. In Morocco there had been several Zionist organizations and parties, paralleling those in Israel, and so there was a natural carryover to this differentiation in Beersheba. Since the Moroccan ethnic association included people of different partisan sympathies, at election time there was a tacit agreement not to hold meetings of the association. On the other hand, in Iraq there had been no parties and only one underground Zionist movement, or so the immigrants claimed. One Iraqi leader explained: "How did we come to Mapai? Abroad we were real Zionists [sic], with no factions and movements. When representatives of the various movements came to divide us, we chased them out. Afterwards, when it was explained to us that if we all enter Mapai, we could benefit the entire community by this, we agreed."[22] Of course, a symbiotic relationship developed between the parties and the ethnic associations. The parties enjoyed what were essentially delivered votes, while the ethnic associations got the leverage needed to get jobs, licenses, favors, and the like.

Zamir contends that this type of relationship between the ethnic groups and the parties prevented what she considers to be the "integration" of the immigrants into Israeli society. She argues that

> when the ethnic group, work group, neighborhood and social groups are all congruent, there is no possibility of intergroup contact or certainly, their integration into one society. This kind of congruence means that ethnic affiliation is the key to social and political appointments — and this slows advancement on the basis of individual worth, and encourages the ethnic leadership stratum.[23]

This argument reflects the prevailing Israeli "melting pot" ethos and the belief that "integration" means the obliteration of ethnic peculiarities. It could be argued against this view that by playing the ethnic game, the parties were — perhaps unconsciously — "integrating" the immigrants into the political system far more effectively than if they had urged people to join parties or participate in politics simply as individuals without specific ethnic identities. Moreover, it is an open question as to whether "integration" is synonymous with homogenization, or whether participation in the same political system, adherence to the same rules and behavioral patterns, and the sharing of some fundamental values — while maintaining separate ethnic identities — is not equally "integration." This is obviously a very large issue, and a very real one in many countries — Canada, Yugoslavia, the Soviet Union, and Nigeria, to mention only a few. It is raised, not out of any presumption that it can be settled here, but because it will be relevant to our future consideration of the "integration" of very different types of immigrants — Soviet and American — two decades after the "Orientals" had settled in Beersheba and other development towns.

Of course, one should not exaggerate the meaning of political recruitment of the sort described above. Its function as a socialization device may be very limited. A researcher into a development town reports that one respondent did not know what a party was, even when this was explained to him in his native language. He could not name a single party — and yet, it turned out, he did have a party membership card! Other people reported that when they had come to register at the labor exchange, it was explained to them that first they needed to have a red membership card (Mapai). While some thought this was "for 'Abu-Lishka' " — the labor exchange official — others affirmed that it was "for Ben-Gurion." "There are not a few cases of people who have two membership cards, one of Mapai and one of another movement. This is known also to the local Mapai leadership, but it sees this as part of the local political reality."[24] Some people simply transferred political patterns from their countries of origin. "In Iraq we knew that you should always support the government. Here the government is Mapai, so you have to be Mapai — otherwise there is no bread."[25]

Despite these initial perceptions, political involvement, even if for the "wrong" reasons, introduced the immigrants to a world whose ways they could not begin to learn had they been left out of it until they — or their children — would acquire the abstract notions and theoretical knowledge that underlay the Western-type system into which they had been thrust so suddenly. Certainly, for the minority who took an active part in politics, rather than the kinds of passive roles played by people described above, political office came to be not only an avenue of political mobility but of social mobility and general acculturation as well. In fact, since the traditional society of the newcomers did "not particularly value those who have party functions, because those functions are still strange to it,"[26] politics became the vehicle for the development of what might be regarded as a "counterelite" to the traditional religious and clan leadership of the immigrant communities. Especially because the newer political elites wielded substantial economic power, they weakened the hold of traditional leadership and provided alternative cues for the immigrants to follow. Moreover, these political elites themselves looked to the national and veteran Israeli leadership for political and social cues, and to the extent that they followed them — which was very considerable, given the highly disciplined nature of Israeli parties — they served as transmitters of "Israeli" values and behavioral patterns to the larger immigrant communities. If the original "instructors" were largely European-origin veterans, their task was carried on by the new and aspiring leadership from the immigrant communities.

As time went on, this two-step transmission process — from veteran Israelis to new immigrant elites to immigrants — proved an effective means of political socialization. A more sophisticated understanding of administration than that represented by the image of "Abu-Lishka" developed, and, slowly, differentiation was made between the dominant party and the government. Ethnicity declined somewhat as a factor in political recruitment, though it remains of great importance. Party appeals and recruitment methods became more sophisticated and less material, though an observer of a development town reports the following as late as 1969:

> The parties pay individuals to recruit new members. One immigrant was encountered who made an acceptable living by recruiting for one party in the morning, for a rival party in the afternoon, and for a third party two or three evenings a week. Neither he nor any of the other non-Western respondents contacted on this point felt there was anything wrong with his conduct; business was business and what the parties stood for was not of his concern.[27]

By the 1970s this kind of recruitment was probably the exception, and the entire process of political resocialization had changed. The change was due to several factors. There were changes in the styles of party competition. The economy had progressed to the point where the basic necessities were much more easily available and dependence on the parties was diminished. The administration of immigrant absorption was altered, increasing the state's role and diminishing that of the parties and of the Jewish Agency. Perhaps most importantly, the nature of the immigrants themselves had changed radically. In the place of dependent and destitute refugees, the 1970s saw the arrival of educated, skilled, and often wealthy immigrants, not from the East, but from the West, not from feudal monarchies and East European dictatorships, but from Western democracies and from the USSR. The change in the nature of the immigrants meant a change in the processes of general absorption and of political resocialization.

IMMIGRATION AND ABSORPTION IN THE POST-1967 ERA

In 1965 immigration fell to nearly half the figure of the previous year, and with the onset of economic recession, it fell by another

50 percent in 1966. In that year only 13,451 immigrants arrived, and in the following year there were only 12,237. Israel's dramatic victory in the "Six-Day War" of June 1967 revived the economy, which now entered a spectacular boom period, ended only by the next Arab-Israeli conflict, the "Yom Kippur War" of 1973. It also made Israel much of the world's hero, though this, too, ended by 1973. Jews, especially, saw Israel in a heroic and even glamorous light. Economic recovery and the image of a nation that had achieved security and was entering a dynamic growth period combined to increase Israel's attractiveness as a country of immigration. Moreover, as we shall see, there were forces at work in the USSR, the United States, Latin America, and elsewhere, which impelled more Jews to emigrate from their native lands. By 1968 immigration increased to 18,087, and in the following year it more than doubled, reaching 37,804. It continued to increase until 1974, when it fell to 31,979, declining to 20,028 in the following year and to 19,879 in 1976.[28] In the 1969-73 "boom" period a total of 227,258 immigrants arrived in Israel.

This period saw dramatic changes not only in the numbers but also in the types of immigrants coming. Whereas in the 1948-51 period half the immigrants had come from Asia and Africa, and in 1952-57 over three-quarters of them were from those two continents, in the post-Six-Day War period nearly three-quarters of the immigrants came from America, Europe, and Oceania, the first time in Israeli history that such a high proportion had come from the Western world. The numbers and origins of the immigrants can be seen in Table 2.1.

The Western origins of most of the immigrants had many implications. Earlier immigrations had been of the "organized group settlement" type, meaning that they had been organized as immigrants from a specific area and brought to a predetermined area, generally settled in agricultural pursuits. Or, in the case of some Europeans and Afro-Asians, they formed fairly compact, homogeneous settlements in a pattern that has been called "gravitation group settlement." Only to very limited extent was the pre-1967 immigration a "chain migration," wherein "migrant communities . . . come into being when persons from a particular township or district in one country settle in a particular locality abroad, establish links with their friends and relatives at home, and encourage them through letter, visits, and offers of assistance to join them."[29] The

TABLE 2.1
Immigration to Israel by Country of Origin, 1968-73

	1968	1969	1970	1971	1972	1973
Eastern Europe,	2,381	6,486	6,627	14,681	34,461	37,206
of which USSR	231	3,019	994	12,839	31,652	33,477
United States	5,024	5,739	6,882	7,364	5,515	4,393
Canada	575	680	792	758	519	393
Latin America	2,290	2,682	4,009	4,426	4,429	4,418
Western Europe	6,979	8,739	8,191	6,207	4,704	3,286
Asia-Africa	13,420	12,941	10,787	8,132	5,911	4,864
Oceania	400	288	389	347	351	318
Totals	31,069*	37,581	37,895	41,930	55,888	54,886

*The discrepancies between these data and the figures of the Central Statistical Bureau are especially great for 1968 and arise from several factors: Some statistics are calculated according to the Jewish calendar year, roughly from September to September, and others according to the general calendar; tourists who settled in the country, returning Israeli citizens, and "potential immigrants," a new category introduced in the late 1960s, were variously classified in the immigration statistics until 1969. For an account of the confusion in statistical records, and the seeming inflation of the data by the immigrant absorption ministry, see "Hahagzamot bemisperai haaliyah vesofrai Haaretz," *Haaretz*, May 14, 1969. In each year there are a few immigrants whose country of origin is indeterminate, and this explains the fact that the totals for each year are a bit higher than the figure obtained by adding the column figures, that is, the figures by continent or country of origin.

Source: Klitat haaliya (Jerusalem: Ministry for Immigrant Absorption, 1972 and 1973).

33

Western immigrants do not fit easily into any of these categories, since most made highly individual decisions and constituted a tiny fraction of the Jewish communities from which they came. The Soviet immigrants, however, represent a chain migration to a considerable extent, especially the Georgians and Central Asians, who constitute about one-third of the total Soviet immigration. The fact that there was almost no "organized group settlement" in the 1960s and 1970s reduced the dependence of the immigrants on the absorbing authorities and made immigration a more individual process for both the absorption authorities and the immigrants themselves. This was reinforced by the fact that the Westerners, especially, did not settle in compact areas, such as the immigrant *moshavim* (agricultural cooperatives) or development towns of the 1950s, but found their own housing on the private market in the major cities and their suburbs, or, like most of the Soviet immigrants, received apartments in immigrant housing projects from the government.

An even more important difference between the earlier and later immigrations, one that contributed most directly to the differences in their absorption, was the higher level of education and skills brought by the American and European newcomers. According to the Immigrant Absorption Ministry, in 1968-69 nearly 33 percent of all the immigrants in the labor force were classified as "academics and members of the free professions," while about 25 percent were employed in crafts and industry, about 15 percent in trade and services, about 20 percent as supervisors and clerks, and the rest in various occupations.[30] There were, for example, 549 engineers, 450 physicians, and 1,109 teachers among the immigrants.[31] In 1970 the proportion of academics and professionals rose to 42 percent. This figure takes on added importance when one realizes that the same occupational category encompassed only 14.5 percent of the Israeli host population in the same year. Thus, while 8 percent of the immigrants were engineers and 5 percent were physicians, only 1 percent of the Israeli population fell in each category.[32] The 1972 figures are quite similar, showing about 20 percent of the immigrants as scientific and academic workers, and another 22 percent classified as "professional, technical and related workers."[33] Later years show the same occupational distribution.[34]

The economic impact of this kind of immigration has been enormous. The growth and development of some of Israel's infant industries were made possible in large part by this massive infusion of technically trained immigrants. The defense and electronic industries, the aviation and shipping industries, and the nursing profession are a few examples of sectors wherein immigrants have played major roles. Their impact on the medical field has been enormous. Fully one-third of all physicians in Israel are immigrants who came between 1972 and 1977, more than half of them from the USSR, and the rest from North America, Romania, Western Europe, and Latin America.[35] Time and again, politicians and economists have pointed out the tremendous resource that this immigration represents to a population that sometimes sees immigrants as a burden, privileged recipients of special tax breaks. It is pointed out that the immigrants bring in a very substantial amount of capital to the country, in contrast to the refugees of earlier years, contributing significantly to Israel's badly needed reserves of hard currency. Moreover, by entering the country with professional training already accomplished, the immigrants save the state the costs of training them in such high-cost professions as medicine. Of course, some of the immigrants require retraining, but others are well ahead of Israeli standards in their fields, and, if appreciated and "exploited" properly, they can be a source of innovation and advancement for the economy. In 1972 the Ministry for Immigrant Absorption pointed out that while in the previous year Israel had spent about $100 million for absorption, the immigrants of that year had brought into the country approximately $150 million. It was noted that they constituted 37 percent of the manpower added to the economy that year and underscored a noneconomic benefit of immigration, or *aliyah*, which is frequently referred to by Israelis. This is the calculation that, given the far higher birth rate among Israeli Arabs than among Jews, only with an additional 70,000 Jewish immigrants a year can the state maintain the present Jewish:Arab ratio.[36]

An economic analysis done by the Jewish Agency concluded that "economic prosperity stimulates immigration tides; the more complex conclusion states that the consumption-production activities on the part of immigration tend to thrust economic processes upward, in the direction of prosperity." Moreover, the additional "human capital" resulting from immigration was calculated at more than $217 million for the period 1968-70, based on an assumption that an average of $20,000 would have had to be spent to train the professionals who immigrated already trained.[37] In 1975 another immigration minister told the parliament (Knesset) that "in the last few years" immigrants had constituted 40 percent of the manpower that had been added to the economy, and about 60 percent of the additional manpower in industry. Moreover, 90 percent of the doctors added to the Histadrut's *Kupat kholim* health care system were immigrants, as were 75 percent of the doctors in the Negev, the southern wilderness and desert area of the country that the state is trying to develop.[38] An immigration ministry publication estimated that in 1971-73 immigrants had brought in $550 million.[39]

The short- and long-range economic importance of this most recent wave of immigration made it obvious that it would have to be treated differently from previous ones. Because the education and culture of the recent immigrants were so dramatically different from any other the state had known, established ways of absorbing immigrants might be not only irrelevant but counterproductive. Therefore, after the Six-Day War, Israel substantially revised its system of receiving and absorbing immigrants from all sources.

IMMIGRATION ADMINISTRATION AND POLICY IN THE 1970S AND 1980S

Encouraging immigration has always been a high priority of Israeli policy. In 1949 the first prime minister, David Ben-Gurion, told the Knesset that "we must speed and make more powerful the stream of immigration to the utmost of our powers, for the ingathering of the exiles is the purpose of our existence and also a precondition of it."[40] After 1967, when many Israelis felt their security situation had improved greatly, there was a turning inward, and a drive to expand and improve the economy and make the society more dynamic, larger, more sophisticated. All this pointed in the direction of a renewed drive for immigration. This became a high priority for the government, or so it seemed.

The logical first step involved the recruitment of immigrants abroad. This was the task of the Jewish Agency, which argued that there were legal barriers in some countries to governmental agencies recruiting immigrants, and therefore, as a nongovernmental agency, it could perform this function (the fact that Australia, South Africa, and other countries maintain government offices abroad for immigrant recruitment was not mentioned). The Agency has representatives (*shlikhim*) abroad whose main task is to recruit and inform potential immigrants, and then, if they should decide to "make aliyah," to help them find jobs, housing, and schooling, arrange transportation, shipment of household goods, and the like. In 1974 there were 108 such representatives operating out of 49 offices in 24 countries. This was in addition to numerous other Agency *shlikhim*, such as those attached to "youth and pioneering" departments, who also engaged in activities designed to promote aliyah.[41]

Recruitment in the diaspora was complemented by efforts to raise Israeli consciousness of the importance of aliyah and to create a receptive atmosphere for the immigrants. Aware of resentments, especially of Soviet immigrants, in certain sectors of the population, former Prime Minister Golda Meir often emphasized how necessary aliyah is and how important it is to receive immigrants with open arms. She said, "There is no State of Israel without a large and powerful aliyah. Without aliyah there is no justification for all the wars and all the sacrifices and all the blood that has been spilled here. This is the essence of our life."[42] The late Moshe Dayan also emphasized the importance of immigration and said that Israelis should even be "prepared to make sacrifices in order to fulfill the needs of those Jews who are ready to come here. . . . We have to adjust and be flexible so that we can fulfill the wishes of potential immigrants."[43]

In 1968-69 a series of measures was adopted designed largely with Western immigrants in mind. These were to ease the transition from developed economies and the immigrants' higher standards of living to Israeli conditions. These measures included "rights" or "privileges" (*zkhuyot*) such as: a lower rate of income tax for the first three years of residence in Israel, with the rate gradually progressing to the point where in the fourth year the immigrant pays full taxes; lower taxation on automobiles (a sales tax of "only" 25 percent instead of the usual 200 percent or so); the right to import goods, tax-free, for personal use during the first three years; mortgages at favorable rates (9 percent interest, instead of the then prevailing commercial rates of about 18 percent), or rental subsidies, or rentals of certain apartments with an option to buy them. A new category of temporary resident, "potential immigrant," was created to accommodate those who were reluctant to make the full commitment to immigration immediately upon arrival. They were given all the rights of a new immigrant for three years, following which they had to decide whether or not they were going to settle permanently and accept Israeli citizenship. For immigrants from North America and much of Latin America and Europe, these "benefits" compared unfavorably to the conditions they had come to expect in their home countries, but, on the other side of the fence, the Israelis saw them as extremely favorable concessions precisely to those who needed them least — educated, relatively wealthy immigrants. The counter-argument was that those who were new in the country did not have the *savoir faire*, the connections (*protektsiia*), or even the language that were advantages enjoyed by Israelis, and that, even with all the "benefits," most of the immigrants — even some from the USSR — were lowering their living standards by coming to Israel. Because of public and financial pressures, and because of abuses by some immi-grants, in the mid-1970s the government limited the "benefits." For example, mortgages were no longer granted for the purchase of especially large apartments, and the tax break on automobiles now depended on the size of its engine, and so on. Nevertheless, resent-ment was expressed by some veteran Israelis, and they were vented particularly against Soviet immigrants. A popular expression was that Soviet immigrants would make a triumphant "V" sign upon arrival in Israel, signifying by that that they would now acquire a villa and a Volvo. Needless to say, such witticisms did nothing to improve relations between veterans and newcomers.

Immigrants with some higher education received additional benefits. On the grounds that the great majority needed retraining, linguistic and otherwise, before they could resume their professions in the new country, they were given the right to live in immigrant hostels for six months, where they would be supported while learn-ing the language in an intensive course (*ulpan*). By 1978 there were 60 such hostels, with a capacity of around 13,000, all over the country. Many *akademaim*, as they are called, actually stay in the hostels longer than six months, since their apartments may not be ready, or they have not found permanent housing. Non*akademaim* also get the opportunity to study in *ulpanim*, but this is usually after working hours in a nonresidential setting. There are vocational retraining programs for people whose specialties are irrelevant to the Israeli economy or too different from the parallel occupations in Israel. An example of the former might be *kolkhoz* economists or Lithuanian language teachers, and the latter would include Soviet lawyers or some types of engineers and physicians. Though some believe that all these measures were designed specifically for Soviet or Western immigrants, they are in fact accessible to all immigrants, irrespective of country or continent of origin, so that Turkish or Iranian immigrants have the same benefits as Canadian or French immigrants.[44]

A long-standing aim of Israeli policy has been the "dispersal of the population" (*pizur haukhlusin*). With about two-thirds of the Jewish population concentrated in the greater Tel Aviv area and coastal strip, the government has tried, for ideological, security, and economic reasons, to encourage people to go to outlying areas. Theoretically, since the government could determine where immigrant housing would be built, it could strongly influence the settlement patterns of the newcomers and direct them away from the center of the country. In practice, the immigrants are concentrated in the coastal area and the larger cities. In 1972, 40 percent of construction for immigrants was said to be in development areas, 10 percent in Jerusalem (which the government was eager to expand and populate for security and political reasons), and 50 percent along the Mediterranean coast.[45] Fully 60 percent of the immigration was to be directed to development areas,[46] but in 1968-69 only 19 percent of the immigrants settled in them.[47] While immigrant families settled *initially* in development areas in the following years, they tended to leave for the established centers as soon as they could (for Soviet immigrants this was perhaps following a pattern they had learned in the USSR). In fact, because housing is not significantly cheaper, and certainly not more attractive, in development areas, and because job and cultural opportunities are far more limited there, the government's policy has been inconsistent and a failure. The major exception is the success of the Negev city of Beersheva in attracting Soviet immigrants. The port city of Ashdod has also attracted large numbers of Soviet Georgian immigrants, and Jerusalem has attracted many Westerners and Soviet immigrants. These three cities, however, are classified as secondary development areas, and not many immigrants have gone to the smaller, younger development areas of the Negev in the south and the Galilee in the north.[48] Since 1977, under the Likud governments, immigrants have been encouraged to go on to the West Bank in settlements established in the 1970s and thereafter.

The kibbutzim, founded by Europeans and not very receptive to the Afro-Asian immigrants, have failed to entice large numbers of the more recent immigrants to take up the communal way of life,

though it is now in many instances a life not of pioneering hard-
ships but of relative comfort and prosperity. There are some West
European and American (especially Latin American) immigrants
who have been socialized in Zionist movements in their home
countries to settle on kibbutzim, but they are a small minority of
the post-1967 immigration. To most of the Soviet immigrants, the
kibbutz smacks of socialism, of the Soviet *kolkhoz*, and of the
"idiocy of rural life" (98 percent of the Soviet Jewish population
was classified as urban in the 1970 and 1979 Soviet censuses). In
the three-year period from 1969 to 1971, only 5,444 out of the total
of more than 170,000 immigrants settled on kibbutzim, and the
trend was clearly downward.[49]

By the late 1960s the methods of recruitment, reception, and
resettlement of immigrants had been modified substantially from the
patterns obtaining earlier. The new, voluntary, educated, Western
immigration was being recruited; all immigrants were granted initially
more favorable conditions than the veteran population; and they
were able to choose their places and modes of residence to a far
greater extent than their predecessors. The costs of immigrant
absorption were high, but the benefits — even the financial ones —
were at least commensurate. Taking a representative year, 1972, we
find the total cost of absorption estimated at about $55 million, of
which about half were direct costs. In "macro" terms, this represented about 8 percent of Israel's gross national product, and in
"micro" terms it meant that about $33,000 were spent on the
absorption of each immigrant family of three. Housing costs were
estimated at about $214 million, and $72 million were expended to
bring immigrants and their goods to Israel (most of this in the form
of loans, much of which is forgiven if the immigrant stays for three
years), on administration, vocational training, transient facilities,
and so on.[50] This enormous operation is administered largely by two
offices, the Immigration and Absorption Department of the Jewish
Agency and the Ministry for Immigrant Absorption.

THE POLITICS AND ADMINISTRATION
OF IMMIGRANT ABSORPTION

In 1948 those in charge of devising Israel's administrative structure did not propose the creation of a ministry of immigration,

though such a ministry did come into being, only to be abolished a few years later. Curiously, the Jewish Agency, which in 1968 and thereafter vigorously opposed the creation of a ministry, favored it in 1948, probably because it was assumed that it would be created directly out of the Agency's immigration department. "Our failure to propose a Ministry of Immigration," writes one of the architects of Israel's administration,

> became a controversial issue between the directorate of the Jewish Agency's Immigration Department and ourselves. They argued that a Jewish State without an Immigration Department was inconceivable. Our contention was that a state permitting free immigration did not need an Immigration Department but agencies for the reception and integration of immigrants, and these would be located within the Jewish Agency. True, an Immigration Ministry was established . . . but later developments confirmed our standpoint.[51]

In 1951, after an intense conflict among the parties over the type of education to be provided to the immigrants in the *ma'abarot* (immigrant camps), the government was dissolved and new elections were held. In the new government there was no longer a portfolio for immigrant absorption. After 1951 immigration activities were divided between the Jewish Agency and various government offices.

By 1968 the new wave and type of immigration made it clear that the Agency's traditional methods of immigrant absorption would have to be modified. Many people expressed the view that the Agency was dominated by an older type of "professional Zionist," appointed largely because of political connections, and that these people were preoccupied with abstract theoretical debates or with petty political infighting. They were said not to be compatible with the new type of immigrant. It is true that the Agency was heavily politicized, a legacy of the Mandatory period. It had not been a "body of full-time, salaried officers, systematically recruited, with clear lines of authority and uniform rules. . . . Administrative style accentuated improvisation and negotiating ability. . . . No code of conduct existed, nor did a common outlook on government or even a commitment to a career as a public official." There was no regular system of recruitment and appointment, no formal system for advancement, little discipline, and no systematic budgetary procedures.[52] In many respects the Agency resembled what Riggs calls the "sala" model of public administration, a style of administration found in many countries making the transition to modernity.[53] The problem was that the "sala" model persisted into the 1960s when the Israeli environment had changed considerably and "sala" characteristics were increasingly criticized by Israelis themselves. With the decline in immigration in the mid-1960s, the World Zionist Congress, the parent body of the Agency, undertook to streamline the Agency and decrease its personnel, but reorganization was hampered by political considerations. As one journalist remarked acidly, "when planning the reorganization, Mr. Pincus apparently forgot one of the fundamental givens of the Agency's structure, according to which the party identification of those in charge of immigration, absorption, and economics is very important, as if the dimensions of immigration and the quality of integration depended upon it."[54]

The Agency was criticized also for its complicated bureaucratic procedures and its failure to recruit more immigrants.

> Even nowadays it happens that an immigrant waits in line for several days. Finally, when his turn comes to ask for a loan . . . the clerk gives him a pile of papers with questions covering everything from the day of his arrival in this world to the day of his departure from it. The climax is reached when the clerk requires . . . 14 co-signers.[55]

When, in the aftermath of the 1967 War, many young people came as volunteers to aid in the civilian sector, they were widely regarded as potential immigrants of high motivation. Out of 7,435 volunteers, however, only 856 had declared themselves immigrants by January 1968.[56] Rightly or wrongly, many blamed the Agency, which was in charge of coordinating the volunteers. All this created pressure from the press and the public for reexamining the administration of immigration and the Jewish Agency's role in it.

In June 1968 the government decided to create a Ministry for Immigrant Absorption (MIA). This decision followed heated debate within a committee set up by the ruling Labor party to consider the issue. Within the committee the representative of the Agency argued essentially for keeping the status quo, though he suggested the creation of a joint agency-government authority to oversee immigration and absorption. "I am opposed to taking immigration and absorption tasks away from the Zionist Organization [Jewish Agency] because this is its main function and without this it has no *raison d'être*, in my opinion."[57] At the opposite end of the spectrum was the proposal of Chaim Herzog, later Israel's ambassador to the United Nations, who suggested that only "immigration in the long run" be left to the Agency, and that all other activities connected with immigration be assumed by the state. A compromise was suggested by Shaul Avigur, long involved in "illegal" and legal immigration, and Arie (Liova) Eliav, then a powerful figure in the Labor party. The basic idea was to have the Agency deal with initial phases of immigration, including recruiting and transferring the immigrant, providing him with temporary housing and language training, with loans to start a business, and so on. The government ministry would assume comprehensive responsibility for "permanent absorption." The creation of the ministry was aimed at achieving all four of the goals that Mosher describes as being those of most reorganizations: changing policies and programs, improving administrative effectiveness, solving personnel problems and responding to "pressure outside the organization."[58] The symbolic purpose of creating the ministry was to raise the importance of immigration in the scale of national priorities and to signal potential immigrants and Israelis that immigration was now a matter of government planning, and that a firm commitment had been made to it. The new minister was Yigal Allon, who served simultaneously as vice-premier. This seemed to signal the importance of the ministry. Eliav, who became deputy minister, says that Allon thought it would be a "British type of 'overlordship,' with the housing and labor ministries subordinated to it insofar as they touched upon immigration. But this was not to come about for strictly political reasons."[59] One of those reasons was that both Prime Minister Eshkol and Finance Minister Sapir supported the Agency's position, the former having worked in the Agency for many years. Thus, the two most powerful politicians in the domestic area had reservations about the new ministry.[60]

Meanwhile, partially in order to meet the criticisms against it, the Agency was reorganizing its Immigration and Absorption Department, and at a time when it seemed that every government ministry — including the MIA[61] — was bringing in a retired general to a top post, General Uzi Narkiss, commander of the Jerusalem sector in the 1967 War, was made director-general of the department. Ironically, when the MIA recruited its staff, those at the top were appointed on the basis of party affiliation and personal acquaintance with the minister and his director-general, but the rank and file were taken from the Jewish Agency. Of 390 MIA employees, 262 were formerly employed by the Agency.[62] This is only one way in which the creation of the MIA failed to break completely with the past and with the Agency.

More important to the functioning of the MIA are the facts that it continues to depend on the Jewish Agency for most of its funds and remains a coordinating agency beholden to the good will of other ministries. It is very far from being an "overlordship." Moreover, until May 1977, when the Likud gained power and assigned the MIA to one of its adherents, the MIA was usually headed by a member of the Mapam party, the distinctly junior partner in the Labor coalition. Under the Likud the ministry has been given to a man who was also head of another, more powerful ministry, and, after the 1981 elections, to the most junior member of the new coalition. These factors make the MIA one of the weakest government ministries. The Jewish Agency has never reconciled itself to sharing administrative jurisdiction with the MIA and has constantly called for the latter's abolition, to no avail.

The Jewish Agency, through its fund-raising activities abroad, supplies a considerable part of Israel's welfare budget. From 1967 to 1969 the budget of the Agency tripled as a result of increased contributions from abroad. In the 1972 fiscal year the Agency funded 63 percent of the health welfare services of Israel, 87 percent of higher education, and 21 percent of elementary and secondary education.[63] The majority of MIA expenditures on the district level come from Agency funds and require Agency approval. This obviously gives the Agency some control of MIA operations, even on a day-to-day basis. The Agency has argued successfully that the monies it provides would not otherwise be available since the government itself could not raise tax-deductible contributions in the United States, whereas the Agency can.

When the MIA was headed by a Labor party minister, and especially one as prestigious as Allon, the Ministries of Labor, Housing, and Finance were willing to cooperate with it, and, according to Eliav, for the most part did its bidding. However, when, after the 1969 elections, Mapam entered the coalition, it received the MIA portfolio. This not only signaled a decline in the importance of the ministry, but also made it unable to coordinate with other ministries. In an internal document, one director-general of the MIA put it this way:

The ministry treads a thin line between those coordination functions which it is supposed to perform and those operational functions it would like to conduct. Moreover, the ministry suffered from the lack of central authority in the government which would enable it to fight for policy directions and the ability to execute policy at all levels. After the elections [1969] the ministry fell into the hands of a minister without portfolio, Sh. Peres, as a temporary "collateral" for seven months, until the permanent [Mapam] minister took office. . . . This situation had a severe effect on the morale of the ministry and on its ability to fight for its image and for its legitimate jurisdiction.[64]

In an interview, Director-General Sherman claimed that the housing minister stopped cooperating with MIA as soon as Peled of Mapam became its minister, so that in 1974 the MIA did not know where immigrant housing would be built nor how many units would be available.[65] This has continued to be the case with most of the ministries. The general attitude is typified by a remark made by an official of the Treasury to an immigrant who had a letter from the MIA exempting her from certain obligations. "I couldn't care less who is the Deputy Director-General of the MIA . . . We don't recognize such letters . . . we have our own problems, our own papers. We are the Ministry of the Treasury." Another Treasury official explained: "Yes, the MIA deals with immigrants, but what they decide is their own business, and we have our instructions."[66]

One more source of MIA weakness is the fact that its legitimacy has been questioned constantly, particularly by Jewish Agency officials. Since what is "initial absorption" and what is "permanent absorption" is not always clear, there are constant jurisdictional disputes between the two bodies. The division of labor, such as it is, leaves the immigrant completely confused. As one MIA district worker put it:

The immigrant does not know who is taking up his case. They drive him crazy. In his immigrant card it says "Jewish Agency," then he comes here and they tell him, "This is the Ministry for Immigrant Absorption, the social worker is an MIA employee getting her salary from the Agency, and she works with forms provided by the Agency!"

It is not surprising that "Agency" and "MIA" have become words of derision among some immigrants. In a 1972 survey, the MIA found that only 13 percent of the Soviet immigrants felt one could rely on the Agency and the MIA for housing recommendations, and 48 percent said they could not be relied upon for anything. Other immigrants had a somewhat more favorable view of the official agencies, but in housing matters, at least, most preferred to rely on friends and relatives.[67] A sample of 591 immigrants over 18, who had arrived between September and December 1969 (nearly two years before the large Soviet immigration began), were interviewed one, two, and three years after arrival. They were asked to evaluate their treatment by the MIA and Jewish Agency (see Table 2.2).

The lack of change over the three years in the view of the agencies is worthy of note; it means that immigrants, who can be expected to be suspicious, harassed, and complaining in the earliest stages of immigration, are not significantly more favorable toward the official absorbing agencies with the passage of time. On the other hand, it should be borne in mind that those who are dependent on official agencies are rarely favorable toward those agencies.

In our own survey of Soviet and American immigrants, we found that 80 percent of the Soviets and 50 percent of the Americans thought the agencies did their jobs "not too well" or "poorly." "Bureaucracy" and "red tape" were the most frequently cited complaints, with both groups complaining that the officials "don't understand the American/Soviet immigrants." One American, who insisted on calling it the "Anti-Jewish Agency," argued that the officials were unsuited to their jobs. "They don't really know what their function is. They make you run around unnecessarily.

TABLE 2.2

Satisfaction with Treatment by Jewish Agency and MIA in percent

	After One Year	*After Two Years*	*After Three Years*
Had dealings with agencies	74	75	80
Completely satisfied	20	19	19
Fairly satisfied	34	35	31
Not so satisfied	20	19	23
Not at all satisfied	26	27	27

Source: Central Bureau of Statistics, *Monthly Bulletin of Statistics — Supplement* 24, no. 6 (June 1973): 138.

Today, for example, I got a paper telling me about the purchase of an apartment. It tells you the square meters, not the price. And the Agency tells you that you must go to Amidar [the Agency housing company] to find how much it is." Calling the Agency and MIA officials "enemies of the *olim* [immigrants]," a Soviet immigrant doctor said they worked "in a purely bureaucractic manner, do not understand the psychology of *olim*, especially those from Russia, and even those who try to work correctly are blocked by the system which requires so many signatures on each piece of paper." Absorption officials were described as "party hacks," "incompetents," "lazy bums with *protektsiia*," and the like. When asked to describe the differences in function and jurisdiction between the two absorption agencies, over one-half of the Soviets and one-third of the Americans could not do so. An American remarked sardonically that the only difference is that "the Jewish Agency keeps score by the number of heads, and the MIA by the noise level of new immigrants." Another remarked that the officials themselves did not know "their own programs, rules, and regulations, so how should I?" The fact that Soviet immigrants generally have a more negative evaluation of these agencies is probably due to their more frequent contact with, and greater dependence on, both the Agency and the MIA. Americans are more likely to find jobs and housing on their own, and are less likely to need the social services and other aid provided by these agencies. In 1980 interviews with nearly 600 Soviet immigrants in Israel, we found that only 14 percent said these agencies did their jobs "very well" or "well." A parallel group of Soviet immigrants in America rated the (private) resettlement agencies much higher.

The immigrants' view of the Jewish Agency and MIA is very important, for they are the official institutions with which they have more direct and frequent contact. Their views of the relationship between the Israeli government and the individual citizen is therefore largely determined by their experiences with these two agencies (they rarely are aware that the Agency is not a government organ). Indeed, we found in our survey a strong correlation (.49) between views of the MIA or Jewish Agency (.43) and the general image of Israeli government as primarily extractive, as opposed to being seen primarily as beneficial.

Unappreciated by the immigrants, unable to persuade the other ministries to accept its priorities, and constantly skirmishing with the Jewish Agency, the MIA has not fulfilled the high hopes held for it in 1968. As early as 1973, after the resignation of MIA Director-General Ashkenazi, one correspondent commented: "The Ministry for Immigrant Absorption, which began four and a half years ago . . . proclaiming the great Zionist goal of the post Six Day War era, appeared this week to be a third class government ministry, weakened in its powers and castrated in its authority."[68] Ashkenazi resigned because of what he described as "the gap between responsibilities and authority," and he pointed to all of the problems with the Agency and with other government ministries. By the end of 1974, six years after it had begun operating, the MIA had had four ministers, four directors-general, and five directors of the Tel Aviv regional office. The Agency, by contrast, remained until mid-1978 with Uzi Narkiss as its director for immigration and absorption, when the Likud put in their own man, Raphael Kotlowitz. In 1977 the Horev Commission report, which called for a single body to be in charge of all immigration and absorption services, seemed to favor the Agency's position, and Agency officials hailed it. The Labor government shelved the report, in effect, but the Likud government promised to act upon it. Coalitional and other calculations[69] have thus far prevented it from doing so.

IMMIGRANTS AND BUREAUCRATS

The decision that, in view of the different type of immigrants coming to Israel after 1967, new procedures for absorption were needed, was a sound one, even if implementation fell short of expectations. One striking indication of the changes involved is the near reversal of the perceived role of the administrators of absorption, the "bureaucrats" of the various agencies that deal with immigrants. Afro-Asian immigrants, unfamiliar with Weberian-type bureaucracies, may have benefitted from Israeli administrative style, but Western immigrants rail against it. On the basis of "impressionistic observations," Elihu Katz and S. N. Eisenstadt found in the late 1950s that there was a process of "debureaucratization" going on whereby, instead of impersonal, businesslike, and specific interactions between immigrants and bureaucrats, they observed "officials relating to clients personally, taking sympathetic account of the status 'new immigrant,' and not confining themselves to their officially relevant roles." They found personal relationships developing between client and administrator, administrators taking on more tasks vis-a-vis the client than those assigned to him by his job, and the "assumption by the bureaucrat of the role of teacher along with (or at the expense of) his other functions. Consider, for example, the bus driver who gets out of the bus to teach the idea of a queue — 'first come, first served' — an idea which is new to many of his new immigrant passengers." Katz and Eisenstadt explain that "the bureaucrat teaches the client how to be a client so that he [the bureaucrat] can go on being a bureaucrat."[70]

Precisely these traits proved to be "dysfunctional" in the eyes of the later immigrants. The "flexible" character of a bureaucracy exasperates Western immigrants who prefer operations closer to Weberian models, as well as Soviet newcomers who came to despise — and to fear — the Soviet bureaucracy and who perceive every bureaucrat as a potential adversary. A systematic survey of 1,649 American immigrants who arrived before March 1966 found that many "describe their contact with Israeli bureaucracy as being problematic in terms of deviations from bureaucratic norms rather than in terms of bureaucratic norms *per se*."[71] A frequent complaint was lack of efficiency, and, as we shall see, this is highly characteristic of the post-1967 immigration as well. Not the fact that they are immigrants, but that they are Western, educated, and of high social status, appears to be the reason for the clash between clients' expectations and Israeli bureaucratic style. A 1968 study of urban adults in Israel concluded that people with high socioeconomic status, East and West Europeans, and veteran settlers are more self-confident vis-a-vis the bureaucracy, but also more dissatisfied with it.[72] A 1973 study of face-to-face encounters between immigrants and officials was highly critical of the latter. Most officials did not have a book of rules and procedures available when dealing with their clients, nor even the files of these clients. Explanations were not given as to why petitions were rejected, nor did officials have decision-making or discretionary powers. These were generally jealously guarded by committees that then transmitted decisions to the client through the official.

> When the immigrant has a request to which the official has no routine answer, the official is not prepared to examine the request (even if he himself identifies with and agrees with the immigrant). It should also be noted that even when certain procedures permit flexibility, the

official does not . . . present all the alternatives to the immigrant, and the limitations of each one.[73]

These observations are confirmed emphatically by the reported experiences of the Soviet immigrants we interviewed and by the general folklore that has developed about immigration absorption in Israel. It must be noted, however, that grousing seems to be intrinsic to the experience of resettlement and that resettlement officials are the easiest, most available targets.

IMMIGRANTS AND THE ISRAELI PUBLIC

Arnold Rose proposes that acceptance of foreigners into a host society is a function of the openness of that society, the immigrants' degree of attachment to their society of origin, and the similarity of the cultures of the country of emigration and the country of immigration.[74] He asserts that "the openness of the host society is largely determined by the policies, programs, and practices . . . of the country of immigration toward immigrants. . . . Most important is the policy of the government."[75] The latter does not appear to be the case in Israel, where the policy of the government is considerably more encouraging of immigration and immigrants than is the attitude of certain sectors of the host society. As an Israeli expression puts it, "we like *aliyah* [immigration], but we don't like *olim* [immigrants]." Because immigration is the raison d'être of a Jewish state, resentment of immigrants is perceived not simply as a social problem but as a failure to grasp the most fundamental ideal and goal of the country. This is the reason that prominent figures take pains to emphasize the benefits that immigration brings and why the press devotes so much attention to the issue of "social absorption" of the immigrants by the host population. On several occasions Golda Meir lashed out against those who resented immigrants, admitting that her generation was in error when it assumed "that everything we know and feel about the nation and the land will be known and felt by every Israeli youngster without our having to explain it."[76] The cabinet discussed the question several times, and Mrs. Meir appointed an advisor to coordinate the absorption efforts of official bodies and voluntary ones. Officials of the Jewish Agency and the MIA spend a good deal of time explaining the "rights" of the immigrants

to the general public and trying to demonstrate the social and economic benefits enjoyed by the entire population as a result of
immigration.[77] Women's organizations, retired teachers, banks, and
youth groups organize activities designed to acquaint immigrants
and Israelis with each other and to promote mutual understanding.
At one time prominent businessmen organized a drive to raise IL100
million for absorption needs, and 8,000 employees of the Histadrut
construction company, Solel Boneh, donated a day's wages for the
same purpose.[78]

Nevertheless, resentment against the economic benefits granted
the immigrants continued at least until 1973, when both immigration
and the controversies around it died down, and then it increased in
1979-80. To some extent the difficulties arose from the fact that
the Soviet immigration in particular got a great deal of publicity and
was portrayed as a miraculous event. This created false expectations
among some that newcomers from the USSR were all heroic idealists
who had suffered a great deal in the Soviet Union and were going to
be grateful for anything done for them in Israel. When this turned
out not to be the case, it became permissible to raise doubts about
the value of this immigration. Two groups in particular stand out
among those expressing doubts or resentment against the immigrants:
young couples in need of housing, and the poorer strata among
the Afro-Asian communities. There were a few isolated incidents
of demonstrations against immigrants and vandalism of their apartments.[79] A group calling themselves "*Sabras* in Need of Housing"
sent a letter to Georgian immigrants saying that "you won't milk
this state as you milk a cow," and another group in Jerusalem
distributed a flyer that said: "We won't let you steal our rights in
this country. You should know that young people who were born
here and fought here are discriminated against here because of you,
the new immigrant. You should know that you are stealing their
rights from young couples and from families with many children. . . .
Why don't you try the *ma'abarot* [immigrant tent cities] and we'll
try the housing projects?"[80]

Several surveys were conducted of the population's attitude
toward immigrants and the benefits they receive. In an MIA survey
of 1969, based on a representative national sample, it was found
that three-quarters of the population saw Western immigration positively, as strengthening the country in various ways. Only 30 percent
felt that the immigrants should receive no economic aid.[81] However,

once the mass immigration from the USSR began, the picture began to change, probably because the Soviet immigrants were perceived as refugees who were being "rescued" rather than as Westerners bringing their capital with them, and because immigration grew to such proportions that the housing situation became critical. People began to perceive a trade-off between immigrant benefits and help to the poor, the latter an issue that had been raised prominently about the same time as the large immigration began. One poll found that 55 percent of the population thought the poor were losing out as a result of immigration, while 35 percent disagreed. However, among those of Afro-Asian origin, 60 percent felt the poor were losing out, while among Israeli-born the proportion rose even higher, to nearly 67 percent of the respondents.[82] In the winter of 1971 a study was done involving 1,100 respondents in three poor neighborhoods. While only 23 percent objected to having Soviet immigrants move into their neighborhood (31 percent of Israeli-born), more than half felt that customs exemptions, mortgage loans, and the like for Soviet immigrants should be either reduced or abolished (62 percent of Israeli-born).[83] The researchers emphasized that the respondents had been taught the notion that seniority — length of time in Israel — was a justifiable criterion for privilege, and that they were now applying it to the new immigrants. They felt that the newcomers were "jumping the queue," and, especially, jumping over them, people who had patiently waited their turn for years. As one Oriental Jew put it in a letter to the editor of *Maariv*, "Is it natural for a new immigrant to come and take everything, while the veteran waits his turn?"[84] Others wrote that they could understand why immigrants from the United States or Western Europe would get tax breaks, since they were used to a higher standard of living, but the Soviets, it was asserted, were not, so why pamper them?[85]

Probably the most reliable survey of popular attitudes is the one conducted by the Israel Institute of Applied Social Research in 1971. A representative sample (n = 1,770) of the adult population was interviewed: 58 percent thought immigrants should continue to receive material assistance, and over half thought this should be done even if this would lower the respondents' own standard of living. However, half the respondents thought that Israeli citizens, rather than world Jewry, were paying the costs of absorption (in fact, through the Jewish Agency, world Jewry pays for most of the cost). When asked to establish priorities among five groups in need of help — slum dwellers, families with many children, young couples, and Moroccan and Soviet immigrants — the two immigrant groups ranked last. Older people and those with postsecondary education were most likely to support aid to immigrants, while those of Afro-Asian origin and those with 5-12 years of schooling were least likely to do so. Illustrating the relative social isolation of the immigrants is the finding that 46 percent of the respondents had not, in the course of the year, conversed with any immigrants about their absorption problems, though 34 percent had done so at least on three occasions.[86]

The subject of immigrant-veteran relations agitated the public and the media and scores of articles were written on the subject.[87] As immigration declined, and when some of the economic benefits given to immigrants were restricted somewhat, resentment began to fade. It should be remembered that aid to immigrants at all times enjoyed fairly wide support. If one compares the reception of immigrants in Israel to their reception in other countries of immigration, the Israeli public appears to be quite hospitable indeed. National surveys in Australia showed that in 1961 only 43 percent, and in 1964, 30 percent, of the Australians wished to see an increase in the number of immigrants. In 1960, 70 percent thought that Asians should be allowed into the country in small numbers only, and 21 percent opposed immigrants speaking in their native languages in public and living together in their own communities.[88] In 1954 in Canada 45 percent thought that immigration was beneficial to the country, but "38 percent expressed an unqualified 'no.' "[89] In both countries, however, there seems to be increasing acceptance both of immigration and of immigrants, though this should not be assumed to be a linear process.

SUMMARY

The post-1967 immigration not only differed from its predecessors in origins and socioeconomic-cultural composition, but it also entered a very different Israel from the one that had greeted earlier immigrants. Seemingly secure, on the verge of an economic boom, the Israeli population's expectations were rising and some believed that the era of sacrifice was at last coming to an end. The Jewish Agency had been reorganized and a new ministry had been created to facilitate the absorption of immigrants. The role of parties, therefore, was presumably diminished, and the modes of absorption and the techniques used were radically different from those that had prevailed a decade earlier. The largest groups of immigrants in the 1967-73 period came from the two superpowers that were increasingly involved in the international affairs of the Middle East. It is to the immigrations from the United States and the Soviet Union that we now turn.

NOTES

1. For an elaboration of this point, see Dan Horowitz and Moshe Lissak, "Authority without Sovereignty: The Case of the National Centre of the Jewish Community in Palestine," *Government and Opposition* 8 (Winter 1973).

2. S. N. Eisenstadt, *The Absorption of Immigrants* (London: Routledge and Kegan Paul, 1954), pp. 62-63.

3. J. Isaac, "Israel — A New Melting Pot?" in *The Cultural Integration of Immigrants*, ed. W. D. Barrie (Paris: UNESCO, 1959), p. 236.

4. Eisenstadt, p. 204.

5. Horowitz and Lissak, p. 61.

6. S. N. Eisenstadt, *Israeli Society* (London: Weidenfeld and Nicolson, 1969), p. 333. According to labor historian Elkanah Margalit, the paternalism and desire for power displayed by rival labor parties in the 1920s disgusted new immigrants who were moved to try to found a united labor movement "which would free the immigrant from his dependence on the parties." *Hashomer hatsair* (Tel Aviv: Tel Aviv University and Hakibbutz Hameukhad, 1971), p. 56.

7. "Meir Veisgal mesaper," *Maariv*, September 19, 1971, p. 9.

8. Ada Sereni, *Sfinot lelo degel* (Tel Aviv: Am Oved, 1975), p. 31.

9. Eisenstadt, *The Absorption of Immigrants*, pp. 218-19.

10. On the concept of "neo-feudalism" and its application to the Israeli case, see Amitai Etzioni, "The Decline of Neo-Feudalism: The Case of Israel," in *Papers in Comparative Public Administration*, ed. Ferrel Heady and Sybil Stokes (Ann Arbor: University of Michigan Institute of Public Administration, 1962).

11. Sh. N. Eisenstadt, *Hakhevra haYisraelit* (Jerusalem: Magnes Press, 1973), pp. 154-55.

12. Peter Y. Medding, *Mapai in Israel* (Cambridge: Cambridge University Press, 1972), p. 276.

13. Ibid., p. 68.

14. Ibid., p. 71.

15. Shevakh Weiss, "Am veeidah," mimeographed (Haifa: May 1974), p. 17.

16. Moshe Lissak, "The Political Absorption of Immigrants and the Preservation of Political Integration," paper presented to the International Political

Science Association Round Table on Political Integration, Jerusalem, 1974, p. 15.

17. Shlomo A. Deshen, *Immigrant Voters in Israel* (Manchester: Manchester University Press, 1970), p. 58.

18. Ibid., p. 77.

19. Ibid.

20. Rinah Zamir, "Tahalikhim khevratiyim beir pituakh: Beersheva 1958/ 59," Vol. 3, mimeographed (Jerusalem: Department of Sociology, The Hebrew University, 1964), p. 51.

21. Ibid., p. 28.

22. Ibid., p. 39.

23. Ibid., p. 55.

24. Hannah Veil, "Ba'ayot kehilatiyot beyishuv olim," mimeographed (Jerusalem: Department of Sociology, The Hebrew University, July 1957), p. 20.

25. Ibid., p. 32.

26. Ibid., p. 41.

27. Sheldon Ruda, "Patterns of Political Integration in a Development Area in Israel," Ph.D. dissertation, Claremont Graduate School, 1973, p. 196.

28. See Central Bureau of Statistics, *Statistical Abstract of Israel, 1974* (Jerusalem, 1975); *Klitat haaliyah 1975* (Jerusalem: Ministry of Immigrant Absorption, 1976), p. 81; and *Haaretz*, January 25, 1977.

29. Charles Price, "Chain Migration and Immigrant Groups, with Special Reference to Australian Jewry," *Jewish Journal of Sociology* 6, no. 2 (1964): 158.

30. Efraim Akhiram, "Herkev haaliyah bishnat 1968/9 uklitatah," *Rivon lekalkalah*, June 1970. The author was director of the ministry's Department of Planning and Research.

31. *Israel Government Year Book 5731* (Jerusalem: Ministry of Education and Culture, p. 245).

32. Efraim Akhiram, "Lekakhim akhadim m'nision klitat haaliyah akharai milkhemet sheshet hayamim," *Rivon lekalkalah*, June 1971, p. 68. For further details, see "Ain nigud bein shtai mesimot," *Al hamishmar*, July 30, 1971, or "Mashmaut klitat haaliyah," *Shearim*, August 30, 1971.

33. Calculated on the basis of data in *Statistical Abstract of Israel 1973*, p. 133.

34. *Klitat haaliyah* for 1973-77.

35. Atallah Mantsour, "Shlish harofim-olim," *Haaretz*, February 7, 1977.

36. *Maariv*, March 22, 1972, p. 4.

37. L. Berger, "Immigration Volume Forecasts," in *Immigration and War Against Poverty* (Jerusalem: Jewish Agency, 1972), pp. 18 and 26.

38. *Maariv*, May 14, 1975.

39. *Aliyah uklitah bishnot hashivim* (Jerusalem, February 1974), p. 9.

40. David Ben-Gurion, *Medinat Yisrael hamekhudeshet* (Tel Aviv: Am Oved, 1969), Vol. II, p. 386.

41. H. Yustus, "Aliyah-shnai ktzavot lah," *Maariv*, January 17, 1974. By 1977 the number of *shlikhim* had declined to about 80, and one-third of them worked also in areas other than aliyah. See *Haaretz*, January 25, 1977.

42. Interview with Dov Goldstein, *Maariv*, January 21, 1972.

43. Interview with Kenneth Harris of the London *Observer*, reported in *Maariv*, January 23, 1971.

44. A discussion of the rationale for immigrant "benefits" may be found in L. Berger, "Takhazit haaliyah litvakh katzar vearokh," *Baayot beinleumiyot* 5, nos. 1-2 (May 1969).

45. Minister of Immigration Peled to the Knesset, reported in *Maariv*, March 15, 1972.

46. Peled to the Knesset, *Maariv*, June 9, 1972.

47. "Aliyat harvakha ainah netulat baayot," *Al hamishmar*, January 12, 1969.

48. For an informed discussion of this subject, see the article by Professor Haim Barkai, "Klitat aliyah upizur ukhlusin," *Maariv*, January 21, 1972.

49. Menakhem Rabat, "Hakibutzim hitoreru liklitat aliyah," *Maariv*, June 1, 1972. Somewhat different figures are cited in *Lamerkhav* and *Hatsofe* of January 28, 1971.

50. *Klitat haaliyah 1972* (Jerusalem: Ministry of Immigrant Absorption, March, 1973), Vol. I, p. 19.

51. Zeev Sharef, *Three Days* (Garden City, N.Y.: Doubleday, 1962), p. 55.

52. Donna Robinson Divine, "Patrons and Saints: A Study of the Career Patterns of Higher Civil Servants in Israel," Ph.D. dissertation, Columbia University, 1970, pp. 39-40.

53. Fred Riggs, "The 'Sala' Model: An Ecological Approach to the Study of Public Administration," in *Readings in Comparative Public Administration*, ed. Nimrod Raphaeli (Boston: Allyn and Bacon, 1967).

54. Naftali Lavi, "Hasokhuut umesimoteha hanitskhiot," *Haaretz*, March 17, 1967.

55. Naftali Lavi, "Haavtalah basokhuut naaset gluyah," *Harretz*, October 2, 1967. See also Eitan Gilboa, "Khamesh hashegiot shebetipul haaliyah," *Davar*, December 25, 1967; and Yustus, "Bemorad haaliyah," *Maariv*, December 30, 1966.

56. *Divrai hakneset*, Vol. 50 (1968), pp. 771-72; Vol. 49 (1967), pp. 2508, 2510, and 2512.

57. *Dapai aliyah*, Vol. 69 (1968), p. 53.

58. Frederick C. Mosher, "Analytical Commentary," in *Governmental Reorganization*, ed. Frederick C. Mosher (Indianapolis: Bobbs-Merrill, 1967), pp. 494-95.

59. Interview with Member of Knesset Aryeh Eliav, May 5, 1972.

60. See *Haaretz*, May 27, 1968, and Naftali Lavi, "Eshkol neged hakamat reshut aliyah," *Haaretz*, January 9, 1969. Eshkol's opposition may have been based also on the calculation that a new ministry entailed renegotiating the cabinet coalition and the possible advancement of Allon, a potential prime minister whose promotion Eshkol did not welcome.

61. The first director-general of the MIA was General Yosef Geva (ret.), former commander of the northern front, and his deputy, Menahem Sherman, was a retired Lieutenant-Colonel. Sherman became director-general in 1978.

62. On this and other details of MIA staffing, see Zvi Gitelman and David Naveh, "Elite Accommodation and Organizational Effectiveness: The Case of Immigrant Absorption in Israel," *Journal of Politics* 38, no. 4 (November 1976): 973-79.

63. Yekhiel Limor, "Dultzin: Habikoret al haaliyah baaretz madigah et anshai hamagbit bekhool," *Maariv*, March 38, 1972.

64. Menahem Sherman, "Hakamat misrad haklitah: mifneh o drikha bamakom," unpublished internal report, n. d., p. 14.

65. Interview on April 14, 1972. At the time of the interview, Sherman was not with the MIA, but with the Tel Aviv municipality.

66. "Inge Deutschkron, olah khadasha," *Maariv*, July 21, 1972.

67. *Klitat haaliyah 1972*, pp. 41 and 35.

68. Eli Ayal, "Lamah hitpater hamankal," *Maariv*, March 2, 1973.

69. For example, the minister until 1981, David Levi, is associated with the Herut wing of the Likud. Were the ministry to have been abolished, the Herut faction would have demanded some other place in the cabinet and a place would have to be found for Levi, who, as a Moroccan-born worker from a development town, has symbolic importance for the Likud. Levi's successor is also Moroccan-born, but is the leader of the small Tami party, formed as a breakaway from the National Religious party in 1981.

70. Elihu Katz and S. N. Eisenstadt, "Some Sociological Observations on the Response of Israeli Organizations to New Immigrants," *Administrative Science Quarterly* 5 (1960/61): 115-24.

71. David Katz and Aaron Antonovsky, "Bureaucracy and Immigrant Adjustment," *International Migration Review* 7, no. 3 (1972).

72. Brenda Danet and Harriet Hartman, "Coping with Bureaucracy, the Israeli Case," *Social Forces* 51, no. 1 (September 1972): 19. "Very new immigrants" were "heavily underrepresented" in this sample (p. 21).

73. Brenda Danet and Miriam Levav, "Dfusai maga bain olim umetaplim," mimeographed (Jerusalem: Ministry for Immigrant Absorption, September 1973), p. v.

74. Arnold M. Rose, *Migrants in Europe: Problems of Acceptance and Adjustment* (Minneapolis: University of Minnesota Press, 1969), p. 33.

75. Ibid.

76. *Maariv*, March 12, 1972. See also her speech to educators, reported in *Maariv*, June 13, 1972, and to university students, *Maariv*, March 9, 1972.

77. See, for example, E. Akhiram, "Olim, vatikim, vedeot kdumot," *Davar*, November 30, 1971; R. Reikher, "Hatavot leolim mishtalmot lamdinah," *Yediot Akhronot*, August 1, 1969; Aharon Geva, "Hem veanakhnu," *Lamerkhav*, May 14, 1971; Natan Dunevitz, "Villa, Volvo, vekhol hashear," *Haaretz*, December 21, 1972.

78. See *Maariv*, January 26 and March 9, 1972.

79. See reports of an incident in Yavneh, *Maariv*, February 27, 1972; of a demonstration in Ashdod, *Maariv*, June 23, 1971; and of an incident in Ramat Gan, *Maariv*, February 21, 1972.

80. *Maariv*, December 16, 1971. The flyer is quoted in Levi Yitzhak Hayerushalmi, "Rotsim lehishtayekh, v'lo yodim lamah," *Maariv*, January 10, 1971.

81. Sarah Frankel, "75% mehaukhlusia mekhayevet aliyat yehudai hamaarav artza," *Hayom*, September 21, 1969.

82. "Mishal: Klitat haaliyah pogaat bekidum shkhavot haoni," *Haaretz*, August 16 and 29, 1971. A less reliable poll in April 1972 found 56 percent agreeing that the Soviet immigration is a burden (*Maariv*, April 13, 1972). Nearly two-thirds of the respondents in a poll taken in late 1971 expressed the opinion that Georgian immigrants who threatened to leave the country if their demands were not met should not be dissuaded from leaving. See *Haaretz*, January 10, 1972.

83. Yokhanan Peres, "Politika veadatiyut beshalosh shkhunot oni," mimeographed (Tel Aviv: Modiin Ezrakhi, Ltd., Hamerkaz lemekhkarim shimushiyim, October 1972), pp. 14-16.

84. Letter by Sami Gabai, *Maariv*, February 7, 1972; see also similar letters in *Maariv*, January 31 and February 2, 1972.

85. Letter by Yosef Meir, *Haaretz*, May 17, 1971.

86. David Katz, "Deot hatsibur al klitat aliyah beYisrael," mimeographed (Jerusalem: Israel Institute for Applied Social Research and Ministry for Immigrant Absorption, December 1971).

87. Some representative examples are Mati Golan, "Ofnah mesukenet," *Haaretz*, May 6, 1971; Geulah Cohen, "Bearba einayim . . . ," *Maariv*, March 10, 1972; Moshe Shamir, "Haaliyah min hamaarav — akhzava hadadit," *Maariv*, July 7, 1972; Matityahu Peled, "Alu, olim, yaalu," *Maariv*, March 17, 1972; Ami Shamir, "Kol hakavod leolim, aval . . . ," *Haaretz*, March 3, 1972.

88. Data taken from Alan Richardson and Ronald Taft, "Australian Attitudes toward Immigrants: A Review of Social Survey Findings," *International Migration Review* 2, no. 3 (Summer, 1968); and Ronald Taft, *From Stranger to Citizen* (London: Tavistock, 1966), pp. 21-23.

89. Raymond Breton, Jill Armstrong, and Les Kennedy, "The Social Impact of Changes in Population Size and Composition" (Ottawa: Department of Manpower and Immigration, 1974), p. 28.

3

AMERICAN AND SOVIET IMMIGRATION AFTER 1967

Professor Mark Azbel, whose 1972 application to emigrate was approved only in 1977, leading a seminar of Soviet "refusenik" and foreign scientists. Courtesy National Conference on Soviet Jewry.

AMERICAN ZIONISM AND ALIYAH

American Zionism never made aliyah the real imperative or end of the movement. The "push" factors present in Europe — anti-Semitism, alienation from mainstream culture, poverty — have not been salient for American Jewry. By and large, Americans identified with any one of the several Zionist organizations in their country have seen their primary function as providing economic and political aid to those who lived in the Zionist homeland, not immigration to it. In fact, several observers sympathetic to Zionism argue that those who consider themselves Zionists have actually opposed aliyah. Benjamin Wohlman asserts that Zionist organizations "were good and loyal in the role of supporters, friends, political fighters and fund raisers, but when the matter of personal realization came up — that was a different matter. There is a great opposition to the idea of *aliyah* and *chalutziyut* [pioneering], and many Zionists will prevent their children from emigration to Israel. . . ."[1]

Several explanations for this seeming paradox have been offered: that American economic, social, and political conditions are not conducive to emigration; that, as a country of immigration, the American ethos discourages emigration; that while American Jews enjoy economic and political security, Israeli Jews do not; American Zionism has usually been hortatory, not ideological. For all these reasons, some are led to conclude that Zionist and Jewish organizations in the United States pursue the goal of aliyah "in a half-hearted manner, as a mere outward conforming with the official principles of Zionism. It is a kind of ritualistic obeisance to unfashionable idols, gestures which serve as substitutes for real activities. The pronouncements are superficial and high-sounding and commit nobody, nor do they lead to action."[2] It is estimated that in the period 1948-60, of nearly 8,000 American immigrants to Israel, only some 2,500 were affiliated with a Zionist youth movement that emphasized aliyah. Considering the fact that there is no refugee immigration from the United States, and that ideological motivations would seem to be the only relevant ones, this is a small proportion.[3] The more obvious point is that the largest Jewish community in the world provided only a tiny proportion of immigrants to Israel until 1967.

In the 1960s and 1970s there were dramatic qualitative and quantitative changes in American immigration to Israel. The proportion of middle class, established professionals increased, and that of the Zionist-affiliated youth declined. A high proportion of immigrants came for what might be called general Jewish reasons rather than specifically Zionist ones, as shall be seen in our discussion of motivations for aliyah. However, this should not be taken as an indication that the attitude toward aliyah has changed very much within the organized Jewish community. Interviews with Israeli aliyah emissaries impressed one observer with the extent to which the activities of the Israel Aliyah Center and access to the American Jewish community to promote *aliyah* are circumscribed by the gate-keepers of American Jewish life — federation executives and lay leaders, rabbis, educators, newspaper editors, Zionist organizations. . . . Quite in contrast to the solidarity with Israel, and the extensive fund-raising and community relations campaigns launched for Israel, in the majority of American Jewish communities the Israel Aliyah Center is an "outsider" and more or less kept apart from the local community. . . . A community leader may, for example, agree to "bless" some departing olim [immigrants] from his community, but refuse to permit a picture of the event to appear in the local Jewish newspaper.[4]

From the viewpoint of some Jewish communal leaders, aliyah conflicts with other priorities, because though it may strengthen Israeli Jewry, it can weaken American Jewry by depleting it of leadership talent, sources of funds, active constituents, and sheer numbers. It may also controvert local communal goals, as in the case of a Jewish community in Brooklyn that had cosponsored an address on aliyah by former Israeli Foreign Minister Abba Eban. "As the audience filed in to hear about Israel's need for Western immigrants, community leaders were passing out flyers urging them to support the . . . campaign to prevent 'white-flight' from the racially changing local community by 'coming to live in Remsen village.' "[5]

Other conflicts arise from the strategy sometimes used to raise funds for Israel. In order to dramatize the need for financial support, United Jewish Appeal advertisements often emphasize Israel's security and welfare problems — emphases that could well discourage people from wanting to live in a country beset by so many troubles. George Johnson also suggests that fund raising and aliyah may conflict because these

reflect two competing views about what it means to be a Jew. The giver is a committed Jew, but he is a diaspora Jew. His problem is not so much that *aliyah* hurts the campaign, but that *aliyah* implies that he is an inchoate Israeli — a notion which runs counter to the major thrust of nearly every major Jewish communal organization, that being a Jew in no way conflicts with being a patriotic American, and must not serve as a basis for distinction or discrimination in the law or society. The diaspora Jew knows . . . that *aliyah* is a statement of the primacy of one's Jewish identity.[6]

For this reason, aliyah has always been portrayed in the United States as an individual decision, the act of a single person. It is not perceived today as a communal obligation, but as the perhaps heroic, perhaps quixotic act of a few who have made a highly individual decision. Indeed, this perception is affirmed by the dimensions of aliyah set against the size of the overall American Jewish community, usually estimated as upward of 5 million. Nevertheless, a far larger number of individuals made the decision to emigrate in the 1968-73 period than had ever done so before — or were to do so in the post-1973 period.

It is very difficult to fix with any certainty the number of American immigrants to Israel before 1967, since many did not accept Israeli citizenship, in order not to lose their American citizenship, and were registered as temporary residents. Some estimates go as high as 10,000, but a careful study found that in early 1967 there were only about 2,400 Americans and Canadians over the age of 15 living in Israel.[7] In 1967 alone a similar number of Americans and Canadians immigrated to Israel, although because of legal and administrative changes in Israel and in the United States it was now easier to declare oneself an immigrant. (For example, acquisition of Israeli citizenship or even voting in an Israeli election or serving in the Israel Defense Force does not automatically mean loss of U.S. citizenship, though it can result in this should one renounce explicitly American citizenship or *volunteer* for the Israeli armed forces.) North American immigration grew to unparalleled dimensions until the decline in the aftermath of the 1973 war and economic crisis (see Table 3.1).[8]

Along with the increase in numbers came a change in the backgrounds of the immigrants. The first waves — or trickles — of American immigrants were mostly young people, moved by Zionist convictions and often oriented to kibbutz life. As time went on, American immigrants were less and less oriented to kibbutz life, and came when they were in their thirties and forties, with professional training and occupations. Increasingly, their motivations were religious, less specifically Zionist and more diffusely "Jewish." Antonovsky found that whereas only 35 percent of his entire study population (American immigrants in the 1948-66 period) could be categorized as "non-kibbutz non-Zionists," 58 percent of those who had come between 1957 and 1966 could be so characterized. Though the more recent American immigrants still represent only a tiny fraction of the American Jewish community, and are by

TABLE 3.1
American Immigrants to Israel, 1948-80

Year	Number	Year	Number
1948-51	1,711	1972	5,515
1952-54	428	1973	4,393
1955-57	416	1974	3,089
1958-60	708	1975	2,803
1961-64	2,102	1976	2,746
1965-68	2,066	1977	2,571
1969	5,738	1978	2,921
1970	6,882	1979	2,950
1971	7,364	1980	2,312

Notes: The figures include "potential immigrants" (*olim bekoakh*), a status chosen by more than three-quarters of American immigrants, enabling them to postpone assumption of citizenship for three years. The figures for 1961-68 include temporary residents; those for 1948-60 do not.

Sources: Statistical Abstract of Israel; Klitat Haaliyah, 1974, 1975, 1977, and 1978; *Monthly Bulletin of Statistics* 32, no. 2 (Jerusalem: February 1981).

definition atypical American Jews, they do now come from a broader spectrum of the community and are a more diverse group than their predecessors.

A DEMOGRAPHIC PROFILE OF AMERICAN IMMIGRANTS IN ISRAEL

There have been changes in the demographic and social character-istics of American immigrants over the decades, but the data are insufficient to examine this systematically. Some studies of the pre-1967 immigration generally conclude that these olim are, modally, members of the second generation of American Jews and were raised in intensively Jewish environments. Their fathers were Jewishly well educated but relatively few had attended college, and the great majority were manual workers, artisans, or small business-men. More than one-third of the families of the olim studied by Antonovsky and Katz had four or more children, and half the total population reported their synagogue affiliation as Orthodox (at the present time it is estimated that no more than 10 to 15 percent of

American Jews are affiliated with Orthodox synagogues). In this
study 37 percent of the respondents attended Hebrew school for
nine years or more, while another study showed 41 percent coming
from Orthodox homes. Almost all had some Jewish schooling in
America, with the modal type being afternoon religious school.[9]

In 1969-70 the Ministry for Immigrant Absorption, the Central
Bureau of Statistics, and the Israel Institute for Applied Social
Research began a longitudinal study of immigrants, interviewing
them two months, six months, one year, two and three years, and
in some cases five years after arrival in Israel. A representative sample
of all immigrants was drawn, and this, along with the longitudinal
nature of the study, makes it a most valuable one. Data from the
study have been analyzed by Goldscheider in his article on American aliyah. He finds "remarkably little difference" in the distribution of American immigrants and the American Jewish population
according to regions. About 70 percent of the American immigrants
were born in the United States, and of these about 60 percent were
children of parents born in the United States, though in the absence
of reliable national data, it is difficult to ascertain how this compares
to the American Jewish population. However, the immigrants are, on
average, about ten years younger than the U.S. Jewish population.
Women are overrepresented among American immigrants (this was
apparently true of the pre-1967 immigration as well). This may be
related to the fact that "about twice as many American olim are
single when compared to the U.S. Jewish population and the contrast
is stronger among women."[10] Goldscheider concludes that "American *aliya* is selective by three major demographic characteristics:
age, sex, and marital status. Olim from the United States clearly do
not represent a demographic cross-section of the American Jewish
population."[11]

Certainly they do not represent the American Jewish population
in terms of their Jewish backgrounds and education, though they
may be somewhat more similar in their general educational backgrounds. "Over 40 percent of the American olim in the survey
had 16 or more years of education compared to 18 percent of
all olim (1969-70) and 6 percent of the Jewish population of Israel
(1970)."[12] Among those whose parents were American-born, 84
percent have a college education.

Of course, the high educational level of the olim is connected
to their occupational status. Over 60 percent of the male immigrants,

and 67 percent of the females, are classified as professionals and this is "clearly extreme even by the distortedly high white-collar concentration . . . of the American Jewish population."[13] Thus, the American immigrants constitute an educational and occupational elite in Israel, and even when compared to the population from which they come, they display very high educational and occupational levels.[14] As we shall see, they are conscious of their elite status and it colors their attitude toward Israelis, Israeli officials, and their role in Israeli society.

RELIGION, IDEOLOGY, AND MOTIVATIONS FOR IMMIGRATION TO ISRAEL

Motivations for emigration from America and immigration to Israel differ from those impelling Jews from countries where they are persecuted or where they perceive their economic or social situations as unsatisfactory. Nevertheless, American immigrants share with others personal motivations, as well as religious and ideological ones. In actuality, it is likely that a complex of motivations impels any ultimate decision to leave one's country, but for analytic purposes we distinguish among four types of motivation: personal: the search for adventure, for a quiet retirement, for reunification with family, for a mate, for a job; religious: a category that often blends into the following one; ideological-Zionist (among the 1969-70 immigrants, 40 percent said they had been active in American Zionist organizations); and affiliative-organizational: by which we mean that a person may have been socialized in a milieu or formal organization that made aliyah "the thing to do" and that immigration, though rationalized in ideological terms, resulted primarily from conformity to behavior taught as desirable. (Nearly half the 1969-70 American olim said their parents were "religious.") Though these immigrants are by no means refugees, they may have been more "pushed" from America than "pulled" to Israel. Antonovsky rejects the notion that the Americans are "an alienated population," but he finds that almost 40 percent say that in "some or many ways" they did not feel at home in America.[15] A graduate of the University of Minnesota, now living in a kibbutz, expressed it this way in 1963:

. . . There is always some kind of imperceptible restraint. Go to a Jewish lodge and bring one non-Jew in, and you find an imperceptible change in the presence of a Goy. You sit up a little straighter, you talk a wee bit more grammatically, you will be a wee bit more polite. It's true. If you called this to the attention of those concerned, they would be offended or deny it. The Goy might not even be aware of it. But I would be. It's the difference between the in-group and the out-group. It was not a question of friction. What is relevant is a feeling of being at ease.[16]

Others objected to what they saw as specific characteristics of American society as they had experienced it: conformity, material-ism, and the danger of assimilating and losing their Jewish identities and culture.[17] The fact that so many American immigrants, of whatever era, age, and background, cite "living with Jews" or "living a fully Jewish life" or being in "one's own homeland" as the primary reason for their move to Israel may mean that the "imperceptible restraints" felt by the ex-Minnesota kibbutznik are widely perceived, and that many immigrants did not feel totally at home or at ease in the United States, even if it is the country of their birth. Still, "push" motivations are cited as important to their migration decision by only a small part of the Americans in the various studies.[18] How-ever, there might be a reluctance to admit — to an interviewer, to oneself — that one was not "well adjusted" to American society, that the "American dream" had not been realized, and that the claims of the melting pot and its liberal interpreters were not fully justified.

It is striking that almost all American immigrants, even those who cite "push" factors, express great affection and admiration for the United States. Isaacs found that "even most of those who described themselves as feeling most excluded as 'Jews' in America tended to insist on the strength of their continued attachment to the political and social ideas they had absorbed as 'Americans' and in their wish to recreate them on Israeli soil."[19] One immigrant described himself and others: "These people are not running away from America. America is still good for them. Their families are still in America. They are not anti-American. In fact, the American who gets here gets more and more pro-American."[20] In most cases, feelings about America are undoubtedly ambivalent, a mixture of pride, shame, guilt, gratitude, resentment, and appreciation. One successful businessman who immigrated in 1972 tried to explain his decision to a skeptical American Jewish friend.

Maybe I am psychologically creating supports for my *aliyah*. If I am, it's subconscious. . . . But I feel the quality of life deteriorating here terribly and I do believe I have chosen an alternative that, on balance, is better. Don't get me wrong, I expect to aggravate myself into an ulcer at 35, on the one hand. And on the other, I love this country. Positively. Not just because it has been good to me or anything so reasonable. I have travelled it and worked in many places, seen much and met many, and I love it. I'm going to miss it more . . . than anyone I know who has gone on *aliyah*. . . . I also know what potential I'm leaving behind. . . . But all these feelings will pass in time or in a generation. And I feel or I hope that other more valuable ones will replace them.[21]

This affection for the United States is in strong contrast to the feelings of many Soviet immigrants toward their former country, though with time some of the Soviets begin to long for some of the nonpolitical aspects of Soviet life: culture, food, friendships, styles of life. One study of immigrants in absorption centers found that Soviets see themselves as quite different from non-Jews in the USSR — and from Israelis as well. This is much less true of immigrants from English-speaking countries. Soviet immigrants were also found to be less positive toward Zionism, Jewish culture, or religion, and so "push" factors appeared more salient for Soviet immigrants, though not as much as one might expect.[22]

All this means, of course, that American immigrants are most likely to portray their decisions to immigrate in terms of the attractions of Israel. The major study of the pre-1967 migrants concluded that over two-thirds were "unequivocally oriented to Israel. Their migration was an act of 'coming to' rather than 'going away from.' " Zionism and Jewishness were the dominant motives, and only 8 percent of the respondents cited dissatisfaction with America as the single most important reason for their coming to Israel.[23] By 1967, however, the year of riots in Detroit, Newark, and other American cities, there was probably more "running away from" than there had ever been. Urban problems, race relations, economic difficulties, the spread of drug abuse, and the constant problem of Jewish assimilation no doubt strengthened the "push" side of the migration equation, though in many cases it may have served not as the primary motivation but as a negative reinforcement of the positive attraction of Israel. As one American immigrant pointed out, the more recent immigrants are more likely to be conscious of emigrating *from* as well as of immigrating *to*. Writing in 1972, Halkin observed that general deterioration in American life . . . has become a conversational staple throughout the United States. Among elderly people this may most frequently have to do with crime in the streets, or inflation . . . or the collapse of Jewish communal life in the old neighborhood; among younger couples, with job insecurity . . . or anxiety about the Jewish education of their children, or about American youth culture generally; among students, with the anti-Israeli and at times openly anti-Semitic rhetoric of the New Left, or the rise of black separatism, which may have done more than anything else . . . to relegitimize a sense of Jewish nationalism in the eyes of the young.[24]

Already in the 1960s there was an increasing proportion of religious immigrants among the Americans. After 1967 this proportion seems to have grown. The published MIA data show that over 33 percent of the American immigrants define themselves as religious, and 48 percent say their parents were religious.[25] Another 33 percent say they are not religious, and the rest say they are "not very" religious. Goldscheider's analysis of the same data leads him to the conclusion that over 33 percent define themselves as Orthodox, and only 25 percent say they are not at all religious or are "secular." What is especially striking is that "fully 43 percent of third-generation Americans on *aliya* define themselves as religious or very religious."[26] This is in sharp contrast to the general trend among American Jewry as a whole, as is the high proportion of immigrants who consider themselves Orthodox. In Goldscheider's words, "what emerge from these data on the religious identification of American olim are patterns of over-concentration and selectivity among religious and Orthodox Jews relative to the American Jewish population."[27] Responses to questions about religious observance confirmed the self-assigned religious identification of the immigrants: Over half observed dietary regulations before immigration, and three-quarters fasted on Yom Kippur. This was true even of the third-generation Americans in the group.

The reasons for this overrepresentation of Orthodox and religious immigrants are probably the attraction of the Holy Land, their perceived need for an intensively Jewish environment in order to fulfill their religious requirements (prayer, education, kosher food, and so on), and perhaps their weaker cultural assimilation into American life, their explicit and implicit rejection of some of its mass culture and social values. Since such observant Jews tend to live in closely knit subcultures in America, it may be that "chain migration" is a factor in their immigration to Israel, as friends and relatives may influence them to follow their lead.

In some contrast to the findings regarding religious affiliation, the survey of the 1969-70 immigrants found that about half the Americans had not been members of any Zionist organization before aliyah. (The same holds for West European immigrants.) There are no precise data on Zionist organizational membership among American Jews, but it is clear that only a small minority of organizationally defined Zionists ever make aliyah. Goldscheider points to "the non-correlation between Zionist organizational affiliation and American *aliya*" and suggests that "American olim are more likely to be affiliated with Zionist organizations but that such affiliation is a consequence rather than a causal factor in the chain of *aliya* determinants."[28] What is probably more important is that the great majority of the immigrants have had a relatively intensive Jewish education in the United States, as all the studies demonstrate. This means that rather than specifically Zionist affiliation and socialization, it is a generally high level of Jewish consciousness, engendered by years of schooling and by reinforcement in the synagogue and in the community that is most directly related to the decision to immigrate to Israel. One might also add another experience that may have been a socializing factor: visits to Israel prior to immigration. Almost 67 percent of the immigrants had visited the country before immigrating, and 18 percent had done so three times or more.[29]

SOVIET IMMIGRATION TO ISRAEL

The Soviet immigration differs from the American one in so many ways: The great majority of Soviet immigrants are not religious, none of them had the opportunity to visit the country before immigrating, very few had ever had formal Jewish education in the USSR, none could belong to a Zionist organization when living under Soviet rule. Yet their educational and occupational profile is quite close to that of the Americans, and although their motivations for immigration were shaped in peculiarly Soviet conditions, there is a common ground of motivation and aspiration for the Soviet and American Jews who have come to Israel in the last decade. In size and political terms the Soviet immigration is far more significant than the American one. It is an immigration that even the most ardent Zionists could only dream of before 1971 and that Soviet officials probably did not envision in their worst nightmares.

From the beginning of 1967 to the end of 1980, 439,488 people immigrated to Israel. Of these, 156,190, or 36 percent, came from the Soviet Union. In the peak years of 1972 and 1973 the Soviet immigrants comprised almost 60 percent of the total immigration, and in the 1970-80 decade they made up nearly half of it. The political, economic, and social importance of this immigration was great in both the country of origin and the country of immigration. Although the Israeli government at first denied that such an immigration existed at all — it was referred to in the 1960s as the "unification of families" immigration — it acknowledged its existence around 1968, but did not release statistics on its dimensions and composition until much later, beginning around 1976.[30] This policy stemmed from Israel's anxiety about offending the Soviet Union and causing it to halt the emigration. The USSR, fearful of internal pressures for expanded emigration opportunities and under attack from its Arab allies for allowing potential soldiers to go to Israel, denied that there was any mass emigration. Soviet media insisted for some time that only old and sick people were being allowed to leave, on humanitarian grounds alone, in order to be reunited with families from whom they had been separated as a result of war and other calamities. As time went on, and the dimensions of the emigration became widely known, this Soviet theme was muted, though not abandoned altogether, and the Israelis felt more secure about publicly acknowledging the size and significance of the Soviet immigration. After 1973 the size of the immigration fell drastically — successively by about 50 percent in 1974-76. In order to press the Soviets to restore previous emigration levels, the Israelis were forced to detail its previous dimensions if their argument was to have any persuasiveness. Thus we have available the data in Table 3.2 that indicate the dimensions and origins of Soviet immigration to Israel.

It can be seen from the table that almost three times as many affidavits (*vyzovy* in Russian), or invitations from relatives, have been sent to Soviet citizens as have actually emigrated. This is because of Soviet restrictions on emigration, reluctance of potential emigrants to make the final decision, the desire by some to have a *vyzov* "just in case," and other idiosyncratic factors. To what extent each of these factors is responsible for the disparity between

TABLE 3.2
Jewish Emigration from the USSR and Immigration to Israel, 1968-80

Year	Number of Visas Issued on Behalf of Israel by Dutch Embassy*	Emigrated to Israel	Number of Affidavits	Transferred in Vienna to Hebrew Immigrant Aid Society
1968-70	4,327	4,263	38,917	—
1971	14,310	12,819	40,794	58
1972	31,478	31,652	67,895	251
1973	34,922	33,477	58,216	1,456
1974	20,181	16,817	42,843	3,879
1975	13,139	8,531	34,145	4,928
1976	14,138	7,274	36,104	7,004
1977	17,159	8,348	43,062	8,483
1978	30,594	12,192	107,212	16,867
1979	50,343	17,614	128,891	34,056
1980	20,319	7,570	32,335	14,078
Totals	250,910	160,166	630,414	91,060

*Since 1967, when the USSR broke relations with Israel, the latter's interests have been represented by the embassy of the Netherlands.

Sources: Ministry for Immigrant Absorption figures, as reported in *Insight* (London) 3, no. 5 (May 1977): 2; and Yaacov Ro'i and Yosi Goldshtain, "Tnuat hayetsia miBrih'm–sikumo shel asor," *Hainteligentsia haYehudit BiVrit HaMoetsot*, no. 4 (June 1980), p. 74; Z. Alexander, "Jewish Emigration from the USSR in 1980," *Soviet Jewish Affairs* 11, no. 2 (1981).

71

affidavits and emigrants is impossible to say and is, of course, a matter of political controversy and polemics.

It can also be seen that nearly all those who obtained visas emigrated to Israel or "transferred in Vienna to HIAS," meaning that they left the USSR with visas for Israel, but changed their destinations in the Vienna and Rome transit points. There they were helped by the American Hebrew Immigrant Aid Society to immigrate to other countries, mainly the United States and Canada, but also to Australia-New Zealand, Western Europe, and Latin America. Between 1971 and 1976, about 13 percent of the Soviet emigrés did not arrive in Israel; but the proportion of those "dropping out" in Vienna rose sharply after 1973, reaching 50 percent of all emigrés in 1976 and 1977, exceeding it slightly in 1978, going over 60 percent in 1979 and 1980, and over 70 percent in 1981. For all of the 1970s, one-third of the Jewish emigrants did not settle in Israel. This, too, has become a matter of controversy within the Israeli and American Jewish communities. Official Israeli sources charge that HIAS is "seducing" the emigrés with promises of a better life in the United States. American Jewish organizations resist Israeli efforts to use administrative measures in order to increase the proportion of emigrés going to Israel, on the grounds that this is a violation of the freedom of choice.

Actually, the reasons for the sharp shift in the destination of the emigrés are several:[31] Israel's worsened security and economic situation following the Yom Kippur war made it less attractive as a country of immigration; difficulties in absorption were reported to their friends and relatives in the USSR by Soviet immigrants; the American economic and employment situations improved in the mid-1970s; and perhaps most importantly, the reservoir of Zionists and Jewishly motivated potential emigrés in the USSR was depleted by the mass migration of the early 1970s, and the later waves of emigrés were motivated primarily by family considerations, political alienation, the desire for economic improvement, and other impulses that would not naturally lead them to choose Israel as their destination.

Indirect evidence for this assertion is provided by the sharp differences in the geographic origin of those going to Israel and those immigrating to the United States. As can be seen in Table 3.3, 35 percent of the Soviet immigrants to Israel have come from Georgia and Central Asia or Daghestan and Azerbaijan (Mountain Jews).

TABLE 3.3
Emigrants from USSR to Israel by Ethnic Groups, 1968-80

Year	Georgia		Central Asia ("Bukhara")		Mountain Jews		Other Jews from USSR		Total
	Percent	Number	Percent	Number	Percent	Number	Percent	Number	Number
1968	–	–	–	–	–	–	100.0	231	231
1969	13.3	400	–	–	–	–	86.7	2,633	3,033
1970	–	–	–	–	–	–	100.0	999	999
1971	33.5	4,300	3.5	450	–	–	63.0	8,069	12,819
1972	34.5	10,900	6.7	2,100	0.2	60	58.6	18,592	31,652
1973	22.2	7,450	11.2	3,750	0.1	325	66.5	21,952	33,477
1974	15.9	2,670	14.7	2,460	9.3	1,570	60.1	10,116	16,816
1975	10.3	870	4.8	410	26.7	2,270	58.2	4,981	8,531
1976	6.8	496	4.4	323	16.6	1,212	72.1	5,243	7,274
1977	5.2	436	9.2	764	10.2	848	75.4	6,300	8,348
1978	7.6	930	13.4	1,630	12.9	1,575	66.1	8,057	12,192
1979	6.5	1,139	18.4	3,237	11.2	1,982	63.9	11,256	17,614
1980	10.8	818	6.6	497	9.3	703	73.3	5,552	7,570
Total	18.9	30,409	9.7	15,621	6.6	10,545	64.8	103,986	160,556

Sources: Insight (London) 3, no. 5 (May 1977): 3; Zvi Aleksandr, "Netunim statistiyim shel hayetsia," *Hainteligentsia hayehudit BiVrihm*, no. 4 (June 1980), p. 76; Z. Alexander, "Jewish Emigration from the USSR in 1980," *Soviet Jewish Affairs* 11, no. 2 (1981).

73

These are areas where Jewish tradition and religion have survived much better than in the European parts of the country. Hence, immigrants from those non-European areas are much more likely to be motivated by messianic visions of Zion, by the yearning to live unfettered Jewish lives, and, because of their traditionalism, to live with their extended families. Moreover, though the table does not show this, about one-third of the total emigration comes from the Western peripheries of European USSR: the Baltic states, Moldavia, West Ukraine, and Transcarpathian Ukraine. Since these areas were absorbed into the Soviet Union only in 1939-40 (and permanently absorbed only at the conclusion of World War II), Jews in these places are less removed from tradition and Jewish knowledge. They have vivid memories of the flourishing Jewish cultural, political, and social life of interwar Poland, Latvia, Lithuania, Romania, or Slovakia, to which their regions had belonged. Soviet censuses show that the percentage of Yiddish speakers is much higher in these areas than in those that have been under Soviet rule since the revolution, and, in general, the level of Jewish knowledge and consciousness is higher in the Western areas than in Russia proper.

About 40 percent of the Israeli immigration has come from what might be called the Soviet heartland, that is, the Russian Republic (RSFSR), most of the Ukraine, and most of Belorussia — the three large Slavic republics. By contrast, about 85 percent of the Soviet immigration to the United States has come from the Ukraine (60-70 percent) and the RSFSR (15-25 percent).[32] These Jews are far less likely than the Israeli immigrants to know very much or care a great deal about Jewish tradition and their own Jewish identities. Better acculturated to the dominant Russian culture of the USSR, and generally occupying higher statuses in Soviet society, they are motivated to leave more by political alienation, the desire to give their children higher education, and family and economic considerations. It is true that the proportion of emigrants from the heartland rose from 11 percent in 1971 to 52 percent in 1976; but since, in 1976, 85 percent of those coming to the United States came from the heartland, it is obvious that the latter phenomenon is not a function of greater emigration from there alone. The correlation between disinterest in Jewishness and coming from the heartland is made clear by the fact that the percentage going to the United States after 1976 is highest — over 90 percent — among those coming from the largest cities, where Jews are most acculturated to the Russian culture: Moscow, Leningrad, Kiev, and Odessa. At the same time, those who came from cities in the peripheral areas absorbed into the USSR in the 1940s — Chernovtsy, Vilnius, Kishinev — have a far lower proportion going to the United States.[33]

The figures in Table 3.3 also show that emigration from various regions has been uneven in timing and scope. For example, 51 percent of the Georgian Jews immigrated in 1972 and 1973, but 51 percent of the Mountain Jews came only in 1974-76. Whether this is the result of decisions by the emigrants themselves or by the Soviet authorities is not entirely clear, and we shall discuss later what can be learned about Soviet policy from the pattern of emigration and immigration.

A DEMOGRAPHIC PROFILE OF SOVIET
IMMIGRANTS IN ISRAEL

The immigrants come from diverse parts of the Soviet Union, and hence from different Jewish subcultures. They differ widely in educational level, occupations, family size, and cultural traditions and outlooks. They do not represent a microcosm of Soviet Jewry, since certain regions are greatly overrepresented and others under-represented. For example, while Georgian Jews form nearly 20 percent of the emigration (1970-80), according to the Soviet census of 1970 they constituted only about 3 percent of the Soviet Jewish population (55,000 out of 2,150,000). By the 1979 census they were only 1.5 percent of the Jewish population (28,000 out of 1,811,000), as more than half of the Georgian Jews had emigrated.

Slightly more than half the Soviet immigration is made up of women, just as more than half the Soviet Jewish population are women. The proportion of women rises in the older age cohorts and is larger among those coming from the territories absorbed in 1939-40 (52.6 percent) and lower in the Georgian and Central Asian groups (50.6 percent).[34]

In the 1972-79 period about 12 percent of the Soviet immigrants were over 65 years of age, in contrast to only 9 percent of the Israeli population in this cohort. The Georgian and Central Asian immigrants were considerably younger than the Europeans: over 33 percent of the former were under 18, while less than 20 percent of the European immigrants fell into this age group. Nevertheless, if one compares the age structure of the emigrants with that of Jews in the RSFSR, the only republic for which such data are available, it is clear that the emigration is younger than the Soviet Jewish population as a whole (see Table 3.4). It is true that the young are overrepresented in most migrations, but their proportion in the Soviet emigration is interesting in light of Soviet claims, largely for Arab consumption, that it is mostly elderly people, unfit for military service, who are allowed to leave for Israel.

Still, viewed from the Israeli perspective, the relatively high proportion of older immigrants imposes a burden on the economy, especially since, unlike American immigrants who receive social security payments in Israel and thereby contribute to Israel's foreign currency reserves, the Soviet immigrants do not receive their pensions after emigration and must be supported by relatives, or, in almost all cases, by the Israeli social security system.

Over 90 percent of the Soviet immigrants arrive with families. There are twice as many single people among the European arrivals as among the Georgians and Central Asians, and the latter groups have larger families than the former: 28 percent of the "Bukharan Jews" have families of six or more people, compared to only 2 percent of the European families. The average Soviet immigrant family has 3.4 people, significantly higher than the average Jewish family size in the USSR (3.2 in 1959; 3.1 in the RSFSR and the Ukraine in 1970, slightly higher in other republics).[35] The Jewish birth rate in the USSR is estimated to be very low, insufficient to replace the Jewish population, but the immigrants to Israel come largely from those sectors of the population with higher birth rates. This migration contributed to the decline of the Soviet Jewish population, as seen in the 1979 Soviet census total of 1,811,000 Jews, down from 2,151,000 in 1970. Of the 340,000 fewer Jews recorded, however, only 177,000 had emigrated. The rest of the decline is explained by higher mortality and lower fertility, at least partially due to the emigration of younger and Asian Jews, and to the consequences of intermarriage. Unless there is some change in the long-term decline of the Soviet Jewish birth rate as well as in the rate of intermarriage, this decline will continue.[36]

As has been remarked, the Soviet immigrants, like the Americans, brought with them a level of skill and vocational training that few previous immigrations had brought. Between 1967 and

TABLE 3.4

Age Structure of Israeli and of American and Soviet Emigrants

RSFR, 1970		Israel								United States			
		1972-75		1974		1975				1974		1975	
Age Group	Per cent	Age Group	Per cent	Age Group	Per cent	Age Group	Per cent			Age Group	Per cent	Age Group	Per cent
1-10	7.0	1-14	18.5	0-14	23.0	0-14	22.0			0-10	13.2	0-10	14.6
11-15	4.2									11-20	15.2	11-20	14.9
16-29	14.8	15-29	26.5	15-29	24.0	15-29	26.0			21-30	19.5	21-30	20.4
30-39	15.8									31-40	18.8	31-40	17.8
40-49	16.0	30-44	19.4	30-44	20.0	30-44	17.0			41-50	16.9	41-50	15.4
50-59	16.2	45-64	22.8	45-64	21.0	45-64	22.0			51-60	7.9	51-60	8.4
60+	26.4	65+	11.2	65+	12.0	65+	12.0			61+	8.2	61+	8.5
Not available	1.6												

Sources: Data on the RSFSR are from the 1970 census, as reported in *Itogi vsesoiuznoi perepisi naseleniia 1970 goda* (Moscow: Statistika, 1973) Vol. IV, p. 373; Israeli data are from *Klitat haaliyah 1975*, and Shmuel Adler and Rachel Klein, "Hatkhunot hademografiyot shel olai Brih"m lefi azorai motza," mimeographed (Jerusalem: Ministry for Immigrant Absorption, January 1977); American data are from HIAS, *Statistical Abstracts* 16, no. 3 (1975). Comparable data for Soviet immigrants to Israel in 1974-79 are in Ministry for Immigrant Absorption, "Haolim MiBrih"m vehanoshrim shehigiu leArha'b—Skira demografit hashvaatit," mimeographed (Jerusalem, 1980), p. 38.

1979, 52 percent of the arriving Soviets stated an occupation. Of these, 42 percent were classified as "professional workers" — 25 percent of them academics, engineers and architects, medical doctors, attorneys, and teachers, and the rest technicians and para-professionals.[37] In absolute terms, this meant that by 1974 nearly 6,000 engineers and architects, nearly 2,000 doctors, and over 500 scientists had entered the country, with several thousand more arriving before the end of the decade. In addition, nearly 25,000 skilled workers (constituting about 30 percent of immigrants with occupations) and 5,000 unskilled workers had also come from the USSR in the 1970s. Again, there are important regional differences among the immigrants: While in 1972-75, about 70 percent of those from the Baltic had definite occupations, among the Georgians this category comprised only 53 percent of the immigrants. This difference arose in large part from the low percentage (40) of voca-tionally trained women among the Georgians and Bukharans compared to the percentage among European women (58). About three times as many of the Baltic immigrants are scientists and academics as are the Georgians and Bukharans. It is interesting to note, however, that in none of the regional groups is there a substan-tial difference in the proportion of men and women who have scientific and academic professions. However, among Georgian and Bukharan immigrants, the proportion of clerks, nurses, and tech-nicians is much higher among women than among men, though these differences do not appear among those from the European areas of the USSR.[38] This occupational profile is roughly similar to that of the Soviet immigrants to the United States, though the higher proportion of immigrants from the Ukraine and the RSFSR raises the proportion of blue-collar workers, artists, and intelligentsia.

The educational and skill levels of the Soviet immigrants are somewhat lower than those of the American newcomers to Israel, though the European Soviets are very similar to the Americans. Nevertheless, by comparison with previous immigrations, or even with present-day immigrants from some other parts of the world, the Soviets are an immediate and valuable addition to Israel's skilled labor force. In contrast to the Americans, however, this does not confer elite status upon them, perhaps because they are widely perceived as refugees, and because the great majority bring no sub-stantial wealth or possessions with them.

THE NATIONAL RENAISSANCE AND THE ALIYAH
MOVEMENT OF JEWS IN THE USSR

Soviet and Western observers alike were astonished when Soviet Jews, generally considered to be "highly assimilated" – and therefore, depending on one's view, either "lost to the Jewish people" or "most successful in drawing closer to other peoples"[39] – displayed signs of awakened and militant nationalism, combined with manifestations of alienation from, not assimilation to, Soviet life and society. The most prominent expression of this national revival has been the desire to emigrate to Israel, viewed as the homeland of the Jewish people. This is not the place for a detailed history and analysis of the Soviet Jewish national reawakening, but a brief analysis is needed in order to understand the context that produced the Soviet immigration to Israel.

There are three long-term factors that explain the emergence of Jewish consciousness in a public and demonstrative way in the USSR. These are the psychological condition of Jews in the Soviet Union; the role of the "Zapadniki," the million or more Jews absorbed by the USSR along with the territorial acquisitions from Poland, Romania, the Baltic States, and Czechoslovakia in 1939-44; and anti-Semitism in the Soviet state and society. These factors existed long before the Six-Day War of 1967 and they shaped the national character of many Soviet Jews, but it was not given public and dramatic expression until 1967 and thereafter. It was the Middle East war, and, especially, the Leningrad trials of 1970-71, that provided the catalyst for the emergence of hitherto subterranean currents as well as for the confluence of the stream of Jewish nationalism and that of liberal political and cultural opposition, with the latter feeding into the former. The result was appeals and petitions to Soviet and non-Soviet authorities to allow Jews to leave for Israel, and public demonstrations and political action toward this end, producing the first mass emigration from the USSR since the aftermath of World War II, and the first peacetime emigration in about half a century.

The psychological condition that underlies Soviet Jewish nationalism is one of dissonance and identity confusion. On the one hand, the Soviet government, having abolished all Jewish schools and most other cultural institutions and severely restricted the Jewish religion, has made it nearly impossible for Soviet Jews to infuse their identity as Jews with meaningful and positive content. On the other hand, by insisting that Jews be officially identified as such (for example, on their internal passports) and by socially regarding them as Jews, Soviet society and government have prevented the Jews from assimilating completely and assuming, say, Russian identity. Thus, Soviet Jews are acculturated, but not assimilated. They have adopted the culture of another social group (only 17.7 percent of the Jews gave a Jewish language as their mother tongue in the 1970 census and only 14 percent in 1979), but they have not adopted that other culture to such an extent that they no longer have any characteristics identifying them with their former culture and no longer have any loyalties to that culture.[40] Soviet Jews are therefore in the dissonant position of being culturally Russian, for the most part, but legally and socially Jewish. In the USSR, where culture and nationality are closely identified, this is an anomalous position.

This split identity creates an internal dissonance whose resolution can be achieved by becoming either wholly Russian or wholly Jewish: Either they assimilate and become Russians in every sense, or they change their cultural and social identities and attempt to become wholly Jewish. Communities under stress usually either hide or attempt to fight back: During Stalinism, most Soviet Jews sought to hide, to assimilate, to become Russian. This attempt failed, as the anti-Semitic campaigns of the very last years of Stalinism showed. Soviet newspapers delighted in publishing the original, Jewish names of cultural and political figures who had adopted Russian surnames. When terror was relaxed, and when others showed that political and cultural resistance is possible in the USSR, Jews began to assert themselves as Jews and to reject the nonoption of assimilation. This *volte-face* was perhaps stimulated in part by the reassertion of ethnic consciousness and of nationalism in other parts of the Western world (parts of France, the United Kingdom, Belgium, blacks and others in the United States, French-Canadians, et al.), as well as in the Soviet Union itself (Balts, Ukrainians, Georgians and Armenians, Crimean Tatars, ethnic Germans). As an emigré who writes about "the delight of being Russian" explains it,

> today every hack in the hierarchy exclaims: "Russia!" (exactly as in the 30's he exclaimed: "Proletariat!") until a sensitive person shudders at the very sound of the word. Yet this debasement of Russian national

values has served to revive other national values — particularly Jewish ones, that now have the advantage of novelty. And persecution could only add an extra appeal, the appeal of a mystery revealed only to the initiated. The tables are turned: at the beginning of the century Jews born of two Jewish parents wanted to be Russian. Now a Russian friend of mine without a streak of Jewish blood in him and having only in-laws in Israel went there in truly nationalistic fervor. My wife gave him as a gift . . . a menorah which had been kept in the family for many generations. . . . This man . . . was one of the pioneers of the exodus in Russia and initiated us as well as many others. . . . The transvaluation of national values was precipitated by the Six-Day War.[41]

Thus, it can be argued that the revival of Jewish nationalism in Russia is, paradoxically another manifestation of assimilationism: When other peoples in the USSR manifest nationalistic feelings, the Jews do likewise. In the Yiddish phrase, *vi es kristelt zikh, azoi idelt zikh* (a multiple pun whose meaning is, "as the Christians go, so go the Jews").

This nationalism might well have been directionless and even contentless, or it might not have appeared at all, were it not for the infusion of Jewish knowledge, consciousness, and aspirations by the Zapadniki into a community that had been cut off from the rest of world Jewry by the early 1920s and had migrated from the *shtetlakh* of the Ukraine and Belorussia to the big cities of those republics and the RSFSR, thereby becoming urbanized, modernized, secularized, and Russianized.[42] Many of the Zapadniki, especially the Zionists among them, were deported to labor camps and prisons in the 1940s, where they transmitted their knowledge of Jewish history and life — now given especial relevance and poignancy by the Nazi slaughter going on around them — to Soviet Jews for whom the glitter of assimilation and the promise of social acceptance had begun to fade.[43] After the war, Jewish life, though severely restricted by the authorities, was much more in evidence in cities such as Riga, Vilnius, and Chernovtsy or Kishinev, than in Moscow, Leningrad, or even the prewar centers of Kiev and Minsk. Jewish theater groups, artists, and writers were active in the newly acquired territories, and such groups as the Jewish choir and theater ensemble in Riga became foci for national expression. They were the direct fore-runners of the aliyah movement since many of the leaders of that movement had been the organizers of the cultural efforts.[44] Already in the late 1950s *samizdat* (underground, literally "self-printed") literature was being produced in Riga, which included an account of the Warsaw Ghetto uprising, David Ben-Gurion's speeches on the Sinai campaign of 1956, material from Simon Dubnov's classic history of the Jews, and, later, materials on the Eichmann trial (1961) in Jerusalem.[45]

When Jews in other parts of the Soviet Union began to reconsider the meaning and potentialities of their Jewishness, they "began to look for the contacts and ties with those who had already stepped on the path of exodus," reports one of the leaders of the aliyah movement in Kharkov.

> People in Riga and in Vilnius were known to receive letters and post-cards from Israel with Israeli landscapes and descriptions of Israeli life and nature. . . . It was known that Jews in the Baltic arranged all sorts of get-togethers colored with Jewish national spirit — songs, food, tradition. They gained such a degree of independence, that they did it even in public — in restaurants, cafes, near the synagogue. The authorities could no longer restrain these activities in the Baltic, though in Central Russia even in 1971 an Israeli postcard or Hebrew textbook was regarded in some cases as an evidence of offense.
>
> Jews from Moscow and other cities began to establish contacts with Riga and Vilnius. . . . The Muscovites began to adopt the methods of Riga. People began to arrange "Shabbats" and gather on the holidays near the synagogue, singing Jewish songs and dancing Jewish folk dances. . . . Probably for people from normally governed countries it won't be clear, that against the background of complete absence of national life these small manifestations look very significant . . . with something of an anti-official flavor.[46]

The experience of Dov Sperling, an early leader of the movement and one of the first to leave the USSR and publicize the struggle of Jews there, is fairly typical. Born in Moscow, he studied at the University of Vilnius where in 1956 he first learned of the existence and nature of Israel and concluded that there was a Jewish nation, contrary to Marxist-Leninist-Stalinist doctrine. While serving two years in a labor camp for "anti-Soviet propaganda," he met Jews from other parts of the country. "Until then I thought I was the only one, but in the camp there were not only students . . . but old Jews too who had been jailed because they were Zionists." Upon returning to his mother's home in Riga in 1959, he found that young Jews there "knew everything about Israel and had begun to fight their assimilation into the Russian culture, and they all spoke of going to Israel.''[47]

Another emigré describes how in 1960 mass celebrations were begun outside the synagogue on the *simkhat torah* holiday, and how Jews began to wear the star of David, study Hebrew clandestinely, and, after the Eichmann trial, organize memorial ceremonies, assuming the character of national reassertion, at the site of the 1941 massacre of Riga Jews.[48]

This audacious approach was imitated by others in the heartland of the USSR. There was also direct involvement by some former Zapadniki who had taken up residence in the interior. Lev Korenblit, one of the defendants in the Leningrad trial, was born in Romanian Bessarabia, survived the Bershad ghetto and a German concentration camp, served in the Red Army, and later settled in Leningrad. Having been active in the Zionist youth movement in Romania, and having a Jewish education, he was able to provide information and guidance as early as 1963-64 to Leningrad Jews seeking to learn more about Jewish culture and history.[49]

One experience shared by Zapadniki and others is encounters with anti-Semitism. It is well known that for the past 20 years and more Jews have had no chance of being admitted to the Soviet diplomatic corps, foreign trade apparatus, military academies, and the higher echelons of the Communist party. Their entrance to certain fields of study and research organizations is severely restricted.[50] This makes a Soviet Jew a second-class citizen, and he is well aware of it. But this is probably not as distressing as the anti-Semitism one may encounter in daily life, for, after all, one may simply choose other fields of endeavor than those closed to Jews, and thus avoid "unpleasantness." One cannot avoid such "unpleasantness" on the street, in school, at work, or in one's apartment house. Some Soviet Jews claim never to have experienced anti-Semitism; others admit having encountered it but dismiss it as one would a pestiferous gnat — annoying, but hardly dangerous; still others are deeply wounded by it and their *weltanschauung* is strongly conditioned by it. Obviously, the latter type is the most likely to think of emigration as a possible solution to the problem of anti-Semitism, a problem whose very existence is denied by the Soviet authorities. (In the words of former Premier Alexei Kosygin, "there has never been and there is no anti-Semitism in the Soviet Union.")[51] Some of the immigrants report how they were scarred by anti-Semitism at an early age, and how this factor was a major one in their decision to emigrate.

Raisa Palatnik, an Odessa librarian arrested for typing samizdat material and who insisted on speaking in Yiddish at her trial, recalls being in grade school with classmates who were all Jews except one Russian girl. "Not one of us could hope to get a gold medal — we all knew it would go to the Russian girl." She remembers that when the "Doctors' Plot" was announced in 1952 she was in the ninth grade. "It was scary to leave the classroom and go into the hallway because from all sides you hear, 'You yids, you poisoned Gorky, you wanted to poison Stalin, you poisoned all our great leaders,' and the atmosphere was very tense. Even the teachers allowed themselves such remarks."[52]

A member of one of the families most prominently involved in the aliyah movement in Riga, Alla Rusinek, describes how she dreaded the first day of school when each child had to announce her name, nationality, and father's occupation.

> First the teacher asks my name. "Milkina, Alla Tsalevna." I always spell my father's name because no one can understand it. Then she asks my nationality and it begins. The whole class suddenly becomes very quiet. Some look at me steadily. Others avoid my eyes. I have to say this word. All the rest say, "Russian, Ukrainian." I have to say this word, which sounds so unpleasant. Why? There is really nothing wrong with its sound, *Yev-rei-ka.* But I never hear the word except when people are cursing somebody or I never see it unless it is written on the walls like an insult. . . . Every time I try to overcome my feelings, but each year the word comes out in a whisper: *Yev-rei-ka.* It seems to me that all the faces of the pupils merge into one grinning mass. Having answered several other questions, I go to my seat, exhausted and upset.[53]

This sort of experience is by no means limited to childhood. It is multiplied several times as one grows older and applies for admission to universities or for jobs. The writer Grigori Svirski describes how he came after the war to Moscow University and was at first denied admission. His friend, a decorated combat pilot like Svirski, was denied admission to the school for diplomats and was told that he was not "of the needed nationality."

> It was in this way that I found out that anti-Semitism exists not only among the uneducated, not only on the kitchen-scandal level, but that

it exists in the highest state level. Can you imagine the terror of it? When you have come back from such a war, a war for Russia in which you were ready to die gladly for your country, to come back from the Barents Sea and find out that you are not part of the "needed nationality," that you are an inferior human being? And that is why, no matter what I wrote later, I always addressed myself to the theme of anti-Semitism. Because it was not only my affair, not only my thought, but my pain.[54]

Anti-Semitism was more intense, open, and perhaps widespread in the 1948-53 period than in the 1960s, so that the emigration movement was not a reaction to a suddenly intensified anti-Jewish sentiment in the country. Its role was to mold the consciousness of some Jews as undesirable aliens in a country that could never be theirs. In the 1960s and 1970s, however, there was an ominous development, reminiscent of the worst years of Stalinism, that did contribute directly to the desire for emigration. This was the closing of educational opportunities that had widened after Stalin's death. Between 1970 and 1973 the absolute number of Jewish *aspiranty* (graduate students) fell from 4,945 to 3,456.[55] Between 1970 and 1976 the number of Jewish students in higher education fell from 105,800 to 66,900. As Alexander Voronel, one of the leaders of the aliyah movement in Moscow has pointed out, education, in addition to being a traditional Jewish value, is of extraordinary importance to Soviet Jews, for it is their only gateway to satisfying work and respectable social status. Voronel argues that one's work becomes all important to Soviet Jews, as this is the one means by which they can gain respect and satisfaction.[56] The narrowing of educational opportunities is therefore perceived as very threatening and is clearly one of the reasons that Soviet Jews, otherwise unconcerned about nationality or politics, leave the country.[57]

THE CATALYSTS: THE 1967 MIDDLE EAST WAR AND THE LENINGRAD TRIALS

The Arab-Israeli War of 1967 had a profound impact on Soviet Jews, as it did on Jews in other countries. There were several reasons why this war made a much greater impression than the 1956 campaign before it, or the Yom Kippur War after it. First, in the weeks leading up to it, both Arab rhetoric and the objective situation made it seem that a second holocaust of millions of Jews was a

real possibility, and after the shattering trauma of the Nazi experience, not even the most assimilated Jew could remain indifferent
to such a prospect. Second, there was a realization that the Soviet
government unequivocally supported those whose declared intention
was to "throw the Jews into the sea," and it did so not merely politically and rhetorically, but by supplying the means of destruction.

> Until June, 1967, Soviet Jews had illusions about co-existence with
> the regime, despite the fact that it wanted to spiritually destroy the
> Jews. But suddenly they realized that the Soviet government identifies
> itself with those who wish to destroy the Jewish state . . . Russia spat
> on the Jewish people "and then we knew that we would never be able
> to live under such a regime."[58]

Soviet propaganda, before, during, and after the war, was so shrill
and one-sided that it could not but arouse the attention of the most
indifferent Jew, especially as the terms "Zionist" and "Jew" were
interchanged rather freely. The massive purge and, in effect,
expulsion of Jews from Poland in 1968, under the guise of an anti-
Zionist campaign, showed where such rhetoric could lead. As is often
the case, Soviet propaganda had a backfire effect on some. A young
engineer, now in Israel, reports that he was indifferent to Israel and
Zionism until 1967. "On the eve of the Six Day War Moscow opened
its offensive propaganda [sic] against Israel . . . I was surprised by
the internal contradictions and exaggerations of this propaganda. The
authors seemed to be accusing me of being a Jew. So I began to be
interested in Soviet Middle Eastern policy."[59]

The third aspect of the war that galvanized Soviet Jewry was the
rapidity and brilliance of the Israeli victory, something that made a
deep impression all over the world, all the more so in the USSR
where the public had been prepared to witness the exact opposite
result. One emigré intellectual asks us to "imagine the scope and
power of this spiritual blast" and describes it in the following terms:

> Able to draw freely on a reservoir of a hundred million men, the Soviet
> inheritors of Russia's 18th century military glory had been preparing
> their Egyptian clients for an invasion of a remote, tiny patch of semi-
> desert, sparsely inhabited by freaks, pictured by 19th century Russian
> humorists as soldiers because nothing was believed to be funnier than
> a Jew forced to fire a rifle. Within six days it became clear that the
> Jewish state was a modern democracy populated by fine, noble,

intelligent Europeans [sic], while the Russian military turned out to be the tragi-comic freaks.[60]

The same point was made, with less historical sweep but with greater poignancy, perhaps, by a teen-ager now living in Israel.

As kids . . . we used to shoot down birds with our catapults [sling-shots]. That poor little dead bird we used to call *zhid* [kike] — yes, even the Jewish boys did this. At that time we didn't stop to think that we ourselves were calling that miserable, helpless creature by the very name that we hated . . . that's how cowardly and helpless we had been. And all of a sudden when the Six Day War was over and won by the Israelis, we Jews realized that we didn't have to be like that . . . bird. We saw that there could be a different kind of Jew who was able to live like a human being.

Another immigrant to Israel, then a Moscow mathematics student, recalls that

after the great fear for Israel before the war came the insane joy after the victory. I can't describe it. Father said, "We were saved," as if we were in the war and threatened by annihilation. And suddenly, for the first time in our lives, we felt that to be Jewish was something to be proud of, honorable, great, and that the newspapers could write what they want but the Russian in the street, and in the store, and also in the university, respects the Jew. Our whole life changed. . . . We thirsted after every word about Israel. At night we searched for the Israeli radio frequency, and we would listen, inebriated, to the news from Israel.[61]

In Kiev, a young radio technician rose to argue with a lecturer on the international situation, expressing his disagreement with the lecturer's depiction of Israel as an aggressor. In August 1968 he and his non-Jewish wife applied to emigrate to Israel. Boris Kochubi-yevsky's application was rejected, and his wife was expelled from the Komsomol. Permission to emigrate was then granted, but withdrawn at the last minute. Instead, Kochubiyevsky was arrested for defaming the Soviet Union and sentenced to three years in prison. Kochubi-yevsky became the first Soviet Jew to renounce his citizenship and to declare himself an Israeli, even while still in the USSR. As he put it, after detailing how members of his family had been killed on charges that they were Petliuraites, Trotskyites, or simply Jews, "In this country I belong to no one. I want to go somewhere where I shall belong."[62]

It was about 1968 that Jews began to become aware that several hundred Soviet Jews had been allowed to leave for Israel, and they began to wonder if it would be possible to do the same. A former resident of Kiev describes events in the Ukrainian capital. A man who worked as a butcher by day and played the accordion at weddings and parties at night, became almost a legend when it was discovered that he got permission to go to Israel.

> The artist-butcher . . . began to go to all the departments . . . and obtained quick permission to go to Israel. I do not know how to explain it. . . . In any case he got his visa and for several days all Jewish Kiev talked only about this. . . . The sensation that this artist made, no matter how you look at it, can only be compared with the sensation from the victory of Israel in the 1967 war. I think the war played the main role, events were "hanging in the air," and our artist was only the stone that started the avalanche.[63]

If the Six-Day War excited an interest in and appreciation of Israel, in a way supplying the "pull" of emigration, it was the Leningrad trial of November-December 1970 that supplied the "push," and that resulted in a mass emigration, beginning in March 1971. Eleven persons, including two non-Jews, were tried for an attempted hijacking of a plane in order to get out of the country, though, in fact, while the hijacking was planned, the defendants were not caught in the act. The plot and trial have been analyzed extensively elsewhere.[64] What is relevant here is that the sentences, announced on Christmas Eve 1970 and which included two death sentences and several long prison terms, aroused an enormous reaction within and without the Soviet Union. Coming at the same time as a trial of nationalist Basques in Spain that had aroused world criticism, the Leningrad trial became a *cause célèbre* throughout the Western world. As Korey remarks, "the Leningrad trial, insofar as the intention of the Soviet rulers was concerned, proved to be a monumental blunder. What had been a minor, though thorny internal problem — the plight of Soviet Jewry — became a major problem of Soviet society and a central human rights item on the agenda of the world conscience."[65] In the course of the trial the defendants were able to raise the full agenda of issues that created the predicament of Soviet Jewry and the desire of many to leave the country. Since the transcript of the trial was circulated in samizdat and abroad,[66] the issues and personalities involved became well known. Three subsequent trials of Soviet Jews in Leningrad, Riga, and Kishinev in the spring of 1971 reinforced the impression made by the first Leningrad trial and kept the issues of Soviet Jewry and emigration very much in the forefront of the news.

Within the USSR the emigration issue had been raised in the Kochubiyevsky trial, by the public renunciation of Soviet citizenship of Yasha Kazakov in Moscow in late spring 1968, and by a petition of 18 Georgian Jewish families sent to the United Nations in August 1969.[67] It was the Leningrad trial, however, that turned the emigration issue into a popular one. People became aware of others desirous of emigrating as well as of world attention to the issue. They were also acutely aware of the hostility of the Soviet authorities toward Jews who wished to assert what they perceived as their legal, national rights. As Sonia Lerner-Levin explains, while the Six-Day War had aroused interest in Israel, it had not led her and others to the conclusion that they should emigrate to Israel. "This came later. . . . This came in December, 1970, when the first Leningrad trial began. Of course, we read every word. We read . . . and were ashamed. . . . Look here, we said at home, here are Jews that don't simply talk about Israel, don't just dream, but they *do* something, and are not afraid of the danger and the punishment."[68] Soviet Jews began to apply for exit visas and by March 1971 the mass emigration had begun. What had been a trickle in 1968-70 turned into a steady stream in 1971.

Feeding that stream was a flow of people from the political opposition to the Zionist movement. Quite a few of the outstanding figures of the latter had begun their "careers as dissidents" in the general political opposition that had emerged in the late 1950s and 1960s. They turned to the movement of aliyah for they felt that, in contrast to political opposition, it had a realistic chance of achieving its aim. For example, the physicist Roman Rutman, who describes himself as totally assimilated, was aroused to political opposition by the 1966 trial of the writers Sinyavsky and Daniel, but he was shocked by the invasion of Czechoslovakia in August 1968.

> I . . . realised two things . . . we had been deceiving ourselves about the future all along, for Russia would never have more freedom than

she has now. . . . Around this time, many of my friends began to be baptised. There was a new-Christian movement afoot and I myself was on the brink of being baptised. But something held me back. . . . I felt an irreparable separation — like the cold space that settles after two lovers split apart. All my life I'd loved my country and then hated her, loved and hated her again. Now I felt nothing for Russia.[69]

This ambivalence toward Russia is typical of those who came to the aliyah movement from political opposition. The Jewish writer, Svirsky, who writes in Russian, expresses it this way: "I am a man of the Russian language, of Russian culture, and nevertheless I want to part with it because of that other, base aspect [anti-Semitism]."[70] Another emigré, living in Jerusalem, expresses her love for the city and for Israel, but admits that "my identity with Russia is so irreversible that the separation from it is very painful. . . . I know it's terrible but I would return to Russia even now. . . . This schism is very painful."[71] Few, if any, of the "pure" Zionists and of those who came from the Baltic feel such nostalgia.

In many ways the "democratic movement," as it is often referred to, and the aliyah movement overlapped. People such as Mikhail Zand, Vadim Meniker, Vitaly Svechinsky, and Yulii Telesin played important roles in both. Some other Zionists were involved in other forms of Soviet dissidence (Mikhail Agursky was associated with Solzhenitsyn's circle, for example). There is no question that the Zionists learned tactics from the democrats, and that there was a good deal of mutual support. Boris Tsukerman provided legal advice to Andrei Sakharov, for instance, and Sakharov has several times publicly supported the right of Soviet Jews to emigrate to Israel. Both groups helped one another to transmit information abroad, and they also aided each other materially and, one might say, spiritually. Yulii Telesin, son of two Yiddish writers prominent in the official journal *Sovetish haimland* (and roundly condemned in its pages after their emigration), notes that "from such as Bukovsky, Litvinov, Grigorenko, Amalrik . . . who had nothing in common with Zionism, I learned how to struggle for my legal right to live in my historic homeland."[72]

There were tensions between the two groups, arising largely from political dissidents' fears that their ranks were being thinned by people going over to Zionism, and by guilt feelings on the part of some nouveau-Zionists for having done so. Within the Zionist group, too, there were differences of opinion regarding the political opposition. Some argued that the Zionist goal was to leave Russia, not reform it. Though their sympathies were with the dissidents, open support of the latter would only give the authorities the excuse to portray the Zionists as "anti-Soviet." Others felt they had a moral obligation to support the dissidents, even after they had succeeded in emigrating. (The Israeli authorities have consistently taken a "hands off" attitude toward the political dissidents and have actively opposed attempts by Soviet immigrants to publicly support political oppositionists in the USSR. When a recent arrival told authorities of his intention to "prevent the Soviet Union from doing to others what they did to me," he was told bluntly: "Not here you wouldn't do any such thing.")[73]

A woman from Kharkov, active in both movements, describes how the

> so-called old guard Zionists — former prisoners, the pioneers of the movement and their followers — positively insisted on the strict separation of "Zionists" from "democrats," and even from Jews who came to the movement from the democratic circles and introduced some new character into the movement. . . . The so-called democrats differed from "traditional" or "classical" Zionists . . . in the manner in which they applied to the authorities; they demanded, rather than asked for something. . . . It is true that a number of these people were more anti-Soviet than nationally minded, at least at the beginning of their activities.[74]

There were also other tactical differences within the movement — between those who insisted on acting within the strict letter of the law and those who were prepared to go outside it; those who sought confrontation with the authorities, and those who strove to reduce them to a minimum; those who renounced Soviet citizenship and declared themselves Israelis, and those who argued that they had nothing against the USSR and even promised to join the Communist party once they had arrived in Israel. These differences and nuances exist to this very day within the dissident and aliyah movements. What is remarkable is that despite these, the overwhelming majority have been able to continue working together and supporting each other.

The aliyah movement gained public attention — no doubt, more outside the USSR than within it — largely through written appeals, letters, and petitions to national and international authorities, but also through such audacious and hitherto unthinkable actions as demonstrations and "sit-ins" in the Kremlin, in the headquarters of the party's Central Committee. By late summer 1969, individual appeals gave way to collective ones, and "for the first time in the history of the Zionist revival in the USSR groups of Soviet Jews appeared publicly, identifying their names and addresses."[75] This change in tactics was due to the spreading realization that some Jews were being allowed to emigrate and that the crack in the wall could be widened. It was also stimulated by the change in Israel's strategy that resulted in publicity being given to the emigration struggle of Soviet Jews, as well as by the mobilization of mass opinion in the United States and Western Europe. The themes and content of these collective appeals varied somewhat, though they all pressed for the right of Jews to emigrate freely. Some quoted Soviet law and international legal documents, or a statement by Kosygin in Paris in 1966 regarding family reunification, as the basis for their demands. Others described forced cultural assimilation and stressed the lack of Jewish cultural opportunities in the USSR. Total alienation from Soviet society and criticism of Soviet policies in the Middle East were among the more audacious and challenging themes struck, though this was characteristic of a relatively small number of cases.[76]

Redlich's analysis of all known signatories of 1968-70 reveals that more than half the petitioners were from the RSFSR and Latvia, while in Georgia collective letters were signed by entire, extended families. When compared to the size of local Jewish populations, it turns out that "petition-signing was highest in Riga and Vilnius, and lowest in . . . Kiev. Moscow, Leningrad, and Minsk were located somewhere in the middle of this scale."[77] Well over half the signers were in their twenties and thirties, and there was a high proportion of professionals, or intelligentsia, among them. By 1971-72 the number of signatories increased considerably in Lithuania, as well as in the Ukraine. Petitions and appeals began to appear also in Moldavia, Kazakhstan, and Kirghizia, and the number of scientists and performing artists signing appeals rose considerably.

In comparison with the political opposition, of whatever stripe, and with other national protest movements, such as the Crimean Tatar, Baltic, or Ukrainian, the Jewish national movement must be considered a success. True, its basic aim has been qualitatively different from those of the other movements. Its purpose is not to change the Soviet system, but simply to leave it. This makes the Jewish movement less threatening to the authorities, as the dangers of "spillover" to other groups is small because the great majority of Soviet nationalities have their historic homelands within the Soviet borders. Of course, this does not mean that Soviet authorities have taken a lenient attitude toward the aliyah movement — the detention of nearly 100 aliyah activists in labor camps, the arrests of hundreds of others, and the refusal of permission to emigrate to thousands is testimony to that. But the authorities have granted permission to over 200,000 Jews (and smaller numbers of Germans and Armenians) to leave the country, which has to be interpreted as a failure for the USSR: a failure to socialize all its citizens fully, a failure to provide satisfactory conditions for large numbers of educated, relatively prosperous people, a failure to achieve the "rapprochement (*sblizhenie*) and friendship of peoples" so often boasted of in Soviet rhetoric. Why the Soviets have failed in these respects is not our concern here; why the aliyah movement succeeded is.

Since the Soviet leadership has not revealed its calculations and motivations in deciding to allow limited emigration — nor is it likely to do so — we can only speculate as to their reasoning and decision making. The Jewish movement may pose a unique danger, as well as a unique opportunity, to the Soviet authorities, and these may explain its treatment. As we have noted, the aim of the Jewish movement is less threatening than that of other dissidents. On the other hand, the composition of the aliyah movement presents a more difficult challenge: While other nationality movements are restricted to a single territory, generally speaking, the Jewish movement has spread from the Baltic through the Caucasus, out to Central Asia and even to Siberia, with its nerve centers in the key cities of Moscow and Leningrad, where access to Western media and tourists is greatest. Thus, for the authorities this became a problem of truly "all-union" scope. Similarly, whereas the political dissidents are mostly members of the intelligentsia, the Jewish movement came to include people of all ages, levels of education, occupations, and social categories. Thus, the movement has cut across geographic and social lines in a way that no other has been able to do. "Vertically," "horizontally," and perhaps numerically, this has been the most comprehensive of the Soviet dissident movements.

Internal pressure for emigration was matched by external pressure. The "Soviet Jewry issue" became a prominent one, culminating perhaps in the "Jackson amendment," which links emigration of Soviet citizens to the granting of "most favored nation" status to the USSR.[78] This pressure complemented and supported the actions being taken within the USSR, and protected it to some extent from severe reprisal. This linkage of internal and external pressure was effective largely because of its timing. After all, Soviet leaders have shown themselves to be quite capable of repressing internal dissidence and of ignoring external demands. In this case, however, in the early 1970s the leadership was pressing hard to expand trade relations with the West, especially with the United States, and to obtain many forms of economic and technological assistance. To achieve these aims it was necessary to gain some public support in the West. Since many of these steps could be taken only by the U.S. government or with government approval, executive and congressional approval became necessary. Perhaps because they take their own propaganda too seriously, Soviet leaders have exaggerated the Jewish presence and power in international financial circles and in American politics. This convinced them that in order to obtain favorable American action on their economic and technological desiderata, they would have to make some concessions to public opinion, especially Jewish public opinion. Perhaps they thought that if the gates were opened, only a small number of "trouble-makers" and "malcontents" would leave, thus ridding the USSR of undesirable citizens and simultaneously placating Western opinion. The Soviet leadership was probably caught by surprise, as were most non-Soviet observers, by the rapid escalation of the emigration movement, by the profundity of Soviet Jewish alienation, and by the determination of both the internal and external forces, political as well as social, to press for unrestricted and expanded emigration.

Whatever the calculus of Soviet decisions,[79] about 1,000 people were granted exit visas in March 1971, and their numbers grew in subsequent months. It is likely that the initial emigrants were motivated primarily by a desire to reunite with families in Israel and by ideological commitments to Jewish nationalism and culture, but as time went on it became apparent that other motivations — political alienation, economic dissatisfaction, family considerations — were impelling people to leave the country.[80] In fact, the Soviet authorities themselves used the vehicle of emigration in order to expel, in effect, dissenting writers and other oppositionists. They were "persuaded" to apply for visas to Israel, even those who were neither Jews nor Zionists, and left the country under the same conditions as the Jewish emigrés, though they then settled in Western Europe or the United States for the most part. Other political dissidents, as well as those who were not actively opposing the regime but were simply alienated from it, began to use the Jewish emigration route out of the country, giving rise to the witticism that "a Jewish wife is not a luxury but a means of transportation." One might say, borrowing Hirschman's terminology, that while "loyalty" had been the only practical option open to the Soviet citizen in the Stalinist period, and "voice" became a possibility with the rise of dissidence in the 1960s, in the 1970s "exit" was added to the list.[81]

It would be misleading to suggest that all individuals leaving the country were doing so willingly or even as a result of a conscious decision. Some, especially children or spouses, were even leaving against their wishes. "Secondary migrants" were simply going along with decisions made by others (the latter is probably especially true of Georgians and Central Asians, among whom the hierarchical family is still quite authoritative). Some children report that their parents explained the emigration decision on the basis of a desire for reunification with family whom they, the children, had never seen. As this rationale was unpersuasive or meaningless to them, they began to search out discrepancies in the Soviet system or look for the meaning of their Jewish identity.[82] It should also be borne in mind that once emigration reaches substantial proportions it acquires a life of its own. Emigration was something so novel, so amazing in Soviet conditions, that the very possibility was attractive to people who had never seriously considered leaving the country before. With travel so restricted to Soviet citizens, it is one of the freedoms they miss most. One emigré, now in the United States, observed that "at first people just wanted to 'try out' life in the United States, but they couldn't do that, so they had to take the final decision to emigrate."[83] Moreover, as a leading student of migration observes,

> migration becomes a style, an established pattern, an example of collective behavior. Once it is well begun, the growth of such a movement is semi-automatic: so long as there are people to emigrate, the principal cause of emigration is prior emigration. . . . When emigration

has been set us as a *social* pattern, it is no longer relevant to inquire concerning the *individual* motivations.[84]

Or, as a woman from Kiev put it simply, "everbody was going, so I went too. I was afraid of being alone, without Jews. All the Jews are going, so should I stay behind?" For most, of course, the process was somewhat more extended and complicated. Navrozov describes how his family was friendly with other families who desired to emigrate, and

> thus those who wished to leave and all their sympathizers were linked in a social entity, cohesive and dynamic, yet inchoate, spontaneous, and self-regenerating. Before last spring I had been an outsider, then my friend's friend got an exit visa! . . . Very soon everyone in Russia who was not an applicant seemed to . . . me insipid, parochial, insignificant, and any activity except the exodus absurd or insane. On the other hand, a novel sense of Jewish brotherhood . . . quickly developed among ourselves and other applicants.[85]

One study of immigrants in Israel found that, indeed, most Soviet emigrants enjoy the support and approval of their relatives and friends,[86] and another study found that they come with their families to a greater extent than do those from English-speaking countries.[87] Half the Soviet immigrants interviewed, but 90 percent of the English-speaking immigrants, had parents still living abroad.

SOVIET EMIGRATION POLICIES AND ADMINISTRATION

Whatever the original calculus and motivations of the Soviet decision to allow some emigration, once the process had been in operation for some years it became possible to discern some patterns in Soviet attitudes and policies. Soviet policy is deliberately ambiguous. Free emigration is unacceptable because it would permit a spontaneous process to go uncontrolled by the authorities, something that runs against the very nature of Soviet rule. However, some selected, controlled emigration is allowed, and this serves several purposes: Western critics can be placated as the need arises; domestic critics can be gotten rid of; Arabs and Israelis may be pressured, if only at the margins. Making emigration an uncertain prospect depresses the number of applications, for the risks involved are too high for many. It also adds to the already impressive leverage that Soviet officials have vis-a-vis the citizens.

Emigration is not conceived of by Soviet authorities, especially local and provincial ones, as a natural right, but as a concession to reprehensible people. Despite the fact that the Soviet Union subscribes to at least three international agreements that provide for the right of every individual to leave his country and return to it,[88] "in Soviet law, a citizen does not possess a right to emigrate at will. . . . The last word . . . rests with the administrative authorities."[89] Emigration is allowed only on the grounds of family reunification. It is a "political dispensation . . . a special privilege conferred . . . by the organs of state and not something . . . a person can claim. . . ."[90] Therefore, the authorities try to persuade potential emigrants to reconsider, to shame them out of their decision, or even to punish them for it and to deny their applications. At the same time as individuals are discouraged, a massive campaign goes on in the media to convince Soviet citizens that emigration is a tragic mistake, at best, and the act of ingrates or traitors, at worst. For those who persist, the emigration process is very often humiliating, demeaning, costly, risky, and exhausting. No doubt this results partially from the inherently laborious and enervating working of the Soviet bureaucracy, and partially from a calculated effort to make the process as unpleasant as possible, intended to discourage all but the most insistent and most durable.

Regulations and procedures governing the granting of a passport and/or exit visa are not published in the USSR, lending credence to our assertion about the Soviet view of emigration. A local office of visas and registration, known as OVIR, accepts applications for permission to leave the country. These are forwarded to the internal affairs ministry of the republic, though there is some evidence that some decisions are made in the local organs of that ministry. With the application to leave, one must submit the following documents: an invitation from relatives abroad (a *vyzov*), since emigration is justifiable only on the grounds of reunification of families; a declaration of intent to leave; an autobiography; character certification from one's place of employment (*kharakteristika*) (no longer required in all cases); permission from one's parents; permission from one's former spouse, if one is divorced; a certificate from the house committee in one's place of residence; copies of birth certificate, marriage license, divorce decree, educational degrees and diplomas, and certificates of death of relatives; and photographs.[91] All these documents must be submitted in person. Needless to say, these requirements present opportunities for harassment, delay, and extortion, since supervisors may refuse to give a *kharakteristika*, house committees may do the same, and vengeful or ideologically antagonistic former spouses or parents may withhold needed permission. In 1980 the proviso that the *vyzov* must be sent by a first-degree relative (parent, spouse, child) living in Israel was enforced very strictly (and vyzovs often do not reach the addressee), thereby cutting the number of emigrants to 40 percent of the number in 1979. In 1981 emigration was cut again by about 40 percent, dropping to the lowest level in a decade. Fewer than 10,000 Jews were allowed to emigrate in 1981.

According to Soviet law, a decision on the application must be rendered within a month. Applicants are notified of the decision in person or by telephone, but almost never in writing. In the great majority of cases, no reason is given for the decision, and in the case of a refusal, there is no judicial recourse, though a periodic review of the application – originally limited to once a year, and since 1976 allowed every six months – may be requested.

Should the application be approved, an application fee of 30 rubles and a passport fee of 300-400 rubles must be paid (it is only 30 rubles for those intending to travel to "socialist" countries). In addition, those leaving the country for permanent residence in Israel must renounce their Soviet citizenship, and for this there is a fee of 500 rubles since it requires a petition to the presidium of the Supreme Soviet for release of citizenship. In 1972-73 an additional fee was imposed, the so-called diploma tax whereby emigrants "repaid" the Soviet state for the education it had granted them, with fees varying by the amount of education received. When this barrier to emigration, very effective against Jews who have high levels of education, was vigorously protested, collection of the fee was halted, though the provision for it remains on the books. (In order to put all of these fees in perspective, it should be borne in mind that the average Soviet monthly wage in the 1970s was around 150 rubles.)

Aside from financial costs, there are other penalties for emigration, though they are by no means uniformly imposed. These include the loss of one's job; public condemnation at a meeting of one's peers or colleagues or in the media; loss of student status in universities; and so on. Emigrés are often socially isolated, except from other applicants. Usually, no more than a month is allowed for departure, and sometimes this is abbreviated to ten days, a period in which a person must liquidate possessions, ship some and pack others; settle all financial and personal affairs; obtain necessary papers; and the like. Some have sold their belongings and apartments and have proceeded to the airport or rail station for the journey out of the country, only to be told that permission had been withdrawn. They must stay in the country, now without an apartment, possessions, or income. Customs regulations are strict, and emigrés, especially those departing by train, are subjected to humiliating searches and often outright thievery by border guards. For example, in order to be taken out of the country, furniture must have been owned for at least a year; only one wedding ring of gold and one piece of jewelry, worth less than 250 rubles, may be taken out. The U.S. congressional investigation of Soviet emigration procedures concluded that the total expense of emigration "can be about 1,500 rubles per adult in a family — the equivalent of an average yearly wage."[92]

Some of the atmosphere surrounding emigration can be appreciated in the reports of the emigrés themselves. One young linguistics specialist, who had been teaching English to applicants for emigration, was called in to the KGB and was told by an official: "I wouldn't say it is illegal, but I would not say it is natural to teach those who wish to leave their own country." The official asked the linguist to report on the activities of the students, claiming that this would enable the authorities to "help them."

> You are an extremely intelligent person, you can observe them accurately, and if we know more about them we can dissuade them. Some of them may even have dangerous intentions and we will be able to stop them without doing them any harm. By providing information you can actually help some of your friends. I should tell you that Jewish emigration is a minor problem and we waste precious time on those light-minded people, but we have serious troubles in Lithuania and elsewhere.

The linguist, frightened and confused, tried to put off the requests that he act as an informer. The KGB persisted, introducing a second official who made some revealing statements about the KGB perception of the emigration "problem." The official's perception in 1974 was that most of the "true Zionists" had already emigrated, and those who remained were trying to persuade others to follow them out of the country. "But the others care for wealth, for adventure; they are not anxious to die for Israel or for any other cause. We should persuade them to change their minds and if we had more information, this would be easier." He then told the linguist of his troubles.

> You heard about that doctor who returned from Israel. He told awful things about Israel, among them that Hebrew is like Chinese and they also write with a brush, and we let him speak on TV, which was certainly a mistake. Now we are getting hundreds of letters — Russians are indignant that such a fool could be a doctor, a professor, and Jews are furious because he slanders Israel. We really should find out how to influence people not to leave.[93]

Having refused to cooperate with the KGB, the linguist was given the choice of giving up his English lessons or of emigrating himself. He decided upon the latter, and two months after applying, he left the country.

Another young professional was born and raised in the RSFSR and held a promising position in what was considered one of the most pleasant and "liberal" research institutes in the country. He had no connection with the Zionist movement, and as late as August 1971, he says, he could not conceive of the idea that all one had to do to leave the USSR would be to apply to do so. However, when his parents died, the idea of applying came to him and he submitted his papers. He made what he calls a "gentlemen's agreement" with the Komsomol — he would resign in order not to embarrass them, and they would not denounce him. The director of his institute called him in for a cordial chat, and tried to get the young researcher to change his mind. One of the arguments he used was, roughly, as follows: "Do you realize how this will affect your colleague X's [a Jew] position? Do you know how much it took to get you in here?" These remarks, made in all sincerity and not without poignancy, only made the researcher reflect on the nature of the system he wanted to leave. Following this conversation, representatives of the district party committee (*raikom*) spent two entire days with the applicant, adopting first a menacing tone and later a conciliatory one, pointing out that Israel was a fascist country, that the emigré might well be unemployed, and so on. At one point, he feels, they tried to provoke him by suggesting, "perhaps you are leaving because you experienced anti-Semitism here." He quickly answered "of course not," in order not to expose himself to the charge of anti-Soviet slander, and in front of two "reliable" witnesses. As a result of his application, several of his articles already in press were withdrawn, but most of his colleagues remained cordial to the very end of the stay in the USSR.[94]

As is well known, others' experiences have not been so mild. A former correspondent of *Literaturnaia gazeta*, which has been playing a leading role in the anti-Zionist campaign, describes the hostility of his colleagues as soon as they learned that he had applied to emigrate. "No one in the office greeted me, no one bade me farewell. People with whom I had worked for years simply cut me." The correspondent's phone was bugged, he was followed and harassed by the KGB, and his application to leave was denied several times.[95]

Not surprisingly, Soviet claims and Western reports regarding the process of emigration vary considerably. Soviet officials insist that the great majority of applicants leave routinely, with the claim made repeatedly that "out of the total number of persons who have submitted applications to emigrate, 98.4 percent have been allowed to do so."[96] At the same time, it was admitted by the same source, Colonel V. S. Obidin, head of the All-Union OVIR, that in 1975 and 1976 alone, over 1,000 people who had been refused permission previously were allowed to leave.[97] Obidin's successor claimed that the number of those "temporarily" refused permission to emigrate was "very small, one might say inconsequential."[98] According to Israeli sources, about 300,000 Soviet citizens have requested vyzovs but have not yet left, and some have concluded that nearly 300,000 people have been refused permission to emigrate. This is misleading for two reasons: it is known that the same person may receive several vyzovs, because several different persons invite him to leave or because the same person issues an invitation several times (since many vyzovs never arrive at their destination); it is also the case that people who receive vyzovs do not always apply to emigrate, either because they have not requested the vyzovs, or because, having requested it, they decide to reconsider or to postpone their emigration. Thus, in Georgia, between 1968 and 1980, 66,144 visas were requested, though, according to the 1970 census, there are only 55,400 Jews in Georgia. Some are "driven to the conclusion that the 1970 population census contained inaccuracies and understated the Jewish population."[99] An alternative explanation is that Georgian

Jews received multiple vyzovs. In light of the strong family ties of the Georgians and their administrative style, on the one hand, and the absence of plausible explanations for "inaccuracies" in the 1970 census, on the other, the latter explanation seems more convincing. Still, even taking into account these factors, the discrepancy between invitations issued and permissions granted is larger than Soviet sources indicate. It would also seem that of those applying, more than 1.6 percent are refused. Evidence for this may be found in a survey of 1,035 emigrés conducted under the auspices of the U.S. congressional commission monitoring implementation of the 1975 Helsinki agreement. Of the respondents, 278 had departed the USSR before the Helsinki accord was signed, and 757 had left after it. Of the pre-Helsinki group, about 30 percent reported that they had been refused permission to leave, whereas among the post-Helsinki emigrés the proportion of refusals declined to 15 percent. In a 1978 congressional study of 235 emigrants, 17 percent reported having been refused permission to emigrate. All three figures are considerably higher than the Soviet statistic of 1.6 percent. Moreover, of the post-Helsinki emigrés who had been refused, 25 percent had been refused three to six times, and 11 percent had been refused eight or more times. Over half of them had been given some reason for the refusal — almost never in writing — the most frequent being possession of state secrets and the absence of close kin abroad.[100]

Almost 20 percent of the respondents had experienced difficulties in receiving their vyzovs, and this was especially true of those in the smaller cities of the RSFSR. Although most of the respondents were over 18 at the time of application, nearly 75 percent had to document parental approval. Nearly all of the pre-Helsinki emigrés, but only 32 percent of the later wave, had to submit a *kharakteristika*, and over 33 percent of the later emigrés had been forced to leave their jobs as a result of their application.[101] Eighty-five percent of the post-Helsinki applicants received their visas within a year of application, but only 68 percent of the earlier applicants did so. "The prospective post-Helsinki emigrants generally had to wait a shorter time for final approval than those who preceded them. . . . Nevertheless, nearly one post-Helsinki applicant in eight had to wait from one to six years for an exit visa, still a lower percentage than the 22 per cent of the pre-Helsinki grouping."[102] In my own survey, including emigrés of a somewhat earlier period and with a substantial overrepresentation of the leaders of the aliyah movement, the time between application and permission was considerably longer. Only 44 percent got out of the country within a year of applying, and 60 percent within two years. In fact, 20 percent of those from the Baltic had waited eight years and more. This is probably due to the presence in the group of several veteran Zionists, and also to the fact that even nonpolitical people in the Baltic areas had applied to leave as early as 1945-48.

Among the others, even the Zionist activists became such only in the 1960s and undoubtedly their first applications to leave came later than those from the Western borderlands. Soviet Jewish emigration activists estimate that the number of "refuseniks" grew from 10,000 in 1979 to 50,000 in 1980-81, plausible figures in light of the drastic reduction in emigration.

So carefully is Soviet emigration policy making (and, of course, policy making generally) veiled from public scrutiny, that we cannot be certain at what level and by whom the major decisions are made. It is striking that emigration has been disproportionately heavy from some areas, and light from others. Until 1980, about 11 percent of the total number of Jews in the USSR (1970 census) had been issued exit permits. If one compares the number of exit permits per republic with the number of Jews in the republic (as reported in the 1970 census), one observes great variation. At one extreme, 59.4 percent of the Jews in Georgia received exit permits between 1968 and 1980; at the other, 0.9 percent of those in Kazakhstan received permission to leave. In Lithuania, 49 percent of the Jews were issued permits, whereas in the RSFSR, where about 37 percent of all Soviet Jews reside, only 4.4 percent of the population have been issued exit permits. This explains why some Jews changed their republic of residence, especially in the early 1970s. Those anxious to leave felt they had a better chance of obtaining permission in the Baltic or in Georgia than in the RSFSR or in Belorussia.

It can be shown that the chances of getting a permit vary significantly by republic, since we know the number of persons requesting a vyzov and the number receiving a permit in each republic. Thus, 84 percent of those requesting affidavits in Lithuania received an exit permit; 62 percent in Latvia; 31 percent each in the RSFSR and Belorussia; and 37 percent in Tadzhikistan. This leads to the conclusion that the disproportions in emigration from different republics are *not* explained solely, or even mainly, by the greater number of applications in some, and the smaller number in others.

The *rates* of granting exit permits vary so widely that one can, in fact, say that it is easier to leave from the two Baltic republics (the number of Jews in Estonia is very small) than it is from Russia and Belorussia. However, it remains true that a greater proportion of the Jews in the Baltic, Georgia, and other peripheral areas apply to leave in the first place. This is no doubt due to higher levels of Jewish consciousness and, in the case of the Baltic and West Ukrainian areas, greater general alienation from the Soviet state generally and from Russian domination especially. A detailed comparison of the number of vyzovs and visas by republic can be made by studying Table 3.5. (Data for 1980, not included in the table, do not alter the picture very much.)

This leaves open the question of how and by whom these variations are determined. Some have suggested that the variation is so great that it must be due to different policies being pursued by republic-level officials or even lower-level authorities. An alternative

Table 3.5
Invitations (Vyzovs) Sent and Visas Issued, 1968-79, by Republic

Republic	Vyzovs Sent	Percentage of Jewish Population in Republic	Visas	Percentage of Visas Granted
RSFSR	101,989	12.6	31,478	30.7
Ukraine	240,372	30.9	87,045	36.2
Belorussia	27,646	18.7	7,265	26.3
Uzbekistan	41,477	40.3	15.668	37.8
Moldavia	48,812	49.7	23,957	49.1
Georgia	65,379	118.0	31,859	48.7
Azerbaijan	27,348	66.2	6,355	23.2
Kazakhstan	1,349	4.9	319	23.6
Latvia	19,169	52.2	11,783	61.5
Lithuania	13,304	56.4	11,109	83.5
Tajikistan	7,457	51.1	2,725	36.5
Kirgizia	996	12.9	312	31.3
Estonia	848	16.0	393	46.3
Turkmenia	247	7.0	113	45.7
Armenia	194	19.4	79	40.7

Source: Zvi Aleksandr, "Netunim statistiyim shel hayetsia," *Hainteligentsia haYehudit biVrih'm*, no. 4 (June 1980), p. 76.

explanation is that central directives have been issued that give higher emigration quotas to some regions, and lower ones to others, in line with national calculations. For example, it would be reasonable for the central authorities to allow Georgian officials to issue more exit visas because Georgian Jews, who are less educated or skilled than those in the RSFSR, are felt to contribute less to the Soviet economy than the scientific intelligentsia concentrated in Moscow or Leningrad. At the same time, Georgian Jews are viewed as a disruptive element in an already troublesome republic and this would be another reason for getting rid of them through emigration. Similar arguments may obtain for the Baltic republics, Moldavia, and the West Ukraine: Each of these areas in its own way poses problems of ethnic and religious dissent to the central authorities, and in the Moldavian republic Jews play a relatively unimportant economic role, though this cannot be said of the more educated Baltic Jews.

It is likely that even if the emigration quotas are set in Moscow, republic and local officials in non-Russian areas are happy to cooperate. The emigration of Jews is welcome from their point of view because Jews overwhelmingly assimilate into the Russian, rather than local, cultures (except in Georgia). Thus, the emigration of Jews removes some agents of Russification and increases the proportion of, say, Lithuanian or Latvian speakers, something many of the local elites desire. Second, Jewish emigration opens up job and housing opportunities for local residents and expands opportunities for mobility of non-Jews. Finally, in some areas traditional anti-Semitism may also be at play, providing another incentive for local officials to cooperate in getting rid of the Jews, even though that is precisely what some of the Jews want. All these factors — differential levels of Jewish consciousness and nationalism; different types of family, economic, and vocational structures; and different calculations and motivations by republic and local officials — may be the determinants of Soviet emigration policy and of the uneven results of that policy. Until, if ever, the authorities make explicit their policy rationales and processes, discussion of those must remain in the realm of informed speculation.

EMIGRATION AND THE SOVIET MEDIA

Soviet authorities try to cure the "disease" of emigration with persuasion, harassment, and outright refusal, but they also attempt "preventative medicine" in the form of propaganda against emigration, portrayed as a betrayal of the motherland as well as a personal mistake for the emigrant. Ever since the revolution, Soviet propaganda has attacked Zionism as a nationalistic ideology serving the interests of British and American imperialism.[103] Before 1948, this was aimed at Zionism in the USSR itself, a powerful political force until the mid-1920s, and at the world Zionist movement. Since 1948, of course, campaigns against Zionism have been linked to criticisms of Israel and its policies. Following the 1967 war, anti-Zionist propaganda was greatly expanded, appearing now as a regular feature in the large-circulation newspapers, in popular magazines, and in special pamphlets and books, as well as in radio and television programs. Such works as Bol'shakov's *Zionism in the Service of Anticommunism*, which appeared in a first edition of 100,000 copies, or Yuri Ivanov's *Beware, Zionism*, which appeared in several languages (Russian, Ukrainian, Czech, English, and others) are obviously designed for mass consumption, and use lurid, vulgar, and odious rhetoric and images, often comparing Zionism to Nazism, to make their points.[104]

One purpose of this literature is to dissuade Jews from emigrating and settling in the Zionist state. Jonathan Frankel concludes that the anti-Zionist press campaigns of the 1960s and 1970s were not directly connected to events in the Middle East, nor is there a direct correlation with rates of emigration (the campaign might have served, inter alia, as a camouflage for stepped up rates of emigration). Rather, he finds, this literature is directly and immediately linked to internal and external public pressures for the right of Jewish emigration.

> The Soviet government was apparently carrying on a kind of strange dialogue with its Jewish citizens. . . . What made this "dialogue" necessary from the governmental point of view was presumably the fact that the protests, the arrests and the trials were published and publicized abroad and that these facts were then relayed back to Russia by Western radio stations. . . . A small sound left Russia but a loud echo was thrown back.[105]

It is difficult to determine the effect of this "dialogue" on readers: Some say that, inadvertently, Soviet propaganda provides some information, however distorted, about the history of Israel and

Zionism while its message is rejected; other readers undoubtedly take these publications at face value, and since there is only one nationality associated with Zionism, associations between Soviet Jews and "imperialist Zionists" are likely to be made. How effective such material has been in dissuading potential emigrés is impossible to determine, but given the generally high educational level of Soviet Jews, and the generally low level of these publications, one doubts that they have had much of the desired effect.

In recent years literature specifically aimed against emigration to Israel has emerged, followed by similar material directed against emigration to the United States and Western Europe. The main targets of this material have been Jews and Soviet Germans. In addition, films, radio, and television have carried similar messages.

Some 20 scattered articles appeared in the Soviet press before 1968 that described the disappointment of Soviet Jews who had been reunited with their families in Israel, and also told of emigrés who had returned, disillusioned, to the USSR.[106] These seem to have been little noticed by Jewish readers.[107] Before 1970 fewer than 30 articles on Jewish emigration were published in the Soviet press. However, in the first three months of 1970, 150 articles on emigration were published, many of which took the form of indignant letters to the editor by Soviet Jews protesting Golda Meir's encouraging Soviet Jews to come to Israel. Following the opening of mass emigration in 1971, we can observe three stages in Soviet media tactics:

A period of about two years (1971-72) where emigration is mentioned in passing, and where attention is focused on statements by prominent Soviet Jews who affirm that they and their fellow Jews enjoy equal rights and excellent opportunities in the "motherland";

In 1972-73 emigration is discussed in some newspapers — *Literaturnaia gazeta* and local newspapers do this prominently — but not in others. For example, in this period *Pravda* carries few stories on the subject;

Following 1974, emigration — or rather immigrants in Israel — is widely discussed in many places. Beginning in 1975, the plight of Soviet immigrants in the United States is also featured.

A study of the Soviet press reveals that in almost all cases it is immigration, not emigration, that is the subject. That is, never is there a detailed explanation of the process of emigration, the way in which one can apply, and so on. Rather, the focus is on the troubles and difficulties, never the attainments and successes, of the immigrants in Israel. Second, the messages are directed at specific audiences: while *Literaturnaia gazeta* emphasizes the difficulties experienced by emigré artists, humanists, and intelligentsia generally, the provincial press concentrates on the problems of working people, those more likely to be reading these newspapers. The journal *Za rubezhom*, popular among educated people because it features carefully selected foreign material in translation, has tended to publish more data on the emigration than other journals, relying heavily on the reports of non-Soviet Communist newspapers and magazines for its articles on the emigration.[108] *Izvestiia*'s technique, especially until 1975, was to quote extensively from foreign sources, including such "bourgeois" publications as *Der Spiegel*, the New York *Times*, the Washington *Post*, and the Israeli press. The Yiddish journal, *Sovetish haimland*, has devoted a good deal of space to the topic, especially since 1973, and almost every issue of the monthly deals with immigration in one way or another. Fairly regular features include a column of wry humor, "jokes from Israel," which concentrates on current difficulties in the state; answers "to readers' inquiries" about Israeli political parties, trade unions, and other institutions, the purpose being to cast them in a negative light; letters from disappointed Soviet immigrants in Israel, and, since 1976, in the United States; editorial attacks on Western protests against Soviet restrictions on emigration; and longer feature articles about specific cases of "Zionist agents" in the USSR and the immigrants they managed "to seduce."[109]

In 1971 a film was shown in Soviet movie houses and on television called "The Loss of the Homeland." It portrayed the difficulties, indeed the horrors, experienced by a Soviet immigrant in Israel, named Samokhvalov. The film ends with a portrayal of Soviet officials meeting to consider his application to return to the USSR and trying to understand why one would want to leave his birthplace for a foreign country.[110] Other films, including one designed for showing abroad, have also been made on this and similar themes.[111]

Soviet television has devoted considerable attention to immigrants' problems, sometimes featuring interviews with people who are said to have returned to the USSR, or are in Vienna hoping to return, after having immigrated to Israel. On January 2, 1977, an extensive program was broadcast. It began by interviewing some emigrants on their way out of the USSR, portrayed the security surrounding them in Vienna, along with shots of the poorest sections of Vienna and Rome, interspersed with film clips of Israeli bombing raids on Arab targets and wounded Arab civilians. Two Americans and a Frenchman were interviewed, admitting that they had brought in "anti-Soviet propaganda" while posing as tourists. Leaders of the aliyah movement were pictured and identified by name, and some were shown embracing Israeli athletes in Moscow, while others were shown receiving gifts and money from Westerners. Emigrants were interviewed while they were boarding the plane taking them out of the country and it was emphasized that their parents are staying behind ("what kind of family reunification is that?"). Finally, some letters were read from disillusioned emigrés.[112]

The Soviet media have devoted a good deal of attention to immigrants who have left Israel, some of whom have requested permission to return to the USSR. No reliable figures are available, but one Soviet source claimed in 1972 that 500 "individual and collective letters" had been received by Soviet organs "in which more than 1,500 former Soviet citizens of Jewish nationality who had left for Israel ask permission to return to the Soviet Union."[113] Most Western sources say that the number seeking to return to the USSR is somewhere between 150 and 300, with only a few dozen actually managing to return. Most of the others have been stranded in Vienna, stateless, jobless, and generally living in miserable conditions. As V. Sil'chenko wrote in the Odessa *Znamia kommunizma* (March 30, 1974), "Our motherland has a good heart. Good — but not all-forgiving. A motherland is not something you can set aside for a moment and then take up again when necessity arises."

In late 1972 a press conference was arranged where people in Vienna explained why they had left Israel and how difficult had been their lot there. *Literaturnaia gazeta* devoted a full page to this event, which it said involved 92 former Soviet citizens.[114] Some who have applied to return to the USSR claim that Soviet representatives in Vienna demanded that they first publicize their criticisms of Israel and that they attempt to dissuade others from emigrating. In fact, the Soviet media have featured several returnees who have done just that, while there are cases reported of returnees who refused to engage in such activities and were subsequently allowed to emigrate once again to Israel.[115] In other cases, Soviet media have quoted extensively from intercepted private letters sent to the USSR by immigrants in Israel.[116] In both Brussels and Moscow, the Soviets have sponsored press conferences featuring disillusioned, embittered emigrants.[117]

In order to discourage people from seeking a better life outside the Soviet homeland, Soviet readers are told many times that native-born Israelis have been emigrating from the country, especially since 1973; that there is a constant danger of war in Israel; that people are unfriendly and especially hostile to immigrants; that Israeli culture is characterized by pornography and appeals to base instincts; that workers are mercilessly exploited; that religious fanaticism is rampant; that the climate is very harsh; that there are strong social prejudices and administrative barriers against non-Jews who might enter as spouses of immigrating Jews. In articles and pamphlets "concerning the plight of immigrants in Israel," authentic names and addresses are often given, with selective quotations from letters written by ex-Soviet citizens. A typical excerpt follows: "I've made an irreparable mistake by leaving the Soviet Union and, together with my wife, going to live with her relatives in Israel. . . . There is racial discrimination. . . . It's virtually impossible to find a job. And . . . there is suspicion, for citizens of Russian origin are not trusted."[118] A woman married to an ethnic Latvian complains that "only in Israel . . . we have seen at first hand how the working class is humiliated and exploited. . . . We are prepared to go through any kind of difficulty, for we do not for a minute lose hope that we shall be forgiven and allowed to return to our homeland."[119] Iosif Fleisher writes from Malzgasse in Vienna, the street where most of those seeking to return reside, that "religious fanaticism and obscurantism, fierce hatred not only of the USSR, but also of us, Soviet people, the humiliating, shameful work we have to do for these cruel masters, all this has made me realise my guilt and my mistake. . . . Cursed be that Zionism which has brought me and my family, and scores of Soviet people, great suffering and torment."[120] One woman went as far as to write: "I'd rather have burned to death together with my children in a concentration camp than lead this sort of life."[121] Both the authenticity and the unrepresentative character of these letters are confirmed by the familiarity of the signers to anyone following this genre of Soviet literature. Riaboi, Liadyzhenskii, Fishkin, Cherches, Shtern, Sneideris, are all names that appear frequently in Soviet sources, with the same stories being told in different variants.[122] These people have been permitted to return, and apparently they have become "professional returnees." Some Israeli journalists have suggested that Soviet officials may have deliberately "planted" such people among the emigrés, in order to be able to discredit the emigration. On the other hand, Victor Louis, described by the New York *Times* as "a controversial Soviet journalist who recently spent some time in Israel and who sometimes carries out missions for the Soviet Security Police (the K.G.B.)," wrote in 1971 that

> the physical ties between Israel and the Soviet Union grow stronger with the passage of every single person who makes the journey, leaving friends and family behind with hopes to meet again. Similarly, the more Russian Jews settle in Israel, the more Israeli citizens there are who feel, however dear their new-found freedom, nevertheless obliged to Russia in all sorts of ways and certainly closer to her than to the United States.[123]

This optimistic view of the Soviet immigration to Israel was expressed in the *Times*, of course, not in any publication accessible to Soviet citizens.

The expansion of German emigration from the USSR has been accompanied by the development of a propaganda literature similar to that concerned with the Jewish emigration, though the literature about the Germans is smaller (as is their emigration) and appears to be concentrated in local newspapers in the areas of German population. In this literature one finds three common themes: the economic difficulties faced by ex-Soviet Germans in the exploitative world of capitalism; the cold and unfriendly attitude of people; the strangeness of Western culture.[124] The tales of disappointment are not as lurid as those concerning the Jews, though in both instances much was made of suicides by a young Jew and a young German who had emigrated. The press is careful not to link the German and Jewish emigrations, probably in order to avoid the impression that emigration is a spreading phenomenon.

THE ARABS, THE SOVIETS, AND JEWISH
IMMIGRATION TO ISRAEL

The testimony of unhappy Soviet immigrants to Israel has been used by some Soviet officials to respond to Arab criticisms of Soviet policy. Responding to an attack by the late Jamal Baroody, the colorful Saudi delegate to the United Nations, Soviet Ambassador Yakov Malik rejected charges that the USSR had been pressured into allowing its Jews to go to Israel. He said that the Soviets had done this in order that Jews could see for themselves how they would be received in "the Israeli paradise." Malik said he had numerous letters testifying to the deep disappointment of the immigrants.[125]

The issue of Jewish immigration to Israel has been a minor irritant in Soviet-Arab relations. Lebanese, Jordanian, Algerian, Libyan, and Egyptian officials, and perhaps others, have openly criticized the USSR for permitting Jewish emigration. Libya and Egypt have done this whenever relations with the Soviet Union, which have been volatile in both cases, took a turn for the worse. Palestinian groups have also joined the criticism at various times.[126] In the early stages of the emigration, Soviet spokesman dismissed it as insignificant to Israel's military position, and on several occasions reassured the Arabs that only the old and infirm were emigrating, and that, in any case, the number of emigrants since 1967 "does not exceed a few hundred . . . all of them old" (statement made in 1971).[127] Such statements did not fool the Arabs, and Hassanan Heikal reported that on April 12, 1972, President Anwar Sadat of Egypt wrote to Party Secretary Brezhnev in Moscow, raising "for the first time" the question of Soviet immigration to Israel, and stating that "there are among them young people, intelligentsia, and scientists who will give Israel a lot of practical help."[128] Once the pretense of a small immigration of elderly cripples could no longer be maintained, the Soviets became defensive and pointed out acidly that while only some tens of thousands of Soviet Jews had gone to Israel, several hundred thousand Jews from Arab lands had immigrated to Israel.[129] Igor Beliaev, a well-known Soviet commentator on Middle Eastern affairs, reminded an audience at Beirut University that over 1.5 million Jews had come to Israel from Arab countries.[130] The Soviet press began to warn its readers that both males and females, newcomers and natives, were drafted into the military, so they could no longer claim so easily that Soviet immigration did not strengthen Israel militarily.[131] Ironically, some Arabs expressed concern not only about the increase in Israel's manpower and military capacity resulting from Soviet immigration, but also about the fact that "these are people who have lived all their lives in a Communist system; what is their influence going to be in the Middle East?"[132]

Yet another angle is seen by the Chinese and the Albanians. The Chinese delegate to the United Nations asserted that connivance between the United States and the USSR allowed the Israelis "to occupy Arab territories and to continue their murderous activities." He charged that "one superpower has been supporting the Israeli aggressors with arms and economic aid and the other is pouring a steady flow of manpower to Israel to supply the Israeli aggressors with sources for troop recruitment and even technical specialists." Not to be outdone in uncovering covert alliances between supposed enemies, the Soviet delegate said that he saw a "touching coincidence" involving China and Israel in that they were united in wishing to "slander the Soviet Union."[133] The Albanians saw the emigration as proof that a "secret deal" was made between the "two imperialist superpowers, and while Brezhnev may have been bowing to U.S. President Nixon's blackmail, Jewish emigration is part of a joint plan to divide and exploit the peoples of the region."[134]

The Chinese and Albanians could have just as plausibly accused Israel and the USSR of having made a "secret deal." Though there had been a tiny trickle of immigrants from the USSR in the 1960s, Israeli censorship kept it from being mentioned in the media, though it was sometimes referred to as immigration of the "reunification-of-families type," a euphemism applied also to immigration from other East European countries. Presumably, the Israelis feared that the Soviet Union would cut off emigration should it be publicized. Leonard Schroeter, who served as an adviser to the Israeli attorney-general for a time, asserts that Israeli policy was set by Shaul Avigur and the special office he headed, which deals with questions of Jews in socialist Eastern Europe.

> His policy was not to publish or acknowledge open letters and appeals.
> . . . He believed that Russian Jews would be freed from the USSR through secret negotiation, the tried method that had been utilized for the illegal immigration [during the British Mandate] and later for securing the emigration for Romanian, Bulgarian, and Polish Jews during the 1950s. When Avigur retired to his kibbutz at the end of 1969, his hand-picked successor, Nechemiah Levanon, attempted to continue his policies. . . .[135]

According to Schroeter, two things forced a change in Israeli policy: Soviet Jews established their own contacts with the West, gaining public attention without Israeli assistance or interference, and, just as importantly, Soviet immigrants in Israel refused to abide by the government's policy of hushing up the issue and began to publicize it in various ways. Thus, when immigrant Yasha Kazakov went to the United Nations and staged a hunger strike to dramatize his family's inability to emigrate, Prime Minister Golda Meir called on him to end his demonstration and criticized his activities and that of another recent immigrant, Boris (Dov) Sperling.[136] It was only 106 days after their first appeal that Golda Meir read the petition of 18 Georgian families to the Knesset and acknowledged, for the first time, individual letters she had received from Soviet Jews wishing to emigrate. After the Leningrad trials, however, in the bright glare of publicity given to the question of emigration, the Israelis changed their policy to publicity and protest, though Levanon's office continues to try to control the activities of immigrants and to influence the strategies and tactics of non-Israelis active on behalf of Soviet Jewish emigration.

SUMMARY

American immigration to Israel after the June 1967 War was spurred by optimism about the future of Zionism and Israel, on the one hand, and by increasing racial and political tensions, along with what some saw as a decline in the "quality of American life," on the other. American immigrants brought with them education and skills that few previous immigrations had brought to Israel. Shortly thereafter, Soviet Jews, with comparable educational backgrounds, began to arrive in large numbers for the first time in half a century. Unlike the Americans, the Soviet immigrants had to struggle hard to leave their country, and the process of emigration was often painful and even dangerous. The desire for emigration to Israel gave birth to one of the most remarkable social and political movements in Soviet history, pitting a small, but significant, ethnic minority against the full force of the Soviet party and state in open and dramatic confrontation. Never before had the USSR seen sit-ins in the very headquarters of the party, public demonstrations, and harsh criticisms of the system by some of its most privileged beneficiaries. The movement's significance spread and was magnified when its existence and its actions led to the involvement of the U.S. Congress, of public and private groups in Western Europe and North America, and to complications in the relations between the two superpowers and between each superpower and its Middle Eastern friends. The issue even attracted the attention of the Chinese and the Albanians. In short, it became a significant international issue, as well as a troublesome domestic problem for the USSR. With all the ups and downs of Soviet emigration, it is fair to conclude that, on balance, the emigration movement has succeeded, certainly when compared to other Soviet dissident movements and causes.

Since the 1967 War, well over 200,000 Soviet Jews have left the country (and some tens of thousands of Soviet Armenians, Germans, and others also did so). If the exit has not always been graceful (usually through no fault of the emigrés), and if there remain large numbers of people desiring to leave but blocked from doing so, the movement has nevertheless succeeded in changing Soviet policy to a far greater extent than have cultural or political dissidents, or those aiming to ameliorate the situation of other nationalities. Clearly, to leave the USSR is far easier than to change it. For the most part, the dissidents have not enjoyed the international support and the political and economic aid given by foreigners that have helped the Jewish dissidents so much. Nevertheless, the outcomes remain what they are and should be seen in the total perspective of the various, and sometimes contradictory, attempts to bring about change in the Soviet Union.

When immigrants have struggled so hard to leave their country, a struggle preceded by years of difficulty in many cases, they are ready, as one social worker put it, "to fall into someone's arms and rest." Instead, they find that they must begin a new kind of struggle, with almost no respite. They find themselves in a strange climate, an alien culture, a different economic and political system from the only one most of them have known. They must adjust to new foods, a new language, new values and patterns of public behavior, and all of this while trying to establish themselves in new jobs and housing. Rather than "falling into someone's arms" they may feel they have gone "from the frying pan into the fire." Having examined the process of emigration, we now turn to that of immigration.

NOTES

1. Quoted in Edward Neufeld, "Zionism and Aliyah on the American Jewish Scene," *Jewish Journal of Sociology* 5, no. 1 (June 1963): 112.
2. Ibid., p. 113.

3. Ibid., pp. 129-31.

4. George E. Johnson, "The Impact of Jewish Community Priorities on American Emigration to Israel," *Analysis*, no. 53 (November 1975), p. 3.

5. Ibid., p. 4.

6. Ibid., p. 5.

7. Aaron Antonovsky, "Americans and Canadians in Israel: Report No. 1, Preliminary Report Presented to the Jewish Agency on the Occasion of the 27th Zionist Congress," mimeographed (Jerusalem: Israel Institute of Applied Social Research, June 1968), p. 2. A thorough survey of the available data led Calvin Goldscheider to conclude that "no more than 9,000 Americans (by the most generous definition) immigrated to Palestine during the British Mandatory Period, averaging less than 300 per year, and less than 3 per cent of all olim. . . . It is not unreasonable to suggest that 30 per cent (plus or minus 10 per cent) of the American olim returned to America." Between 1948 and 1960 another 5,528 declared immigrants arrived (temporary residents are not included in this figure), and between 1961 and 1966 another 4,763 Americans declared themselves immigrants. See Calvin Goldscheider, "American Aliya: Sociological and Demographic Perspectives," in *The Jewish American Society*, ed. Marshall Sklare (New York: Behrman House, 1974), pp. 347-53.

8. Goldscheider's figures for the years before 1969 are considerably higher than the ones presented here and are based on "unpublished official data in the files of the Central Bureau of Statistics, Israel" (p. 353, Table 2). For example, for 1965-68 his figures add up to 2,595 and those for 1961-64 add up to 3,085. These are figures for immigrants only — the number of "temporary residents" is much higher. I am at a loss to explain the discrepancy between the published and the "unpublished official" figures.

9. See Aaron Antonovsky and David Katz, "Americans and Canadians in Israel: Report No. 2, Presented to the Jewish Agency" (Jerusalem: Israel Institute of Applied Social Research, March 1969), pp. 4-8; and Gerald Engel, "North American Settlers in Israel," *American Jewish Year Book* 71 (Philadelphia: Jewish Publication Society, 1970), pp. 164-65. One-third of the 1969-70 American immigrants defined themselves as "religious."

10. Goldscheider, p. 365.

11. Ibid., p. 366.

12. Ibid., p. 368. A slightly different figure (36.7 percent) is shown for American immigrants in the official report of the survey, *Monthly Bulletin of Statistics — Supplement* 25, no. 5 (May 1974), Table B. However, Goldscheider has refined the data and done his own tabulations and we have confidence in them.

13. Goldscheider, p. 371.

14. Roughly similar findings were obtained from a sample drawn from the membership lists of the Association of Americans and Canadians in Israel and from the files of the American section of the Jewish Agency. See Harry Leib Jubas, "The Adjustment Process of Americans and Canadians in Israel and their Integration into Israeli Society," Ph.D. dissertation, Michigan State University, Department of Secondary Education and Curriculum, 1974, pp. 104-09. In this sample of 1,178, who filled out a mail questionnaire, 23 percent said they had some college education, and 27 percent were college graduates.

15. Antonovsky, pp. 19 and 21.

16. Harold B. Isaacs, *American Jews in Israel* (New York: John Day, 1967), p. 89. This book is based on about 50 interviews with "settlers and would-be settlers" in 1963.

17. See Engel, p. 168.

18. See Aaron Antonovsky and David Katz, "Americans and Canadians in Israel, Report No. 3 Presented to the Jewish Agency: Integration into Israeli Life," mimeographed (Jerusalem: Israel Institute of Applied Social Research, May 1969), p. 13; Engel, p. 167, says that the "attraction [to Israel] seemed stronger than their disturbance about America."

19. Isaacs, p. 121.

20. Ibid., p. 229.

21. Private communication.

22. Tamar Horowitz and Khava Frankel, *Olim bemerkazai klitah* (Jerusalem: Henrietta Szold Institute, 1975), Research Report No. 185, Publication No. 538, pp. 144-45. The same conclusion is reached by Ephraim Tabory and Bernard Lazerwitz, "Motivation for Migration: A Comparative Study of American and Soviet Academic Immigrants to Israel," *Ethnicity* 4 (1977): 96.

23. David Katz, "Why Did They Come to Israel," in *Abraham David Katz: Jew, Man and Sociologist*, ed. Aaron Antonovsky (Jerusalem, 1975), p. 23. (This article was Chapter 4 of Katz's doctoral dissertation, completed shortly before he was killed in action in the October 1973 War).

24. Hillel Halkin, "Americans in Israel," *Commentary* 53, no. 5 (May 1972): 59.

25. See *Monthly Bulletin of Statistics*, p. 31.

26. Goldscheider, p. 379.

27. Ibid., p. 380. Over 40 percent of Tamar Horowitz's sample of immigrants from English-speaking countries called themselves "traditional," and 26 percent said they had an Orthodox affiliation in the United States, 29 percent Conservative, 12 percent Reform, and 20 percent had no religious affiliation.

28. Ibid., pp. 376 and 377.

29. *Monthly Bulletin of Statistics*, p. 31.

30. Nevertheless, Israeli and Jewish Agency sources would "leak" data to foreign correspondents, whereupon the Israeli press would publish the figures, attributing them to the foreign source. Thus, *Maariv* would regularly summarize the articles of Harry Trimbourne of the Los Angeles *Times*, which contained information obviously obtained from official sources.

31. These are more fully explored in Zvi Gitelman, "Soviet Jewish Emigrants: Why Are They Choosing America?" *Soviet Jewish Affairs* 7, no. 1 (1977). See also David Harris, "A Note on the Problem of the Noshrim," *Soviet Jewish Affairs* 6, no. 2 (1976). Soviet immigrants in Israel are divided on the question of how to treat the "drop-outs," and the leadership of the Union of Soviet Immigrants split on the issue. See the different views expressed in *Maariv*, November 1, 1976, and in the articles in *Maariv* by Meir Gelfond, July 7, 1976; Shmuel Shnitzer, September 24, 1976; Avraham Tirosh, September 20, 1976; and David Markish, July 28 and September 27, 1976.

32. See HIAS, *Statistical Abstracts*, Vols. 17 and 18.

33. In 1976, 94 percent of those emigrating from Odessa did not immigrate to Israel. The same was true for 86 percent of those from Kharkov, 80 percent from Kiev, 71 percent from Moscow, and 70 percent from Leningrad; however, only 16 percent of those leaving Kishinev and 9 percent of those leaving Chernovtsy (both cities absorbed into the USSR only in 1944) did not go to Israel. See *Insight* 3, no. 5 (May 1977): 9 and 4, no. 5 (May 1978): 3. See also Yehuda Kesten, "Yotsai Odessa mesarvim laalot," *Haaretz*, February 16, 1977. and Z. Alexander, "Jewish Emigration from the USSR in 1980," *Soviet Jewish Affairs* 11, no. 2 (1981): 17.

At various times, the Israelis have accused Soviet officials of granting exit permits precisely to those who were most likely to "drop out" at Vienna and not come to Israel; they have suggested various means by which Soviet emigrants could be dissuaded from going elsewhere; they have sent Soviet immigrants from Israel to Western Europe to try to persuade the emigrants to continue on to Israel; and in late 1981 they announced that the Jewish Agency would not assist any emigrant who did not intend to go to Israel. The Israeli press has eagerly reported difficulties of Soviet immigrants to the United States (the American and Soviet presses have also featured such stories, with the three national presses generally drawing different conclusions from their stories, of course). For an example of such a story, see Daliah Mazuri, "Migruziia el Arhab," *Maariv*, September 17, 1976. This recounts the adventure of a Georgian Jew who came to Israel in 1973, was unemployed, and left for Paris and then for "Greenwald" [Greenville], South Carolina. From there he and his family went to San Francisco where he worked as a janitor for $800 a month, netting only $500, according to the story. This left the family on the borderline of poverty. When he lost his job, he decided to return to Israel. "Now he tells his Georgian neighbors about his adventures in the great land of America — violence, crime, prostitution. . . ."

34. Data from Shmuel Adler and Rakhel Klein, "Hatkhunot hademografiyot shel olai Brihm lefi azorai motsa," mimeographed (Jerusalem: Ministry for Immigrant Absorption, January 1977). The following section relies heavily on this source. The same tendencies hold for the 1974-79 period. See Ministry for Immigrant Absorption, "Haolim miBrih'm vehanoshrim shehigiu leArhab — Skira demografit hashvaatit," mimeographed (Jerusalem, 1980), p. 31.

35. In Belorussia it was 3.3 and in Moldavia, 3.2. See *Itogi vsesoiuznoi perepisi naseleniia 1970 goda* (Moscow: Statistika, 1974), Vol. VII, pp. 275-78, 340-41.

36. On demographic trends among Soviet Jews, see Zvi Gitelman, "Poriyut hayehudim bivrit hamoetsot," *Shvut*, no. 5 (1977) (English version: "Correlates, Causes and Consequences of Jewish Fertility in the USSR," in *Modern Jewish Fertility*, ed. Paul Ritterband (Leiden: E. J. Brill, 1981).

37. "Immigration from U.S.S.R. from Six Day War Through 1974," mimeographed (Jerusalem: Ministry for Immigrant Absorption, December 1974), p. 4. See also Adler and Klein, and MIA, "Haolim miBrih'm vehanoshrim," pp. 51-52.

38. Adler and Klein, Tables 6 and 7.

39. The latter is, of course, the official Soviet view, as expressed, for example, in M. I. Kulichenko, *Natsional'nye otnosheniia v SSSR: tendentsii ikh razvitiia* (Moscow: Mysl, 1972), p. 498.

40. On the difference between acculturation and assimilation, see Arnold Rose, *Sociology: The Study of Human Relations* (New York: Alfred A. Knopf, 1956), pp. 557-58.

41. Lev Navrozov, "Getting Out of Russia," *Commentary* 54, no. 4 (October 1972): 50. Edward Kuznetsov, who was sentenced to a 15-year term for his part in the Leningrad hijacking attempt, writes how a Soviet police official could not believe that a person registered as a Russian would want to change it to Jewish. He refused to make the change and advised Kuznetsov to "write to Moscow." Edward Kuznetsov, *Prison Diaries* (New York: Stein and Day, 1975), pp. 38-39. Kuznetsov was released in June 1979.

42. For a description of these processes, see Zvi Gitelman, *Jewish Nationality and Soviet Politics* (Princeton, N.J.: Princeton University Press, 1972).

43. See, for example, Meir Gelfond's description of the Zionist education he received in a labor camp, "Tiurmenye vstrechi," *Sion* no. 1 (1972), pp. 11-19. See also A. Feldman, "500 dnei VI alii," *Sion* nos. 2-3 (1972), pp. 92-93.

44. See David Garber, "Choir and Drama in Riga," *Soviet Jewish Affairs* 4, no. 1 (1974).

45. Information supplied by Leah Slovin to Leonard Schroeter, author of *The Last Exodus* (New York: Universe Books, 1974), p. 64. This is the most comprehensive and reliable account of the Soviet aliyah movement. The author openly sympathizes with the more militant elements in the movement.

46. Lina Volkova-Yakobson, unpublished manuscript, 1972, p. 2.

47. Quoted in Iver Peterson, "Soviet Jew Who Got Out After 11 Years Tells How Difficult It Was," New York *Times*, December 6, 1969.

48. M. Perakh [Mark Blum, now known as Mordechai Lapid], "Pepel Rumbuli probudil serdtsa zhivykh," *Nasha strana*, November 25, 1971, p. 4. See also "The Memorial at Rumbuli," *Jewish Frontier* 38, no. 6 (June 1971).

49. See Dov Goldstein's interview with Korenblit, *Maariv*, August 17, 1973.

50. A comprehensive analysis of Soviet anti-Semitism is William Korey's *The Soviet Cage* (New York: Viking, 1973).

51. Statement made at a press conference in New York, and later repeated in Ottawa and Copenhagen. See Ibid., p. 3.

52. Quoted by Irina Kirk, *Profiles in Russian Resistance* (New York: Quadrangle, 1975), pp. 165-66.

53. Alla Rusinek, *Like a Song, Like a Dream* (New York: Charles Scribner's Sons, 1973), p. 20. See also her article, "How They Taught Me I Was a Jew," New York *Times*, March 4, 1971.

54. Quoted in Kirk, pp. 243-44.

55. *Vestnik statistiki*, no. 4 (1974), p. 95.

56. Alexander Voronel, "The Aliyah of the Russian Intelligentsia," *Midstream* 22, no. 4 (April 1976).

57. See Gitelman, "Soviet Jewish Emigrants."

58. David Giladi, summarizing statements by Soviet immigrants at the Twenty-Eighth World Zionist Congress, in *Haaretz*, January 25, 1972.

59. Ephraim Feinblum, quoted in *Jews in Eastern Europe* 5, no. 1 (April 1972): 25. On the reaction of Soviet Jews to official propaganda regarding the Arab-Israeli conflict, see Yeshayahu Nir, *The Israeli-Arab Conflict in Soviet Caricatures 1967-73* (Tel Aviv: Tcherikover, 1976). Nir asked 118 Soviet immigrants to react to Soviet caricatures on the Arab-Israeli conflict as part of his study.

60. Navrozov.

61. The first quotation is from Chasya Pincus, "Family and School: Some Preliminary Observations on Adolescent Russian Immigrants in Israel," *Jewish Social Studies* 34, no. 3 (July 1972): 256. The second quotation is from Dov Goldstein's interview with Sonia Lerner-Levin, *Maariv*, March 18, 1977. Mrs. Lerner-Levin is the daughter of Professor Alexander Lerner, one of the prominent scientists refused permission to emigrate.

The role of the Israeli radio is quite important in the history of the aliyah movement, though there is controversy over it. See Tsvi Zinger, "Golos Izrailia pronikaet za zhelenyi zanaves," *Nasha strana*, February 14, 1975, p. 8.

62. A partial account of the Kochubievsky affair is found in Peter Reddaway, ed., *Uncensored Russia* (New York: American Heritage Press, 1972), pp. 301-06.

63. Izrail' Kleiner, "Anekdotichna tragediia," *Suchasnist'*, no. 78 (July-August 1973), p. 225.

64. The best accounts and analyses are those of Korey, *The Soviet Cage*, Chapter 11, and Schroeter, *The Last Exodus*, Chapters 10 and 11. See also Renee Beermann, "The Soviet Trials: Some Legal Aspects," *Soviet Jewish Affairs*, no. 2 (1971).

65. Korey, p. xiii.

66. The unofficial trial transcript is found in the samizdat publication *Exodus (Iskhod)*, no. 4 (1971), published in English as a supplement to *Soviet Jewish Affairs*, no. 1 (June 1971). See also Richard Cohen, ed., *Let My People Go* (New York: Popular Library, 1971), Chapter 3. For *Iskhod*, see *Evreiskii samizdat* (Jerusalem: Centre for Documentation of East European Jewry, The Hebrew University, 1975), Vols. 2 and 3. Sixteen volumes of this publication have appeared, and they contain the original texts of Jewish samizdat, beginning with the Riga *Iton* of 1970 and ending with the series *Evrei v SSSR* of 1975 and after. Some of the earlier samizdat publications are reprinted also in *Posev* (Munich), seventh special edition, March 1971, and ninth special edition, October 1971.

Several of the Leningrad trial defendants have subsequently emigrated to Israel and have given their views on the hijacking affair and trial. See, for example, the six-part series by Sylva Zalmanson, wife of Edward Kuznetsov, in *Maariv*, September 13, 16, 20, 25, 27, and 30, 1974. Lassalle Kaminsky's story is told in Aharon Dolav, "Hasekher nifratz — hamayim zormim," *Maariv*, September 5, 1975; and Lev Korenblit's in the interview with Dov Goldstein, op. cit. Mary Khanokh, wife of one of the defendants, tells her story in *Maariv*, December 10, 1971. More details became available after the release in 1979 of some more of those tried. See, for example, Judith Cummings, "Leningrad Hijacking: A Desparate Act," New York *Times*, April 30, 1979. Interviews with two of those released are in the Jerusalem *Post*, May 4, 1979. One of them, Mark Dymshitz, describes how he was a Communist, an air force pilot married to a Russian, but became politically alienated and Jewishly conscious when he was refused a pilot's job in Leningrad because of his Jewish nationality. On the impact of the trial, see Esther Markish, *The Long Return* (New York: Ballantine, 1978), p. 269.

67. For a reproduction of the original document, see Shimon Redlich, ed., *Evrei i Evreiskii narod: petitsii, pis'ma, i obrashcheniia Evreev SSSR* (Jerusalem: Centre for Documentation of East European Jewry, 1973), Vol. I, p. 19. This is the first in a series of volumes that reproduce appeals and letters regarding civil rights and emigration by Soviet Jews to various authorities.

68. Interview with Dov Goldstein.

69. Interview in *Village Voice*, December 30, 1971, quoted in *Insight* 2, no. 4 (April 1976): 2.

70. Quoted in Kirk, p. 255.

71. Maya Ulanovskaya, quoted in ibid., pp. 274-75.

72. Quoted in Reddaway, p. 51.

73. As told by the wife of Anatoly Radygin, in Kirk, p. 43. On *Israeli* political debates regarding the strategy appropriate to the Soviet Jewry issue, see Dan Margalit, "Hamemshala nevokha beinyan Yehudai Brit Hamoetsot," *Haaretz*, March 3, 1970. Betty Gidwitz notes that "protests on behalf of persons still in the Soviet Union must conform to . . . guidelines, considered restrictive by some, established by the Israeli government for foreign policy reasons." "Problems of Adjustment of Soviet Jewish Emigres," *Soviet Jewish Affairs* 6, no. 1 (1976): 39.

74. Manuscript by Volkova-Yakobson, p. 4. For another analysis, see Roman Rutman, "Jews and Dissenters: Connections and Divergences," *Soviet Jewish Affairs* 3, no. 2 (1973).

75. Shimon Redlich, "Jewish Appeals in the USSR: An Expression of National Revival," *Soviet Jewish Affairs* 4, no. 2 (1974): 27.

76. See Ibid., pp. 29-32.

77. Ibid., p. 32. For a complete geographic analysis of the petitions, see pp. 32-34.

78. In early 1975 it was announced that the USSR had cancelled the 1972 Soviet-American Trade Agreement that had been amended to include the "Jackson-Vanik" provisions. It has been argued, convincingly in my view, that not the Jackson-Vanik amendment — which concerned most-favored nations and which was of relatively little importance to the Soviets who do not export many finished products to the United States — but the "Stevenson amendment," which set a ceiling of $300 million on credits to the USSR over a four-year period, caused the Soviet leadership to cancel the trade agreement. The most detailed and persuasive analysis of the whole affair is William Korey's, "The Story of the Jackson Amendment, 1973-1975," *Midstream* 21, no. 3 (March 1975).

The campaign for Soviet Jewry conducted in the United States is the subject of William Orbach's, *The American Movement to Aid Soviet Jews*

(Amherst: University of Massachusetts Press, 1979). The author is sympathetic to the more militant elements in the movement.

79. For an attempt at analyzing the Soviet bureaucratic politics of emigration policy, see William Korey, "Soviet Decision-Making and the Problems of Jewish Emigration Policy," *Survey* 22, no. 1 (Winter 1976).

80. On the motivations of migrants generally, see S. N. Eisenstadt, *The Absorption of Immigrants* (London: Routledge and Kegan Paul, 1954), pp. 3-4; and N. H. Frijda's "Three Factor Theory of Emigration," as discussed in Arnold Rose, *Migrants in Europe: Problems of Acceptance and Adjustment* (Minneapolis: University of Minnesota Press, 1969), p. 9.

81. Carole Pateman ignores the "exit" option in her discussion of the consequences of frustrated political expectations. However, as the experiences of China, Cuba, Vietnam, Uganda, and many other countries demonstrate, "exit" may be the most available option to those who are politically alienated or threatened. See Carole Pateman, "Political Culture, Political Structure and Political Change," *British Journal of Political Science* I, Part 3 (July 1971): 297. For a discussion of the "exit" option, see Albert O. Hirschman, "Exit, Voice and the State," *World Politics* 31, no. 1 (October 1978).

82. As reported in Pincus, p. 257.

83. Quoted in Gitelman, "Soviet Jewish Emigrants."

84. W. Peterson, "A General Typology of Migration," in *Readings in the Sociology of Migration*, ed. Clifford J. Jansen (London: Pergamon Press, 1970), p. 63.

85. Navrozov, p. 51.

86. Jeffrey A. Ross, "Interethnic Relations and Jewish Marginality in the Soviet Baltic," paper presented to the Sixth Conference of Baltic Studies, Toronto, May 1978, p. 12. Ross found that Jewish friends supported the emigrants in their resolve to leave to a greater extent than did non-Jewish friends. There are, of course, some notable exceptions to the general support of friends and relatives. One prominent aliyah activist, 50-year-old Vladimir Slepak, has been refused an exit visa since 1970, ostensibly on the grounds that his 84-year-old father, Semion Ignatevich (formerly Solomon Izrailovich), a convinced Communist, refuses to give the son permission to leave. See the report by David Shipler, New York *Times*, November 26, 1976. In June 1978 Slepak was arrested on charges of "malicious hooliganism" (he had displayed a banner that said he should be allowed to join his son in Israel). Slepak was sentenced to five years in exile.

87. Horowitz and Frankel, p. 158.

88. These are the Universal Declaration of Human Rights (1948), which is not legally binding on states, the International Convention on the Elimination of All Forms of Racial Discrimination (1965), and the International Covenant on Civil and Political Rights (1966). See William Korey, "The 'Right to Leave' for Soviet Jews: Legal and Moral Aspects," *Soviet Jewish Affairs* no. 1 (June 1971).

89. George Ginsburgs, "Soviet Law and the Emigration of Soviet Jews," *Soviet Jewish Affairs* 3, no. 1 (1973): 4.

90. Ibid.

91. For details of these documents and procedures, see Commission on Security and Cooperation in Europe, *Report to the Congress of the United States on Implementation of the Final Act of the Conference on Security and Cooperation in Europe: Findings and Recommendations Two Years after Helsinki* (Washington, D.C., August 1, 1977), pp. 105-10. On Soviet law and emigration, see the following articles in *Soviet Jewish Affairs*: George Ginsburgs, "Soviet Law and the Emigration of Soviet Jews," 3, no. 1 (1973); Yoram Dinstein, "Freedom of Emigration and Soviet Jewry," 2, no. 4 (1974); and George Ginsburgs, "Current Legal Problems of Jewish Emigration from the USSR," 6, no. 2 (1976).

92. *Report to the Congress*, p. 115. This includes 300 rubles for the exit visa, 500 for the renunciation of citizenship, about 200 for the trip to Vienna, up to 100 rubles for repairs to one's apartment and trips to Moscow, 90 rubles exchanged into Western currency, and the rest for shipping to Vienna or to Israel.

93. Recollections of an emigré linguist, written at my request in March 1976, a year after he had emigrated.

94. Personal interview in November 1974.

95. See Viktor Perel'man, "My Last Day on Literaturnaia Gazeta," Radio Liberty Dispatch, August 13, 1973. For similar experiences among scientists, see Mark Azbel, *Refusenik* (Boston: Houghton Mifflin, 1981).

96. Statement by Colonel V. S. Obidin, Chief of the All-Union OVIR Office, quoted in Vladimir Itkin, "Myl'nye puzyri i real'nye fakty," *Izvestiia*, January 23, 1976. This is one of the longest and, because of the place of publication, most authoritative Soviet articles on emigration.

97. Ibid.

98. Novosti interview with K. Zotov, quoted in *Sovetishe Yidn: Faktn un tsifern* (Moscow: Sovetskii Pisatel', 1980), p. 86.

99. *Insight* 3, no. 5 (May 1977): 6.

100. Commission on Security and Cooperation in Europe, pp. 3-6. See also the Commission's "On Leaving the Soviet Union: Two Surveys Compared" (Washington, D.C., May 1, 1978).

101. Ibid., p. B-5.

102. Ibid., p. B-4.

103. One of the very first Soviet Yiddish publications was Zorakh Greenberg's, *Di tsionisten oif der idisher gass* (Petersburg: Commissariat for Jewish Affairs, 1918).

104. For examples of this plentiful genre, see Vladimir Bol'shakov, *Sionizm na sluzhbe antikommunizma* (Moscow: Izdatel'stvo Politicheskoi Literatury, 1972); Evgenii Evseev, *Sionizm: ideologiia i politika* (Moscow: Moskovski; Rabochii, 1971), printed in 70,000 copies; Evseev's *Fashizm pod goluboi zvezdoi* (Moscow: Izdatel'stvo Tsk Vlksm, 1971), published in the series "1,001 crimes of capitalism" and in 75,000 copies; T. K. Kichko, *Iudaizm i sionizm* (Kiev: Znannia, 1968). (This Ukrainian pamphlet, of which 60,000 copies were printed, is by the author of the notorious *Iudaizm bez prikras*, published in 1963 but withdrawn from circulation after worldwide protests against its Nazi-like text and caricatures.) One of the most publicized of this genre is Yuri Ivanov's *Ostorozhno, Sionizm!*, published in at least two Russian editions of 75,000

copies each. The first Ukrainian version (*Oberezhno: Sionizm!*) was published in 70,000 copies. A description and analysis of this kind of literature is found in William Korey, "Anti-Zionism in the USSR," *Problems of Communism* 27, no. 6 (November-December 1978).

Frequently, anti-Zionist materials are attributed to authors with obviously Jewish names, in order to convey the impression that Jews themselves are critical of Zionism and to preclude charges of anti-Semitism against the Soviet authors. Thus, the Ukrainian journalist M. Fridel and the Belorussian journalist V. Begun (whose nationality is not clear) are frequent authors of anti-Zionist articles and pamphlets. See, for example, Begun's *Polzuchaia kontrrevoliutsiia* (Minsk: Belarus, 1974). See also, for other examples, S. Daichman, *Chorna dushu sionizmu* (L'viv: Vidavnitstvo Kameniar, 1972), and Ya. Valakh, *Sionizm – Znariaddia reaktsiy* (Kiev: Vidavnitstvo politichnoi literaturei Ukraini, 1972).

105. Jonathan Frankel, "The Anti-Zionist Press Campaigns in the USSR, 1969-1971: An Internal Dialogue?" *Soviet Jewish Affairs*, no. 3 (May 1972), 10. See also Zeev Ben-Shlomo, "The Current Anti-Zionist Campaign in the USSR," *Bulletin on Soviet and East European Jewish Affairs*, no. 5 (May 1970), and the extensive collection of appended documents.

106. Yosef Govrin, "Israel-Soviet Relations: 1964-1966" (Jerusalem: Soviet and East European Research Centre, January 1978), Research Paper No. 29, p. 108. See summaries of such articles in *Jews in Eastern Europe* (London) 3, no. 5 (October 1966).

107. Frankel cites two articles, one in December 1969 and the other in February 1971 that appeared in *Izvestiia* and that mentioned Soviet Jewish emigration to Israel "in small print." pp. 24-25. Most of the previous articles were published in republic provincial newspapers in the Western borderlands, where relatively large numbers of people had applied to emigrate.

108. For articles containing accurate, but partial, data, see "Zagovor sionistov protiv Arabov," *Za rubezhom* (*ZR*), no. 20 (May 10-16, 1974); "Zhelaiushchikh poekhat' v Izrail' vse men'she," *ZR*, no. 35 (August 23-29, 1974); "Begstvo iz zemlii obetovannoi," *ZR*, no. 11 (March 7-13, 1975).

109. Some representative examples include a wide-ranging survey of articles from the Soviet and foreign press, "Di gesise fun der aliye," *Sovetish haimland* (*SH*), no. 4 (1976); "Vitsn fun Yisroel," a fairly regular feature; "Aktivistn fun der'aliye' oig oif oig mit zikh," *SH*, no. 5 (1976); and "Mentshn on a haim," *SH*, no. 12 (1976). An especially interesting item is the article by Jozef Erlich of Odessa, "Oifn smakh fun mein farbindungen mit der tsionistisher agentur," *SH*, no. 7 (1976). This article describes how an Odessa journalist discovers that his good friend, Shifrin, is a Zionist agent, and how the journalist, playing double agent, meets in Vienna with Nechemia Levanon, erroneously identified as "secretary-general of the Israeli foreign ministry." (Levanon was actually head of an office, technically attached to the Foreign Ministry, but dealing exclusively with Jewish activity in the USSR. Levanon has worked in the Israeli embassies in Washington and Moscow, and has been identified in other Soviet sources as a "colonel in the Israeli Secret Service.") Erlich also implicates the political dissenters, Natalia Gorbanevskaia and Zinaida Grigorenko, in his description of Zionist subversion.

For an article on the plight of Soviet Jews in America, see "Der shans, velkhn es git Amerike," *SH*, no. 7 (1977). Articles from the provincial press (Minsk, Kiev, Kishinev, Smolensk) on the horrors of emigré life in Israel and the United States are translated in *SH*, no. 4 (1979), pp. 9-21. A similar collection, this time including Canada as well, is "Der veg in opgrunt," *SH*, no. 7 (1981).

110. See *Maariv*, December 26, 1971.

111. See the report by Vladimir Matlin, originally in the Los Angeles *Times* and translated in *Maariv*, July 9, 1974.

112. Reported in detail in *Maariv*, February 4, 1977.

113. V. Gorbunov, N. Gudkov, and M. Trakhman, "Pravda o 'zemle obetovannoi'," *Literaturnaia gazeta*, January 12, 1972. This article, filling an entire page, is composed of brief interviews with several emigrés who want to return to the USSR.

114. V. Gorbunov and N. Gudkov, "Sionistkie doktriny i razbitye sud'by," *Literaturnaia gazeta*, November 22, 1972.

115. See *Maariv*, March 21 and 23, 1973. One of the most curious cases is that of Grigori Vertlib, an early aliyah activist in Leningrad who, after a struggle, gained an exit permit. He left Israel disappointed and tried to reenter the Soviet Union, was asked to write critical articles about Israel (which were published in *Leningradskaia pravda*), but did not return to the USSR. See *Maariv*, May 14, 1974.

116. See, for example, *Maariv*, April 2, 1972.

117. Christopher Wren, "7 Soviet Jews Say Israel Was Harsh," New York *Times*, February 7, 1976, and "4 Jews Asking Return to Soviet Assert They Were Abused Here," New York *Times*, February 13, 1976. For an earlier story on immigrants disillusioned with the United States, see Christopher Wren, "Soviet, to Deter Emigrants, Tells About Jews who Returned from U.S.," New York *Times*, December 11, 1974, and the complementary story by C. Gerald Fraser, "Jews' Host in U.S. Tells of Problems," in the same issue.

118. *The Deceived Testify* (Moscow: Novosti, 1972), p. 12. This is a translation of *Svidetel'stva obmanutikh*, which has appeared in at least two Russian editions. For a description of other such pamphlets, see *Nasha strana*, January 31, 1971, p. 3, and February 7, 1972, p. 3. For a summary of radio broadcasts on the subject, see "The Soviet Media Image of Emigration," Radio Liberty Dispatch 190/74, June 25, 1974.

119. *The Deceived Testify*, p. 11.

120. Ibid., p. 20.

121. Ibid., p. 19.

122. See, for example, the pamphlet by B. Prahye, *Deceived by Zionism* (Moscow: Novosti, 1971), a translation of *Obmanutye Sionizmom*, where some of these names appear. See also A. Golikov and N. Sorin, "Sionistskii durman," *Ogoniok*, no. 7 (February 1971).

123. "Israel in Soviet Eyes: II," New York *Times*, September 8, 1971. Louis, who sought medical treatment in Israel, wrote in the first part of the article: "The Jewish people are renowned for their fondness for going to the doctor and, after all, Israel is a good place to go in any case" (September 7, 1971).

124. For examples, see Hulda Grad, "Bitter Lesson," *Freundschaft* (Tselinograd) May 27, 1976, translated in Joint Publications Research Service (JPRS),

Translations on USSR Political and Sociological Affairs, no. 745 (August 4, 1976), and the article by Hans Odes, "In Front of and Behind the Facade," *Freundschaft*, June 15, 1976, translated in JPRS, ibid. Earlier articles include Karl Balke, "We Yearned for Our Homeland," *Freundschaft*, September 4, 1974; Paul Loeffler, "Confession of an Emigré," *Freundschaft*, October 30, 1974, JPRS, no. 583 (December 11, 1974). Other such articles are translated in JPRS, nos. 550, 551, and 580 in 1974.

125. *Maariv*, February 27, 1972.

126. For Arab criticisms of Soviet emigration policy, see the New York *Times*, January 30, 1972, and October 2, 3, 5, and 6, and November 6, 1973. In May 1975, Egyptian Foreign Minister Fahmi, in a press conference, demanded that all immigration to Israel from the USSR and United States be stopped. See *Maariv*, May 11, 1975.

127. Quoted in Korey, *The Soviet Cage*, p. 198.

128. From Heikal's book, *The Road to Ramadan*, serialized in *Maariv*, April 27, 1975.

129. Radio Moscow in a broadcast to Algeria, quoted in *Haaretz*, August 27, 1973. See also the statement by Soviet Deputy Minister of the Interior Boris Shumilin, distributed by Novosti and reprinted in *Maariv*, April 8, 1972. Radio Moscow's Arab-language broadcast on August 21, 1978, made the following points: the "imperialist media and its agents" exploit the emigration to "create doubts about the Soviet Union, the Arabs' honest, sincere ally"; the number of emigrés had declined; the number not going to Israel has increased; the "number of Jews who emigrated from the Arab countries to Israel is more than 10 times greater than those who emigrated from the Soviet Union."

130. Quoted in Jean Riollot, "The Arabs and Soviet Jewish Emigration to Israel," Radio Liberty Dispatch, May 2, 1973, p. 2.

131. See, for example, "Khozhdeniia po mukam," *Sovetskaia Moldavia*, August 8, 1970.

132. Quoted in Henry Tanner, "Cairo Approves Austria Attack," New York *Times*, October 3, 1973. According to Tanner, "Cairo and other Arab governments have discussed the issue with the Russians over the last three years. . . . But, according to informed sources, Leonid I. Brezhnev, the Soviet leader, has reacted coldly."

For an analysis of the relationship between Jewish emigration from the USSR and Soviet-Arab relations before 1967, see Yaacov Ro'i, "Emdat Brit Hamoetsot legabai haaliyah kegorem bimdiniyutah klapai hasikhsukh hayisraeli-aravi (1954-1967)," *Behinot*, no. 5 (1973).

133. See New York *Times*, April 1973.

134. See Albanian statements quoted in *ABSEES* (Glasgow), July 1973, p. 123.

135. Schroeter, *The Last Exodus*, pp. 126-27. This passage was originally published in Schroeter's, "The Origins of the Georgian Aliya," *Midstream*, May 1974, p. 65.

136. See *Haaretz*, March 30 and April 2, 1970.

4

SOCIAL AND ECONOMIC ABSORPTION OF SOVIET AND AMERICAN IMMIGRANTS IN ISRAEL

Soviet immigrant teachers in a re-training course. Courtesy The Jewish Agency.

Political socialization does not occur in a vacuum, but in an economic and social context. Research in the United States has shown that children living in an economically depressed rural environment develop far less benevolent images of the president than do children growing up in more prosperous environments.[1] We can expect that the economic and social adjustments made by immigrants will affect their perceptions of the political system — its efficiency, equity, and impact on them and on the society they have entered. Economically dissatisfied immigrants may turn to oppositionist parties more than those who have found the economic system to their liking and benefit; those who feel socially rejected may be attracted to political

127

movements that claim to speak for the alienated. Others may feel impelled to associate themselves with mainstream parties as part of their effort to be accepted by the host population. Still others may perceive politics as irrelevant or secondary to their pressing economic and social needs, and may defer the "luxury" of political involvement to a time when their more pressing needs will have been taken care of. It may be that immigrants' personalities will impel some to try to become as involved in the new society as possible, while others may be more withdrawn and cautious about venturing into social and political *terra incognita*.

When studying European refugee immigrants who came to Israel shortly after the state was established, Judith Shuval discerned two patterns of early acculturation. "On the one hand, there was a pattern of 'approach' to the new society with an attempt to draw close to the new way of life; on the other, there was a pattern of 'withdrawal' and what seems to be a rejection of Israeli values and a return to the immigrant society."[2] Those who "approach" the new society seek to become "integrated" into it.

It is very difficult to define "integration" or terms that are often used interchangeably with it, such as "absorption" or "adjustment." A minimum, operational definition might be that the immigrant does not leave the country; at the other extreme, some believe that "to be fully absorbed, the immigrant must be socially invisible."[3] If one defines integration or absorption in terms of similarity to the host population, many questions immediately present themselves: Since the host population is not homogeneous, which subgroup must the immigrant resemble in order to be considered "integrated?" At what point in the process of coming to resemble the host population, or part of it, can it be said that integration has been achieved? Is the process of becoming integrated a linear one, or is it marked by fluctuations and variations? Is integration a uniform process, or do people become "integrated" in one area of life, while remaining "unintegrated" in others? These questions are important, but they need not be resolved in order for us to deal with the subject at hand, the *process* of absorption or integration of Soviet and American immigrants in Israel. We are concerned, not with the terminal point, if there is one, but rather with the road that is taken. Our task at present is to describe the road and the scenery around it, rather than determining where the road ends and how it does so. Later on, when we take up political integration or absorption, we will be concerned with "final destinations," but here we shall try to describe the social and economic experiences of the immigrants, without making judgments about final outcomes.

The process of immigrant absorption in Israel is different from that in other countries in several ways. First, immigrants come largely from one religious-ethnic group. This greatly simplifies their relations with the host society, which is dominated by the same group, as well as the question of their own ethnic identity. Jews who have gone from North Africa to France, for example, are not sure whether to define themselves as North African Jews, North Africans, Jews, Frenchmen, or combinations of these categories.[4] Those who have gone to Israel are much more likely to limit their definitions to Jew, Israeli, or, in a minority of cases, to add North African to either of the two primary identities. Second, immigration is not restricted in any significant way, so that immigrants do not have to worry about barriers to their relatives joining them if the latter so desire. Third, Israel's commitment to immigration is not based on economic needs or demographic calculations alone, but on ideological commitments that are fundamental to its existence. Therefore, the immigrant should be more confident than his counterpart in other countries that he will not suddenly be perceived as an undesirable burden. He is aware that in official rhetoric he has a positive image and that the population is being urged to welcome and even honor him. Rather than threatening the existing population, immigration is said to guarantee its existence.

Nevertheless, as we have seen earlier, immigrants are by no means universally admired or even welcomed in Israel. By the same token, they are often critical of their new home and experience difficulties in adjusting to it. Some of these difficulties are "objective" — they are due to a lack of fit between educational, vocational, or housing opportunities, on the one hand, and immigrant expectations, on the other. Other difficulties are "subjective" — they reflect the lack of fit between the values, outlooks, and aspirations of the host population and the immigrants. S. N. Eisenstadt, basing himself on observations of the immigrants of the 1950s, distinguished among six types of immigrants and attempted to describe their specific adjustment processes as resulting from the interplay of their characteristics with that of the host society.[5] Many of the criticisms of Israel made by several types of 1950s immigrants were also made by the immigrants of the 1970s. Jewish activists from Central Europe and the closely knit immigrant groups from Bulgaria and Yugoslavia in the 1950s all had a tendency to accept the fundamental values of the society but to criticize it for bureaucratic inefficiency, politicization of administration, the concentration of political and administrative power in the hands of the veteran settlers, and their reluctance to accept fully the new immigrants.[6] Eisenstadt also describes some immigrants in terms that aptly describe post-1967 American immigrants who fail to find satisfaction in Israel and who frequently return to the United States. He found, among some immigrants from East Central Europe and from Iraq, a tendency to accept some of the dominant values of Israeli society but to reject its collectivism.

> Whatever reference groups and standards they have are mostly those of their countries of origin; outside the instrumental field they have no tendency to extend their social relations in the absorbing society. Besides a somewhat vague and generally positive identification with that society (but not with its collective values), they have little social or cultural orientation towards it. Whatever social solidarity and expressive gratification they have is confined to their private groups, and can be extended only with difficulty.[7]

This type of immigrant, in both the 1950s and 1970s, generally failed to study Hebrew intensively, evaluated negatively the Israeli educational system, and shirked some of the obligations that Israel imposes on its citizens, new or old.

A third type of immigrant described in the 1950s and reappearing in later years is the Zionist activist, who comes to Israel with the greatest of expectations and who therefore is in danger of suffering the most profound disillusionment. Judith Shuval found, among former displaced persons immigrating to Israel from Europe, that those with Zionist backgrounds and ideologies were better insulated against disappointment with the reality of Israel than those without such backgrounds. However, when the Zionists did suffer disappointment, it tended to be deeper than that of the non-Zionists.[8] One has the impression that this has remained true for the Soviet immigration. For a minority of Zionist activists, especially those from the interior of the USSR, disappointment with Israel led to greater depression and more extreme reactions than that observed among those less overtly committed to Zionism in the USSR and among those whose notions of Israel were developed at least partly through personal knowledge of Jewish culture and traditions, rather than emerging from a process of ideological searching.

ADJUSTMENT PROBLEMS OF SOVIET AND AMERICAN IMMIGRANTS

The Israeli, Soviet, and American presses, each from its own perspective and motivations, have dealt extensively with the problems of immigrants to Israel. Some of the problems — learning a new language, finding housing and employment, adjusting to the economy and cultural mores — are shared by all immigrants to a greater or lesser degree. Other problems are more specific to newcomers from a particular country.

Soviet immigrants enter with several special disadvantages: their knowledge of Israel is very partial, having been filtered through Soviet propaganda. They have had no opportunity to tour the country or meet Israelis abroad, and thereby to form impressions or collect information that will make their post-immigration adjustment easier. Most of the Soviet immigrants from Europe are unfamiliar with Jewish history, customs, and religious traditions, and are equally unfamiliar with Western mass culture, private enterprise, political democracy, and social mores. For many of them, Israeli society is "anarchic," permitting public and private behavior that, they claim, would not be tolerated in the USSR. They are disturbed by what they see as youthful disrespect toward adults, a popular culture that seems without redeeming social value, and sometimes decadent or pornographic. They are troubled by what they see as cold and competitive relations among the citizens, and passivity by the government that, they feel, ought to provide more social services (free medical care and higher education, for example), on the one hand, and intervene more forcefully to curb undesirable actions of citizens and the media, on the other.

Many Soviet immigrants expect the state to provide them with employment, and they do not display the same individual initiative in seeking employment, or customers, as do immigrants from capitalist countries. They are puzzled by, and suspicious of, a system in which one employer will pay different wages from another, though the same work is to be performed by both. They find housing costs appallingly high, but are dazzled by the availability and assortment of consumer goods. They are sometimes ambivalent toward the freedom of expression they find: On the one hand, they find it appealing in principle and beneficial in political and social matters; on the other hand, they find it abused when they hear or read criticism of Israeli policy or leaders, or the expression of radical or bizarre views. Soviet immigrants have also been chagrined to discover that their vocational skills are not always considered up to par by the Israelis, who, like other Westerners, find some Soviet immigrants to be overly specialized (this is true particularly of engineers), inadequately trained (physicians, social scientists), or possessing skills irrelevant to the economy in which they find themselves (teachers of Russian literature, bridge builders, coal miners). This presents not only a problem of employment, but also those of recovering self-esteem and willingness to adapt to the demands of the new environment. Similarly, those who were active on behalf of Jewish and Zionist causes in the USSR have found that, after an initial period of excitement and publicity, Israeli society no longer treats them as heroes and they fade from public consciousness and concern. Some of them feel that Israel should adopt the Soviet practice of rewarding people symbolically, whether with pictures on a "billboard of honor," or with lapel pins, or ceremonies of one sort or another. All of these, of course, are part of the larger problem of making the transition from one social system to another.[9]

For Americans the problems are quite different. In a sense, they come to Israel "from the opposite direction" of the Soviets. To many of them there is too much government "interference" in Israel, too much "socialism," though sometimes the same people will complain of the government's failure to do this or that, to provide one service or another. Like some Soviet immigrants, Americans sometimes complain about Israeli mass culture, not because it is so different from the American version, but because it is so similar. Some expected to find a country of Zionist idealists, or at least of people of high culture whose tastes run more to Bach than to the Beatles. Most have visited Israel before making aliyah, so they have some prior knowledge of the climate, physical appearance, and public life of Israel. But they often repeat the anecdote about the person who was shown heaven and hell while still alive, was impressed by the physical delights of the dissolute society of hell, and when, years later, arriving at the pearly gates and choosing hell over heaven, was promptly beaten, boiled, and flayed. Asking his hosts in astonishment what had happened to the good life as he had seen it, he is told, "The first time you were a tourist; now you are a resident, and are being treated as such."

Though they arrive with more capital than most Soviet immigrants, many Americans soon feel the pinch of Israel's economy, and in most cases they are unable to maintain the standard of living to which they were accustomed in the United States. Professionals often find Israeli practices and procedures in their fields to be archaic, inefficient, and unreasonable, while almost all Americans complain of excessive bureaucracy and red tape. Whereas many Soviet immigrants are anxious to be accepted by Israelis as social peers, some American immigrants assume a studied indifference toward other Israelis, at times openly expressing their feelings of superiority to the "Israelis" who are referred to as "they." Like many Soviet immigrants, however, Americans are suspicious of Israeli officials and are on their guard against "being taken," or "being shuffled around." While only a few Soviet immigrants have tried to establish new settlements or join social and economic experiments, some Americans have done so. Thus, a few kibbutzim (Gezer, Admit) are populated largely by Americans who, in the 1960s, sought to break with conventional middle class life in the United States, and whose different paths — political activism, drugs, "dropping out" — ultimately led them to more modified experimentation in Israel. Other settlements, such as Neve Ilan outside of Jerusalem, were designed and planned by potential immigrants while still in the United States. This is a *moshav shitufi*, a cooperative where all income is shared but where families live in separate units. Other attempts at forming "American" concentrations in a planned way have run into what the Americans perceive as Israeli duplicity, rapaciousness, and inefficiency. Thus, a plan to settle 1,000 religious American families of modest means in Beit Shemesh, an area the government would like to see developed by Western immigrants, has dragged on for over a decade with few tangible results. Other Americans who participated in a rental housing scheme arranged by the Ministry for Immigrant Absorption suddenly found their rents raised and their future occupancy in doubt. A plan to settle 2,000 American families in the North Sinai town of Yamit never came off, and the same fate befell a plan to settle Canadians near the coastal city of Netanya.[10] An Israeli journalist sympathetic to those who felt cheated by the rental scheme wrote:

A group of new immigrants, mostly Anglo-Saxons, demonstrated this week at the Jewish Agency convention. The demonstrators demanded something no veteran Israeli would think of expecting: that the Israeli government should keep its word. Anglo-Saxon immigrants don't run wild in government offices, turn over tables or attack officials. They conscientiously gather documents which say black on white what was promised to them. . . .[11]

Perhaps one reason American immigrants can be militant in the pursuit of what they see as their rights is that they have a guaranteed avenue of retreat. They are, of course, dependent on the government and Israeli society for many things that affect their adjustment, but should they fail to find satisfaction in Israel, they can always return to the United States. This may not be an easy step, as it involves dismantling the Israeli household and reestablishing the American one, once again seeking employment, housing, perhaps schooling, and, in many cases, having to explain to friends why the immigrants "had failed." Often this arouses much ambivalence, for returned immigrants might not wish to present a negative picture either of Israel or of themselves, and yet they feel obliged to offer explanations of their return. To explain that they could not make ends meet might arouse the response either that they should have known this before, or that had they been true idealists this should not have mattered. This is but one instance of the many doubts, questions, and suspicions that arise in the minds of returning immigrants themselves and among their acquaintances. Nevertheless, the option of returning, unavailable to the great majority of Soviet immigrants and to many from other countries, remains open to the American. While this is, of course, an advantage, it can also work to impair the immigrants' adjustment efforts. "An immigrant who knows he can return to his old environment and is still in close contact with his family or friends may be impaired in his preparedness to change. . . ."[12] Of course, even those who eventually return to the United States must go through at least the initial stages of immigrant absorption, though in some cases it is this very process that makes them decide to return.

There are objective measures of "absorption," or measures of how close immigrants come to Israeli norms in housing, employment, language, and standard of living as measured by possession of material goods. These do not necessarily predict to subjective assessments of adjustment that are made by the immigrants themsevles. In between the "objective" and "subjective" are measures of social contact between newcomers and veteran Israelis; though, again, how important these are and how they are interpreted by the immigrants cannot be readily ascertained simply by noting the frequency of such contacts. In the final analysis, the "absorption" *of* immigrants is also absorption *by* immigrants — absorption of the country's values, styles, mores, and behavior patterns. From the government point of view, successful absorption can be measured by the extent to which material needs of immigrants are satisfied. From the society's point of view, absorption is measured by the degree and nature of contacts between newcomers and the rest of society. From the viewpoint of the immigrants themselves, however, what is crucial is what value and meaning they place on material possessions, on their place in the social system, and on the ways of the society around them as they perceive and interpret them. The immigrants are judged by the society, but they judge it as well. Since society's judgment affects their own, both of these are part of the ultimate determination of whether immigrants will stay or leave.

Therefore, it is erroneous to measure immigrant adjustment solely by "objective" measures, though this is a fair indicator of the success or failure of the government or society to supply the prerequisites — and they are only that — of immigrant satisfaction. Without these material prerequisites, however, it is difficult to imagine satisfaction and adjustment. Thus, it is important to answer two questions: To what extent does the Israeli government succeed in providing the material prerequisites of immigrant adjustment? How is the immigrant's judgment of Israeli society, himself, and his decision to immigrate conditioned by his "objective" economic and social situation in Israel?

To answer these questions we shall examine data on housing, employment, and material possessions of immigrants, their knowledge of Hebrew, their social contacts, and their evaluations of their standards of living and general satisfaction in Israel. At the risk of creating an erroneous impression of general dissatisfaction and disappointment, we shall conclude with a look at some of the least-satisfied immigrants — those who leave the country — in order to sharpen the picture of satisfaction and dissatisfaction. Some specific groups of Soviet immigrants, widely reputed to be "problematic," will be discussed only to emphasize the individual and subjective nature of the immigrant absorption process and the specificity of its problematic aspects. "Success stories" will not be told in such detail because, while they are more numerous, they are easier to imagine and understand than the "failures." It should be remembered that the latter are the exception, not the rule, among American and Soviet immigrants.

HOUSING

There are several choices immigrants in Israel have in regard to housing. They can, of course, purchase apartments, as most Israelis do, and they receive mortgages on more favorable terms than others. There is a very small rental market in Israel, but immigrants can rent apartments owned by the Ministry for Immigrant Absorption, in most cases with an option to buy them on favorable terms after a certain period. Immigrants with higher education are housed temporarily in reception centers or hostels, where, in addition to room and board at a nominal charge, they receive intensive Hebrew language instruction. When all these options are unavailable or unsuitable for one reason or another, immigrants can rent apartments on the free market and they will receive rental subsidies, or they will be housed in hotels and other temporary accommodations until more permanent quarters can be found. All this applies to all immigrants, irrespective of age, sex, or country of origin.

Table 4.1 shows the percentages of immigrants in each type of housing at different periods. It is based on a sample of immigrants

TABLE 4.1
Immigrant Housing by Type and Period of Residence in Israel
(in percent)

	Two Months	Six Months	One Year	Two Years	Three Years
Permanent housing	50	64	78	87	93
Of which:					
Family-owned dwelling	6	9	14	30	39
Rented, unfurnished	41	51	60	55	52
Temporary housing	50	36	22	13	17

Source: Israel-Monthly Bulletin of Statistics — Supplement 24, no. 6 (June 1973): 142.

from all countries who arrived in 1969-70, and it should be remembered that in later years the housing market was considerably tighter. (For example, in 1978 only 22 percent of those who had been in the country three years were in a family-owned dwelling.) By the end of five years, 95 percent of the immigrants who have remained in the country have obtained what is considered "permanent housing."[13]

A greater proportion of Soviet immigrants than the average find permanent housing within one year. They tend to cluster in the central region of the country and in the coastal cities of Haifa and Tel Aviv and their suburbs. Americans are less attracted to Haifa, but much more attracted to Jerusalem, to which religious immigrants are especially drawn. The differences in location among various immigrations can be observed in Table 4.2, based on the distribution of the 1971 immigration. The great majority of Soviet immigrants live in apartments of two and three rooms (living room and one or two bedrooms), housing designed for immigrants and quite adequate for the typical Soviet family that has three or four members (Georgian and Central Asian families are larger).[14]

Housing for Soviet immigrants generally compares very favorably with their housing conditions in the USSR (except for Georgians and Central Asians, many of whom had spacious housing in their native republics). However, they are very critical of the procedures by which they have obtained housing. Nearly half the Soviet immigrants surveyed in 1972 claimed that recommendations regarding housing that had been made by the Jewish Agency or MIA were completely

TABLE 4.2
Location of Immigrant Residences
(in percent)

	North America	USSR	Eastern Europe	Asia- Africa	Western Europe/ Oceania
Development areas	9.3	17.4	9.4	23.9	18.6
Central region	15.0	25.6	30.2	25.4	24.0
Tel Aviv	29.3	24.1	24.7	33.8	33.2
Haifa	13.2	28.0	26.5	11.3	9.1
Jerusalem	31.7	4.9	9.2	5.6	15.1

Source: Ministry for Immigrant Absorption, *Klitat haaliyah, 1972* (Jerusalem, 1973), p. 38.

unreliable, and nearly the same proportion felt that the advice given by the Union of Soviet Immigrants was equally useless.[15] Still, once having obtained their apartments, Soviet immigrants are very much satisfied with them, though they are less satisfied with the neighborhoods in which they live than are American or West European immigrants.[16] Of a representative sample of 1,566 Soviet immigrants who had arrived in Israel between 1960 and 1971 (before the mass immigration), nearly 67 percent reported their living conditions to be better than what they had been in the USSR, 15 percent judged them to be the same, and 22 percent thought they were worse. In their view, housing was the area in which they had experienced the greatest improvement as a result of the move from the Soviet Union to Israel. For the great majority, housing in Israel reduced the density of the household from what it had been in the Soviet Union.[17]

Obviously, this is not the case for most American immigrants. Many American immigrants go from private houses to apartments when they move from the United States to Israel, and their living space shrinks. For those who purchase apartments on the private market, and they are many, they find themselves paying considerably more than they would in the States for apartments that are substantially smaller and less equipped than the homes they had in America. Nevertheless, though it may take them some time to find satisfactory housing, large majorities of those surveyed by the MIA express satisfaction with their dwellings.[18]

In general Israel provides immigrants with a high standard of housing, especially in comparison with other countries of immigration. It can be safely assumed that housing is not a major sore point for most immigrants, although it is obtained with considerable anxiety and expense.

EMPLOYMENT

Immigrants everywhere face the task of finding employment that suits their talents, training, and expectations, and that provides them with a living wage. Specific groups of immigrants have both particular advantages and difficulties. American immigrants to Israel are advantaged, compared to Soviet immigrants, in that they have ample opportunity to explore employment possibilities before immigrating. There is a program, known as "Tour v'aleh," which organizes tours by potential immigrants for the purpose of exploring employment conditions and opportunities in their fields in Israel. Contacts with potential employers can be made from abroad, and in some cases contracts are signed even before the immigrant arrives in Israel. Obviously, none of this is possible for Soviet immigrants.

The difficulties of Soviet immigrants are compounded by the great difference between the organization of work in the USSR and in Israel (or other Western countries). Whereas in the USSR the state finds a person his job, and in some cases assigns him to it, individual initiative is required to find a job in the free market system of the West. Since there is little unemployment in the Soviet Union — officially, there is none at all — to be without employment is a strange, frightening, and demeaning experience to those coming from there. Often, Soviet immigrants who have not completed their stay at a reception center and the language course will leave in order to take a job that has been offered, fearful that should they wait to complete their course, another employment opportunity will not come along.

Some immigrants expect the state to supply not only jobs but also customers to those who have chosen to go into private enterprise. There are many stories heard in Israel about the tailor, or shoemaker, who was provided with a shop and the tools of his trade, but then demanded a list of customers, as he claimed he would have been given for his state-owned shop in the USSR. For many other immigrants the main problem is either the irrelevance of their vocations to the Israeli economy or their overspecialization in terms of that economy's needs. The scales of the Soviet and Israeli economies are so enormously different that many people who were respected and needed specialists in the USSR find no demand for their skills, considered exotic or overly narrow, in Israel. The practice of teamwork in the USSR also means that many, even professionals, have experience in only specific phases of operations performed entirely by one or two people in Israel. This is particularly true of technicians, engineers, and even of medical personnel. For some specialties there is only limited place in Israel. This would include train engineers, or professors of Russian history or Central Asian languages, or certain types of geologists, astrophysicists, and the like.

As Israeli employers came to the realization that there would be a steady flow of Soviet immigrants, some began to employ them for periods up to six months, and then dismissed them just before the employee gained tenure or job security, since there was always another immigrant ready to fill the job. This was done in a different way in the scientific and academic fields. The Jewish Agency provides funds to scientific and academic institutions that enable them to employ immigrants for up to three years. At that point, the institutions must absorb the immigrants into their regular budgets, and this is not always possible. Of course, many of these same people would not be carried even for three years in any other Western country, but this is small comfort to the immigrant who finds himself without prospects of employment in his field.

Despite their comparative advantage, American immigrants also encounter difficulties in the employment area. Some find that promises made by potential employers when the immigrants were still abroad are not honored, or that conditions of employment suddenly change. Others find no market for their skills and specialties, and still others claim that Israeli methods and practices are outmoded and inefficient. They find it difficult to work in such conditions and even more difficult to gain acceptance for their innovative suggestions. Like the Soviet immigrants, some Americans find their occupations not in great demand in Israel: rabbis (especially non-Orthodox ones), certain kinds of teachers, retailers, and others. Of course, those whose professions are highly specific to particular cultures — lawyers are the best example — must either retrain or find some other occupation.

Israel's retraining courses have successfully transformed Uruguayan lawyers into Israeli social workers, Soviet economists into accountants, American biology students into agronomists, and teachers from France into teachers of French in Israeli high schools, to give but a few examples. In many instances, people have remained in their respective professions but have qualified for Israeli practice. This is true especially of law and medicine. In 1974, 116 retraining courses were available to immigrants, and 2,600 enrolled in them.[19] Fields of study included social work, data processing, retailing and marketing, tax inspection, teaching, and a variety of technical fields.

Despite the best efforts of the state — and they have been considerable — there remain problems for Soviet immigrants that are rooted in cultural and systematic differences between the USSR and Israel. Between 1967 and 1975, when 100,000 Soviet immigrants arrived and contributed 51,900 people to the labor force, 20,500 entered Israeli industry. Of these, about 16,500 were workers and 3,500 were technicians and engineers. About one-quarter of the blue-collar workers were Georgians, a considerable number of whom were not industrial workers in the USSR but who had been retrained in Israel. They included Georgian women, few of whom worked at all in the Soviet Union, and many of whom were employed in the Israeli food and textile industries. Though Soviet immigrants are generally highly regarded as workers, respect for them as employees does not easily transform itself into a desire to have them as friends. This, at least, is the view of many Soviet immigrants. One woman put it this way:

> There is something wrong in Israel. There is no contact among people. Everyone thinks only of himself. . . . Friends from work are friends only at work. We don't visit each other at home. They don't invite me, and I don't invite them, because we don't have such a relationship. They come to visit when someone is sick. . . . Relations are good, but not warm. . . .[20]

Whatever their social discontents, industrial workers and technicians find attractive employment opportunities in Israel. Scientists have a harder time. Scientists in the USSR are a privileged group, enjoying generous funding for research, high salaries, and access to perquisites, such as private automobiles and country homes, which few Soviet citizens can obtain. Moreover, there is a vast network of research institutes in the USSR that allows people to do research on a full-time basis and requires no teaching of them. The Israeli situation is more like that in the United States: much of the country's scientific research is conducted in universities, so that teaching is the activity that makes research possible, and research grants are awarded on a competitive basis from year to year, rather than being included in the government's budget. Moreover, there are practically no private foundations in Israel, and the state itself cannot support research to the extent this is done in wealthier countries. The ex-Soviet scientist has to scramble for a job and for funding at the same time. He did not do this in the USSR, and he finds it both degrading and frustrating.

In the USSR the emphasis is on applied research, whereas in Israel there is more emphasis on basic or pure research. Moreover, because political controls are imposed in the USSR even in purely scientific fields, Soviet scientists are not always aware of professional developments outside their own country and they have difficulty getting access to scientific publications, let alone attending scientific meetings abroad. When Soviet scientists arrive in Israel they sometimes find that they lag behind their Western colleagues, or that methods, approaches, and techniques are very different from those they have worked with. In addition, they find themselves part of a surplus of scientific talent in relation to the present capacity of the Israeli academy and economy. Because of their different orientation and their conviction that Israeli industry and the economy need applied research — which most informed Israelis will agree with — several immigrant scientists have proposed that applied research institutes be set up to employ primarily Soviet immigrants. These would simultaneously employ productively immigrant scientists and also make a needed contribution to the Israeli economy. From time to time small groups of immigrant scientists have formed nascent institutes, but none of them seems to have established itself solidly, from institutional, financial, and official points of view.[21] Some of the scientists claim that short-sightedness, bureaucratic obstacles, and ill will on the part of the Israeli authorities have prevented the successful implementation of their plans and have frittered away a potential resource of enormous value to Israel's scientific and economic growth, as well as to its domestic social and world scientific standings. The counterarguments are not always clearly expressed but center on claims that the scientists do not have as much to contribute as they claim, since they are overly specialized and have not proved the worth of their projects to the specific needs of Israel, or that the enormous funds needed for such enterprises are not available. Moreover, such projects would further isolate the Soviet scientists from their colleagues, as well as from Israeli society generally, and this is seen as highly undesirable.

Soviet physicians present other specific problems. Immigrant physicians constituted one-third of all doctors in Israel by 1977, and of the immigrants, more than one-half were from the USSR.[22] In the country's largest polyclinic system, the Histadrut's *Kupat kholim*, approximately one of every four doctors is a recent immigrant from the USSR, more than half of them women. On the one hand, this organization has provided employment for a great number of immigrant physicians, but, on the other, it is low-prestige employment, especially for those who had hospital appointments in the USSR and see themselves reduced to "assembly line" general practitioners with an enormous case load, frequently in polyclinics located outside the major centers. Soviet doctors find that the *lingua franca* of medical science and practice in Israel is English, and that they must reacquire a professional vocabulary. The style and even the substance of medical practice differ from what they had been used to. For example, Soviet medicine seems to be far more conservative in the use of new drugs than Western medicine, and Soviet equipment in provincial hospitals and polyclinics is often antiquated by Western standards. On the other hand, Israeli medicine lags behind that of the Soviets in such areas as chronic diseases, gerontology, and preventative medicine.[23] The image of Soviet doctors in Israel quickly became a negative one, and immigrant doctors have protested that their qualifications are unfairly questioned.[24] A representative sample of Soviet doctors who had arrived in 1972 generally had a higher evaluation of Soviet than of Israeli medicine, though they did not idealize Soviet medicine. Those in hospitals had a more favorable view of Israeli medicine than those in polyclinics, and it is significant that over half those interviewed were working in polyclinics. Clearly, most had experienced downward occupational mobility: while 82 percent had been specialists in the USSR, only 27 percent were certified as specialists in Israel; 40 percent of the doctors had worked last in the Baltic region, and only 14 percent in the Russian republic.[25] In sum, while their role in Israeli medicine is numerically large, the status of Soviet immigrant physicians is low relative to their expectations and to that of Israeli-trained physicians and others trained in the West. Since Soviet emigrés in the United States have had great difficulty qualifying to practice medicine,[26] it appears likely that the differences between Soviet and Western medicine are, indeed, substantial. Without attempting to judge which kind of medicine is "better," the fact is that the difference creates difficulties for the Soviet emigré physician. Still, Soviet-trained physicians have a far easier time finding a position in their profession in Israel than do those who have immigrated to the United States.

A third professional group prominent in the Soviet immigration is the artistic one, broadly defined. In the 1969-74 period about 4,500 artists — musicians, actors, stage directors, writers, graphic artists, and screen-writers — came to Israel from the USSR. While the skills of musicians and graphic artists are easily transferred from one culture to another, those of writers or even cinematic professionals are not. Of course, musicians and artists coming from the Soviet Union may be unfamiliar with modernist trends in the West, but their adaptation is relatively easy. Again, the small and strained Israeli economy is hard pressed to support artists, something the Soviet economy does generously and on a large scale. However, many Soviet musicians have been accepted into Israeli orchestras, and new groups, such as the Haifa and Beersheba orchestras, were formed to accommodate immigrant musicians, a high proportion of them from the USSR. Music conservatories and smaller music instruction classes have been greatly expanded by Soviet immigrants, and, judging by radio and television programming, classical music has experienced a revival in Israel. Prominent conductors, such as Yuri Aharonovich and Rudolf Barshai, have been given jobs with existing or new musical groups, though not all of these efforts have succeeded.[27] Pianists, violinists, cellists, singers, and other musical artists have made their reputations in Israel and are beginning to make them in the Western world generally. Some dancers, including the well known husband-wife team of Valery and Galina Panov, have done likewise. There are quite a few jazz musicians who have found their niche in Israel, and for them the West provides greater opportunity for artistic growth, if not for financial remuneration, than did the Soviet Union.

Actors and directors have more serious problems than musicians, because of the importance of language in their work. A few actors have found their place in the Hebrew and Yiddish theaters, but notions of establishing a Russian-language theater ran into financial and even ideological barriers, as the government seemed reluctant to promote culture in a non-Jewish language. It does, however, support Russian-language publications, presumably because their content concerns Israel and Jewish matters. Probably least successful has been the absorption of film directors. According to one source, nearly 100 scriptwriters and directors immigrated to Israel in the 1969-74 period. About 70 of them came from the USSR and Romania. A fund of 1 million Israeli pounds was established by the Ministry for Immigrant Absorption to give each a chance to make one film, and then the artist was to make his own way.[28] So far, the results have been discouraging to everyone. The Israeli film industry has never really gotten off the ground, despite the fact that Jews have pioneered the film industry in the United States, that

Israel offers excellent climatic and topographical conditions for film-making, and that there are experienced film-makers and actors in the country. The Soviet immigration has not done much to change the picture.

Athletes have made highly visible contributions in Israel. Americans, including immigrants, brought basketball to Israel and made it the nation's most popular sport after soccer. In the decade 1966-76, 54 Jewish basketball players came from the United States to Israel, and about a dozen remained as immigrants.[29] In 1977, when the Macabee-Tel Aviv team won the European cup, basketball's popularity reached new heights and "the Americanization of Israeli basketball" was much discussed.

While American athletes complain about the difficulties of making a living competing in an amateur league, they are in a better position than most immigrant Soviet athletes. Especially prominent in soccer, wrestling, and boxing, and in women's track and field, these immigrants, like scientists and artists, had been treated well by the Soviet state. Israel has neither the means to support athletes very much nor a tradition of doing so. It was no surprise, therefore, that the former middleweight youth champion of the Ukraine, ranked third in the entire USSR, decided to leave Israel and try making a boxing career in Europe. "I'm only 22, and have no skill aside from boxing. I have desire, strength, and my future lies ahead of me. I would love to stay in Israel and I will always be an Israeli, even in Europe, but . . . as a boxer I have no choice but to leave Israel."[30] A free-style wrestler from Baku, former youth champion of the USSR, complained that even the most elementary facilities for training were not available in Israel. "Today I've given up hope completely. It hurts me to say so, but I'm very sorry that I came to Israel. . . . If I have no choice I'll give up the sport, throw away all the years and all the work I've put in, and go to work so that I'll have something to live on. . . ."[31] While top athletes have not found a very supportive environment in Israel, the interest that many Soviet immigrants have in active sports has been felt in the gymnasiums and on the athletic fields of Israel.

Not surprisingly, Israeli chess has been greatly bolstered by the arrival of Soviet immigrants, and the sport is dominated by Soviet-born players. Alla Kushnir is one of the top-ranking women players in the world, and other recent immigrants have performed very well in European tournaments.

Whatever the difficulties of particular vocational groups, the overall employment picture for immigrants is a bright one. According to official statistics,[32] of the immigrants arriving in 1969-70, 69 percent had been in the labor force in their home countries in the two years prior to emigration. In Israel, after one year, 55 percent were employed; by the end of the third year the proportion had risen to 60 percent. After five years nearly all of those in the labor force were employed. Among Soviet immigrants, the proportion of employed is higher — 66 percent after one year in Israel. (Of the 1977 Soviet immigrants in the labor force, 83 percent were employed by the end of the first year.) About 15 percent of those with higher education change their vocations, most of them trained in the humanities and social sciences, and those immigrants who are over 55 years old experience difficulties in obtaining employment, as one-third of those in the labor force are unemployed.[33] In general, a somewhat higher proportion of Soviet immigrants are in the labor force compared to American ones, presumably because among the latter there are both more retirees and more people who are independently wealthy or whose income continues to come from the United States. Of the employed Americans, 44 percent are in the public and services sector, while only 33 percent of the employed Soviets are located there. Among both groups, there is a shift over time from industry and construction to public and service sector employment. After one year in the country, 28 percent of the Americans and 46 percent of the Soviets were employed in industry and construction, but after five years only 23 percent of the Americans and 37 percent of the Soviets remained in this sector.[34] Occupationally, there is a significant decline among both immigrant groups in the proportion of those classified as workers. This is in line with a general tendency in the Israeli economy as a whole, where the service sector has been expanding more rapidly than the industrial. The parallel trends among immigrants are seen in data on the 1969-70 immigration, where nearly one-quarter of the immigrants who started out as workers in industry, construction, and transportation had shifted to sales or to services by the end of their third year in the country.[35]

Satisfaction with one's job seems to increase with time in Israel, presumably because the immigrants become better acquainted with working conditions and find their proper levels.[36] After two years in the country, about three-quarters of all immigrants report that they are "completely satisfied" or "fairly satisfied" with their jobs.[37] Soviet immigrants rely on the official employment services of the state to a far greater extent than do the Americans, as this is the kind of system with which they are familiar, and with which middle class Americans are less familiar. Perhaps because of their more frequent contact with the employment services, Soviet immigrants in absorption centers report far less satisfaction with them than American immigrants.[38] The MIA studies indicate somewhat higher job satisfaction among American than among Soviet immigrants. In the study of pre-1971 immigrants, a larger proportion of Soviet immigrants reported that the work they did in Israel was similar to that which they had done abroad, but their level of job satisfaction was somewhat lower than that of American, West European, or Afro-Asian immigrants.[39]

One measure of the economic success of the immigrants is their possession of durable goods. Within two years after arriving in the country, nearly all immigrants have a refrigerator and the great majority have television sets. Not surprisingly, more Americans possess such items as tape recorders, phonographs, and automobiles than East Europeans, with 65 percent of the Americans owning private vehicles three years after arrival.[40] Washing machines, sewing machines, and mixers are also owned by large proportions of both American and European immigrants. For most Americans, this represents a continuation of their situation in the United States, but Soviet immigrants acquire possessions in Israel that they did not have in the USSR. The Horowitz-Frankel survey found that only 14 percent of the Soviet immigrants claimed to have had an automobile in the USSR (in the Russian republic and the Baltic, about 18 percent). Among Soviet immigrants in Detroit, Michigan, 29 percent reported in 1976 that they had had an automobile in the USSR, though in 1974 only 4 percent of the entire Soviet population had automobiles.[41] In Israel, by the third year of their stay in the country more than 33 percent of the immigrants from European USSR and 10 percent of those from Asia have automobiles. It should be remembered that because they enjoy tax benefits, immigrants rush to acquire durables during their first three years in the country, so that possession of these items is not quite as good an indicator of economic resettlement as might be supposed.

Not only does the objective material situation of Soviet immigrants improve when they move to Israel, but so does their subjective evaluation of their standard of living. In the study of pre-1971 immigration from the USSR, Shuval and Markus found slightly more than 50 percent of the Soviet immigrants who saw their standard of living as having risen in Israel, while only 22 percent felt it had declined, and 27 percent thought it had remained the same;[42] but half the respondents felt that their Israeli income was less adequate than their Soviet one, both in terms of current needs as well as savings. The apparent discrepancy between a higher standard of living and a less adequate income is explained by Shuval and Markus by the greater availability in Israel of consumer goods, making possible a higher standard of living but also leading to rising expectations and different patterns of consumption, thus creating a need for higher income. In the government survey of the 1969/70 immigrants, two years after arrival, 54 percent of those from Eastern Europe felt their standard of living was higher in Israel than in their countries of origin, and only half that proportion felt it was lower. By contrast, only 10 percent of the Americans felt it had risen in Israel, and 67 percent felt they had a lower standard of living in Israel than they had in the United States. Compared to all other immigrants, East Europeans experienced the sharpest rise in their standards of living when immigrating to Israel.[43]

It would be reasonable to suppose that immigrants' material situation and their perception of change in their material status would influence their overall satisfaction with their new country and, more specifically, might influence their political attitudes and behavior. This supposition will be examined explicitly when we discuss our particular groups of Soviet and American immigrants.

LINGUISTIC ACCULTURATION

In Israel, acquisition of Hebrew language facility is viewed not only as a practical matter but as an ideological goal. In the nineteenth and twentieth centuries there was among East European Jews a *kulturkampf* around the question of which language, Yiddish or Hebrew, was to be regarded as the authentic language of the Jews. Non-Zionist Yiddishists pointed out that Hebrew was a language used mainly in rabbinical correspondence and religious literature, and to a small extent by ideologically committed Hebraists. Zionists, however, saw the revival of Hebrew as a language of daily use as part of the renaissance of the Jewish people. Casting off

Yiddish, or other venaculars adopted after the exile from the Palestinian homeland, would be part of the restoration of the Jewish people to its historic homeland and the purging of its culture from alien influences that had penetrated during the long exilic period. Jewish Communists, on the other hand, succeeded in persuading Soviet authorities that while Yiddish was the language of the proletarian masses, Hebrew was the language of the class enemy, the clergy and bourgeoisie, and of the politically hostile Zionists. This resulted in Yiddish gaining a total monopoly "on the Jewish street" in the USSR, as all Jewish institutions in the USSR operated exclusively in Yiddish. Even Hebraic elements in Yiddish were purged, and the orthography was reformed to accentuate the differences between Yiddish and Hebrew.[44] This sharpened the political lines drawn around the languages, and the Zionists in Palestine mounted a successful campaign to make the public use of languages other than Hebrew a matter of social opprobrium. The slogan of "Ivri, daber Ivrit!" (Hebrew [person], speak Hebrew!) became a popular one, with the result that many children of immigrants never learned their parents' language, just as had happened in the United States, guided by its "melting pot" ideology. Whatever the linguistic and psychological prices paid, the end result was that Hebrew is unquestionably the dominant language of the country, the *lingua franca* of Jews and Arabs alike. Perhaps because Hebrew has unquestionably won the battle of the languages, the ideological fervor attached to the learning of Hebrew has diminished, though acquisition of the language remains a social and ideological, as well as practical, attainment for the immigrant.

As indicated earlier, Israel invests considerable sums and effort in the *ulpan* network, language training courses that stress the rapid acquisition of practical skills, especially in oral communication. The Ministry for Immigration Absorption's surveys indicate rapid progress in learning Hebrew on the part of the immigrants. About one-third of all immigrants claim to be able to converse freely in Hebrew, one year after immigration, and the same proportion say they read a Hebrew newspaper at least once a week.[45] By the end of three years, half the immigrants claim fluency in Hebrew, though only 38 percent claim to read a Hebrew newspaper at least weekly. (Only 8 percent say they were fluent in Hebrew already in their country of origin.)[46] The rate of language acquisition slows considerably as time goes on, so that by the end of the fifth year only 53 percent claim fluency in Hebrew; 31 percent say they speak Hebrew with difficulty, and 16 percent not at all.[47]

In general, Americans claim a better knowledge of Hebrew than Soviet immigrants, undoubtedly because of better prior knowledge of the language. Whereas there is a large network of instruction in Hebrew in the United States, in the USSR, Hebrew can be studied only privately and in semilegal conditions. Soviet immigrants seem to make greater efforts to learn Hebrew than do American ones, no doubt because they start from further behind, and their language, unlike English, is not widely spoken by Israelis, nor is it taught in schools, while English is the dominant foreign language in schools at all levels. Thus, while after both two and five years Americans claim greater spoken and reading fluency than Soviets, the comparative advantage of the Americans declines.[48] Soviet immigrants appear to be more concerned than Americans with learning Hebrew, and they are less satisfied with their progress, probably not because their progress is slower, but because their desire and expectations are greater.[49] That the Soviets make greater efforts is indicated by data on media use: After one year in Israel, despite the fact that Americans have considerably greater knowledge of Hebrew, slightly more Soviet immigrants than Americans read a Hebrew newspaper, though fewer listen to radio news in Hebrew. Though both immigrant groups have newspapers available in their native languages, the Soviets appear to make greater efforts to read a Hebrew newspaper, whether a standard one or one in "easy Hebrew" designed for immigrants.[50] Among both American and Soviet immigrants, women appear to acquire Hebrew more quickly than men, at least in the immigrant absorption centers, though this tendency is more pronounced among the Americans.[51] These differences may disappear at a later stage when men enter the labor force and women do not, or do so later than men.

ENTERING ISRAELI SOCIETY

Although Israel is a society of immigrants, its dominant mores and social patterns are defined by the "veteran" population. It is they who "set the tone" in culture and social life, as well as in the economy and politics. This was probably more the case vis-a-vis the less educated Afro-Asian immigrants of the 1950s than it is for the Western and Soviet immigrations, but it remains at least partially true today. Therefore, social acceptance and identification — by others — as "an Israeli" are quite important to many immigrants.

Social acceptance of immigrants is obviously less manipulable by government policy than housing, employment, or learning Hebrew. It depends on interaction between immigrants and veteran settlers, on their mutual subjective perceptions and desires. Indeed, this is the area that immigrants find most difficult and that seems to trouble them the most. It is widely believed, by both immigrants and veterans, that social relations between the two groups are not very extensive, nor are they always harmonious. According to press reports, confirmed by my own observations and conversations, immigrants feel that Israeli society is "closed," while some Israelis argue that immigrants "stick to themselves" and make no serious efforts to mix with nonimmigrants.[52] As noted in our discussion of Israeli attitudes toward immigrants, a large social distance between immigrants and the host population is nothing new in Israel, nor in any other country of immigration. MIA surveys of immigrants clearly point to a very slow process of expanding social contacts on the part of immigrants. After only two months in the country, 20 percent of all immigrants reported meeting frequently with veteran Israelis, but after three full years, when most immigrants are no longer officially classified as such, only 28 percent reported frequent social contacts with "Israelis." After three years in the country, 37 percent of the immigrants claimed that they had no social contact at all with non-immigrant Israelis.[53] Not unnaturally, immigrant satisfaction with their social life does not improve over time (see Table 4.3).

TABLE 4.3
Immigrants' Satisfaction with Social Life by Time in Israel
(in percent)

	Two Months	Six Months	One Year	Two Years	Three Years
Absolutely satisfied	34	24	25	20	21
Fairly satisfied	39	47	42	49	49
Not so satisfied	18	20	24	21	21
Not at all satisfied	9	9	9	10	9

Source: Central Bureau of Statistics, *Monthly Bulletin of Statistics — Supplement* 24, no. 6 (June 1973): 136.

For both Americans and East Europeans, there is no relationship between the immigrant's age and his satisfaction with social life.[54] Americans, however, are more generally satisfied with their social life than European immigrants and Soviet newcomers, whether after one, two, or three years in Israel.[55] Among all immigrants, it seems that those from the USSR are most sensitive to the problem of social integration and most troubled by it. Moreover, this is one of the very few instances in which Soviet immigrants compare Israel *un*favorably with the Soviet Union.

In the Soviet Union, according to the pre-1971 immigrants, they enjoyed an intensive social life, 70 percent reporting that they met with friends several times a week. Nearly all the respondents asserted that they were satisfied with their Soviet social life, but in Israel only slightly more than half were prepared to make a similar statement. Moreover, their social circle appeared to be quite narrow — even among those who were in Israel for ten years, 77 percent reported their social contacts were mostly with people from their own country of origin. Among the post-1967 immigrants, the picture is much the same: After two years in Israel, 41 percent of the Soviet newcomers claimed that their social life was worse than it had been in the USSR; whereas 90 percent met with friends at least once a week in the USSR, only 46 percent did so in Israel. Younger immigrants and those living in smaller towns and in development areas had more frequent social contacts than older ones and those residing in the major urban centers.[56] Nevertheless, it was the younger Soviet immigrants who complained more about social life, probably because their needs and expectations were greater.

Soviet immigrant social contacts are more restricted than those of American immigrants and most others. After one year in Israel, half the Soviet arrivals claimed not to have met with Israelis except on rare occasions.[57] Even after five years in the country, by which time Americans claimed to meet almost as frequently with native-born Israelis as they did with immigrants from the United States, only 9 percent of the East Europeans reported frequent social contacts with Israelis.[58] Over half the Soviet immigrants reported that they did not meet with immigrants from other countries, while only one-quarter of the Americans made this assertion.[59] Still, as we shall see, Soviet immigrants identify as Israelis to a much greater extent than do American ones or those from Western Europe.

Why do Soviet immigrants appear to be less socially integrated into Israeli society than American ones? As we saw, at least initially, they are less linguistically equipped than Americans to make contacts with Israelis, especially as non-Hebrew-speaking Americans can use English in many social situations. Second, Americans have higher social status in Israeli society than Soviets and may be sought out more by Israelis. At the same time, Soviet expectations of social life are greater. Americans are used to living in private houses and spending much leisure time alone with the television set. They find Israeli social life, now moving from a style more akin to that of the Soviets toward some semblance of the American one, not all that different from what they expect. These are only generalizations about aggregates of people, and, obviously, there are individual Soviet immigrants who have far more frequent and intensive social contacts with native Israelis than individual American immigrants. The nature of the immigrant's social contacts depends on many factors: his residence, his linguistic facility, his values and tastes, his personality, and the like.[60] We can only point to objective circumstantial and cultural factors that would make one or another pattern of social integration more likely among specific immigrant groups, always bearing in mind that there will be a great deal of individual variation in this area.

IMMIGRANT SATISFACTION AND IDENTIFICATION

Judging by the studies conducted on behalf of the Ministry for Immigrant Absorption, there does not seem to be any great change in immigrants' satisfaction with their lives in Israel over the first three years of their stay, nor is there great variation by continent of origin. After one year in Israel, about two-thirds of the immigrants reported that they were at least fairly well satisfied, and this remained true after the second and third years. By the end of three years, however, the proportion of satisfied Americans reached some 80 percent, whereas it was somewhat lower for other immigrants.[61] This may be due to the departure of substantial numbers of American immigrants, leaving only the most satisfied in Israel. In fact, within five years after their arrival, 37 percent of Americans surveyed by the ministry had returned to the United States. Of the West Europeans, 34 percent had left, and among East Europeans, only 7 percent had departed (It is much more difficult for East Europeans to return to their countries of origin, and, in many cases, it is also more difficult for them to emigrate to third countries.)[62] Those between the ages of 18 and 29, men, and single people are the most likely to leave.

Despite their self-described social isolation, Soviet immigrants identify strongly with the Israeli state and its people, and they consider themselves primarily Israeli, to a greater extent than other immigrants. According to Shuval and Markus,

> it seems that Soviet immigrants feel good in Israel, and so their Israeli identification in the first period in Israel is higher than that of other immigrants. The older ones have higher Israeli identification but are more downcast while among the young the opposite is the case. It seems that Jewish background plays a role in Israeli identification, while general morale is influenced by age. . . . Israeli identification increases with the length of one's stay in Israel, while general morale is stable over time. Men feel more Israeli and have a higher morale than women.[63]

Shuval and Markus compared the Israeli identification and general morale of Soviet immigrants who came after 1967 with previously unpublished data gathered from other immigrants who had arrived after 1969 (see Table 4.4). Soviet immigrants arriving in the large immigration after 1971 were more than twice as likely as Americans to identify as Israelis one and three years after immigration, and more certain that they would stay in the country.[64] In the 1970s only 10 to 13 percent of the Soviet immigrants thought they might not stay in Israel, but about 40 percent of the Americans were not sure they would stay. This is, in fact, a very accurate reflection of the proportions actually staying after five years. These data support our findings, to be reported later, on the higher Israeli identification of the Soviet immigrants, while American immigrants wish to retain their identities as Americans and resist the "melting pot."

Whether or not an immigrant stays permanently in Israel does not appear to depend on any single material or psychological factor or even on definite combinations of such factors. "Successful absorption" does not depend on a success in a *particular area* of absorption. Shuval and Markus conclude: "One cannot assume that a positive pattern [of absorption] in one area implies a parallel positive pattern

TABLE 4.4
Israeli Identification and General Morale of Immigrants after One and Two Years
(in percent)

	Soviets		Americans		West Europeans		Afro-Asians		Israeli Urban Sample
	One Year	Two Years	One Year	Two Years	One Year	Two Years	One Year	Two Years	
Identification									
Feel they belong in Israel	74	78	—	57	57	68	68	72	
Identify as Israelis	59	65	—	25	22	39	45	55	
Sure to stay in Israel	90	90	—	60	52	61	71	76	
General Morale									
Not worried	25	27	—	21	23	32	14	22	22
Good morale	52	53	—	53	53	51	32	37	40

Source: Yehudit Shuval and Yehuda Markus, *Dfusai histaglut shel olai Brit-Hamoetsot*, Part 1 (Jerusalem: Israel Institute of Applied Social Research, 1973), p. 21.

in other areas," though social life, job satisfaction and the adjustment of the immigrants' children are related to general morale and to one's identification as an Israeli.[65] They see employment and social life as more important to the absorption of the immigrant, with housing and language acquisition less associated with the level of identification of the immigrant. Absorption, in their view, is not a "unidimensional process." Different patterns of successful absorption are established by differentiated adjustments in each sphere of life, and so there does not seem to be any single assured pattern of successful immigrant absorption.[66]

Basing himself on the panel study of 1969-70 immigrants, Louis Guttmann concludes much the same thing when he shows that satisfaction with any particular aspect of immigration is not very strongly correlated with certainty of staying in Israel, though there is a reasonably strong positive correlation between general satsifaction and satisfaction in specific areas. Guttmann finds, however, that "the best predictor of staying in Israel does not come from specific areas [job, housing, etc.] but from the immigrant's initial feeling upon arriving in Israel."[67] That is, the best predictor of whether an immigrant will want to stay after two years in Israel is how strongly he wanted to stay upon first arriving. This is not a tautology; it means that a strong subjective commitment to "make it" in Israel is more important than objective material circumstances in determining whether or not the immigrant will become a permanent resident of Israel. In the government study of 1969-70 immigrants, 72 percent of all immigrants declared that they were "sure to stay in Israel." Among East Europeans, 88 percent declared themselves sure of staying, though among Americans, only 60 percent could do so. This turns out to be an accurate predictor for the groups since 60 percent of the Americans and about 90 percent of the East Europeans and Soviets are still in Israel five years after arrival.[68] So whether or not an immigrant will stay may be predictable and appears to depend more on his original intentions than on his subsequent economic and social situation, though presumably the former may be modified by dramatic experiences in regard to the latter. Not surprisingly, among all immigrant groups there is a direct relationship between age and certainty of staying: The older the immigrant, the more sure he is that he will stay in Israel.

IMMIGRATION AND REEMIGRATION

"In countries receiving immigrants there exists always an almost parallel movement of emigration. This movement is composed mainly of newly arrived immigrants who return to their country of origin or leave for another country."[69] It is generally not appreciated how large is the volume of reemigration from the traditional countries of immigration. Between 1857 and 1924, for every 100 immigrants to Argentina, there were 47 emigrants; in Australia, between 1906 and 1924, there were 70 emigrants for every 100 immigrants; and in the United States, between 1908 and 1924, there were 34 emigrants for every 100 immigrants.[79] Unlike in other countries, in Israel emigration is an ideological, social, and political issue. Emigration is generally stigmatized, with many thinking of it in terms of desertion or treason, while more charitable views are that it is simply a manifestation of weakness and personal inadequacy. The very terms used to describe immigrants and emigrants signal the values attached to each: The immigrant is called an *oleh*, one who goes up (a term deriving from the Biblical description of the obligatory holiday pilgrimages to Jerusalem), whereas the emigrant is called a *yored*, one who goes down, and perhaps not only in a physical sense. No less a personage than former Prime Minister Yitzhak Rabin referred publicly to the estimated 300,000 Israelis who had emigrated as "dregs and weaklings." Emigration is seen as weakening Israel militarily, politically, and morally, and government agencies and public organizations often discuss how to "prevent *yeridah*" (emigration) and how to attract emigrants back to the country. Isolation and condemnation have alternated with the extension of material incentives and moral appeals as tactics designed to return the emigrants. Reemigration of recent immigrants is especially painful because it reflects badly on the immigrant absorption process. Cases of immigrants who are about to leave the country are widely reported in the newspapers, and a great deal of wringing of the hands and shaking of the heads ensues. However, precise data on emigration are very hard to come by, since a considerable number of the emigrants never officially declare their intention to leave for good, and often depart saying — in many cases with all sincerity — that they are leaving only "temporarily," to study abroad, to work for a while, or simply to tour other countries. Moreover, it is not clear at what point an Israeli residing abroad becomes a yored: after one year, after five, or ten? Even those who acquire non-Israeli citizenship may return at some point, so there are no easy definitions of a yored.

In the government study of 1969-70 immigrants, an attempt was made to ascertain precisely how many immigrants left Israel for good. It was found that already within the first two months of arrival, 2 percent of the immigrants had left; by the end of the first year, 8.7 percent were gone, though among those classified as "potential immigrants" (mostly Americans and West Europeans), the percentage was 20.4.[71] By the end of the second year, 12 percent had gone, and by the end of three years, 15 percent (including 31 percent of "potential immigrants" and 8 percent of "immigrants.")[72]

Within the first two years in the country, 25 percent of the immigrants from North America and from Western Europe had left, while about 5 percent of those from Eastern Europe and Asia-Africa had done so.[73] By the end of the third year, the emigration figures had risen to 30 percent for the Americans; and by the end of five years, as noted previously, 37 percent of the American immigrants, 34 percent of the West Europeans, but only 7 percent of the East Europeans had departed.[74] Interestingly, there is not much variance by education or profession among the emigrants, though blue-collar workers are somewhat less likely to leave than others.[75]

Most East Europeans who leave Israel go to Western Europe and North America, and most could not return to their native countries even if they wanted to. The East Europeans have some difficulties in obtaining permission to immigrate to Western Europe and America, or even to enter as students or tourists. This may explain why there is not a higher proportion of East European emigrants from Israel. On the other hand, it may be that for a variety of reasons — lower material expectations, better cultural adjustment, higher ideological motivation — the East Europeans are less tempted to leave Israel than those from the West. After all, among West European immigrants to Australia there are significant differences, depending on country of origin, in emigration rates.[76] There are as yet no systematic studies of emigrants that would permit generalizations about their motivations for leaving, though much can be inferred from the demographic characteristics of the emigrants.[77] For example, the high proportion of young, single emigrants indicates that those with fewer family responsibilities and commitments are freer to change their country of residence than older, "more settled" people. A perceptive observer of American immigration to Israel, himself a "successful" immigrant, expresses doubt that emigration, at least of Americans, can be explained systematically.

> What it ultimately boils down to is a matter of chemical reaction, and though we know enough to class them with the volatile substances, we still do not know very much about the chemistry of the Jews. Are some born with a valence for like and some with a valence for unlike, are some suddenly ionized in mid-course so that they change from one to the other? We do not know, nor, when the sociologists have finished scoring the last questionnaire and tabulating the last punch card, are we likely to know much more.[78]

Another "successful" immigrant, a well-known scholar from the USSR, offered us the following theory during the course of a long interview.

> According to my own observations, each immigrant goes through three stages: the primary ecstasy, lasting 2-3 months; the psychological crisis; the period of adaptation. The crisis does not depend directly on one's job and flat. These factors might only aggravate or facilitate the crisis. . . . When the crisis is over, the period of adaptation starts. . . . The problem of psychological adaptation remains the most complicated one — the problem of transition from "oleh," to a citizen of Israel, to an Israeli. I know people who hold good positions in the Israeli intellectual elite. Though they came to Israel after the Second World War, they told me that this problem still exists for them, that they did not adapt psychologically.

According to this conception of the process of immigration, even some of those who are in the country 20 or 30 years feel themselves not completely a part of their adopted society, a feeling no doubt shared by many "first-generation" citizens all over the world.

THE SOVIET GEORGIANS: A SPECIAL CASE

To many Israelis and other "outsiders," the "chemistry"of the Georgian Jews is completely unknown. Constituting about 20 percent of the Soviet immigration, Georgian Jews have gotten unfavorable publicity in Israel because of their "clannishness," expressed in their insistence on living among other Georgians and as close as possible to members of their extended families. Their religious fervor and economic behavior have also been targets of criticism. Especially in 1971-72, when the Georgians were 46 percent of the Soviet immigration, they were given considerable attention in the media and in public and private discussion. Perhaps for this reason the Ministry for Immigrant Absorption made a special study of Georgian immigrant absorption. The Georgian immigration turned out to be younger and less educated than other Soviet immigrants. Only 44 percent of the Georgians had been employed in the USSR, and of those employed, 42 percent had been skilled workers and another 23 percent were employed in sales.[79] Only 9 percent of the Georgians could be classified as *akademaim*, those with post-secondary education, while 25 percent had only four years of schooling, and 62 percent had grade school education. Women were less educated than men, and few had worked outside the home in Georgia. However, after one year in Israel, more than half of the Georgians were employed, and of those, 64 percent had been channeled into industry. Already there was a noticeable shift from industry to transportation and services, a trend that would be accelerated in later years.[80] Georgian women were, in most cases for the first time, working outside the home, mostly as unskilled laborers in the textile and food-processing industries. Compared to other Soviet immigrants who had come at the same time, Georgian incomes were low: While 40 percent of other Soviet immigrants earned between 700 and 800 Israeli pounds a month, only 18 percent of the Georgians did so. Not surprisingly, Georgians were considerably less satisfied with their incomes than other Soviet newcomers.

Relatively few of the Georgians were studying Hebrew formally, and the immigrants were slow to learn the language. Thirty-three percent of them said they had not read a daily newspaper in the USSR, and 84 percent were not reading a Hebrew newspaper in Israel, although 37 percent claimed to be readers of the Russian-language daily.[81] After a year in Israel nearly one-half said they could not speak Hebrew at all and only one-quarter were listening to the news in Hebrew.[82]

Their linguistic isolation was accompanied by social isolation. They expressed strong preferences for Georgian neighbors, and only 19 percent were eager to live among Israelis. Nearly 75 percent had no social contact with immigrants from other countries or even areas of the USSR, and few had contacts with veteran Israelis not of Georgian origin, or even with Israelis of Georgian origin.[83] At the same time, twice as many Georgian immigrants as other newcomers felt that they were being "discriminated against" by the Jewish Agency and the Ministry for Immigrant Absorption.

Although 90 percent of the Georgians found permanent housing within one year, they were less satisfied than other immigrants with their accommodations, claiming that in Georgia extended families were able to live quite comfortably under one roof, but in Israel their apartments were too small to permit this. This may be one of the reasons that 58 percent of the Georgians expressed the view that their standard of living was *lower* in Israel than it had been in the USSR, while only 36 percent of other Soviet immigrants felt this way. In fact, Georgians do possess fewer durables, including automobiles, than other Soviet olim. Yet 67 percent of the Georgians claimed that they were "completely" or "quite" satisfied with their general situation, and only 13 percent claimed to be "not at all satisfied." Moreover, 96 percent said they were sure that they would remain in Israel.

Nevertheless, much publicity was given to a letter sent by four Georgians to Nikolai Podgorny, then chairman of the Presidium of the USSR Supreme Soviet, asking to be allowed to return to the Soviet Union. The press devoted considerable attention to rumors about Georgian Jews leaving Israel.[84] While it appears that few actually left, and even fewer tried to return to Georgia, the Georgians voiced their complaints to the point where they were invited to meet with Premier Golda Meir. They said that their religious needs were not being met and that Israeli housing and social policy frustrated their desire to live among other Georgians. Mrs. Meir, never noted for flexibility, refused to support "Georgian isolationism" and expressed doubts about the need for religious facilities. The religious parties had made a political issue of the Georgians' religious needs, charging that the Mapam-dominated Ministry for Immigrant Absorption was deliberately trying to wean the Georgians away from their centuries-old traditions.[85] The Agudat Yisrael party even brought a motion of no confidence in the government to the floor of the Knesset, as shall be described in Chapter 8.

Very quickly the Georgians were stereotyped as volatile, violent, suspicious, clannish, ignorant, fanatical, and demanding. Their distinctive looks and dress made them easy targets for ridicule, and to combat this, the Israeli press tried to inform the population of the history, traditions, and outlooks of the Georgians. Several articles discussed the injustices of anti-Georgian prejudices and emphasized the importance of dignity and self-respect to the Georgians. Violent behavior was explained as a reaction to insults and challenges to the worth of the Georgians.[86] It is hard to say whether such articles influenced public opinion, and one gets the impression that Georgian immigrants still rank very low on the Israeli social scale.

This does not mean that they have been ignored by the political parties. Whatever one may think of Georgians, they represent a significant number of potential voters, and, as geographically concentrated, less educated, and economically dependent people, perhaps they could be mobilized politically in the same ways as the earlier North African and Middle Eastern immigrants. The religious parties and the Labor party have been especially active among the Georgians, as shall be discussed in a later chapter, but the results of these political efforts are not clear. There is some evidence, to be cited later on, that the Georgians have remained largely outside the political arena and have not been successfully mobilized by any of the parties to any significant extent.

"BUKHARAN" JEWS

Jews from Central Asia are generally labelled "Bukharan," though they may be from other cities of Uzbekistan (Tashkent and Samarkand have the largest concentrations) or from other republics of Central Asia (mainly Tadzhikistan and Kazakhstan). The label is a cultural, rather than a geographical, one and refers only to those Jews of Judaeo-Persian culture, and not to Jews of European origin who migrated to Central Asia. In 1970 there were about 160,000 Jews in the Central Asian republics. By the end of 1980 about 15,000 had immigrated to Israel, most of them from Uzbekistan and Tadzhikistan. Though they did not arouse the same interest nor generate as much publicity as the Georgians, some of their problems are similar. Bukharan Jews have a long history of settlement in Palestine/Israel and have much-admired traditions, but the recent immigration is a relatively uneducated one and occupied lower rungs of the Soviet occupational ladder. However, occupations such as shoemaking, carpentry, and tailoring offered the possibility of illegal, but tolerated, side income in the USSR, so that even people with higher levels of education chose these occupations.[87] Though not as powerful as among the Georgians, religious tradition still exercises a strong influence in the Bukharan community, which is similar to the Georgian one in its extended families and clans. Like the Georgians, Bukharans usually lived in large one-story homes divided into smaller units for individual families, and in Israel they had to shift to small, modern apartments. Some Islamic traditions influenced the Central Asian Jews — for example, in regard to the roles of women — and these are not easily assimilable into the modernized, rather secularized Israeli society and economy. Unlike the Georgians, however, the Bukharans appear to lack the strong sense of communal solidarity and the internal financial system that could protect the community and defend it against the surrounding society. In one locale such defense was necessary because the local population, mostly of North African origin, considered the Bukharans "primitive," thinking of them as "Georgians" and calling them such. According to an anthropological study in this area, the population very much resented the immigrant benefits that the Bukharans received, arguing that these might be due to educated Europeans but not to these "primitive Georgians."[88] Not surprisingly, a considerable number of the recent immigrants left the area and drifted to the poorer sections of the big cities.

SUMMARY

Thus was the new type of immigration, in the main a Western, educated, relatively affluent immigration, settled into Israeli society and received by it. Whereas material difficulties were severe for previous immigrations, it seems that social and psychological transitions were more salient to the post-1967 immigrants, though material and psychological adjustment were clearly related.

Having surveyed the general picture of the mutual adjustment of Soviet and American immigrants and the host population, we can now turn to our specific concern with one aspect of their adjustment, the political one. As the immigrants learn the language, customs, foods, and values of the society — to the extent that they do — do they also acquire its political mores? They have brought with them political cultures and subcultures. How do these shape the acquisition, rejection, or transformation of Israeli political culture? These are the major concerns of our investigation into the political socialization of Soviet and American immigrants to Israel.

NOTES

1. Compare David Easton and Jack Dennis, "The Child's Image of Government," *The Annals of the American Academy of Political and Social Science* 361 (1965), with Dean Jaros, Herbert Hirsch, and Frederic J. Fleron, Jr., "The Malevolent Leader: Political Socialization in an American Sub-Culture," *American Political Science Review* 62, no. 2 (June 1968).

2. Judith T. Shuval, *Immigrants on the Threshold* (New York: Atherton, 1963), p. 119. It is interesting that Shuval found the "approach" pattern more characteristic of non-Europeans, whereas the Europeans tended toward the "withdrawal" pattern.

3. W. D. Borrie, *The Cultural Integration of Immigrants* (Paris: UNESCO, 1959), p. 47.

4. A survey in the late 1960s of North African Jewish immigrants in France found that the modal identification was "Jew," but that substantial numbers chose "Jew and Frenchman," "North African Jew," or "Frenchman." Doris Bensimon-Donath, *L'integration des Juifs nord africaines en France* (Paris: Mouton: 1971) p. 203. See also the study of Moroccan brothers who settled in France and in Israel by Michael Inbar and Chaim Adler, *Ethnic Integration in Israel: A Comparative Case Study of Moroccan Brothers Who Settled in France and in Israel* (New Brunswick, N.J.: Transaction Books, 1977), esp. pp. 65-70.

5. S. N. Eisenstadt, *The Absorption of Immigrants* (London: Routledge and Kegan Paul, 1954), pp. 146ff.

6. Ibid., pp. 148 and 161.

7. Ibid., p. 164.

8. Shuval, p. 75.

9. Some of the better descriptions of the problems faced by Soviet immigrants include: Betty Gidwitz, "Problems of Adjustment of Soviet Jewish Emigrés," *Soviet Jewish Affairs* 6, no. 1 (1976); the series by Eliahu Salpeter in *Haaretz*, March 19, 21, 22, and 23, 1971; Sol Stern, "The Russian Jews Wonder Whether Israel is Really Ready for Them," New York *Times Magazine*, Apirl 16, 1972; the series by Mati Golan in *Haaretz*, December 17, 19, and 20, 1971; the series by Shabtai Tevet in *Haaretz*, March 29, 31, April 4, 7, 8, 12, 17, 18, and 21, 1972; Avraham Tirosh in *Maariv*, July 6, 1973; the series by Yehuda Litani in *Haaretz*, September 1974; Naomi Shepherd, "The Soviet Jews in Israel: Coping with Free Choices," New York *Times*, April 27, 1975. An observer of Soviet refugees in Switzerland lists the following traits as being typical: intensive ties to the homeland; vocal rejection of rules that the refugees could not understand; great thirst for knowledge and certainty about their vocational desires; a tendency to stay with the group and no desire for privacy; group solidarity and mutual help. See Maria Pfister-Ammende, "Displaced Soviet Russians in

Switzerland," in *Uprooting and After*, ed. Charles Zwingmann and Maria Pfister-Ammende (New York: Springer Verlag, 1973), pp. 79-90.

10. On the Beit Shemesh affair, see Aharon Dolav, "Kakh hivrikhu hashiltonot olim-muomadim m'arhab," *Maariv*, December 6, 1974; on the rental matter, see Yosef Vaksman and Amos Levav, "Mah erkah shel modaah mitaam misrad haklitah," *Maariv*, June 2 and June 25, 1975. On Yamit, see Aharon Dolav, "Kakh nigozah . . . ," *Maariv*, June 13, 1975.

11. Shmuel Shnitzer, "Korat-gag akumah," *Maariv*, June 20, 1975.

12. Abraham A. Weinberg, "Mental Health Aspects of Voluntary Migration," in Zwingmann and Pfister-Ammende, *Uprooting and After*, p. 112.

13. *Olai tashal: Khamesh hashanim harishonot beyisrael*, supplement No. 19 to the *Monthly Bulletin of Statistics* 27, no. 4 (1976): 54.

14. In Tamar Horowitz and Khava Frankel's study of immigrants, they found 52 percent of Soviet immigrants had two-room apartments, and 25 percent were in three-room apartments. *Olim bemarkazai klitah* (Jerusalem: Henrietta Szold Institute, 1975), Research Report No. 185, Publication No. 538, p. 131.

15. Ministry for Immigrant Absorption, *Klitat haaliyah 1972* (Jerusalem, 1973), p. 40.

16. Yehudit Shuval and Yehuda Markus, *Dfusai histaglut shel olai Brit-Hamoetsot*, Part 1 (Jerusalem: Israel Institute of Applied Social Research, 1973), p. 124.

17. Ibid., Part 2 (*Tahalikhai hizdahut im hakhevrah hayisraelit*) (Jerusalem, 1974), p. 61.

18. See the data in Shuval and Markus, Part 1.

19. "Professional'naia podgotovka i perepodgotovka novykh olim," *Nasha strana*, April 11, 1975.

20. Quoted in Levi Yitzhak Hayerushalmi, "Lemaalah m'esrim elef nikletu betaasiyah," *Maariv*, January 31, 1975.

21. See, for example, Avraham Peleg, "Kemakhtsit hafizikaim hayehudim . . . ," *Maariv*, February 21, 1974, and the series by the same author on Soviet immigrant scientists in *Maariv*, January 15, 22, and 29, 1976. See also the series by Nakhman Favian in *Haaretz*, July 30, August 1, and August 5, 1973.

22. Atallah Mantsour, "Shlish harofim – olim," *Haaretz*, February 7, 1977.

23. A good discussion of these matters is found in Eli Ayal, "Rofim olim verofim yordim," *Maariv*, March 10, 1972. See also Ofra Eligon, "Harofim merusiia merapim balev," *Maariv*, February 21, 1975.

24. See, for example, *Maariv*, February 10, 1972.

25. Yehudit Shuval and Arnold Schwartz, "Tahalikhai klitah shel rofim olim mibrit hamoetsot," mimeographed (Jerusalem: Israel Institute of Applied Social Research, November 1976), pp. 39, 79, and 15.

26. Of 47 Soviet physicians who entered the United States in 1973, 28 took the licensing exam required of foreign medical graduates, and all failed. See George E. Johnson, "Which Promised Land? The Realities of American Absorption of Soviet Jews," *Analysis*, no. 47 (November 1, 1974).

27. Aharonovich had been conductor of the USSR Radio and TV Symphony Orchestra, a position he attained at age 30. He conducted the Haifa

Symphony for a time, but in recent years has conducted mostly in Western Europe. Barshai, former conductor of the Moscow Chamber Orchestra, emigrated later, and a chamber orchestra was formed for him. He was provided by the government with what is, by Israeli standards, a luxury apartment, and this expenditure aroused some negative public reaction. For Aharonovich's fascinating biography, see Zvi Lavi, "Im LeYuri Aharonovich ein avodah be Yisrael, lemi yesh avodah?" *Maariv*, November 5, 1974.

28. See Shraga Har-Gil, "26 hadakot shel Viktor Nord," *Maariv*, March 11, 1975, and Talilah Ben-Zakai, "Haomanim haolim . . ." *Maariv*, March 20, 1975. Quite a few Soviet cinema professionals have left Israel, seeking work elsewhere.

29. An interesting account of the experiences of several of these players is found in Mordechai Rosenblum, "HaAmerikanim-notnai haton," *Maariv*, December 1, 1976.

30. Khaim Zilbershmidt in *Maariv*, February 4, 1975.

31. Rami Mishaev-Miron, quoted in Yisrael Rosenblatt, "Healuf shenishbar," *Maariv*, February 5, 1976.

32. Central Bureau of Statistics, *Monthly Bulletin of Statistics – Supplement* 24, no. 6 (June 1973): 143.

33. *Klitat haaliyah 1972*, p. 53.

34. *Olai tashal*, pp. 58-59.

35. Central Bureau of Statistics and Ministry for Immigrant Absorption, *Immigrants Arrived in 1969/70: The First Three Years in Israel*, Special series No. 483 (Jerusalem, 1975), p. xx.

36. *Monthly Bulletin of Statistics* 24, no. 6, p. 131.

37. *Monthly Bulletin of Statistics* 24, no. 9 (September 1973): 132.

38. Horowitz and Frankel, p. 177.

39. Shuval and Markus, Part 1, p. 26.

40. *Monthly Bulletin of Statistics* 24, no. 9, pp. 136-36, and *Immigrants Arrived in 1969/70*, pp. 9 and 27 (Tables 6 and 17). See also *Klitat haaliyah, 1978* (Jerusalem, 1979), p. 22.

41. See Zvi Gitelman, "Recent Emigrés and the Soviet Political System: A Pilot Study in Detroit," *Slavic and Soviet Series* (Tel Aviv University) 2, no. 2 (Fall 1977): 49.

42. Shuval and Markus, Part 1, p. 56.

43. *Monthly Bulletin of Statistics* 24, no. 9, and *Immigrants Arrived in 1969/70*.

44. For details, see Zvi Gitelman, *Jewish Nationality and Soviet Politics* (Princeton, N.J.: Princeton University Press, 1972), pp. 276-85.

45. *Monthly Bulletin of Statistics* 22, no. 7 (July 1971): 60.

46. *Monthly Bulletin of Statistics* 24, no. 6, p. 141.

47. *Olai tashal*, p. 55.

48. For the relevant data, see *Monthly Bulletin of Statistics* 24, no. 9, pp. 138-39, and *Olai tashal*, pp. 58-59.

49. See *Klitat haaliyah 1972*, p. 77, and *Immigrants Arrived in 1969/70*, pp. 11 and 29 (Tables 7 and 18).

50. *Klitat haaliyah 1972*, p. 68.

51. Horowitz and Frankel, p. 87.

52. See, for example, Menachem Shmuel, "Anakhnu margishim kan kezarim," *Maariv*, July 17, 1975; "Obshchestvennaia absorptsiia," *Nasha strana*, January 1, 1975.

53. *Monthly Bulletin of Statistics* 24, no. 6, p. 136.

54. *Monthly Bulletin of Statistics* 24, no. 9, p. 143.

55. *Immigrants Arrived in 1969/70*, pp. 15 and 33 (Tables 9 and 20).

56. Shuval and Markus, Part 1, pp. xix, 71, 78, and 80-81.

57. *Klitat haaliyah 1972*, p. 65.

58. *Olai tashal*, pp. 58-59.

59. Data cited in Shuval and Markus, Part 1, p. 65.

60. An anthropological study of American immigrants concludes that people's "social network structure . . . remains constant in different cultures." This argument, based on interviews with 19 families, is made by Pearl Katz, "Acculturation and Social Networks of American Immigrants in Israel," Ph.D. dissertation, State University of New York at Buffalo, 1974. Katz defines acculturation in terms of social networks and says: "Those immigrants who were unacculturated to Israeli society — as defined by their social network patterns — were not acculturated to American society. Furthermore, their parents or grandparents were not likely to have been acculturated to East European [non-Jewish] society. . . . Most of the immigrants in the study who were acculturated to Israeli society have been acculturated to American society" (pp. 3-4). This raises several problems. First, defining acculturation in terms of social networks alone takes no account of the immigrant's subjective perceptions of himself in his new society, job, and so on. Second, acculturation often takes place into a specific subculture, so that one may be "acculturated" into the subculture defined as "Americans in Israel." More importantly, Katz's hypothesis about the constancy of the tendency to acculturate logically implies that those who were "assimilated" in America (that is, had social networks including many non-Jews) adjust *better* to Israeli society than those whose social network was largely Jewish. Aside from the prima facie unlikeliness of this hypothesis, there is a great deal of evidence that religious Americans — who were less likely to have non-Jewish friends in the United States — adjust more easily to Israeli society and are more likely to stay there. They would seem, therefore, to "acculturate" better in Israel, unless Katz is prepared to argue that they may be more likely to stay in Israel but are less likely to "acculturate" — in which case her concept of acculturation is grossly misleading, if not altogether useless.

If one extends her arguments to Soviet immigrants, it would follow that those from the Soviet heartland, who had broader and less ethnocentric social networks in the USSR, should "acculturate" better than Zapadniki, who had relatively narrower networks and were less involved with Russians or Balts. In fact, it is the Zapadniki who "acculturate" more rapidly and more extensively.

61. *Immigrants Arrived in 1969/70*, p. 13 (Table 18). After two years in the country, American, West European, and East European immigrants report the same levels of satisfaction, but those from Africa and Asia report somewhat lower levels (71 percent of the latter report satisfaction, compared to 80 percent

and more of the other immigrants). *Klitat haaliyah, 1972*, p. 18. Fin ings are much the same for immigrants who came in 1973-77. See *Klitat haaliyah, 1978*, p. 115.

62. *Olai tashal*, p. 52.

63. Shuval and Markus, Part 1, p. xiv.

64. See *Klitat haaliyah, 1978*, pp. 116-17.

65. Shuval and Markus, Part 1, pp. 1-5.

66. Ibid., p. 76.

67. Haviva Bar-Shimerling and Eliahu Louis Guttmann, "Hashnatayim harishonot beyisrael: tmurot behistaglut olim khadashim," mimeographed (Jerusalem: Israel Institute of Applied Social Research and The Hebrew University, Faculty of Social Sciences, September 1975), p. 3.

68. *Monthly Bulletin of Statistics* 24, no. 9, p. 127, Table 1. A study of over 600 North African Jews in France, done in 1966-67, found that 67 percent of those between the ages of 15 and 25 thought they might emigrate to another country — and two-thirds of these named Israel as that country — while only about 40 percent of those between 25 and 40 considered emigrating — of these, 87 percent thought they would go to Israel. Bensimon-Donath, p. 227.

69. Moshe Sicron, *Immigration to Israel, 1948-1953* (Jerusalem: Falk Project for Economic Research in Israel and Central Bureau of Statistics, Special Series No. 60, August 1957), p. 40.

70. I. Ferenczi, *International Migration* (New York, 1929) Vol. I, quoted in ibid., p. 41.

71. *Monthly Bulletin of Statistics* 24, no. 7 (July 1971): 69. Of the "potential immigrants," 55 percent were from North America.

72. *Monthly Bulletin of Statistics* 24, no. 6, p. 145.

73. *Monthly Bulletin of Statistics* 24, no. 1 (January 1973): 125-27.

74. *Olai tashal*, p. 52.

75. *Klitat haaliyah 1972*, Vol. II, p. 15.

76. See Ronald Taft, *From Stranger to Citizen* (London: Tavistock Publications, 1966), p. 26, n. 1.

77. A pilot study of 58 Soviet immigrants who were about to leave Israel found social and interpersonal relations were the primary disappointments of these people, and that the lack of cultural and vocational opportunities were among the most important reasons for leaving. See D. Elizur and R. B. Elizur, "Factors Affecting the Intention to Leave Israel Among Immigrants from the U.S.S.R.," *Immigration and Israel's Survival* (Jerusalem: The Jewish Agency, 1975). For a study of some Israeli immigrants who returned to Austria, see F. Wilder-Okladek, *The Return Movement of Jews to Austria after the Second World War* (The Hague: Martinus Nijhoff, 1969).

78. Hillel Halkin, "Americans in Israel," *Commentary* 53, no. 5 (May 1972): 63.

79. "Klitat olai Gruziia tokh hashana harishona lehagi'am," mimeographed (Jerusalem: Ministry for Immigrant Absorption, September 1973). A brief note about this internal report is found in *Maariv*, December 29, 1974. On the history of Georgian Jews and their Zionist tradition, see Mordechai Neishtat, *Yehudai*

Gruziia (Tel Aviv: Am Oved, 1970), and Natan Eliahshvili, *Hayehudim hagruzim beGruziia ubEretz Yisrael* (Tel Aviv: Tsherikover, 1975).

80. See Menakhem Rahat, "Kaitzad shukhne'u olai Gruziia shelo lifnot el harokhlut," *Maariv*, May 8, 1972.

81. "Klitat olai Gruziia," p. 7.

82. Ibid., p. 14.

83. Ibid., p. 9.

84. See, for example, "Hitakhdut olai Gruziia," *Al hamishmar*, November 30, 1971; "N. Peled umishlakhat olai Gruziia," *Davar*, December 2, 1971; *Haaretz*, December 7, 1971; *Yediot akhronot*, December 24, 1971; and "Asarot mishpakhot me'olai Gruziia rotsot lakhzor leRussia," *Maariv*, November 26, 1971.

85. See *Maariv*, November 28, 1971, and January 16, 1972. According to the latter article, the Georgian representatives demanded that those who were in charge of Georgian absorption be themselves religious; that Georgians be settled in compact groups of at least 200 families, with a synagogue for each such concentration; that Georgians not be forced to work on the Sabbath; and that they be allowed to meet their families arriving at the international airport. "Mrs. Meir argued against the isolation of Georgian *olim* because, in her opinion, immigrants from different diasporas should live together. She also said she didn't understand the need for separate synagogues since anyone who wanted to pray could enter a synagogue and do so." [Georgian Jews' ritual differs from that of other Jews.] She hinted that the delegation may have been inspired by certain political parties, something the delegates denied vehemently. For complaints of religious discrimination, see *Davar*, October 26, 1971, and *Hatsofe*, October 27, 1971.

86. See, for example, Amnon Nadva, "Yehudai Gruziia regishim likhvodam," *Haaretz*, December 2, 1971; interview with Rabbi Yehudah Butrishvili, *Maariv*, December 3, 1971; Khanokh Bartuv, "Mah koev leAvraham Jinjikhashvili," *Maariv*, January 28, 1972; interview with Eliahu Debarashvili, *Maariv*, May 26, 1972; and Avraham Tirosh, "Motsiim baaretz shem ra leGruzinim," *Maariv*, March 18, 1974. A good anthropological study of a Georgian immigrant community is Yitzhak Eilam's, *Seker antropologi shel hakehillah haGruzinit beAshkelon* (Jerusalem: Research Department of the Ministry for Immigrant Absorption and Department of Sociology and Cultural Anthropology, The Hebrew University, May 1974). See also Eilam's *Hagruzinim beYisrael* (Jerusalem: Kaplan School of Economics and Social Sciences, The Hebrew University, 1980).

87. See Rinah Ben-Shaul, *Olai Bukhara-Beit Shemesh: mekhkar antropologi* (Jerusalem: Research Department of the Ministry for Immigrant Absorption and Department of Sociology and Cultural Anthropology, The Hebrew University, September 1975), p. 38.

88. Ibid., p. 83.

5

IMMIGRATION AND POLITICAL RESOCIALIZATION

Amateur Jewish teachers of Hebrew, a language almost no Soviet Jew is allowed to learn, but the main language of Israel. Courtesy National Conference on Soviet Jewry.

A Swedish scholar of migration and politics, Tomas Hammar, has said of the literature on migration and on political socialization that "in the latter we find very little about migration, in the former not much about politics."[1] This book uses both in order to understand better what happens politically to the immigrants and, at the same time, to contribute to neglected aspects of migration and political socialization. The process of immigration involves mainly *adult* political socialization, or *re*socialization, a process about which relatively little is known.

Political socialization, according to Greenstein, may be conceived of in two ways.

> Narrowly conceived, [it] . . . is the deliberate inculcation of political information, values, and practices by instructional agents who have been formally charged with this responsibility. A broader conception would encompass all political learning, formal and informal, deliberate and unplanned, at every stage of the life cycle, including not only explicitly political learning but also nominally nonpolitical learning that affects political behavior, such as the learning of politically relevant social attitudes and the acquisition of politically relevant personality characteristics.[2]

We shall examine the "narrow" form of political socialization of the immigrants, but we shall also be more broadly concerned with who learns what, from whom, under what circumstances, and with what effects.

RESOCIALIZING ADULTS

There has been a great deal of research and theorizing on the political socialization of children, and, to a lesser extent, of adolescents. However, as one of the leading students of political socialization points out, "there is extremely little in the whole area of adult political socialization."[3] Despite almost ritual repetitions in the literature that political socialization is a lifetime process and that there is such a thing as adult socialization, there seems to be a dominant assumption that socialization in childhood is more important.

Jennings and Niemi point out that

> it is . . . regularly noted that some systematic changes do occur during . . . adult life. However, the extent of, and, especially, the rate of, these changes are not always clear. Nor has there been any careful delineation of just what things do vary systematically over the life cycle. The most common view seems to be that except for a few matters affecting all age-groups to some degree, such as voting turnout, and changes caused by cataclysmic events . . . changes during adulthood are relatively small and of minor importance.[4]

Greenstein, for example, argues that "political orientations learned during the initial school years or the late preschool years often have a greater impact on the individual's adult political behavior than do orientations that are learned later in life." The reason for this, according to Greenstein, is that orientations acquired in childhood have been "adopted without conscious consideration of alternatives, and [are] likely to have an unquestioned character that makes them both influential for behavior and resistant to change."[5] Even one of the few students of adult socialization thinks that childhood social- ization is "usually much more effective than adult socialization." Orville Brim suggests that this is due to the different relationships between socializers and socialized in childhood and adulthood: Whereas the child relates to the socializing parent or teacher emotionally and affectively, and power can be introduced into the relationship by the socializer, "agents of adult socialization . . . typically appeal more to the reason and self-interest of the person being socialized, and use power only as a last resort." For this reason, adult socialization usually limits itself to a "concern with behavior rather than with motivation and values."[6]

The assumption that what is learned in childhood is more basic than that which is learned later on is pervasive in Western psychol- ogy. In regard to political orientations this "primacy principle" comprises three assumptions: political orientations are learned during childhood; this childhood learning further shapes any subsequent modifications of these orientations; and these modifications can only be small, since "fundamental political orientations tend to endure through life."[7]

The "primacy principle" has been challenged by some noted social scientists,[8] and it has been tested by political scientists using Survey Research Center data on U.S. elections. Using cohort analysis as a substitute for panel data, Searing, Wright, and Rabinowitz found that the sense of political efficacy and the sense of trust underwent substantial change over time, in contrast to partisan identification, which remained more stable. Contemporary events, or *zeitgeist* factors, were found to affect political behavior to a much greater extent than the aging of the individual. Searing, Wright, and Rabino- witz conclude that the data

> do support the primacy principle . . . but reveal magnitudes of change that are simply too great to be ignored. Persistence apparently depends not only on how deeply an orientation is embedded but also on how it is reinforced through life. Indeed, our most surprising finding is the

pervasive impact of contemporary events; the character of post-adolescent experience has considerable significance for orientation development and change.[9]

All of this suggests two alternative hypotheses regarding the political resocialization of immigrants. Either the primacy principle is applicable even to those moving physically from one political system and culture to another, with any consequent change being on a superficial, behavioral level, for basic political orientations have been established in the country of the immigrants' birth. Or immigration involves uprooting to such an extent that even "primordial beliefs" about politics are affected and, if not displaced, at least substantially modified.

If one were to extrapolate from the literature on political socialization, one would favor the first alternative. Even without challenging the validity of the primacy principle for "normal" situations, however, one is still led to question whether it would hold for immigration. After all, just as the language and possibly the conventions of dress and manners that one learned as a child in one's native country become irrelevant, and in some cases even "dysfunctional," in the country of immigration, so too might the political orientations. One who has been taught to question and challenge authority and to act on one's conscience might find himself in a very difficult situation indeed were he to act on these principles in a new country whose political system were authoritarian. Second, by the very act of emigration, some people might be renouncing the culture of their childhood. If they choose to immigrate to a different political system, they may be explicitly renouncing the values and political beliefs dominant in their native land. Third, migration is for many a "cataclysmic event" on a personal level and may have the same political effects on the individual as cataclysmic social or economic events (for example, the Great Depression). Just as such social and economic events may change the political physiognomy of a generation, so might the experience of uprooting and transplantation bring about an individual's political reorientation. Finally, recalling Brim's argument that childhood socialization is more effective and longer lasting because of the nature of the socializer-socialized relationship, we might suggest that for immigrants — at least for some of them — the relationship between socializer and socialized is like that which "normally" obtains in childhood. After all, like a child, the immigrant is basically dependent. The socializer has more power vis-a-vis the immigrant than he does in relation to other adults, and he may even be the focus of an affective attachment on the part of the immigrant who wishes to identify with his new country. The immigrant's capacity for independent judgment and evaluation is, in most cases, quite limited, at least during the first period of his arrival in the country. Our earlier description of the role of the "instructor" in absorbing immigrants in Israel should illustrate the point. In fact, as was pointed out, it is well known that many immigrants explicitly rejected the socialization of their childhoods and adopted the values and behavior of the role models provided by the new political system. Immigrant resocialization may be heavily infused with emotional content, as in childhood socialization, for the political system will strive to gain the affection, not just the passive loyalty, of the new citizen. Certainly, the "Americanization" efforts of late-nineteenth- and early-twentieth-century America and the Zionist socialization of Israeli immigrants relied a great deal on emotional appeals.

For all these reasons, it makes sense to consider an alternative to the primacy principle, at least in regard to immigrants: immigration is such a special case of adult resocialization, resembling childhood socialization in several crucial ways, that it is possible that fundamental political orientations, and not just external behavior, may be transformed in the process of immigrant political resocialization.

There are, however, some powerful arguments against equating immigrants with children for the purposes of political resocialization. After all, we know very well that immigrants sometimes do not learn the language and the ways of their adopted country and that they remain within their childhood cultures. Might not the same hold for the political realm? Immigrants might be part of a "latent culture," one that "has its origin and social support in a group other than the one in which the members are now participating."[10] Their behavior might be at least tolerable by the "manifest," or majority, political culture, but their values and beliefs might be those imported from the antecedent political culture in which they were originally socialized. A related possibility is the rejection of the manifest culture, expressed in passive withdrawal. The antecedent political culture may be challenged, but if no substitute is offered, or is attractive, then according to Anthony Wallace, the "Principle of Conservation of Cognitive Structure" will come into play. That is, previous conceptions will not be wholly abandoned until new ones are adopted. "Individuals for years will cling to a disordered socio-cultural system, in which events do not follow reliably upon their supposed antecedents, rather than face the anxiety of cultural abandonment."[11] Trotsky put it more directly: Consciousness lags behind reality. Immigrants may remain betwixt and between: They are aware that their previous political culture is irrelevant to the dominant one in their new home, but they cannot quite bring themselves to abandon it entirely and substitute the host society's culture for it. Or they may outwardly adopt a new political culture but only superficially, so that they are apt to shift easily with the political winds.[12] A third possibility is that the immigrant is strongly committed to a set of political ideals that are not the same as those dominant in the host society (or his original homeland, for that matter). Such a person "often ignores the principle of situational adjustment, pursuing his consistent line of activity in the face of a short-term loss."[13] In other words, he refuses to be resocialized and to conform with mainstream values and behavior patterns. Such, for example, are those Soviet immigrants who in the late 1960s and early 1970s bitterly opposed the welfare socialism of the Labor governments, as well as their methods of handling Soviet Jewish and other world issues, and who did not fit in easily to the absorption framework of Israel.

We have, then, arguments for viewing immigrant resocialization as no different from what is assumed to be adult political socialization in general: A process of usually incremental change, outweighed in importance by the socialization that takes place in childhood. There are other arguments that would lead us to consider immigrant resocialization as more analogous to childhood than to adult social-ization, and hence would expect it to involve more dramatic and fundamental transformations. Still, there are psychological observations that might make us hesitate, and to consider whether or not immigrants can be as easily *re*socialized as children are socialized, in light of the possibilities of "latent culture," the reluctance to abandon previously held beliefs, and the possibility of "commit-ment." Thus, we shall leave our original two alternative hypotheses as just that: assumptions that have a prima facie plausibility, though they seem to contradict each other, and that have to be answered empirically rather than logically. We should hasten to add that our limited data cannot supply a definitive empirical answer to such large questions; but the exploration itself is worth the journey.

IMMIGRATION AND SOCIALIZATION

Migration is not simply individual behavior, nor is it random. It cannot be explained solely in physical (distance) or biological (age) terms, as it once was.[14] Migration is a social process, in part, linking two social systems. Therefore, to fully appreciate a particular process of migration one needs knowledge of both systems.[15] The more recent realization that migration is also a process involving socialization or resocialization[16] obliges an analysis of the impact of migration upon the absorbing or host society as well as on the individual, and of his socialization before migration. The international migrant, especially, is likely not to be a "typical" member of his original society, nor is he likely to share all of the characteristics of the population that will receive him as an immigrant.

> Even before they leave, migrants tend to have taken on some of the characteristics of the population at destination, but they can never completely lose some which they share with the population at origin. It is because they are already to some degree like the population at destination that they find certain positive factors there, and it is because they are unlike the population at origin that certain minus factors there warrant migration.[17]

Thus, the study of immigrant resocialization should involve, as our case study does, analyses of: the system from which the immigrant came and his particular place in it; the changes in the immigrant as he moves from one society to another; the relevant characteristics of the host society and of the immigrant's place in it; and the mutual impact of immigrant and receiving society.

Stanton Wheeler distinguishes between "developmental socialization systems" and "resocialization systems." The purpose of developmental socialization is "the training, education, or more generally the further socialization of the individuals passing through." The formal purpose of resocialization systems, on the other hand, "is to make up or correct for some deficiency in earlier socialization."[18] In the case of immigration the "deficiency" is defined by the host society.

Since we are dealing with adults, resocialization must involve *de*socialization, the *"un*learning" of values, beliefs, attitudes, and behavioral habits acquired in a different setting. Desocialization of immigrants is both spontaneous and planned. As the immigrant's language, cultural habits, social status, and previous social roles become irrelevant in the host society, these may be abandoned, either with enthusiasm and hastily, or grudgingly and slowly. Many immigrants will engage in "defense acts aimed at salvaging parts of the socio-personal system,"[19] resulting in a partial retention of functionally, but not psychologically, useless characteristics (modes of dress, insistence on certain formalities or refusal to adopt others that are native to the host society, reading only the immigrant press). Others will totally reject the new society and attempt to re-create their old one. Spontaneous pressures for desocialization are ever present, however, and in most cases, they are effective in substantially desocializing the newcomer.

Planned desocialization includes programs designed to teach the new culture, and almost always by implication to renounce the old one. Governments or civic associations aim to "integrate" the immigrants as rapidly and as completely as possible. Israeli policies of population dispersal, language teaching, taking immigrants on tours of the country, and giving them short courses in its history and current situation are designed to desocialize and resocialize simultaneously. In the language courses (*ulpanim*), the very first lessons stress that despite the different countries of origin of immigrants, they are all one people and Hebrew is their common language. Thus, one of the most widely used Hebrew texts contains the following passages in the very first lessons:

> Where are you from, Menashe? I am from Kishinev. . . . Where are you from, Shimon? From America. . . . And Hannah, where is she from? From France. Where are you from, Yitzhak? From Argentina. You are from Argentina, he from Russia, she from France. Now he and I and she are all in Israel, at the Hebrew University in Jerusalem. Thank God! . . . The teacher says that a good pupil speaks Hebrew not only in class, but on the street. . . . Englishmen speak English, Frenchmen speak French, and Arabs speak Arabic. The Jews are one nation and speak the Hebrew language.[20]

The message is clear: Jews in Israel, no matter their geographic origin, should speak Hebrew, not their native tongues.

American socialization of immigrants has also stressed "unlearning." An American educator, writing in 1909, described southern and eastern Europeans as "illiterate, docile, lacking in self-reliance and initiative, and not possessing the Anglo-Teutonic conceptions of law, order, and government." He argued that "our task is to break up these groups or settlements, to assimilate and amalgamate these people as a part of our American race, and to implant in their children so far as can be done, the Anglo-Saxon conception of righteousness, law and order, and popular government. . . ."[21] Other educators and civil leaders spoke of "absolute forgetfulness of all obligations or connections with other countries because of descent or birth," or stressed that immigrants "must be induced to give up the languages, customs and methods of life which they have brought with them." Even President Woodrow Wilson declared that "America does not consist of groups. . . . A man who thinks of himself as belonging to a particular national group in America has not yet become an American."[22] "Americanization" was desocialization with a vengeance. At least until the recent "ethnic revival," it succeeded in the acculturation, if not in the assimilation, of the immigrants.[23] Nevertheless, in the United States as well as in Israel, it is likely that the desocialization process owes more to spontaneous social pressures than to planned programs.

Whether spontaneous or planned, desocialization will occur simultaneously with resocialization and can be separated from it only for analytic purposes. Rivkah Weiss Bar-Yosef sees "successful adjustment . . . as a dynamic balance of desocialization and resocialization, where the desocialization tendencies are slowly eliminated while the resocializing forces expand." Resocialization is not a linear process, nor, of course, is the overall adjustment of the immigrant. "Absorption is not a well ordered temporal sequence of phases of adjustment, but a fluid exchange between the immigrant and society."[24]

Neither desocialization nor resocialization necessarily occurs among immigrants, despite spontaneous and planned pressures for both. A study of immigrants to Canada concludes that "the mere fact of migration to another country did not fundamentally alter a person's sense of who he was, how he should behave, or where he belonged."[25] This was especially true of British or American immigrants who retained the same occupation. "Evidently they did not experience the degree of 'desocialization' that appears to be a necessary precondition of any fundamental change in political loyalty as shown by a desire for naturalization."[26] However, when an immigrant experienced a marked change in "status-personality," accompanied by acute insecurity, he was open to resocialization. Eisenstadt reports analogous findings in Israel.[27]

Assuming that the immigrant has been desocialized to an extent allowing for resocialization, can we predict the likelihood and extent of resocialization? Studies in Australia led Ronald Taft to identify three linked stages of resocialization, one being a prerequisite for the next stage. The three psychological stages of what Taft calls "assimilation" are satisfaction, identification, and acculturation. Satisfaction with life in Australia is a prerequisite for identification with that country, "and both satisfaction and identification were found to be prerequisites for a relatively high level of acculturation."[28] The process is more spiral than linear: A minimum of acculturation will contribute to social and occupational adjustment, which will increase the immigrant's satisfaction, and this will make him more eager to further acculturate, and perhaps then he will identify more with his new country.[29] Alan Richardson, accepting this schema, suggests that there is a pattern of initial elation, arising from novelty, social freedom, and self-justification, followed by depression, due to culture shock, nostalgia and nonacceptance by the host population, and then followed by a return to a moderated favorable evaluation. A similar pattern has been discerned among Israeli immigrants.[30] Our impression from Soviet and American immigrants in Israel, and Soviet immigrants in the United States, is that this cycle of elation, depression, and moderated favorable evaluation is quite common among immigrants. The "spiral" relationship among satisfaction, identification, and acculturation also seems to obtain among the Soviet and American immigrants.

Although attempts have been made to identify the variables most affecting the successful resettlement of immigrants — and it is not always clear whether "successful" from the point of view of the immigrant or of the dominant groups in the host society — there has been little systematic, cross-cultural testing of the actual operation and relative importance of these variables.[31] There are suggestive findings regarding the role of variables such as education and time in the new country, and we shall explore these variables in our own case, but thus far no comprehensive multivariate theory of immigrant resettlement has been developed.

Even less developed, indeed almost nonexistent, is work on political aspects of immigration. Tomas Hammar, one of the few political scientists who has studied immigration, identifies three main areas of political analysis of international migration: migration policies, the politics of migrants (how migrants behave politically), and political resocialization of migrants.[32] There have been studies of migration policies, but studies of the other two areas hardly exist. While this book attempts to deal with all three areas, one must agree with a remark made in regard to Australia, but even more applicable elsewhere, that "clearly there is room for further intensive research on migrants and political behaviour."[33] Paul Wilson, who has written a book on politics and immigrants, may have exaggerated only a bit when he wrote in 1973: "There is virtually no work being done on adult political socialization generally and the political resocialization of immigrants specifically."[34] Wilson's study of British and Italian immigrants in Brisbane, Australia, Hammar's work on immigrants and migrant workers in Sweden, and this book appear to be the only ones that are devoted to the political resocialization of immigrants, though there have been a few doctoral dissertations dealing with the politics of immigrants.

IMMIGRATION AND POLITICAL RESOCIALIZATION: METHODS OF A CASE STUDY

As will be recalled, the case study of Soviet and American immigrants in Israel was to deal with five more general issues: how the Israeli political system attempts immigrant resocialization; whether, in fact, the immigrants are resocialized; by whom are they resocialized; how extensive is the resocialization; and what parts of the antecedent political culture are more and less easily changed? Chapter 2 outlined how the Israeli system attempts to resocialize immigrants and how it has done so in the past. Attempts to socialize Soviet and American immigrants specifically will be described in forthcoming chapters.

We now turn to the question of whether and to what extent the immigrants are resocialized. In so doing we are raising the issue of the "primacy principle" and the relative importance of resocialization in adult life. We are asking which political beliefs and behavior seem to be firmly embedded by earlier socialization, and which can be replaced or eliminated by resocialization. Whereas in earlier chapters we focused on the socializing *system*, we are now turning to the *individual* being socialized, in concurrence with the argument of Jennings and Niemi "for an approach to political learning which takes into consideration the needs of individuals as well as system structures."[35] In regard to the individuals who are the targets of the socializing system and its agents, we ask four groups of questions:

Who are the immigrants and how do they change with the passage of time in the new country?

What are immigrants *able* to do politically with their political knowledge, skills, resources; does their ability change with time?

What do the immigrants *actually* do — what is the nature and degree of their political interest, partisanship, affiliation, and participation?

How do the immigrants evaluate the political system and their own relationship to it, and how do these change over time?[36]

Common to these questions is the issue of change, for immigrant resettlement and integration or resocialization is a dynamic process. In order to study a dynamic process, one should ideally measure and describe changes over time, and a few socialization studies have done this. A panel study, that is, interviewing and reinterviewing the same group at different points in time, is one way to study a dynamic process, but it involves certain difficulties. It is, of course, time consuming and hence expensive, and it raises difficult methodological problems.[37] The first problem is that of "history": events occur between the two interviews and these may account for the changes observed. On the other hand, observed changes may be due to "maturation," natural processes, such as growing older, which might well influence a respondent's attitudes and behavior. Third, the very fact that a person was interviewed once may sensitize him to certain issues and might be "contaminating" his responses during the later interview.[38] Distortion may result also from changes in the measuring instrument, so that not quite the same questions are asked in the two stages of interviewing. There is also the possibility that the change observed is due simply to the instability of the measures involved, a problem in all social science research, magnified when small samples are involved. Finally, there is the problem of regression toward the mean. Independently of any conscious or induced changes in the period between interviews, there is a *statistical* likelihood of change, as those who scored "high" on a measure are likely to score lower, and those who scored "low" are likely to score higher, as there is a general regression toward a statistical mean.

The panel of Soviet and American immigrants with which this study operated may have been affected by some of these problems. "History" should not be viewed as a problem in our context, for one of our concerns is precisely the effect of major events, such as the Yom Kippur War, on the political outlooks of the respondents. Conscious efforts were made to ascertain the effect of such events. The "maturation" problem is more serious, not because the physical aging that took place in the three years between the first and second interviews would have much effect on one's political outlook and behavior, but because in that period many respondents changed their status from immigrant to citizen, from student to employee, and the like. Since those questions that were repeated in the second state were formulated exactly as they had been in the first, there is no reason to attribute observed change to differences in "instrumentation." There is a possibility that the earlier questioning sensitized respondents to issues that were raised in later interviews, but the passage of three years filled with far more meaningful, memorable, and exciting events than an interview makes us doubt that this was the case. Our discussions with respondents and observation of their responses to our second request for an interview led us to believe that there was little, if any, of this type of biasing. Probably the most serious methodological defect of this panel is the small number of respondents, which increases the chance that the changes observed between 1972 and 1975, the two years in which the interviews were conducted, are due to the instability of the measures involved. Thus, percentage differences are not to be taken too literally, but where there are striking and consistent differences between 1972 findings and those of 1975, or between different groups of respondents, we can treat them as "real" differences, though we would not want to be as certain of the magnitude of those differences. In any case, the reader can judge for himself how meaningful and plausible these differences are. Without wishing to minimize the difficulties posed by the method used in the study and by the small number of respondents, it should be pointed out that some believe that "any experiment is valid until proven invalid. The only invalidation comes from plausible rival explanations of the specific outcome. . . . But unless one can specify such a hypothesis and the direction of its effects, it should not be regarded as invalidating."[39] In such an undeveloped field as immigrant political resocialization, it seems that even putting forth plausible hypotheses and testing them is justification enough for reporting them, providing material for further explorations in the field.[40] As Arend Lijphart has observed, "often, given the inevitable scarcity of time, energy, and financial resources, the intensive comparative analysis of a few cases may be more promising than a more superficial statistical analysis of many cases. In such a situation, the most fruitful approach would be to regard the comparative analysis as the first stage of research, in which hypotheses are carefully formulated, and the statistical analysis as the second stage, in which these hypotheses are tested in as large a sample as possible."[41]

One way of minimizing what Lijphart calls the "many-variables-small N" problem is to focus the comparative analysis on comparable cases, that is, on those similar in a large number of important characteristics that one wants to treat as constants, but dissimilar in those variables that the researcher wishes to relate to each other. This is what we have done with a group of Soviet and American immigrants to Israel. Rather than selecting a random sample from each immigration, which was not possible owing to financial and political constraints, we have chosen a group of Soviet immigrants and one of American immigrants who are alike in several important ways, but who differ in characteristics we wish to relate to each other. Thus our respondents — perhaps they should more properly be called informants — are not statistically representative of Soviet or American Jewry, nor of Soviet and American Jews who have immigrated to Israel. We cannot generalize from these groups to larger ones, but we can compare the process and outcomes of the political socialization of two types of immigrants, other things being equal. To insure that "other things" are, indeed, equal, the groups were matched on crucial variables. The purpose of this matching was "to minimize differences due to extraneous variables."[42] Thus, in his study of participant citizenship in six countries, Alex Inkeles was trying to determine whether similar *relationships* among indicators of modernity existed in different countries, whether modernization processes were similar, rather than in generalizing to national populations. He therefore drew purposive, unrepresentative samples matched to each other, in all respects but occupation.[43] I have done the same in all respects except country of origin. In their study of Moroccan brothers who settled in France and in Israel, Michael Inbar and Chaim Adler also worked with a matched and nonrepresentative sample. Their view of what they had accomplished describes our assessment of our own effort.

> We conceive of our research as a *case study*. In this perspective, the data should be seen as involving a pair of matched brothers, with sixty-five replications. . . . It is our belief that speculations based on an internally valid case study . . . have at least as much justification as speculations based on no study at all. At the very least they have the built-in legitimacy shared by all scientific endeavors: they stimulate replications of whatever findings are at the heart of a controversial argument.[44]

Since they do not know if their sample is representative, they make no such claims for it. "At the same time . . . because we do not know that it is unrepresentative either, and because the design of the study insures that, other things being equal, the results are likely to meaningful . . . , we shall dare speculate about the implications of our findings."[45]

The respondents, or informants, for this study were selected according to several criteria. As will be recalled, Soviet and American immigrants were chosen in order to see how entry into a political system from quite different "directions" affects the political socialization of the entrants. While there are no significant regional differences among American Jews, Soviet Jews are a much more heterogeneous population in many ways: they differ from each other in language (Yiddish, Russian, Judaeo-Persian, Georgian, Tat, and other Soviet languages), in dress, religious and social customs, family structure, levels of education, and historical and political experience. Thus, for example, Georgian Jews are generally less educated, and are mostly skilled and unskilled workers or clerks, with relatively large and hierarchical extended families, while Jews from the RSFSR generally have very high levels of education, are well represented in the intelligentsia, have only one or two children, and are Russian by culture and atheists by conviction. Even within European, or Ashkenazic, Soviet Jewry, there are important differences. Most basic is the difference between those from the Western borderlands of the country and those from its Slavic heartland. The former come from the Baltic republics, especially Latvia and Lithuania, and the formerly Polish areas of West Ukraine, the formerly Romanian territory of Moldavia, and the Transcarpathian Ukraine, which had been in Czechoslovakia between the world wars. Their common denominators, from our point of view, are a more recent experience with unfettered Jewish cultural, social, and political life than that of Jews in the Slavic heartland, and a shorter experience with Soviet rule, and hence with Soviet political socialization. Jews from the three Slavic republics — Russia, the Ukraine, and Belorussia — on the other hand, have been cut off from the mainstream of Jewish life and culture for more than half a century and also live in areas that have been Sovietized since at least 1921. Because of these two fundamental differences, the group of informats was selected so as to represent "Zapadniki" (Westerners) and "heartlanders" equally. The idea was to see whether the Westerners, because of their stronger Jewish identification and their shorter Soviet experience, would have been politically socialized less effectively in the USSR than the heartlanders, and how this might affect their resocialization in Israel.

Because this is a study of *political* socialization, and since there is overwhelming evidence from a great variety of political systems that men are more politically involved than women, it was decided to limit the inquiry to males. Furthermore, since education is also positively correlated with political interest and activity, the group was further narrowed to include only those with at least high school education ("middle school" in the USSR). Only those between the ages of 18 and 60 at the time of interview were included, on the assumption that younger and older immigrants would have less interest in politics. Finally, the Americans and Soviets were matched as to their date of arrival in Israel. The first set of interviews was conducted in the spring of 1972, and the earliest a respondent could have arrived was in 1968; the latest, six months prior to the interview. This was based on the notion that the post-Six-Day War immigration is qualitatively different from its predecessors, and that a person in the country for less than six months is unlikely to know very much about the political system. Finally, the immigrants were divided into two "waves": those who arrived in Israel between 1968 and 1970; and those who had come in 1971 and early 1972. This was done to allow comparison of Soviets who came before the mass emigration with those who followed and also to build in a dynamic comparison. In other words, by dividing the immigrants by time of arrival, it might be possible to measure the effects of time in Israel on whatever dependent variables we were interested in studying. In sum, the American and Soviet groups were matched on the variables of sex, age, level of education and time of immigration to Israel. All of them had been urban or suburban dwellers in the United States and USSR, and almost all were so in Israel, with the great majority residing in the three major urban centers of Jerusalem, Haifa, and the Greater Tel Aviv area.

Since it was not possible to draw representative samples, respondents were identified and located largely through a "snowball" technique among the Soviet immigrants and from the lists of the Association of Americans and Canadians in Israel (AACI). In the case of the Soviets, when a person was located who matched our demographic criteria, he was asked for the names and addresses of other male Soviet immigrants with more than secondary education who had immigrated at the time periods specified. This led to an overrepresentation of aliyah activists in our group, since we started with some of the better-known leaders of the movement and they naturally referred us to others they knew from the movement. We estimate that 20 percent of our Soviet respondents were prominently identified with the movement in the USSR. It may be that these people are more politically conscious or informed than other Soviet immigrants, at least initially.

Americans were chosen by going through the lists of the AACI, picking out those who met our demographic requirements, and then selecting a random sample of potential respondents from the new list. We had expected that Soviet immigrants might be reluctant to give us an interview, fearing that we were government agents seeking information or simply being unfamiliar with personal interviews for research purposes. Our expectation was that Americans would be much more cooperative. In fact, it turned out that of 160 Soviet immigrants approached for an interview, only 12 refused to grant one, but fully one-third of the Americans refused. Thus, 148 Soviet immigrants and 54 Americans were interviewed in 1972. We pretested the questionnaire with 22 Soviet and 12 American immigrants and even then noticed the greater willingness of the Soviets to be interviewed. Soviet immigrants were flattered by the request for an interview, taking it as an indication that a "scientific researcher" was interested in their opinions. For many, this was the first time they had ever been interviewed on social and political issues and their approach to the matter was very serious and considered. The Americans, on the other hand, may well have been jaded by years of being asked what brand of soap they preferred, which candidate they intended to vote for, and so on. Moreover, there have been quite a few studies of Americans in Israel, most of which have used the AACI lists to identify respondents.

All interviews were conducted either in Russian or in English, even when respondents claimed fluency in Hebrew. The interviews were done in the homes of immigrants, with a few taken in their places of work. With the permission of the subjects, interviews were tape recorded, although in about a dozen cases — almost all of them Soviets — permission to tape was not granted and the interview was taken down in writing. The first set of interviews was done during May-August 1972, and the second set during April-July 1975. Each interview in both years was coded separately by two coders. Significantly, although almost exactly the same instrument was used to interview the Soviets and the Americans, the Soviet interviews averaged one hour and 35 minutes, while the American interviews took only 55 minutes. Soviet respondents took more time to think about their answers and tended to give longer and more involved responses. Very often the formal interview was preceded or followed by an extensive conversation over a glass of cognac, vodka, or tea, allowing us to gather much relevant information not included in the formal instrument. This was the case with both groups of respondents.

Our experiences are remarkably similar to those of other researchers in Israel and Australia. The large-scale study of pre-1971 Soviet immigrants done by Shuval and Markus also found a great willingness to cooperate on the part of the olim and encountered no problem with respondent fatigue, though many of the interviews lasted an hour and a half and more. Markus' impression is that the immigrant is very eager to talk to an interviewer since he is lonely and has a great deal of which he wants to unburden himself.[46] Markus found the most effective interviewers to be themselves recent Soviet immigrants, and so we adopted the same technique. Research among Dutch immigrants in Australia showed that Dutch interviewers elicited more truthful information than did Australian ones.[47] Wilson, in his study of immigrant political participation, found that very similar questionnaires were answered in 45 minutes by British immigrants, but in 70 minutes, on average, by Italian ones.[48] His response rate was also very high. In Israel, among Soviet immigrants, the real difficulty seems to be not in getting them to agree to an interview, but in locating them in the first place. In the Shuval-Markus study, nearly 33 percent of the potential respondents could not be located. About 2 percent of those approached for an interview refused to grant one.[49]

When presenting the analysis of the results, we shall make several kinds of comparisons: between the Soviet and American immigrants; between Zapadniki and heartlanders among the Soviets; between the findings of 1972 and those of 1975. With regard to the last, by and large the comparison will be between responses of those who were interviewed in both years, designated as the "1972/75 group." In this way, we will be measuring change, or lack of it, among the same group of people. However, where appropriate, there will be observations concerning the group that was interviewed only in 1972. We shall see whether this group, which includes those definitely known to have left Israel, differs in meaningful ways from those who were reinterviewed successfully.

Three other data sets are referred to here. One is a national survey of Israelis conducted before and after the 1973 elections by a team from Tel Aviv University headed by Professor Asher Arian. The data used here are from a representative sample of 1,066 respondents interviewed in January 1974 and a May 1973 sample of 1,905. Several of the items on the questionnaires were phrased exactly as those on our questionnaire.[50] Along with the national sample, the 1973 Israeli electoral study included 800 recent immigrants who were interviewed separately. The survey that was taken in May 1973 included 243 Soviet immigrants who had arrived between 1969 and 1973. Of the 243, 79 came from the Baltic republics (Zapadniki, by our definition), another 79 came from the Slavic heartland, and 85 were from Soviet Georgia. They responded to a questionnaire in Russian. Those who conducted the survey claim that this was a "representative" urban sample of immigrants, though no information is available as to how the sample was drawn. American immigrants were also interviewed, but Americans, Canadians, and even Latin Americans were lumped together, making meaningful analysis impossible.

The third set of data referred to was gathered from a representative sample of 132 Soviet immigrants in the Detroit metropolitan area in the summer of 1976. Since our aims in that survey were quite different from our concerns here, the data are not very comparable and will be referred to only occasionally. It is interesting to note, however, that we found the same willingness to cooperate among the Detroit immigrants as among the Israeli ones.

We turn now to the analysis of the data, beginning with the first of our questions: Who are the respondents, what were their experiences before coming to Israel, and what changes can be observed in their social and economic condition in Israel?

NOTES

1. Tomas Hammar, "Migration and Politics: Delimitation and Organization of a Research Field," paper presented to the Workshop on International Migration and Politics, European Consortium for Political Research, Grenoble, France, April 1978, p. 16.

2. Fred I. Greenstein, "Political Socialization," in *International Encyclopedia of Social Sciences*, ed. David L. Stills (New York: Macmillan and The Free Press, 1968), Vol. 14, p. 551.

3. Jack Dennis, ed., *Socialization to Politics* (New York: John Wiley, 1973), p. 444.

4. M. Kent Jennings and Richard J. Niemi, *The Political Character of Adolescence* (Princeton, N.J.: Princeton University Press, 1974), p. 252.

5. Greenstein, p. 554.

6. Orville G. Brim, Jr., "Adult Socialization," in *International Encyclopedia of Social Sciences*, p. 558. See also his "Socialization Through the Life Cycle," in *Socialization After Childhood*, ed. Orville G. Brim and Stanton Wheeler (New York: John Wiley, 1966), p. 21.

7. Donald Searing, Gerald Wright, and George Rabinowitz, "The Primacy Principle: Attitude Change and Political Socialization," *British Journal of Political Science* 6, no. 1 (January 1976): 83.

8. See, for example, Howard Becker, "Personal Change in Adult Life," *Sociometry* 27, no. 1 (March 1964).

9. Searing et al., p. 113.

10. Howard A. Becker and Blanche Geer, "Latent Culture: A Note on the Theory of Latent Social Roles," *Administrative Science Quarterly* 5, no. 2 (September 1960): 306.

11. Anthony F. C. Wallace, *Culture and Personality* (New York: Random House, 1961), p. 161. A study of East European refugees concluded that "habits of thought are slow in subsiding; and consistent attitudes do not follow every turn of the reality on which they bear but tend to perpetuate themselves as long as the latter can be interpreted in their light." Siegfried Kracauer and Paul L. Berkman, *Satellite Mentality* (New York: Frederick A. Praeger, 1956), p. 8.

12. In his study of Australian immigrants, Michael Kahan found that non-British immigrants were unstable in their voting behavior. He concludes that the non-British immigrant "has not yet crystallized his place in the Australian polity, representing a source of support still to be permanently harnessed by either the

labor or non-labor camps." "Some Aspects of Immigration and Political Change in Australia Since 1947," Ph.D. dissertation, Department of Political Science, The University of Michigan, 1970, p. 113.

13. Becker, pp. 49-50.

14. J. J. Mangalam and Harry K. Schwarzweller, "General Theory in the Study of Migration: Current Needs and Difficulties," *International Migration Review* 3, no. 1 (Fall 1978): 8. The authors claim that "our current knowledge about migration and phenomena concomitant with migration tends to be fragmentary, noncumulative, and non-sociological" (p. 17).

15. J. J. Mangalam and Harry K. Schwarzweller, "Some Theoretical Guidelines toward a Sociology of Migration," *International Migration Review* 4, no. 2 (Spring 1970): 12.

16. Frank E. Jones, "A Sociological Perspective on Immigrant Adjustment," *Social Forces* 35 (October 1956).

17. Everet S. Lee, "A Theory of Migration," in *Migration*, ed. J. A. Jackson (London: Cambridge University Press, 1969), p. 296.

18. Stanton Wheeler, "The Structure of Formally Organized Socialization Settings," in Brim and Wheeler, p. 68.

19. Rivkah Weiss Bar-Yosef, "Desocialization and Resocialization: The Adjustment Process of Immigrants," *International Migration Review* 2, no. 3 (Summer 1968): 29.

20. Aharon Rozen and Yosef Ben-Shefer, *Elef Milim* (Tel Aviv: Akhiasaf, 1976), pp. 7, 26.

21. Ellwood P. Cubberly, *Changing Conceptions of Education* (Boston: Houghton Mifflin, 1909), quoted in Milton M. Gordon, *Assimilation in American Life* (New York: Oxford University Press, 1964), p. 98.

22. Quoted in ibid., pp. 100-01.

23. For an elaboration of this argument, see ibid., pp. 105-14.

24. Weiss Bar-Yosef, p. 43.

25. Anthony H. Richmond, *Post-War Immigrants in Canada* (Toronto: University of Toronto Press, 1967), p. 274.

26. Ibid.

27. S. N. Eisenstadt, "Studies in Reference Group Behavior," *Human Relations* 7, no. 2 (1954), quoted in ibid., p. 276.

28. Ronald Taft, *From Stranger to Citizen* (London: Tavistock Publications, 1966), p. 46.

29. Ibid., p. 54.

30. Alan Richardson, "A Theory and a Method for the Psychological Study of Assimilation," *International Migration Review* 2, no. 1 (Fall 1967): 6-14. For Israel, see Haviva Bar-Shimerling and Eliahu Louis Guttmann, "Hashnatayim harishonot beyisrael: tmurot behistaglut olim khadashim," mimeographed (Jerusalem: Israel Institute of Applied Social Research and The Hebrew University, Faculty of Social Sciences, September 1975), p. 38.

31. One descriptive attempt at outlining a model of resettlement, tested in Toronto in 1969-70, is John Goldlust and Anthony H. Richmond, "A Multivariate Model of Immigrant Adaptation," *International Migration Review* 8, no. 2 (Summer 1974).

32. Hammar, p. 6.

33. Ian H. Burnley, "The Absorption of Immigrants in Australia," in *Australian Immigration: A Bibliography and Digest*, ed. Charles A. Price (Canberra: Australian National University, 1971), p. A-38. The bibliography cites only nine studies touching on political aspects of immigration in Australia — six of them are masters or doctoral theses (at least two have subsequently been published).

34. Paul R. Wilson, *Immigrants and Politics* (Canberra: Australian National University Press, 1973). For some earlier observations on immigrants in Australian politics, see Alan Davies, "Migrants in Politics," in *New Faces: Immigration and Family Life in Australia*, ed. Alan Stoller (Melbourne: F. W. Cheshire, 1966).

35. Jennings and Niemi, p. 15.

36. The last three questions are called by Hammar "dimensions" of the politics of migrants ("Migration and Politics," pp. 30-31).

37. See, for example, Donald T. Campbell and H. Lawrence Ross, "The Connecticut Crackdown on Speeding: Time Series Data in Quasi-Experimental Analysis," in *The Quantitative Analysis of Social Problems*, ed. Edward R. Tufte (Reading, Mass.: Addison-Wesley, 1970).

38. Such an effect is reported by James W. Hottois, "Panel Research in the Study of Social Change," paper presented at the 1969 Annual Meeting of the American Political Science Association, New York.

39. Campbell and Ross, p. 123.

40. Judith Shuval, Elliot Markus, and Judith Dotan report reinterviewing 340 of an initial sample of 780 Soviet immigrants who had arrived after 1967. The second interview took place in 1974, three years after the first one. In their summary report, there is no methodological discussion of the panel. *Patterns of Integration over Time: Soviet Immigrants in Israel* (Jerusalem: Israel Institute of Applied Social Research, August 1975), pp. 11, 18, and 21ff.

41. Arend Lijphart, "Comparative Politics and the Comparative Method," *American Political Science Review* 65, no. 3 (September 1971): 685.

42. Hubert M. Blalock, Jr., *Social Statistics* (New York: McGraw-Hill, 1972), 2d ed., p. 235.

43. See Alex Inkeles, "Participant Citizenship in Six Developing Countries," *American Political Science Review* 63, no. 4 (December 1969). See also Alex Inkeles and David Smith, *Becoming Modern* (Cambridge, Mass.: Harvard University Press, 1974), pp. 48, 126-29.

44. Michael Inbar and Chaim Adler, *Ethnic Integration in Israel: A Comparative Case Study of Moroccan Brothers Who Settled in France and in Israel* (New Brunswick, N.J.: Transaction Books, 1977), p. 21.

45. Ibid.

46. Interview with Elliot Markus, Israel Institute of Applied Social Research, Jerusalem, September 9, 1971.

47. Taft, p. 28.

48. Wilson, Chapter 3.

49. Yehudit Shuval and Yehuda Markus, *Dfusai histaglut shel olai Brit-Hamoetsot*, Part 1 (Jerusalem: Israel Institute of Applied Social Research, 1973), p. 160.

50. See Asher Arian, ed., *The Elections in Israel, 1973* (Jerusalem: Jerusalem Academic Press, 1975).

6

EMIGRANTS' EXPECTATIONS AND THE REALITIES OF RESETTLEMENT

Registering as new immigrants. Courtesy National Conference on Soviet Jewry.

The immigrants' demographic characteristics and political socialization in their countries of origin are likely to affect directly their political resocialization in Israel. Therefore, in this chapter we outline some of the demographic characteristics of the immigrants we interviewed, their political experiences, their views of former countries, and changes in their social and economic status during their first years in Israel. We shall also consider the degree to which they have become "integrated" in Israel, and we will examine the characteristics of the least integrated, those who have left the country.

Information on the age structure of the Soviet immigration to Israel before 1972 is not available, but analysis of Israeli data on the immigration between 1972 and 1975 reveals that of the adults (over 18) coming from the Soviet Union, half were over 45 years old.[1] The age structure of our own sample is quite similar, but our sample of heartlanders is substantially younger than the heartlander immigration as a whole, and the sample of Zapadniki is somewhat older. Our respondents arrived between 1968 and 1972, and the Israeli national data are for 1972-75, so it is impossible to determine how similar the age structure of our group is to the overall 1968-72 immigration. It is more important to point out some possible implications of the fact that our Zapadniki are considerably older than the heartlanders. It makes it more likely that the Zapadniki will have stronger Jewish backgrounds, as many of them grew up in pre-Soviet Eastern Europe. Second, as we shall see, the Zapadniki are generally lower on the socioeconomic scale than the heartlanders, and this may be due in part to age: The younger heartlanders may have had a greater opportunity for education and social mobility. Third, if we assume that age is associated with differences in political values, attitudes, and behavior, the age difference between the two Soviet immigrant groups will have to be borne in mind when analyzing their politics. In this connection it should be pointed out that the age composition of our American respondents was more like that of the heartlanders. As we shall see, Americans and heartlanders turn out to be more similar in their political attitudes and values than Americans and Zapadniki, and the similarity in age may play some role here, though we believe that other factors are more important.

Most of the immigrants arrive in family units, especially the Soviets. In 1975, only 11 of our Soviet repondents and one American were not married. Though 18 Soviet men had married in Israel, only two of them married native-born Israelis, whereas the three Americans who married in Israel all married Israeli natives. As is the case in the USSR, European Soviet immigrant families are small. Nearly 70 percent of all Soviet immigrants, excluding Georgians and Central Asians, are members of two- or three-person families,[2] and this is the case among our respondents and those in the 1973 Israeli election study.

Because our respondents were deliberately selected to have at least high school education, they obviously differ in this regard from the total Soviet immigration, though it should be remembered that about 40 percent of the entire immigration had at least some postsecondary schooling. In our groups, 67 percent had some higher education — 47 percent obtained a degree — and the rest had high school diplomas. In the Israeli election study, 23 percent were found to have higher education, 37 percent had some secondary schooling, and the rest had only elementary education. There are significant educational differences by region, as is the case in the USSR itself. For example, over half the Georgian respondents in the Israel election study had only an elementary education (including 15 percent who had no education at all), and only 8 percent had higher education, while among the Zapadniki and heartlanders over 30 percent had higher education. It is interesting to note, however, that 55 percent of the *fathers* of the Georgian respondents had not had any formal education at all, pointing to the rapid rise in educational levels in Soviet Georgia. Among our own respondents, heartlanders have higher educational levels than Zapadniki, and Americans had more education than either group of Soviets, as can be seen in Table 6.1.

The relationship between education and immigrant adjustment is not clear. In studies of immigrants in Toronto, as well as of Soviet immigrants in Detroit, it was found that education and satisfaction were negatively correlated, and a study in Israel showed that the highly educated were overrepresented among those immigrants who left Israel. On the other hand, an Australian researcher asserts that more education is conducive to acculturation.[3] It has often been remarked that more educated Soviet immigrants, whether in Israel or in the United States, find adjustment more difficult, as their

TABLE 6.1
Educational Levels of Soviet and American Respondents
(in percent)

	Heartlanders	Zapadniki	Soviets (total)	Americans
High school	25.4 (18)*	39 (30)	32.4 (48)	3.7 (2)
College incomplete	12.7 (9)	24.7 (19)	18.9 (28)	18.5 (10)
College degree	60.6 (43)	35.1 (27)	47.3 (70)	18.5 (10)
Graduate education	—	—	—	53.7 (29)
No answer	1.4 (1)	1.3 (1)	1.4 (2)	—

*Absolute numbers are in parentheses.

cultural and vocational expectations are higher than those with less education. Thus far, there has been no convincing demonstration that the more educated leave Israel in greater proportions than the others, and our own experience was that in 1975, only one-third of those with higher education could not be located in Israel, whereas *two*-thirds of those with high school education (32 of 48) could not be found. Of course, not all of the latter are likely to have left the country, and the greater geographic stability of the more educated may be due to a lack of job mobility as much as it is to job and housing satisfaction, but this difference in the "sample survivability" of the two groups is worth noting. It may influence the changes we shall be observing between responses obtained in 1972 and those given three years later.

As could be expected from the data on education, those at the higher rungs of the occupational ladder were more easily located in 1975 than those lower down. Almost all the engineers, scientists, physicians, and other Soviet and American professionals who were interviewed in 1972 were located in 1975. The great majority were still working in their original fields, especially among the Soviets. However, of 15 Soviet artists (including cinematographers, writers, and musicians), only 2 were still in their original fields, attesting to the difficulty of changing cultures. Also, those who come as skilled workers tend to move out of that category. In 1972 there were 28 skilled workers among the Soviets, but by 1975 only 15 remained in that category. A few American professionals and skilled workers entered either business or the civil service in Israel, finding their original occupations irrelevant to the Israeli economy or not rewarding financially. It is striking that over three-quarters of the Soviet respondents were employed in the public sector, but only half the Americans were. This can be explained by several factors: Soviet immigrants are more used to public employment and more fearful of working for a private "capitalist" than Americans; the large, publicly owned enterprises are more likely to employ Soviet immigrants, especially technicians and engineers, than the smaller, privately owned ones; Americans bring capital with them, whereas Soviets do not, and this enables the former to open private businesses (about 20 percent of the Americans were in business, but none of the Soviets were).

Respondents in the Israeli election study are more evenly distributed on the occupational scale than our own respondents, due to our purposive sampling, but the Zapadniki and heartlanders in the election study are quite similar to our own respondents in that nearly half are professionals, and most of the rest are skilled workers or clerks. By contrast, only 19 percent of the Georgians are ranked as professionals, 37 percent are skilled workers, and 34 percent are unskilled workers. While 11 percent of the Soviets and 14 percent of the Americans were unemployed in 1972, only 1 percent of the Soviets and 3 percent of the Americans were unemployed by 1975. It is significant that fully 20 percent of the Soviets who did *not* reappear in 1975 were unemployed in 1972, while only 4 percent of those who were employed did not reappear. Obviously, the former are more likely to have left the country or to have moved within it.

In sum, by 1975, 71 percent of the Soviets and 53 percent of the Americans were working as professionals; 18 percent of the Soviets and 10 percent of the Americans were employed as skilled workers; and the rest were mostly clerks, businessmen, or students.

When we inquired about fathers' occupations, we discovered that the heartlanders were already pretty much second-generation intelligentsia, or sons of skilled workers and civil servants who took the "next step up" the occupational ladder into the professions. On the other hand, nearly one-third of the Zapadniki were of bourgeois class backgrounds, and the greatest number came from the East European Jewish working class. While one-third of the Americans were also from professional families, two-thirds came from the Jewish proletariat and businessmen, for the most part the small businessmen of the large urban centers. If we accept the equivalence of Soviet and American professional categories, it would appear that heartlanders achieved entry into the higher professional categories earlier than Americans, at least within our groups of respondents. This makes sense because the 1917 revolution opened enormous possibilities to Jews in Soviet Russia where the intelligentsia had largely disappeared, whereas it was not until after World War II that American society reduced the professional barriers to Jews and many Jews acquired the financial means to enter higher education.

Their education and occupational skills enabled the immigrants to achieve relatively high incomes very soon after their arrival. Comparing the income distribution of the immigrants in our study, those in the Israeli election study, and the Israeli national sample in that study, we found the income distribution among the immigrants rather similar to that of the nonimmigrant population, except that because of the high proportion of professionals among them, our group of interviewees fell disproportionately into the high income group (see Table 6.2). There are several things in this table that deserve comment. First, 16 percent of the veteran Israelis refused to disclose their income, while the immigrants, not yet terrified by the tax inspectors, were more forthcoming (though 5 percent of the 1973 immigrants did not answer the question on income). Second, since the 1972 Soviet immigrants from our study were highly educated, and excluded Georgians and Central Asians, we can understand why twice as many of them fell into the high income category as among the 1973 immigrant sample. In the latter sample, we found only 10 percent of the Georgians in the "high" category, but 25 percent of the Europeans were in it. Third, it is obvious that the Americans were far better off than either the Soviet immigrants or the Israeli population as a whole.

In 1975 the income distributions of the group interviewed in 1972 had not changed very much. However, comparison of the 1972 incomes of those who reappeared in 1975 with those who did not reveals that the former group (the "1972/75 group") had significantly higher incomes in 1972 than those who were not reinterviewed in 1975[4] (see Table 6.3). As mentioned earlier, the number of unemployed was higher among the 1972 group, and this depressed their incomes, but it probably does not account for the entire income difference between the two groups. We should not underestimate the importance of income as a factor in the satisfaction of the immigrants and their intention to stay in the country.

TABLE 6.2
Income Distribution of Immigrants and Israelis
(in percent)

	Low	Medium	High
Soviet immigrants, 1972 (our study)	25.4	32.5	42.1
Soviet immigrants, 1973 (Israeli study)	33.4	42.0	19.4
American immigrants, 1972 (our study)	12.3	10.2	77.6
Israelis, 1973 (Israeli study)	29.0	36.0	19.0

Source: Israeli data collected by Prof. Asher Arian, Tel Aviv University, 1973.

TABLE 6.3
Incomes of Soviet 1972/75 and 1972 Immigrants
(in percent)

	Low	*Medium*	*High*
1972-only group	47.6	17.4	34.0
1972/75 group	21.8	32.2	47.0

Even if low income by itself may not drive an immigrant to reemigrate, it may be both a cause of discontent and an indicator of other discontents. Low income, for example, may limit an immigrant's housing opportunities or social contacts (he may be "ashamed to be seen among people," as one put it), and it may lead to apathy, depression, or hopelessness.

THE JEWISH BACKGROUND OF THE IMMIGRANTS

Israel defines itself as a Jewish state, though with substantial non-Jewish minorities. Therefore, one might assume that immigrants with stronger Jewish backgrounds and consciousness would feel more at home and would find adjustment to the Israeli political system easier than those for whom Jewishness may be little more than an accident of birth or of someone else's categorization. For this reason we inquired about the immigrants' attachment to the Jewish religion, the Jewish atmosphere in homes in which they were raised, the language of their parents and the one they considered their native tongue, and so on (see Table 6.4). From such questions we were able to construct a summary index of the Jewish background of the respondents. (For details on this index, see Appendix A.)

In light of Soviet restrictions on Jewish culture and Judaism, it is no surprise that Americans have much stronger backgrounds than the Soviet immigrants. Similarly, having come under Soviet rule only in the 1940s the Zapadniki have stronger Jewish backgrounds than the heartlanders.[5] Even younger people born in the Baltic republics after Sovietization have greater Jewish knowledge and consciousness than their counterparts in the Ukraine or the RSFSR, for their parents have transmitted their knowledge and memories

TABLE 6.4
Jewish Background of the Immigrants
(in percent)

	Heartlanders	Zapadniki	All Soviets	Americans
Weak	62.0	28.6	43.8	3.8
Medium	33.8	57.0	46.6	57.4
Strong	4.2	14.3	9.6	38.9

directly to the younger generation, whereas in the heartland it is only grandparents or, often, great-grandparents, who retain even a fading memory of Jewish cultural life before its forced decline. How these differences in Jewish knowledge and background affect immigrant adjustment and political resocialization shall be examined later.

By their own self-definition, the Americans are considerably more religious than the Soviets. However, unlike in regard to the overall measure of Jewishness, Zapadniki do *not* display greater religiosity than heartlanders. This is the case both in our own study as well as in the Israeli election study: In our study 14 percent of the heartlanders and 4 percent of the Zapadniki called themselves religious, and in the other survey 20 percent of the heartlanders and 10 percent of the Zapadniki put themselves in this category. (In the latter study, nearly 60 percent of the Georgians defined themselves as religious, as might be expected.) Why is the proportion of religious among the heartlanders greater than that among the more culturally Jewish Zapadniki? While no definite answer can be given here, we should note that Jewishness was a more positive, "natural" identity in the Baltic, Moldavia, or Transcarpathian Ukraine, but in the heartland it was largely a state-imposed category devoid of positive content. For heartlanders, especially the young intelligentsia among them, the discovery of the content and implications of their Jewishness was a difficult, often dramatic, process; for most Zapadniki it was an assumed and unquestioned part of their existence. Among some members of the intelligentsia in the 1960s, especially in Moscow and Leningrad, a search for spiritual alternatives to the materialistic doctrines of Marxism-Leninism led some to experimentation with Buddhism, Hinduism, and Russian Orthodoxy. Like many of their counterparts in the West, some Soviet intelligentsia searched among the more mystical doctrines for alternative ideologies. As one traveller to the Soviet Union observed: "It has ... become fashionable among Moscow intellectuals — especially among Jews, as a Jewish intellectual from Leningrad wryly put it! — to cultivate ties with Russian Orthodox priests. ..."[6] There were quite a few instances of conversion by young Soviet Jews to Russian Orthodoxy — some of these people are now in the West — and others delved into more exotic religious philosophies.

The emergence of the Jewish national movement toward the end of the 1960s slowed this trend, as the national movement attracted dissatisfied *intelligenty*. Many discovered that Jewishness and Jewish cultural history were inextricably bound up with Judaism as a religion, and they found that their search for spiritual alternatives could be satisfied with Judaism. Some of the leaders of the Jewish national movement became practicing Orthodox Jews, and even some prisoners in labor camps began to observe Jewish rituals, despite severe punishment. Yosef Mendelevich, who served ten years for his part in the Leningrad hijacking affair, refused to eat non-kosher food or violate the sabbath and wore a skullcap during his term at hard labor. By the time Mendelevich and others arrived in Israel, they were fully committed to religious Judaism. Several entered academies of religious learning, and others settled in religious areas.

Among the Zapadniki, however, most of the nationally conscious had not come to Jewishness by way of dissatisfaction with Soviet ideology or spiritual life, but simply as an outgrowth of their upbringing, largely in nonreligious, but culturally Jewish and linguistically Yiddish, homes. They arrived at Zionist conclusions, not through a process of abstract reasoning or intellectual search, but as a result of their almost visceral desire to live a Jewish cultural and social life. For them, Zionism was enough. Coming to Israel meant not the fulfillment of an abstract program of principles such as national self-determination or of religious ideals, but rather the possibility of living among Jews and within a Jewish cultural environment.

There are two other findings that require comment. The Soviet constitution guarantees freedom of religion (at least for adults) as well as freedom for antireligious activity, but subsidizes only the latter, investing millions of rubles annually in antireligious propaganda and agitation. The antireligious effort is as old as the revolution itself, and, from all reports, most people in the USSR today, especially in the European urban areas, are not religious believers. The Soviet state encourages not just agnosticism or lack of belief, but urges its citizenry to become militant atheists and to fight "religious manifestations" actively. However, surprisingly few of our respondents identified themselves as "antireligious," though as urban, educated people they would have been the most likely of all Soviet citizens to be atheists, and perhaps militant ones (see Table 6.5). Thirty-six percent said they were "neither religious nor traditional," but only 16 percent declared they were "antireligious," implying conscious and perhaps active opposition to religion. This relative lack of militant atheism may be due to a general disinterest in actively fighting religion, often reported in Soviet publications. Some Soviet surveys have found that the majority of Soviet youth consider adherence to a religious faith among the lesser "social evils."[7] These immigrants, undoubtedly generally positive toward their Jewish identities, may well be aware of the close link between the Jewish religion and Jewish identity, and even if they are not personally religious, they are not committed to an antireligious posture, since that could be taken as an anti-Jewish one.

If the proportion of antireligious is surprisingly low, that of "traditional" is amazingly high. Over one-third of the respondents in both our study and the Israeli election one defined themselves as "traditional (or said they "observe a little" in the Israeli election

TABLE 6.5
Religious Self-Definition of Immigrants
(in percent)

	Heartlanders		Zapadniki		Soviets		Americans	
	1972	1975	1972	1975	1972	1975	1972	1975
Religious or very religious	14.4	6.4	3.9	6.5	8.9	6.5	26.5	34.4
Traditional	33.3	41.9	37.7	21.7	35.6	29.9	45.3	37.9
Neither religious nor traditional	33.3	45.2	37.7	60.9	35.6	54.5	18.9	17.2
Antireligious	14.5	6.5	16.9	10.9	15.8	9.1	3.8	10.3
Other	4.3	—	3.9	—	4.1	—	5.7	—

study). We were puzzled by this finding, and so in 1975 we asked respondents to explain what they meant when describing themselves as "traditional." The great majority explained that even in the USSR they had tried to observe some Jewish holidays, not out of religious conviction, but because of a desire to identify as Jews, to "maintain the tradition of our people," or simply out of sentiment for the memory of childhood experiences. One person from the Ukraine described how they would have a party around Hanukkah time, and after an old man who remembered something of the ritual lit a few candles and said a blessing, there would be general merriment and much vodka. This, he explained, was an example of "carrying on the Jewish tradition."

Between 1972 and 1975 there was an increase in the proportion of Soviets who saw themselves as neither religious nor traditional, with a concomitant fall-off in the "traditional" category. This is most pronounced among the Zapadniki. Closer analysis reveals that this is not due to differences already existent in 1972 between the 1972/75 and 1972-only Soviet groups, for both had pretty much the same religious profile. In other words, we seem to be observing a real shift in the immigrants' religious self-definition. A possible explanation lies in the meaning of "traditional" to the Soviets. It might be that some Zapadniki who observed customs and traditions in the USSR for the reasons we cited found that in Israel this no longer was considered "traditional" behavior, but was simply part of the custom of the country, even of the "secular" population. "Traditional" (*mesorati*) is used in Israel to mean someone who may be religious and even observant of many rituals, but not all or most of them. Since Orthodoxy is the dominant mode of religious expression in Israel, those who do not conform fully to it tend to be thought of as "traditional," while nonreligious people are thought of as "secular" (*khiloni*). So what was considered "traditional" in the USSR is not the same as the understanding of "traditional" in Israel. The Zapadniki therefore revised their self-definition and saw themselves as neither religious nor traditional. Among the heartlanders, who seemed to show an increase in *both* the traditional and nonreligious categories between 1972 and 1975, there really was no such change, since there were more 1972/75 (those reinterviewed in 1975) heartlanders in these categories than the 1972-only group. Moreover, in the USSR heartlanders were less likely to act "traditionally" than Zapadniki because of the cultural differences between the two groups, and so they did not have to revise their notions of traditionalism in Israel to the extent that the Zapadniki did.

Among the Americans, the 1972/75 and 1972-only groups differed markedly on religious identification. Of the 1972/75 group, 70 percent called themselves "religious" or even "very religious," but only 13 percent of the 1972-only group did so. Obviously, among those who could be located in 1975 the religious were greatly overrepresented, remembering that only 27 percent of the original 1972 group had defined themselves as religious. We note that in 1972, Americans with a weaker Jewish background tended to say their expectations of Israel had not been fulfilled, while the opposite is true of the religious. This finding fits well with a widely accepted belief that religious Americans are much more likely to adjust in Israel, and settle permanently, than nonreligious immigrants. After all, many of the Americans immigrate precisely for religious reasons – to find religious fulfillment, to live in a religious community, to give their children a religious education – and these needs are met in Israel. Moreover, the religious immigrants tend to be middle and lower middle class in America, and their material expectations and "needs" may be more modest than those of the more affluent. The religious come from the big cities, where many lived in apartments, so the adjustment to Israeli cities and apartment living is easier for them than for the exsuburbanite Americans who find it much more difficult to replicate their life-styles.

The immigrants were asked to describe "the Jewish atmosphere in your parents' home when you were growing up." As could be expected, two-thirds of the Americans and three-quarters of the Zapadniki came from strongly Jewish homes, but only one-third of the heartlanders described their parents' home as "strongly Jewish" or even "quite Jewish." While nearly two-thirds of the Zapadniki said their parents spoke Yiddish at home, only about one-third of the heartlanders remembered Yiddish as the language of the house. Not a single Baltic immigrant remembered Latvian or Lithuanian as the language of his parents. Interestingly, among the 1972/75 group, especially the heartlanders in it, the proportion of Yiddish speaking parents is greater than among the 1972-only group. Overall, in the homes of half the Soviet immigrants, Yiddish was the language spoken.

As for the immigrants themselves, only 15 percent claimed Yiddish as their "native language" (*rodnoi iazyk*), while two-thirds called Russian their native language. Among the Zapadniki, however, slightly more than half gave Russian and one-fifth listed Yiddish as their native language. Again, despite the fact that Latvian and Lithuanian are official languages of those Baltic republics, and the titular nationalities there stress the use of those languages, only two of the Baltic immigrants claimed them as their native language. Traditionally, the Baltic languages were considered rural, peasant languages, and the urbanized Jews did not often adopt them as their first language; but even in the Soviet era, when large numbers of Lithuanians and Latvians migrated to the cities, Jews, while gaining facility in these languages, did not adopt them as their own.

Though more than 20 immigrants said Yiddish was their native language, only 9 claimed to have read the sole Yiddish journal published in the USSR, *Sovetish haimland*. (Only 5 percent of the Detroit immigrants said they had read it.) Even those who asserted that they had "never" read it were quite prepared to offer an opinion of the journal. Comments ranged from the mild "an agitational journal" to the more pungent "the usual quisling journal. It's not even worth having an opinion about. It's a Soviet counterfeit piece, a collaborationist journal." While "official" Jewish culture in the Soviet Union was rejected by the immigrants, a significant number were active in unofficial − and unapproved − Jewish activity, which took on an increasingly political coloration in the 1960s and 1970s.

Almost all the Americans were members of at least one Jewish organization in the United States, though only 11 listed a Zionist organization among their memberships. There being no legal Jewish organizations in the USSR, Soviet immigrants were asked whether they had been affiliated with a group that "concerned itself with the Jewish problem." Nearly two-thirds claimed such affiliation, and almost half said they were active in such a group. Contrary to what one might expect, there is no difference on this score between the 1972/75 and 1972-only groups. Actually, we have the impression that Zionist activism in the USSR does not predict to successful integration in Israel. Some of the most active fighters for aliyah in the Soviet Union became among the most "difficult cases" in Israel, and, as we shall see, some left Israel altogether. For some, the clash between an ideal formulated in the abstract while in the USSR and the realities of daily life in the Jewish state was so sharp that it led to bitter disappointment and frustration. For others, the transition from militant activism in the subculture of Soviet dissidence − with all its danger, excitement, and drama — to a workaday existence in a state where they became just another Soviet immigrant — was too deflating and disappointing. As Shuval noted of an earlier group of European immigrants, "the frustration of disappointment has a deeper effect on the active Zionists than it does on those who came to Israel with no ideological commitment."[8]

The somewhat greater proportion of activists among the heartlanders confirms our impression that many of the Zapadniki were not, for the most part, militant fighters for the program and principles of the Zionist movement, but rather people whose modest aim was to live among "their own kind" in a state of their own. However, among the activists the Zapadniki had become involved before the heartlanders. Nearly 50 percent of the Zapadniki claim to have been actively involved in a politically oriented Jewish group before the 1967 Middle East War, but only 20 percent of the heartlander activists were involved at that time. In fact, nearly half the heartlanders did not become actively involved until after 1970, the year of the Leningrad and other trials. More Zapadniki than heartlanders were "thinking about aliyah" before 1967, and more claimed they had made the decision to emigrate before then, though they could not act on it until 1968 and after. Though nearly two-thirds of the Americans say they "thought about aliyah" before 1967, the actual decision came after 1967 for almost all of them. Of course, the time span between decision and immigration could be much shorter for the Americans than for the Soviets, whose departure from the USSR depended primarily on the Soviet government, not on themselves.

IMMIGRANT BACKGROUNDS AND "WAVES"

In order to assess the effects of time spent in Israel, respondents were divided into those who had arrived in Israel between 1968 and June 1970, and those who had come between January 1971 and May 1972. There are some meaningful differences in the Jewish backgrounds of the people in each "wave" of immigration. The American group was evenly divided into those who came in the first and second waves (27 people in each), but 79 percent of the Soviets (n = 117) came in the second wave and 21 percent (n = 31) in the first, reflecting the fact that the mass emigration from the USSR did not begin until March 1971. Americans and Soviets who came in the first wave tended to have better Jewish backgrounds than those who came later. It turns out that earlier arrivals from the USSR felt less at home there, had stronger Jewish backgrounds, and were more "pulled" to Israel than "pushed" from the USSR. The same can be said for the first-wave Americans. The Soviets and Americans of the first wave were more likely to be located in 1975 than the later immigrants. Perhaps this can be understood in terms of a kind of "critical period of adjustment." It is generally believed that if the immigrant "sticks it out" for three years or more, the probability of his leaving Israel declines greatly. Those who were interviewed in the spring of 1972 had already been in the country at least two and a half years, and in 46 cases, at least three years. Most of the "dropouts" of the first wave had probably left by the time of the interview, whereas the second wave was still "shaking down."[9] Moreover, people in the first wave are more likely to be in permanent housing than people in the second.

The sample interviewed in the Israeli election study came somewhat later than our respondents. Nearly 90 percent of the Israeli election sample arrived in 1971-73, so they had been in Israel at most two years when they were interviewed (two-thirds had been in Israel less than two years). This should be borne in mind when discussing their responses to questions about Israeli politics. Knowledge of Israeli politics is more limited among this group than among our own respondents, who also have the advantage of higher educational levels. The Israeli sample does resemble our own, and indeed the overall pattern of immigration, in that those from the Slavic heartland came to Israel later than those from the Baltic republics and other Western border areas.

EMIGRATION AND IMMIGRATION: EXPERIENCES IN THE "OLD COUNTRY" AND ADJUSTMENT IN THE NEW

The immigrants' experiences in the "old country" must have had an influence on their resocialization in Israel. Each individual had a unique family and personal experience, and each had his subjective evaluation of life experiences in the United States or the USSR. However, we can generalize about attitudes displayed by the respondents toward their native countries and make some inferences about how these condition their reactions in Israel.

Not surprisingly, Americans have a far more positive view of the United States than Soviet immigrants do of the USSR. None of the American respondents renounced his American citizenship. Even those who said they came to Israel in order to escape negative aspects of American life remained interested in American affairs and were anxious to see the United States solve its problems. When asked in 1972 what was the major problem facing the USSR, a number of Soviet immigrants replied that they were not at all interested in the USSR or its problems. Not a single American gave a similar response when questioned about American problems. Among those who did comment on Soviet problems, nearly one-fifth pointed to foreign policy issues, especially the Sino-Soviet conflict (the "yellow peril," as one put it), and a similar proportion saw the main problem as the necessity for the ruling elite to control a discontented population. By 1975, one-quarter of the Soviet respondents claimed to be unconcerned with the problems of the USSR and would not discuss them. One respondent's rambling answer captures the frustration and hopelessness expressed by many. He thought the main problems of the USSR were "the border with China and the problem of liberalization." He went on to say:

> The whole system doesn't mesh well. I was a member of the presidium of the Society for Soviet-German friendship and I had to meet with all kinds of people, even some from Norway. . . . But the USSR doesn't interest me, I hate the system, I don't believe in it and will never do so. Jews might live there peacefully for a few years, if they are completely assimilated, but if something should happen, they will be completely annihilated. When there's a dictatorship, you can't even know their problems. Their problems are theirs, not our business, let the Soviet people solve their own problems, we have enough of our own. I don't want to give them advice. Let the intellectuals like Solzhenitsyn do so. . . . Under a dictatorship it is forbidden even to give advice.

Those who were willing to identify and discuss Soviet problems were pessimistic about the possibility of solving them, and few believed that Soviet citizens could play any role in the solutions. Over half the immigrants thought the citizenry can have no effect on Soviet problems, but about one-fifth did suggest protest, organization, and even revolution. "Only a revolution will help over there," said one, and another added that the solution is "revolution, but this time without Jewish participation!" Some expressed doubt that a revolution would occur, since "a nation has to be thoroughly enslaved in order to revolt, and compared to the past, people live better in the USSR. The intellectuals can't put up with things as they are, so they come out for democracy, but I don't think the people can change anything in the near future." The picture that emerges is of hostile indifference to Soviet problems, or pessimism that they can be solved, especially by "ordinary people."

Soviet immigrants compared the Soviet government unfavorably with the Israeli. While over half the Soviets saw the Israeli government acting generally on behalf of the people, only 8 percent saw the Soviet government doing so, and nearly 80 percent said it acted solely in accord with its self-interest. Similarly, according to 75 percent of the immigrants, Soviet bureaucrats serve their own interests primarily and neglect those of the people. Generally, Soviet immigrants tended to see the Israeli government as more beneficent than extractive, while American immigrants perceived the reverse.

In 1972 the American problems most often cited by Americans were racial conflict and national disunity over the Vietnam War. Three years later nearly 30 percent of the respondents identified economic problems as the most serious ones facing the United States, no doubt in light of the economic difficulties experienced after 1973. The racial issue faded somewhat, but the problem of defining the national purpose and the goals of foreign policy remained prominent in the minds of the immigrants. Some were disturbed by cultural and social trends, and there was frequent reference to drug abuse. One respondent perceived a "social and cultural revolution going on." He explained that "what happened is that many younger people have no respect for the older generation . . . and many have a sense of ennui, of tiredness and fatigue and despair with life in general. . . . They're turning to drugs, or passivity, or extremism, all undesirable. There are also extreme forms of behavior in sex. . . . I feel American society is kind of sick." He felt that "only a shift back from the left" will alleviate the situation, which can be aided by "the actions of responsible people who don't allow everybody to do their own thing." Many of the respondents echoed this fear that things are changing in America, away from traditional values and to extreme behavior in many areas of life. A successful professional identified the fundamental problem as "the vanishing of the middle class. When you have a strong middle class you have a stable society, and we're becoming a society of haves and have nots in America. . . ."

A young immigrant, on the other hand, thought that America's problem was that "the country is too materialistic. There's not much social value there." It is striking that, no matter their viewpoint, most Americans referred to America in terms of "we" or "our," whereas none of the Soviet respondents used these terms and quite naturally referred to the Soviet people as "they." Moreover, in contrast to the Soviets' view that the citizenry could do little or nothing to solve the problems, nearly all the Americans expressed ideas about how the citizens could help solve the problems America faces.

As might be expected in a group of urban, well-educated Jews, the majority (57 percent) of the Americans said they had identified as Democrats while in the United States, with most of the rest "Independents" (most of whom "leaned" toward the Democrats), and only 2 percent Republicans. Nearly 40 percent claimed to have participated in peace or antiwar demonstrations. At the same time, the great majority in both 1972 and 1975 agreed with the view that "blacks in America have gone too far in their demands." A high proportion of the 1972/75 group lived in the older neighborhoods of the large cities, and they were the ones most likely to be faced with the problem of "changing neighborhoods," street crime, and competition for jobs from blacks and other racial minorities.[10] This 1972/75 group was also more negative in its view of the contemporary situation in the United States, most of them agreeing in 1972 that "everything considered, life in the U.S. was better ten years ago." The view that American life has deteriorated is also more typical of those who came in the earlier wave. In sum, those who thought American life had deteriorated tended to be religious people from the large cities, well beyond their student years, arriving soon after the 1967 War, and somewhat conservative in their politics, though identifying themselves as Democrats (undoubtedly those of the Lyndon Johnson variety, rather than the McGovern and Eugene McCarthy brands).

The contrasting attitudes of Soviet and American immigrants toward their native countries may stem in part from their very different perceptions of anti-Semitism in those countries. While there is no way to measure accurately the intensity, frequency, scope, and geographic-cultural distribution of anti-Semitic attitudes in the USSR, we can ascertain the subjective perceptions of anti-Semitism of the respondents (see Table 6.6). The contrast between the two

TABLE 6.6
"Did You Feel Anti-Semitism in the United States/the Soviet Union?"
(in percent)

	Heartlanders		Zapadniki		Soviets		Americans	
	1972	1975	1972	1975	1972	1975	1972	1975
Often	35.2	40.6	34.2	21.7	34.7	29.5	5.7	6.7
Sometimes	50.7	34.4	42.1	45.7	46.3	41.0	41.5	36.7
Rarely	11.3	21.9	14.5	23.9	12.9	23.1	32.1	50.0
Never	2.8	3.1	9.2	8.7	6.1	6.4	20.8	6.7

groups of immigrants can be seen more immediately in Figure 6.1, based on responses to the question given in 1975.

FIGURE 6.1
Encounters with Anti-Semitism

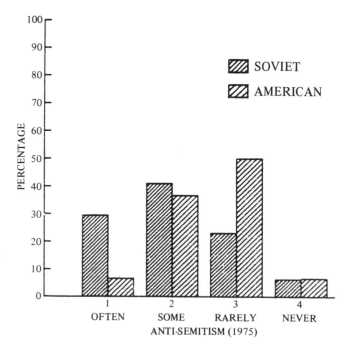

Source: Compiled by the author.

That the Soviets encountered anti-Semitism more frequently than Americans should come as no surprise. Less expected is the finding that heartlanders reported somewhat more frequent anti-Semitic encounters than Zapadniki. This turned out to be the case also with respondents in Detroit who were asked the same question. Why should this be so? Is there really "more anti-Semitism" in the Slavic heartland than in the Western territories? There is no strong *prima facie* reason for believing so. Is it because there is some relationship between education and experiences of anti-Semitism? The heartlanders in Israel as well as in Detroit had higher educational levels than the others, and they reported more frequent anti-Semitic encounters. It turned out that there was such a correlation between higher education and more frequent experiences of anti-Semitism among our Israeli respondents, irrespective of area of origin. The better-educated were more likely to feel anti-Semitism since they aspired to more responsible and prestigious positions and were exposed to the unacknowledged, but very real, Soviet quota system, and to others feeling that Jews were "intruding" where they do not belong. Moreover, for the past decade and more, admission to institutions of higher education has been difficult for Jews, and the very fact of having higher education increases the chances for exposure to anti-Semitism. A third possibility is that those who had a weaker Jewish identification and did not consider themselves Jewish in any way except legally — precisely those who had acculturated into the Russian culture and who had higher education, especially in the heartland — were more disturbed by anti-Semitism than others. After all, anti-Semitism robbed them of what they desired above all: to be accepted on an equal footing by the cultural and social elite of Russian society.[11] Jews who "know their place" do not attempt "to pass" or to "intrude" to the same extent and may not be so pained by anti-Semitism. They are more likely to expect it and to have no illusions on that score.[12]

Why the changes in the Soviet immigrants' perceptions between 1972 and 1975? The data for the 1972/75 and 1972-only groups are nearly identical, and when the responses of the same individual in both years are compared, it becomes certain that the perceptual change is real. In 1975, 23 people reported less frequent anti-Semitic experiences than they had three years earlier, and 13 reported more frequent encounters. Are unpleasant memories fading, as immigrants begin to remember mostly the "good things" in their previous countries? Or perhaps in 1972 did the immigrants feel a greater need to reassure themselves that they had made the right decision in emigrating, and so they dwelt more on the darker sides of their lives in the USSR, remembering more of the unpleasant incidents? We have no way of answering these questions, but offer these as hypotheses.

Among the Americans, the change in three years is in the opposite direction. They are no longer as sure as they were in 1972 that they "never" encountered anti-Semitism, and some who thought in terms of "never" now thought in terms of "rarely." It is possible that in 1972 Americans felt psychological pressures that were opposite to those felt by the Soviets. American olim may have felt it necessary to prove that they were not "running away" from anything in the United States but were coming to Israel of their own free will, that they were "pulled," not "pushed." Americans in Israel will often talk about how good things were in the States, especially in their first few years when they are frustrated by the problems of resettlement, but later on, as the initial traumas are successfully overcome and one becomes more acclimated, the tendency to do this diminishes. By 1975 they were not so sure that they had "never" run into anti-Semitism in the United States. They no longer had to explain – even to themselves – why they came to Israel.

Closely related to perceptions of anti-Semitism are feelings of "belonging" in one's former country. Again, one finds that Americans said they had "felt at home" much more frequently than the Soviets. In both 1972 and 1975, when over 80 percent of the Americans said they had felt at home in the United States, less than 40 percent of the Soviets made the same claim, and over 33 percent of the Soviet respondents said they had "never" felt at home in the USSR. Among the Soviets, the 1972-only group felt more at home than the others, and this was especially true of the heartlanders, who felt at home to a greater extent than the Zapadniki. The latter, like many ethnic Balts, may have seen the Soviet system as something alien imposed upon them after World War II, rather than something they had grown up with. This estrangement was compounded by the Jews' feeling that they were not part either of the local non-Russian or Russian cultures, whereas Jews from the Slavic heartland had a greater involvement in and affection for Russian culture. Some heartlanders who despised the political system still retained admiration and even affection for Russian culture and its traditions. As one put it: "In recent years I have seen two different countries: the Russia of Tolstoy and Solzhenitsyn, and the Russia of Stalin and Brezhnev." On the other hand, despite their professed comfort in being part of American society, American immigrants reveal at times that they were fully aware of their marginality. This was apparent in a comment of one of the respondents: "One of the things that gives me a kind of perverse pleasure is that this is the one country where Jews are a majority and the people who are uncomfortable are the minority group, which is what we are in the rest of the world. . . . This is the one country where the shoe is on the other foot."

Though many of the Soviet immigrants express strong negative feelings toward their country of origin, they do see some aspects of the Soviet Union in a positive light, and this has been the case with other groups of Soviet emigrés. In their study of pre-1971 Soviet immigrants, Shuval and Markus asked respondents to say whether they had suffered a loss, made a gain, or experienced no change in several areas, as a result of their move from the Soviet Union to Israel (see Table 6.7). The greatest loss was experienced in social life and the greatest gain was in the standard of living. As we shall see, our respondents reported similar changes.

The Harvard Refugee Project, sponsored by the U.S. Air Force and involving some 3,000 people who left the USSR during and

TABLE 6.7
Changes in Five Areas in the Transition from the USSR to Israel
(in percent)

	Type of Change		
	Loss	*Similar*	*Gain*
Nature of social life	38	33	29
Family relations	29	50	21
Social status	28	40	32
Standard of living	22	27	51
Influence in the family	7	70	23

Source: Yehudit Shuval and Yehuda Markus, *Tahalikhai hizdahut im hakhevrah haytisraelit*, Part 2 (Jerusalem: Institute of Applied Social Research, 1974), p. 41.

after World War II, was the first, and remains the largest, study involving Soviet emigrés. The project found that even among the most anti-Soviet emigrés there were some valued and appreciated aspects of Soviet life. While "many reject[ed] the notion that there is *anything* desirable" in the Soviet system, it turned out that there were institutions and ways of doing things in the USSR that were evaluated positively. Among our respondents also there were those who claimed there was nothing Israel could learn from the USSR, but they, too, missed certain features of the Soviet system. Therefore, like the Harvard Project authors, we can conclude that the "assertion that 'nothing' of the present system should be kept . . . can be regarded more as an expression of generalized hostility toward things Soviet than as evidence of literally complete rejection of the entire Soviet institutional apparatus."[13] The Soviet refugees of the 1940s tended to evaluate positively the social welfare services provided by the state, as well as the nationalization of the economy. Nearly 30 years later, similar sentiments were expressed by a very different group of Soviet emigrés. Over half of our Soviet informants cited welfare services, or civility and culture, as areas in which Israel could learn from the USSR. As time goes on, Soviet respondents begin to emphasize "culture" less, perhaps because they have become acculturated in Israel, and talk more about efficiency, hard work, and devotion to one's job, claiming that the Soviet employee and worker are more conscientious than their Israeli counterparts. A former Muscovite, who while still a young man was imprisoned for Zionist activity — his family was caught teaching Hebrew, using the Israeli Communist newspaper as a text — provided a good summary of the major points made by the respondents: "There is a low cultural level here, pornography, vulgarity, poor upbringing [*vospitaniie*] of the youth, a lack of intellectual interest among young people, poor relations among certain strata of the population, crime . . . poorly developed social services. . . ."

Regarding the relationships among people, another former Muscovite said, "*chelovek cheloveku volk* [men treat each other like wolves]. There a man is not alone. Here they are terribly indifferent to each other. I miss the collective where I work, where they respect me." It seems that human relations at the workplace appear especially inferior in Israel to those in the USSR. "In the Soviet Union it was understood that work is not just an obligation, but a need. Moreover, work was valued more from a moral point of view. . . .

The Russian people have an especial respect for work. The Jewish people has just started working and does not yet have a sufficient respect for labor." Another comment: "At work there isn't the slightest feeling of mutual relationships, of warm human relations. I lost my group, my spiritual cocoon. Of course, there are good people here, but it's a different life, we sing different tunes. . . ." One complaint was simply that "there are no meetings at work, so how can I get to know my coworkers?" In a similar vein, it was observed that "there [in the USSR] people are less isolated at work. Here I live in one city, work in another, and have my friends in a third." In trying to explain the differences in human relations between the two countries, one immigrant offered the following thesis:

> There, life is hopeless and dark. So this relationship among people, relations of "the soul," is very developed there, and this spruces up [*ukrashchaet*] the life of the individual. In Israel, a man is free, but alone, in his own little corner. In Russia there is no freedom, so in order to escape the influence of the environment, they hide in a group of two, or twenty, or thirty people. I noticed this phenomenon in the labor camp. When life became unbearable, we banded together in groups, and such strong friendship developed in these groups, and there was so much self-sacrifice, that spiritual contact was stronger than in family relations. This was the natural defense of the soul against tyranny. . . . This cannot be repeated in a free country . . . here life is too multifaceted [*mnogogranna*], but that's the price you pay for the freedom of the West.

The Soviet immigrants feel that medical services should be administered by the state and be provided free of charge. Education is seen as a major Israeli shortcoming, and it is perceived in broad terms, including the education of adults as to proper public behavior. One person understood Israel's problems as due to the fact that "Israel is an Eastern country, while Moscow and Riga are in Europe." Nevertheless, Israel should strive to emulate the European models. More frequent prescriptions were to crack down on violators of public order and sanitation, to introduce more discipline into the schools, or as one put it, "to establish a strong legal system, to teach people to respect the law, and if this does not work, teach them to fear the law." Several respondents suggested that "you need some dictatorship here, otherwise there will be nothing left in a few years." "Hooligans" and violators of public order were to be dealt with more firmly, and children were not to be spoiled. Even the press was criticized for being too free and irresponsible. "They publish in the papers what we don't need to know, they wash dirty linen in public, and the enemy can make use of this."

There were others who took a very different view of what could be learned from the USSR. As mentioned, some thought there was "nothing" worth emulating, or all that could be learned was negative: "How not to build socialism, how not to implement an ideology, how not to allow one party to have such influence, how not to have a gargantuan and expensive bureaucracy. . . ." Some mentioned somewhat mundane lessons that could be learned: certain technical processes, some production techniques, and so on. At a more abstract level was the telling insight that what was missing was "concrete goals. In the USSR, the goal was to emigrate. Here, clothes and a car – that isn't enough of a goal."

Americans were much more homogeneous in their assessment of what Israel could learn from the United States. Nearly 70 percent stressed efficiency, with another 10 to 20 percent citing civility, tolerance, and politeness. One American explained his feelings rather colorfully.

> Having come here I understand why in America they had the Boston Tea Party when they rebelled against the Stamp Act [sic]. I never understood what the Stamp Act was until I came to Israel and realized that every piece of paper you sign has to have stamps affixed to it and they have to be paid for in advance, and each page has to have the right stamp on it, and you have to buy it at the corner candy store. Now the woman there may be selling a chocolate candy bar to someone and you've got to stand in line, and when you finally get back with the stamps, they might not be the right denominations for the right pages, and if they are, they tell you the fellow who was supposed to take care of it has now gone out to tea. . . .

Other Americans miss a "middle road in religion" and feel Israelis could learn tolerance and pluralism from the American Jewish community and the United States generally. Consumer protection, public sanitation, higher ethical standards (for example, "individuals not cheating on taxes") are also cited as positive American lessons to be learned. Israelis are seen as narrow minded, not open to new ideas, lacking in civic pride and responsibility, and too tolerant of public wrongdoing. One person asserted that "there's a significant minority of people here who are really obnoxious, overly aggressive, almost bordering on being psychopathic, horning in on you in line, etc." "That's why it's important to me to retain my Americanisms while becoming Israeli," was one conclusion drawn. Trying to be fair-minded, one respondent remarked that "with it all there are a lot of things Americans can learn, too, from the standpoint of a human feeling and contact in doing things – that's missing in the States, so it's not all one-sided."

From the critical comments about Israel, we may deduce what aspects of Soviet and American society the immigrants value. Those who had been arrested in the USSR or whose parents were purge victims were, of course, more hostile to the Soviet system than the others.[14] But even they missed the close interpersonal relations and free welfare services of the USSR, whereas the Americans remembered fondly what they perceived as civility and efficiency. Obviously, immigrants may also miss familiar foods, sights, even sounds and smells, but we have focused on systemic characteristics that are widely admired, even by those who express hostility or indifference toward their former countries.

We have examined some of the attitudes toward their native countries displayed by the immigrants and have gotten a glimpse of some of their activities there that might give us clues to their political socialization, thereby allowing a fuller understanding of the political transformations, or at least challenges, they will face in Israel. In order to complete the picture of relevant experiences before coming to Israel, we must inquire, as best we can, into the motivations of the immigrants for leaving their home countries.

MOTIVATIONS FOR EMIGRATION

The reasons people migrate from one place to another have intrigued scholars for a long time, though there is no widely accepted general and systematic theory of migration. N. H. Frijda offers a "three-factor theory of emigration," which seems to explain our particular cases rather well. The first factor is dissatisfaction, usually of an economic nature, with the migrant's native land. Second, "a special stimulus to leave the community, either through the pull of ties with emigrants or through the push arising from orientation which differs from that of the community and a lesser degree of adhesion to that community and the people who comprise it." The third factor is a "more specific motive . . . in the shape of longings which already contain the germ of 'somewhere else.' "[15] As ethnic minorities – and in the case of the Soviet Jews, disadvantaged ones – the immigrants may well have felt "a special stimulus to leave the community." As conscious and, for the most part committed, Jews, they may have been "pulled" to the reborn Jewish state.

Aliyah is suffused with emotional, ideological, and political significance, so it is difficult for Israelis to speak about it in value-free terms. It is especially difficult for immigrants, since they feel pressured to conform to society's image of aliyah as a noble act stemming from idealistic motivations. Furthermore, the immigrant is often trying to justify his immigration to himself, rationalizing what has turned out to be a difficult, even if ultimately rewarding, experience. Discussions of motivations for immigration must therefore be treated with caution, and questions about motivations are likely to involve some telling interviewers what the respondent thinks they want to hear, or what the society expects them to say. Shuval, Markus, and Dotan, in discussing aliyah motivations with successive waves of Soviet immigrants, observed that "motives for immigrating were . . . remarkably similar in all groups, despite the fact that the most recent groups are somewhat less Jewish in their background and are more alientated from Soviet society."[16] David Katz's American immigrant respondents gave "Zionism" or "Jewishness" most often as the primary reason for their aliyah, with only 8 percent citing dissatisfaction with life in America. "Pull" reasons accounted for more than two-thirds of the responses.[17]

Soviet emigrés who have gone to countries other than Israel displayed a similar uniformity in citing their motives for emigration. In its 1977 survey of over 1,000 emigrés, the U.S. Congress' Helsinki Commission found over 50 percent saying they left because of "discrimination on the basis of nationality," 31 percent cited the desire to be reunited with family abroad, and 35 percent stated "because of limitations on my civil rights" (because multiple answers were permitted, the total exceeds 100 percent).[18] In our study in Detroit we found that family reunification, political alienation, and the desire to escape anti-Semitism were the most frequently cited reasons for leaving the USSR.[19]

Among our 1972 Soviet respondents, 63 percent cited variations on a Zionist theme as their primary motivation for aliyah, 9 percent cited family reasons, 8 percent mentioned political alienation, and others talked about the desire to live among Jews, to escape anti-Semitism, or to improve their economic situation. Among the Americans, there was a wider range of motivations cited, with only 28 percent speaking in terms of Zionism, and significant numbers giving childhood socialization, religion, prior impressions of Israel while touring, or simply "adventure" as motivations for leaving the United States and settling in Israel. (Six of 24 Americans in the 1972-only group say they came for "adventure," but only one of 30 in the 1972/75 group cited this. Presumably, having had their true adventure, the others left the country.) Nearly three-quarters of the Americans had visited Israel before making aliyah, half of them more than once, and this is quite typical of the American aliyah generally.[20]

Some explained their immigration in abstract, philosophical, and principled terms, while others gave more personal, emotional, or even cynical explanations. Some of the most persuasive statements cited more than one reason. A young, religious American described his motivations as "basically Zionist. We felt that Israel was our homeland and a good place to bring up our children. And also we were from New York City and things are very bad there." Some came not so much for themselves, as they saw it, but for their children: "We don't spend as much time worrying about the ideals of our children as we would have in the States." Others were frank to say that their motivations were less than Zionist-idealistic:

> I was a district manager for a company and I reached a point where I didn't care to go farther and Israel offered a challenge in language and a new way of life. I'm not Zionistic. I feel myself Jewish from a social point of view. Economically, it was to my advantage, since I had saved money. . . .

A very different response came from a resident of Jerusalem.

> I was involved in Jewish War Veterans . . . and I saw that American Jews are very apathetic about what was happening in the States. In 1966 there was a convention in Israel and this was a pilot trip for me. Then I volunteered for the Six-Day War. I came in 1968 with a group

and toured a lot, and was very impressed with Israel. Finally, my wife agreed to the idea, and a year later, after being at aliyah meetings, we became interested in the Neve Ilan Moshav and joined it. . . . We left the moshav group a few months later and became regular immigrants.

Soviet immigrants tended to talk in more abstract and principled terms when explaining their immigration. They spoke of "repatriation of the Jewish people to our homeland," the achievement of "national self-determination" and the like. Some cited specific events that triggered their decision to emigrate, a decision that could not be implemented until years later. A medical doctor said he decided to emigrate "in 1947, when there was a revolution in the United Nations and Israel was established." Another gave 1948 as the year of decision. "Since 1948 I have understood that I am a temporary resident in the USSR and I lived accordingly. I was and am a Jew. I believe that all Jews should live in Israel." A former resident of the Baltic area says he decided to go to Israel in 1936 "when Hitler became the chancellor in Germany [sic]." A young man who dabbled in dissidence in Moscow said: "I thought seriously about emigration in 1968, during the occupation of Czechoslovakia, in which I took part myself."

Others cited no specific events, but said that the idea of leaving the USSR was a long-standing one. "I heard it always in my parents' conversations. That's how I was raised. I imagined Israel to be paradise on earth, and I was intent on going to Israel since childhood, I don't know why. Perhaps it's because of anti-Semitism in Russia, which I felt constantly. . . ." Others also claimed that they always felt "estranged" in the USSR, that their parents had "explained everything" to them. One said that "the experience with Gomulka showed that sooner or later it would be necessary to leave."[21] Finally, there were those who made no attempt to conceal the fact that their immigration was not of their own doing, or that they regretted it. One man said simply, "my wife nagged me" [*zhena sagitirovala*], while another said "my family forced me to come." Yet another said, "I came by mistake. There was no other place to go, so I came here."

Sometimes people find it easier to talk about why others do something than to explain why they have done the same. This is why we asked why *other* Soviet/American immigrants decided to make aliyah. To this query the respondents gave more complex and less "idealistic" answers. Political alienation, job opportunities, running away from problems, and seeking adventure were more frequently mentioned as typifying *others'* reasons for going to Israel, while "Zionism" was mentioned less frequently. Some Soviet newcomers distinguished among different geographic and cultural groups, or among different age groups in analyzing motivations for emigration. An immigrant from Estonia suggested that most Georgian immigrants were "pulled" to Israel, but the "Tbilisi intelligentsia" was "more pushed." "As for those from the Baltic and Russia, they are basically pulled. They want to see an Israel such as the one they had imagined. A third group — that's the one from Odessa, unfortunately, a large number. They want to improve their material situation. They are more pushed than pulled, and they are not what the country needs."[22] One veteran of the Communist underground in Lithuania, a Party member for 37 years until his son applied for emigration and then he was expelled, explained emigration in terms of "hatred for the Soviet power, which despite the beautiful theory, is completely counterfeit." "Roughly speaking," explained another, "you can divide them into three groups: those younger people who see their Judaism as a form of democratic protest; the middle-aged from the Baltic and the Ukraine who still have some traditions and idea about Zionism; and the Moscow and Russian Jews, also middle-aged, but whose attitude toward Judaism is different from that of the younger generation."

Americans tended to divide motivations simply into attraction to Israel for idealistic reasons, on the one hand, and "running away" from problems in the United States, on the other.

> The Americans I've talked to have immigrated for many reasons. Some for noble reasons, like the experiment of building a new country, working on the land, and so forth. Others, for reasons such as my own, religious reasons, if you want to call them noble or not. Others come for reasons which I consider not only not noble, but doomed to failure, namely, they're running away from something and I think there's no end to running. Not only that, but I think you can better solve your problems in the country you've been born in, and in the language you speak fluently, and whose culture you're used to. . . . The person who is running can't solve his problems here. I think what will happen is he'll just have more problems on top of his other ones, and he'll leave, and he'll be worse off than when he started.

Among the problems most frequently mentioned were marital difficulties, the fear that children would be involved with "the drug scene," the loss of a job, or the search for a mate. A few cited disenchantment with political and social trends in the United States. "Why do others immigrate? If they're like me, they're disenchanted with the United States. . . . I wanted something to believe in. It's hard to believe in that country. A nation is a bunch of people who share a common idea. America isn't this any more." Even among the first wave, more motivated by Zionist and religious considerations and having thought about aliyah for some time, the decision to move was triggered by the dual perception that Israel was in a better situation than it had ever been, and that, after the 1967-68 urban riots, America was in crisis.

By 1975, when questioned about motivations for immigration, the respondents began to talk about *themselves* in terms more similar to the ones they had used to talk about *others* in 1972. Among the Soviets, only 12 percent cited "Zionism" as their primary motivation, with a similar proportion mentioning social pressure, political alienation, and family considerations. Among the Americans, too, there was a decline in the proportion who talked in terms of Zionistic motivations. Since the 1972/75 group had been the one to explain immigration in terms of Zionism to a slightly greater degree than the 1972-only group, this change is quite definite. One can think of two plausible explanations for this change: either Zionist rhetoric was seen as the "appropriate" response in 1972 and was no longer perceived this way in 1975, or it was an authentic response in 1972, but after living several years in the Zionist state it had lost much of its meaning, since the ideal has been fulfilled on the personal level and people forget how much it meant to them outside of Israel. The humdrum of daily life tends to obscure abstract ideals, and one's concerns tend to be more prosaic. A "Zionist" response may be no longer be seen as appropriate because "Zionism" has a somewhat mocking connotation in Israel and is seen by many as an insincere posturing, covering up less-than-idealistic motivations and calculations. Immigrants, who are at first chagrined to learn that "Zionism" is used cynically by many, may have learned to avoid the term after three to five years in the country. Still, in 1975, 62 percent of the Americans and 43 percent of the Soviets maintained that most immigrants were "pulled" rather than "pushed" to Israel, though 46 percent of the Soviets (23 percent of the Americans) thought they were "equally pulled and pushed."

EXPECTATIONS OF ISRAEL

One's motivations for emigration should influence one's expectations of the host country. In Australia it was found that "when emigration from the native land had been difficult, assimilation was facilitated. Similarly, it was facilitated if the immigrant came to Australia through being unhappy in his own country rather than being attracted to Australia, presumably because of lower expectations."[23] The evidence from Israel points in the opposite direction: Those who came to Israel primarily to escape difficulties at home were less likely to be happy and to stay in Israel.

Among the Soviet immigrants, 40 percent talked about a Jewish environment and culture as their primary expectation of Israel, while another 25 percent mentioned personal, professional, or economic expectations. However, among the 1972/75 group, 45 percent cited "Jewish" expectations, and only 13 percent cited personal ones, whereas among the 1972-only group, only 33 percent cited Jewish expectations, while 22 percent cited personal ones. There were also more people in the 1972/75 group who gave political freedom as their prime expectation of Israel. The reasonable assumption is that the expectations of the 1972/75 group were better fulfilled than those who could be located only in 1972; a Jewish milieu and political freedom were more easily found in Israel than professional or economic achievement. It should be pointed out, however, that in 1975 there was a definite shift among both Soviets and Americans in their recollection of their expectations of Israel. Especially among the heartlanders and the Americans, there was a drop in the proportion citing "Jewish" expectations, and a rise in the proportion who spoke in terms of personal, professional, and economic fulfillment. This may be the result of response set being weaker in 1975, or because the more abstract and idealistic expectations have faded in memory. Those expectations that have been fulfilled — political freedom and Jewish fulfillment — recede in the memories of the respondents, as they have been fulfilled almost "automatically," with little effort on the part of the newcomers. This shift in response distribution over the three years is parallel to the one observed in stated motivations for emigration.

To what extent have the immigrants' expectations been fulfilled in their estimation? From Table 6.8 it is clear that the expectations of the Zapadniki have been fulfilled to a greater extent than those of the heartlanders. We return to the hypothesis previously suggested: The Zapadniki had a less idealized and abstract conception of Zionism; their basic desire was to live in an environment where they would not feel as aliens, and thus their expectations were "more modest" and more easily fulfilled than those of the heartlanders, whose concept of Zionism was at once more abstract and more ambitious or demanding.

It can be seen that among the Soviets between 1972 and 1975 there was a substantial rise in the proportion of those whose expectations had been "completely" or "mostly" fulfilled (from 52 to 82 percent), though among the Americans the rise was more modest. However, in both cases fewer people were willing, in 1975, to say that their expectations had been "completely" fulfilled. This may indicate that the initial euphoria pointed to by Australian scholars has worn off, though the immigrants still feel that, on balance, their expectations have been met. It is also possible that there was a greater perceived need to tell the interviewer in 1972 that "all" expectations had been fulfilled. Actually, the apparent rise in the proportion of those whose expectations were fulfilled was due to the differences already present in 1972 between the 1972/75 group and the 1972-only group. Table 6.9 compares the two groups of respondents. The 1972/75 group, those who were still in the country

TABLE 6.8
Extent to Which Expectations Have Been Fulfilled
(in percent)

	Heartlanders		Zapadniki		Soviets		Americans	
	1972	*1975*	*1972*	*1975*	*1972*	*1975*	*1972*	*1975*
Completely	39	31	46	31	43	31	31	7
Mostly	5	45	13	55	9	51	17	45
Somewhat	39	21	28	12	34	16	23	31
Not at all	17	3	12	2	15	3	29	17

TABLE 6.9
Fulfillment of Expectations, 1972/75 and 1972-Only
(in percent)

	Soviets		Americans	
	1972/75	*1972-Only*	*1972/75*	*1972-Only*
Completely fulfilled	42.3	40.1	33.3	28.0
Mostly fulfilled	14.1	6.0	22.2	11.3
Somewhat fulfilled	36.6	28.7	18.5	28.2
Not at all fulfilled	7.0	25.2	25.9	32.5

and could be located three years after the first interview, judged the fulfillment of their expectations more positively in 1972, and the relative dissatisfaction of the other group may explain their absence three years later.

Some of the immigrants' comments about satisfaction emphasized the points made about the relationship between the nature of one's expectations and the chances that they would be fulfilled. One Zapadnik, who said his expectations were "completely" fulfilled, defined his expectation simply as "to feel myself at home." An American explained this in greater detail:

> I expected to be able to live without having to justify my existence as a Jew. . . . When I worked in the States, and when I didn't show up on a holiday, or I left early on Friday [in order to observe the Sabbath] I had to explain myself, and most people understood, but I still had to explain it, and the burden of proof was on me. I felt that in coming to Israel, I wouldn't have to do this any more.

Several Soviet immigrants differentiated between their material expectations, which they said were fulfilled, and their "spiritual" or "moral" expectations, which were not. "My economic expectations have been fulfilled, my moral ones, no. Everyone here is divided according to the country from which they came, and only children can overcome this. If this continues, I will try to leave Israel." A dentist from the Transcarpathian Ukraine defined his expectations as "being able to contribute my efforts to the good of the country, and that people would understand me. I hoped for a country without bureaucracy." Had these expectations — which sound as if they had been defined after he had come to Israel — been fulfilled? "Not in the least." Analysis of our other data reveals that the Soviet immigrants whose expectations were not fulfilled had a low sense of political efficacy, tended not to be members of Israeli organizations, felt at home in the USSR and identified as "Russians" in Israel, and favored political systems characterized by elite control of decisions and strong leadership.[24]

In 1975 the immigrants were asked what had disappointed them most about Israel. Inefficiency and purposelessness were mentioned most often by the Americans, and the Soviets added to these "disorder, lack of discipline." Another disappointment cited by both groups was the lack of enthusiasm for aliyah or, especially, olim. Said one American, "I've seen a great deal of very distorted views of the 'privileges' that are extended to immigrants and claims of abuses of those privileges, when, in fact, these 'privileges' represent nothing compared to the sacrifices made by people from Western countries to come to live here." Waste, inefficiency, environmental pollution, and a lack of idealism and of ethical conduct were other disappointments listed by Americans. Another complaint was that the evils that plagued America were infiltrating Israel — crime, juvenile delinquency, drugs, "the things that pushed us out of the States." "Keeping up with the Joneses" was another such "imported" problem. "When we came here four and a half years ago, you didn't see the Pontiacs and Chevys on the roads. The society has changed from a slow, easygoing society to a fast, affluent one. My boss lives in an exclusive area in Ramat Gan, and there everyone has Pontiacs. If you don't have a Pontiac or a Cutlass, you're a nothing, a nobody." Others cited "small things" of daily life — "to drive in Israel is a very punishing experience." And one summed it up simply, saying, "Jews in general pretend to know it all."[25]

On the other side, the most positive aspects of living in Israel are seen by Soviets and Americans as living among one's own people. An equal number of Soviet immigrants cite freedom and democracy as the major benefit of Israeli life, while family relations and the friendliness of people are mentioned by Americans. Some cite the excitement and vitality of life in Israel, while others talk about the informality of the people. These evaluations do not change over three years, and they are made equally by Zapadniki and heartlanders.

It is interesting to compare our findings with roughly analogous ones from the panel study of 1969-70 immigrants, conducted by the Ministry for Immigrant Absorption. In that study, immigrants were queried about satisfaction with their standard of living in Israel, their social lives, and with their leisure time use. They were also asked about their satisfaction with their "situation in general." Results of the latter question are presented in Table 6.10. It can be seen that after the first two months, when "euphoria" and "culture shock" may both be at work, there is little change over time in immigrants' satisfaction. The question asked here is roughly similar to our own inquiry about the fulfillment of expectations, and referring back to Table 6.8, we find that the Soviets' assessment of the extent to which their expectations have been fulfilled, three years after the first interview, is remarkably similar to the responses regarding satisfaction given three years after the 1969-70 immigrants arrived in Israel. The Americans in our study, on the other hand, were considerably less satisfied than the Soviets or the 1969-70 immigrants, and the same MIA study showed that a higher proportion of Americans leave the country than any other major immigrant group.

When all is said and done, whether or not an immigrant will be happy in the new country and judge that his expectations have been met, is not determined by the kinds of factors we have been considering — demographic characteristics, motivations for emigration,

TABLE 6.10
Immigrants' Satisfaction with Their "General Situation"
(in percent)

	After Three Years	Two Years	One Year	Six Months	Two Months
Completely satisfied	25	22	25	22	33
Fairly satisfied	53	56	48	47	36
Not so satisfied	15	15	19	20	19
Not at all satisfied	7	7	8	11	12

Source: Central Bureau of Statistics, *Monthly Bulletin of Statistics — Supplement* 22, no. 12 (December 1971): 136.

views of the "old country," and expectations of the new — though it is *influenced* by them. For in addition to these considerations, one must take account of personal traits and predispositions. Eisenstadt points to "the predisposition to change" as crucial to successful adaptation. Those with no predisposition to change were found to identify positively with the new country only if they could maintain their social status and income as it had been in their country of origin.[26] Of the several types of immigrant groups and their styles of adaptation that Eisenstadt sketches in the 1950s, the "self-transforming cohesive group" seems to characterize the Soviet and American immigrants of the 1970s:

> They have many criticisms to make of the absorbing country and its institutions, but these are derived from its basic social values which, on the whole, they generally accept. Their criticism is directed mostly against: a) inefficiency on the part of the officials; b) growing political influence and bureaucracy in the social structure; c) lack of readiness on the part of the old inhabitants fully to accept the new immigrants; d) the concentration of political and bureaucratic power among the old inhabitants. . . . Consequently, there is more pronounced criticism of the government, the Jewish Agency, etc., positive identification being mainly oriented towards the Jewish people, the State as such, etc. They believe, however, in the possibility of correcting these things. . . .[27]

This type of immigrant group, according to Eisenstadt, is likely to be "absorbed" successfully.

Satisfaction is crucial to resettlement because it both reflects what has gone on in the past and presumably predicts to the future of the immigrant and his relationship to the host society. A study of Dutch immigrants in Australia found that while length of residence was not significantly correlated with either satisfaction or "assimilation," "it was highly correlated with identification and acculturation for those subjects who were satisfied. In other words, once a certain level of satisfaction is reached, the longer the immigrant stays, the more assimilated he becomes."[28]

By 1975, four-fifths of the Soviet immigrants seemed to have crossed a threshold of satisfaction that should have enabled them to become more "assimilated" or "integrated" into Israeli society. Only slightly more than half of the Americans had done so, and perhaps even those who were still in the country were not moving rapidly toward "assimilation." Of course, much depends on how we define "assimilation" or "integration." We shall soon take up this question, but in order to do so we must look at some objective indicators of changes in the economic and social status of the immigrants and in their culture. Analysis of the immigrants' subjective perceptions of how they have adapted to Israel and of their evolving socioeconomic status should complete the answers to the first and second of our basic questions: Who are the immigrants and how are they changing, and what are immigrants *able* to do politically with their developing political knowledge, skills, and resources?

THREE YEARS AFTER: SOCIAL, ECONOMIC, AND CULTURAL CHANGE

It has been pointed out that already in 1972 both Soviet and American respondents had attained income levels that were higher than that of the Israeli population as a whole. This remained true in 1975. We also found that in 1972, the 1972/75 group had substantially higher incomes than the 1972-only group. We were able to construct an index of socioeconomic status (SES), which included income, education, and self-ascribed social class. In both 1972 and 1975 Americans ranked higher on SES than Soviet immigrants, and heartlanders scored ahead of Zapadniki (see Table 6.11). We also found that the 1972/75 group was higher in SES than the 1972-only group, and this was true for all groups of immigrants, though SES alone may not be sufficient to predict whether immigrants will stay in the country or stay in the same location.

Just as important as measures of SES in ascertaining the status of the immigrants are the immigrants' own feelings about their standing

TABLE 6.11
Means and Medians of SES Scores for 1972/75 and 1972-Only Groups

	Heartlanders		Zapadniki		Soviets		Americans	
	1972/75	1972	1972/75	1972	1972/75	1972	1972/75	1972
Means	6.938	6.282	6.717	6.000	6.808	6.157	8.867	8.458
Medians	7.167	6.000	7.300	5.417	7.227	5.786	9.333	8.500

in the new society. The MIA studies and the Shuval-Markus project demonstrate that while Soviet immigrants generally experience a rise in their standard of living, they do feel some losses in other areas. Among our own respondents, 75 percent of the Americans in both 1972 and 1975 claimed that their standard of living had declined as a result of their move to Israel, and less than 10 percent felt it had risen. By contrast, 69 percent of the Soviets felt that their standard of living had improved over what it was in the USSR. The less dramatic improvement in standard of living perceived by the heart-landers is understandable, because the Moscow-Leningrad intelli-gentsia, a large proportion of the heartlanders, had a higher Soviet standard of living than the somewhat less educated Zapadniki.

Respondents were asked not only about their standard of living but about their "social status," as they perceived it. Had it changed since coming to Israel, and if so, in what direction? There were no differences between the 1972/75 and 1972-only groups. More Zapad-niki than heartlanders thought their social status had risen, though nearly half of both groups saw no real change in their social status. Again, the Russified intelligentsia of the heartland enjoyed a higher social and cultural status in the USSR than the provincial Zapadniki, and now they found themselves living on the edges of Israel's major metropolitan centers, and also taking a loss in their vocational stand-ing. The vocational and residential status of the Zapadniki had not changed as much, and as people with higher Jewish consciousness, they may have felt more accepted by Israeli society. In 1972 half the Americans perceived no change in their status, and the rest were evenly divided between those who saw a decline and those who saw it as having risen. However, by 1975 only one American felt his social standing had declined, 16 felt it had stayed the same, and 12 saw it as having risen. This perceived rise in status may have resulted from the fact that the Americans were no longer seen as olim, as immi-grants, but they were still regarded as "Anglo-Saxon," and therefore as having high status. One person explained that "in America I was part of the great middle class. It has changed partly because of being labelled an 'Anglo-Saxon,' as well as having a small American income."

THE MEDIA AND ACCULTURATION IN ISRAEL

Israel has a highly developed press, with several morning dailies and two large-circulation afternoon dailies, all in Hebrew. In addition, there are daily newspapers in English, Arabic, Russian, Polish, Romanian, and Yiddish, and other newspapers in French, German, Spanish, Hungarian, Georgian, and other languages. The great majority of the non-Hebrew newspapers are owned by a holding company that has been controlled by the Labor party. These newspapers are generally skimpier than the Hebrew ones and are obviously designed for those immigrants who will not "graduate" to a Hebrew paper (the Jerusalem *Post* is something of an exception, since it serves a high-status immigrant community, and, more importantly, it is widely disseminated abroad and, within Israel, to the foreign community). Russian-language publications flourished with the arrival of the Soviet immigration. There are several journals in Russian, and, at present, a daily newspaper (at one time there were two dailies). The journals are quite varied, with some directed toward the Zionist intelligentsia, others toward a mass public seeking entertainment, and still others have a religious character. Some of the publications are sponsored by political parties, while others are published by individuals or organizations of immigrants.[29]

In 1972, when there were two Russian dailies, about half our Soviet respondents claimed to read two newspapers. Very few Soviets or Americans read no newspaper at all, but the Soviets claimed to read more than the Americans. The 1972/75 Soviet group read more newspapers than the other Soviet immigrants. Even in 1975, 56 Soviet respondents said they read one or two Russian-language publications, and 22 claimed to read three or four, so that not a single Soviet immigrant had ceased reading Russian altogether.

We inquired about the exposure the immigrants had to the Hebrew language media, surely a measure of their Israeli acculturation. Three things stand out: in 1972, the Zapadniki were most attentive to these media; by 1975, the heartlanders were just as attentive; in both years, the Soviet immigrants were more attentive than the Americans, who nevertheless also showed a considerable increase from 1972 to 1975 in their exposure to non-English media. The Soviets assimilated Hebrew more rapidly, but all groups turned to the Hebrew media as time went on, even though they may have continued to read in their native languages. Among both Soviets and Americans, the 1972/75 group showed more attentiveness to the media, but this group substantially increased its exposure to the Hebrew media over the course of three years. The trend toward Hebrew can be seen in the following data: in 1972, 72 percent of the Soviets reported that they were reading Russian newspapers primarily; by 1975, exactly the same percentage said they were reading Hebrew newspapers primarily. Among the Americans, the trend is weaker: 35 percent read Hebrew in 1972, and in 1975 this grew to 43 percent. Among the Soviets, over 50 percent read *Nasha strana*, the daily newspaper, 25 percent read the weekly *Klub* — "an informative magazine, on a popular, non-intellectual level, which provides the monolingual reader with current, newsworthy material from a variety of Western sources," as Edith Frankel characterized it —[30] and 10 percent read the weekly *Nedeliia*, which supported the Likud party and was highly critical of the Labor government. (*Nedeliia* claimed a circulation of some 3,000 in 1976.)

About half the immigrants listened to the radio or watched television several times a day. Americans were somewhat more frequent television watchers, perhaps because there were many English-language programs (with Hebrew titles). Both Americans and Soviets substantially increased their radio listening and TV watching over the three years, and the proportion of television viewing rises as the immigrants become more affluent and able to purchase a set and as they can get away from the English, Russian, and Yiddish broadcasts on the radio to the television, where Hebrew and English (and Arabic) are the only languages. Just over half the Soviets said that Israeli politics was their main interest on the radio and television, with foreign news next. Among the Americans, Israeli politics took third place after foreign news and economic affairs. This is another clue to the Americans' greater interest in events in the United States and elsewhere, and the Soviets' greater desire to be involved in Israeli society and its affairs. The great majority of all groups of respondents believed that the information supplied by the Israelis is trustworthy. Given the frequent exposure to the media and the faith that the immigrants had in it, one would assume that the media played a significant role in the general and political socialization of the newcomers.

While the media may be an important agent of socialization, it does not seem to be the exclusive, or even primary, source of political information for the immigrants. Only among the 1972/75 group of Americans is there a strong correlation between media exposure and the level of political information (gamma = .47, Tau b = .40, signif. = .001). By 1975 this relationship disappeared, perhaps because additional sources of information — friends, colleagues —

were available. Using our 16-item index of political information (including items on political personalities and their party affiliations, political parties, government ministers, and so on), the immigrants scored as shown in Table 6.12 on level of political information. (For details on construction of this index, see Appendix B.)

Because in the United States they had free access to information about Israel and because of their socialization before coming to Israel, Americans had a lot more information about Israeli politics than Soviets, despite greater Soviet interest in politics after having arrived in Israel. However, the 1972/75 Americans had considerably more knowledge of Israeli politics than the 1972-only group: While 53 percent of the 1972/75 group scored "high," only 29 percent of the others did. (These data are not in Table 6.12.) The 1972/75 Soviets were also better informed than their fellow immigrants, though the difference was not as great as in the American group.

Heartlanders and Americans scored higher in 1975 than they had in 1972, but Zapadniki did not. Moreover, Zapadniki scored lower than heartlanders even in 1972. One would have expected Zapadniki to know more about Israeli politics, given their stronger Jewish backgrounds and generally lesser ambivalence about becoming Israeli. However, they seemed to know less about Israeli politics than the others and did not improve their knowledge with time. The reason for this may be that they were less educated than the others, or perhaps our earlier hypothesis is relevant here: The Zapadniki did not view Israel in the same political-ideological way that the heartlanders did. They were more interested in living in a Jewish society than in a Jewish state, to make an artificial distinction for a moment.

TABLE 6.12
Levels of Political Information
(in percent)

	Heartlanders		Zapadniki		Americans	
	1972	*1975*	*1972*	*1975*	*1972*	*1975*
Low	38.1	28.1	39.0	34.8	26.0	3.3
Medium	33.8	40.6	39.0	50.0	31.6	13.3
High	28.2	34.4	22.0	15.2	42.6	83.3
1972 mean score	9.042		8.987		10.093	

They were less concerned with the principles, programs, and politics of the state than they were with daily life in a Jewish milieu.[31]

Americans were able to identify more Israeli politicians and their correct party affiliations than the Soviets, and they were able to name more political parties (in fact, twice as many, on average, as the Soviets). The Soviets generally named the two major parties, Labor and Likud, and the Communist party, whereas the Americans were much more familiar with the minor parties. In 1972, one-quarter of the Soviets could not say which party Premier Golda Meir was affiliated with, though in both years the prime minister and ministers of defense and foreign affairs were the most frequently mentioned as "prominent personalities." It is interesting that the minister for immigrant absorption was mentioned by only 10 respondents in 1972, and none in 1975. Apparently, he was not seen as very relevant to the immigrants. Between 1972 and 1975, two years before the Likud came to power, there was an increase in the frequency of mention of the Likud, especially among the Soviets, and of Menachem Begin, its leader.

Asked to describe how decisions were made in the national government in Israel, over 50 percent of the Soviets could not answer the question in 1972. By 1975, over 80 percent were prepared to offer an explanation of the decision-making process. Those Soviets who did answer the question in 1972 tended to identify the formal institutions of decision making, the Knesset and the cabinet, and to describe the formal procedures followed. Americans, by contrast, focused on an often unspecified "elite," and they generally expressed negative opinions about how decisions were made. By 1975 the Soviets were sharing these views. "In the Labor party there is a narrow group of people, linked together by family and financial ties, who take decisions without having a critical attitude toward the problem." Another Soviet newcomer said: "Sapir [then the finance minister] decides — sometimes it's someone else — and then the Knesset rubber-stamps it." An American talked about the "inner cabinet which meets every Sunday night" as the real ruling body (what was known as "Golda's kitchen" up to 1974). One American said that outside the defense area "the decision-making is about the sloppiest batch of compromises and political deals I have ever seen in all my life. And it is a direct result of a parliamentary type government in which a coalition is the only way to keep power." Neither the Americans nor, of course, the Soviets were used to the kind of decision making typical in coalitions, and both found the process less than satisfactory. The point is, however, that after three years and more in the country, the immigrants had a fairly realistic notion of how decisions were made, and had gotten beyond the formal descriptions of the process.

Thus, by 1975 the immigrants had greatly increased both their exposure and attention to the Israeli media, even the Hebrew media, and they had gained considerable information about Israeli politics. However, it is not clear that there is a causal relationship between the two, and there may be important sources of political information other than the media. We have also seen that the 1972/75 group was in 1972 more attentive to the media and better informed on politics. Together with its higher income and employment levels, stronger Jewish background, and more positive reasons for immigration to Israel, this group seemed already in 1972 to be better integrated into Israeli life and to have a better probability of staying in Israel and "making it." Americans, while more knowledgeable about certain aspects of Israel, were nevertheless linguistically and culturally assimilating less rapidly than the Soviets. Within the Soviet group, the initial cultural advantages enjoyed by the Zapadniki were wiped out by the rapid progress the heartlanders made in three years, a trend that might be due to the different levels of education of the two groups.[32]

BEYOND RESETTLEMENT: THE INTEGRATION OF THE IMMIGRANTS

The resettlement of immigrants entails initially the largely technical tasks of providing housing, employment, minimal linguistic training, and other means for survival in a new society. If we look beyond physical survival, we are dealing with the question of "integration" or "absorption," namely the extent to which immigrants become "part of" the society in something more than the physical sense. How do we know when immigrants have become "part of" the new society — how do we know why they are integrated? There are two ways of approaching this question, one from the viewpoint of the immigrant, and the other from the viewpoint of the host society. The first involves the subjective feelings of the immigrant, and the second involves developing criteria or measures according to which a person can be judged as integrated or not. Theoretically, it is possible that an immigrant would feel — and assert — that he is "part of" that society, that he has been accepted by it for what he is, and that he is comfortable in it even though he does not speak the language of the new country (or does so minimally), has no friends other than people from his own country of origin, and has not adopted the values and morals of the host society. This same person will be regarded by others as unintegrated, since they posit certain criteria — language, dress, social contacts, values — for what they consider "integration." Conversely, it is possible that a person will meet all the outward criteria for integration, and yet not feel himself fully accepted by or "part of" the society, as some of our American respondents have acknowledged. Moreover, societies are so large, complex, and differentiated, that it is almost always misleading to talk of integration into "a society." In reality, people — and not only immigrants — generally become "part of" a *sub*society, a "*sub*culture," a group within society whose values and life patterns are not shared by others in the same society. The attempt to determine the nature and extent of immigrant integration is therefore fraught with difficulties.

Shuval and Markus list nine types of measures of "absorption,"[33] but in their study they used only three types of measures. These combine instrumental and subjective ones, the former actually measuring integration from the viewpoint of the host society, and the latter from the perspective of the immigrant. Since absorption or integration is a process, one ought to take measures at different points in time, in order to see whether the process is, indeed, taking place, and at what rates. We have seen that there is marked linguistic change among our respondents over three years, and that by the end of that time the questions of housing and employment have been pretty much settled. On the other hand, there does not seem to be much spatial dispersal of the immigrants, but this is more a function of the housing market than of sociological factors. As we shall see, the immigrants feel that most people in the host society still regard them as "new immigrants," and the information we have cited on Israeli attitudes confirms this impression. It is more difficult to deal with measures that test the psychological adaptation of the immigrant and his adoption of the norms and values of the new country. Because of our reluctance to accept a partial view of integration — as defined *either* by the host society *or* by the immigrants — we include these in our discussion of integration.

This discussion includes the subjective assessments of the immigrants themselves: whether they feel themselves "Israeli" or "Russian" or "American," whether or not they wish to lose their previous identities and become "Israelis," whether they think of themselves as "new immigrants," whether they see themselves living in Israel in the future. It also includes indicators from the society's perspective — the immigrants' social contacts, their linguistic assimilation, their conformity to Israeli patterns of political and social behavior. There are two cautionary notes that must be struck about this discussion. First, as Shuval, Markus, and Dotan put it, not only is it impossible to determine "how long" it takes for an immigrant to be "integrated," since this "depends on the substantive issue involved and on the measures of integration being considered," but integration is not a "uni-dimensional process." That is, "an immigrant can show positive integration in some life areas and negative integration in others. The overall process is not uni-dimensional nor is there any one 'best' measure of integration. . . . At different phases of the process, some dimensions are emphasized more than others."[34] Second, even with the combination of "subjective" and "objective" measures, one cannot be certain about the integration of any particular individual, at least as he himself would judge it. Shuval, Markus, and Dotan argue that Israel is so pluralistic and consists of so many subcultures that it makes sense to speak of "integration" only as a subjective measure. They also find, as a result of their panel study, that "with the exception of language ability, prediction of integration scores from T_1 to T_2 [the first point in time to the second] is likely to be poor [and] prediction is generally weak from T_1 to T_2 with respect to scores on specific integration variables."[35] However, we have been able to develop an "index of integration" that, combining subjective and objective measures, seems to predict integration over time — at least over three years — remarkably well. (Appendix C tells how we constructed our index and what its components are.) That is, knowing the score of an immigrant at T_1 (1972), we could have predicted with great certainty whether or not the person would be in Israel at T_2 (1975). Of the immigrants who were located only in 1972, 70 percent of the Soviets and 88 percent of the Americans scored "low" on integration in that year, whereas only about 50 percent of the 1972/75 groups had the same score. The differences between the 1972/75 and 1972-only groups can be seen in Table 6.13.

TABLE 6.13
"Index of Integration" Scores, 1972

	Heartlanders		Zapadniki		Soviets		Americans	
	1972/75	*1972*	*1972/75*	*1972*	*1972/75*	*1972*	*1972/75*	*1972*
Low	59.4	74.3	34.8	64.5	44.9	70.0	56.7	87.5
Medium	31.3	25.6	47.8	25.8	41.0	25.7	40.0	12.5
High	9.4	—	17.3	9.7	14.1	4.3	3.3	—

In all immigrant groups, the 1972/75 subgroups scored significantly better on integration already in 1972 than the others did.
These are the people who reappear in our sample in 1975. Moreover,
scores on integration in 1975 were substantially higher for all groups.
Even the 1972/75 group scored higher in 1975 than it did in 1972.
When responses for each individual in 1972 and 1975 are compared,
we find that 35 Soviets and 15 Americans had higher scores in 1975
than they had in 1972, and only 12 Soviets and 3 Americans had
lower ones. Clearly, the immigrants are becoming more "integrated"
with the passage of time. In both years, Americans scored lower than
the Soviets. Zapadniki scored considerably higher than heartlanders
in 1972, but by 1975 the difference between them had narrowed
greatly, just as was observed in other respects.

Those who have been in Israel longer achieve higher scores on
integration, and this may be due to our measure including such items
as language use. Those with a stronger Jewish background are also
more likely to score higher on integration, though the relationship
between background and integration is not very strong. There is
an interesting relationship between age and integration. If we divide
the immigrants into three age groups, we find that the younger
group scores best on integration in both years. However, the older
group scores better than the middle group. In 1975, for example,
38 percent of the young, 22 percent of the old, and 17 percent
of the middle group scored "high" on integration. A plausible
explanation for these differences is that the older people have the
strongest Jewish backgrounds, especially among the Soviets, and so
they adapt to Israel without having to change very much; the
younger people are prepared and able to change in order to "fit
in." It is the middle generation that has the greatest difficulty

adapting: They do not have as strong a Jewish background and motivation, but they do have families, vocations, and fairly set ideas
about their goals, and they are less able to compromise and change
than the younger newcomers.

How do the immigrants themselves perceive their relationship
to the rest of Israeli society? As noted, none of the Americans had
severed all ties with the United States by renouncing American
citizenship, though by 1975 almost all of them had acquired Israeli
citizenship as well. Three to six years after aliyah, when *none* of
the immigrants is officially an *oleh* — that is, is classified by the
government as an immigrant — 10 percent of the Soviet and American immigrants "always feel themselves to be an *oleh khadash* (new
immigrant)." Fifty-five percent of the Soviets and 43 percent of the
Americans, however, "never" feel like immigrants, and the rest feel
like immigrants occasionally. The Zapadniki claim to feel less like
immigrants than the heartlanders.

A related question of subjective identity is whether the immigrants feel themselves to be Americans or "Russians" in Israel.
In 1972, 38 percent of the Soviets, but only 8 percent of the Americans, said they "never" felt "Russian" or American. By 1975, 65
percent of the Soviets and 20 percent of the Americans made that
claim. Zapadniki felt Israeli to a somewhat greater extent than
heartlanders: After all, they had never felt "Russian" in the USSR
and had felt more Jewish than the more acculturated residents of the
Slavic republics. Even the heartlanders, however, said they retained
their former identities less than the Americans, few of whom claimed
"never" to have felt American. Despite the fact that the Americans
had strong Jewish backgrounds, they clung to their American
identity. They were less linguistically assimilated than the Soviets
and they did not *want* to lose their identities as Americans to the
same extent the Soviets wanted to lose their "Russian" identity.
As one put it: "I don't have any desire to assimilate because I don't
think much of the Israelis. I'm an American living in Israel — we
feel we're above them culturally and socially." This frank statement
expresses a viewpoint that we heard often, even from those who were
well settled in Israel. Some felt that, as Americans, they bore a sort
of "white man's burden," that they were in Israel to "educate the
wogs." A businessman from Philadelphia, explaining why he did not
want "to become Israeli," said that "if we want to do any good to
this country, we should not give up our standards. . . . We should

communicate with the Israelis and show them what can be done, and not give up after we've knocked our heads against the wall. . . ." Another put it less charitably and more pompously: "The few good things that have come here have come because of the Americans." All these statements were made by people still in Israel in 1975! Other Americans explained their lack of assimilation, not as a result of their desire to stay "American," but because the others regarded them as Americans and would always do so. The immigrants claimed that their outlooks, values, methods, even their sense of humor, were different and were regarded as distinctly "American" by Israeli natives. Moreover, while the Americans did not say so, it was clear that they felt no political or social need to reject their former country, but the Soviets did. Finally, the Soviets were not usually regarded as "Russians" in the USSR, and they found it less than flattering to be so named in Israel, though some felt more Russian in Israel than they ever did in the Soviet Union. As one put it: "I feel myself Russian, a guest, temporary. Here I feel Russian, just as in Russia I felt myself to be a Jew. . . . My friends are all from Russia, and they are very few. I have a couple of acquaintances who are *sabras* [native-born Israelis], but they're not friends." Almost all the Soviet immigrants would prefer to have at least half their friends "Israelis," though few Americans felt this way, most preferring American friends. Most Soviets said that they would like very much to be considered Israeli, but that the society did not regard them as such. "I felt myself a *vatik* [veteran] from the very first day, but unfortunately, some of the *vatikim*, especially the youth, see us as Russians, and I can feel this every day." A few, however, said that they had come to feel, for the first time in their lives, that they really belonged in a country and that they were an integral part of it.

Those who did feel themselves Russian in Israel were less integrated and less likely to remain in Israel. The 1972/75 group felt much less "Russian" (or "American") than the others, and even they felt less Russian or American by 1975. Those who felt Russian felt more at home in the USSR than the others, had weaker Jewish backgrounds and lower incomes in Israel, and they said their expectations were not very much fulfilled. They would have preferred to live with other immigrants from the Soviet Union or even from Poland and did not wish to live among veteran Israelis.

The wish to be regarded as Israeli, which we shall encounter in other contexts, comes through also in a study of Soviet immigrant students that was done among 500 who arrived in 1972. The students were asked how they would like to be seen by Israelis, and how they thought they were actually identified (see Table 6.14). The sharp contrast between the desired and actual identities as "Russians" and "Israelis" seems to confirm the remark quoted above regarding young people's views of the Soviet immigrants.

Not a single American agreed with the notion that "immigrants should adopt Israeli ways as soon as possible," but nearly one-third of the Soviets did. Most of the Soviets agreed that Israel should strive for ethnic homogeneity, but most of the Americans thought that the various ethnic groups and cultures should retain their own ways. It is somewhat ironic that the Soviets should have been in favor of a "melting pot" in Israel, since they were discriminated against in a system nominally committed to ethnic pluralism, but favoring the dominant Russian culture and people. Either they had accepted Soviet-type *practice*, or they were simply so eager to "become Israelis" that they were attracted to the idea of an ethnically undifferentiated society.

In the Israeli election study of 1973, immigrants were asked whether they felt themselves Israeli: 58 percent answered affirmatively, 20 percent negatively, and the rest gave less definitive answers (there were no differences among Baltic Jews, heartlanders, and Georgians on this question). As we did with our own survey, we were able to construct an index of integration based on 13 variables from the Israel election study (see Table 6.15). As might be expected, the immigrants from the Baltic scored highest on the index, the Georgians lowest, and the heartlanders were in between, but closer

TABLE 6.14
Desired and Actual Identity of Soviet Immigrant Students
(in percent)

	Desired	Actual
Primarily as a Jew	58	34
Primarily as a Russian	2	62
Primarily as an Israeli	40	2

Source: Ministry for Immigrant Absorption, *Klitat studentim olim mi-Brih"m*, Report No. 1 (Jerusalem, December 1975), p. 24.

TABLE 6.15
"Index of Integration" — Israel Election Study
(in percent)

	Balts	*Georgians*	*Heartlanders*	*Soviets*
Low	11.4	40.0	19.0	23.9
Medium	41.8	31.8	38.0	37.0
High	46.8	28.2	43.0	39.1

to the Zapadniki. This may lend some validity to our own comparative findings. (Details of the index are found in Appendix D.) The
Zapadniki (Balts) in the study had been in the country somewhat
longer than the others, listened to the radio and watched television
more than the others, and were more proficient in Hebrew. When
detailing the problems the immigrants were concerned with, the
Zapadniki were more likely than the other Soviet immigrants to
mention economics, a most salient problem to other Israelis. Heartlanders and Georgians focused on problems related to immigration
and absorption. This was an indication that the Zapadniki had
moved beyond concerns with resettlement to those of the "average"
Israeli citizen.

Where do the immigrants see their future? Both in 1972 and
1975 the great majority of the immigrants we interviewed thought
they would still be in Israel five years hence, though by 1975 more
than one-third of the Soviets thought they would move elsewhere
within Israel, indicating, perhaps, that they had rising expectations,
and that they were no longer dependent on government housing.
However, there is a sharp contrast between the 1972/75 and 1972-
only groups. Twice as many Soviets from the 1972-only group said
they would *not* be in Israel or that they weren't sure they would be,
and the same difference appeared between the two American groups.
One student expressed the simple hope that in five years he would
"live like a normal person." Others had more ambitious and idealistic
visions. A politically active newcomer from the Baltic expressed the
hope that he would help "raise the intellectual level of the country."
Another saw himself living in Gaza where he would be building a
new city; while yet another hoped to be building a new town near
the Jordan River, "when Judea and Samaria will finally be ours."

His Israeli nationalism was mixed with what sounded like a Russian idea of a good time: "There will be a beautiful environment, friendship, bars, clubs, movies, we'll drink plenty of vodka, light the fireplace. . . ."

Other people had no desire to remain in Israel. An unemployed filmmaker said bitterly that he did not know where he would be living, except that "it would not be in Israel. Because here they don't need people who do something or think better than the locals, they're afraid of that. So anyone who is cultured and has creative experience and the will to work loses himself here." Louis Guttman's notion is that the best predictor of staying in Israel is one's declared intention in the early stages of arrival:[36] If one firmly intends to stay, one generally does. This appears to hold true for our group, as was seen in the comparison of the 1972/75 and 1972 groups on their vision of the future. What happened to those who did not stay in Israel?

THE "YORDIM"

By speaking with neighbors and friends, we were able to ascertain that of the 54 Americans interviewed in 1972, eight had left the country for good. Another seven could not be located and it appears that four or five of these had also left. Nine others were abroad temporarily, in military service, and so on, and could not be interviewed. Of the 148 Soviets interviewed in 1972, 15 definitely had left Israel, 18 could not be located (some of them are very likely to have left the country), and the rest were unavailable for various reasons — travel abroad, military service, and so on. One had died and three were too ill to be interviewed. The Americans who left the country had all gone back to the United States. Of the Soviets known to have emigrated, three went to the Federal Republic of Germany, three to the United States, two to Canada, two to England, and one each to Iran and New Zealand. The whereabouts of three others are unknown to us.

Thus, at least 23 people, and probably around 35 all together, had become *yordim*, people who "go down" from Israel. From the information they supplied in 1972, we see that they are a younger group than those who stayed in Israel, and that they were mostly professionals earning good incomes (one-third of ex-Israelis who became U.S. citizens in 1975 were professionals; two-thirds were natives of Israel).[37]

As already indicated, our "index of integration" proved to be a good predictor of leaving or staying in Israel. Every one of the Americans who left had scored low. Those who left also had lower scores on measures of information about Israel, perhaps because, not intending to stay, they had little incentive to learn about the country. They did not identify with political parties to the same extent that the others did, and the few who did identify with a political party — all Soviets — leaned toward the parties of the left or left-center.[38]

A larger proportion of the Soviets who left had weak Jewish backgrounds, though a few with a fairly strong background also left Israel. Only one of the Americans who left had such a background. Those who left also cited Zionism half as frequently, but political alienation from the USSR twice as frequently, as those who stayed, when asked about their motivations for emigration. Those who came for "adventure" departed.

These findings indicate that reemigration is not random, but it should be stressed that the decision to leave is a highly individual one, and it is often painful and traumatic. Especially in Israel, it is suffused with feelings of shame, guilt, failure, and even betrayal. People leave often not because they are dissatisfied, but because spouses or children do so, because there are family ties pulling them away, and for a whole variety of other reasons that are as many as there are reemigrants.

The most dramatic story we heard, a most atypical one, concerned an immigrant from a small central Russian city who had been arrested for dissident activity in the late 1950s and while serving a term in prison had come around to Zionism. When he was released, he also became a practicing Jew, wearing a skullcap in public and his children doing the same, despite the fact that their mother was not Jewish. Isolated in this provincial city, he built up in his own mind a highly idealized picture of Israel. After some difficulty, the man succeeded in leaving the USSR and came to an absorption center in Beersheba. Much to his consternation, he found that he was the only observant Jew among the center's residents. Still, when he left the center, his wife was converted to Judaism and his children attended a religious school in the Tel Aviv area. He himself was employed as a mechanical engineer in the defense industry and was doing well economically. According to a close friend of his, however, he was constantly shocked and embittered at the negative aspects of Israeli life: crime, corruption, bureaucracy, secularism, and the like. He became more and more depressed and suddenly gave up religious observance. Neighbors reported that for hours at a time they would hear Soviet patriotic songs being played on a phonograph or tape recorder in the engineer's apartment. He stopped working and sat at home for long periods of time, listening to the songs. One day he announced his intention of leaving. His wife and children, by now quite happy with life in Israel, begged him to stay; but he insisted. In the middle of the Yom Kippur War, with Israel fighting for its survival, he and his family boarded a plane for Rome. After a few months of studying English, he was granted entry to New Zealand, where he was living as of 1976.

SUMMARY

In this chapter we have tried to gain an understanding of how the background of the immigrants — their demographic characteristics, their previous political experience, and their assessment of it — influences their resocialization in Israel. How well immigrants adapt to the new country influences their political adaptation, so considerable attention has been devoted to the question of integration, absorption, or adaptation, and an explicit comparison has been made between those who left the country by 1975 and those who remained. Knowing something about the linguistic, social, and psychological adaptation of the newcomers enables us to assess their abilities to operate in the political arena. How they actually do operate there is determined by the interaction of their own abilities, interests, and attitudes with the activities of socializing agencies that introduce the immigrants to the system. The post-1967 era saw major changes in the organization and dynamics of immigrant political resocialization. Although the role of the parties and trade unions became less visible, and the new type of immigrant seemed less malleable, political organizations competed vigorously for the attention and loyalty of newcomers, who, under Israeli law, can become voters within a year of their arrival. These organizations would seem to have a significant role in inducting the immigrants to Israeli politics, and an analysis of the interplay between them and the immigrants will give us insights into the immigrants, the organizations, and the political system itself.

NOTES

1. Based on recalculation of data found in Shmuel Adler and Rachel Klein, *Hatkhunot hademografiyot shel olai Brih"m lefi aizorai motsa*, mimeo-graphed (Jerusalem: Ministry for Immigrant Absorption, 1975).

2. Ibid.

3. The Toronto study is John Goldlust and Anthony H. Richmond, "A Multivariate Model of Immigrant Adaptation," *International Migration Review* 8, no. 2 (Summer 1974). The Israeli data are from the panel study of 1969-70 immigrants and are reported in Central Bureau of Statistics, *Monthly Bulletin of Statistics – Supplement* 24, no. 1 (January 1973): 127. Ronald Taft argues that "a young, well educated person finds acculturation . . . comparatively easy." *From Stranger to Citizen* (London: Tavistock, 1966), p. 69.

4. Since there was so little income variance among the Americans, no significant differences appeared between the 1972/75 and 1972 groups. An Israeli study of 1,000 Soviet immigrant families found that their incomes and living standards were significantly higher than they had been in the USSR and, more significantly, than the Israeli national average. Gur Ofer, Aharon Vinokur, and Yehiel Bar-Haim, "Report on Absorption and Economic Contribution of Soviet Immigrants," Ministry for Immigrant Absorption, Bulletin No. 193/194 (December 1980).

5. Tamar Horowitz and Khava Frankel found that while 35 percent of the Baltic immigrants they interviewed had attended a Jewish school, only 8 percent of those from the Slavic republics had done so. *Olim bemerkazai klitah* (Jerusalem: Henrietta Szold Institute, 1975), Research Report No. 185, Publication No. 538, p. 138.

6. George L. Kline, "Religious Ferment Among Soviet Intellectuals," in *Religion and the Soviet State: A Dilemma of Power*, ed. Max Hayward and William C. Fletcher (London: Pall Mall, 1969), p. 68. See also William C. Fletcher and Anthony J. Strover, *Religion and the Search for New Ideals in the USSR* (London: Pall Mall, 1967).

7. See the *Komsomol'skaia pravda* poll cited in Bohdan Bociurkiw, "Religion and Soviet Society," *Survey* (London), no. 60 (July 1966).

8. Judith T. Shuval, *Immigrants on the Threshold* (New York: Atherton, 1963), p. 75.

9. In his study of Cuban refugees in the United States, Richard Fagen observed distinct occupational and educational differences between two waves, the first being better educated and more heavily managerial and professional in its occupational composition. See his *Cubans in Exile* (Stanford, Calif.: Stanford University Press, 1968), p. 69.

10. In fact, there is a positive correlation (.32) between identifying oneself as religious and feeling that "blacks have gone too far."

11. For the anti-Semitic experiences of a Jew who has no positive feelings toward his Jewishness and feels himself completely Russian culturally, see Efim Etkind, *Notes of a Non-Conspirator* (Oxford: Oxford University Press, 1978).

12. Some Soviet respondents qualified their answers on anti-Semitism. An immigrant from Estonia said that he had not experienced anti-Semitism in contacts with Estonians, but he had "often" in contacts with Russians. Several others pointed out that up to a particular period they had not felt such anti-Semitism, but that they encountered it more frequently thereafter. As one said, "I always felt anti-Semitism, but after 1948, when it increased greatly, I felt like a second-class citizen."

13. Alex Inkeles and Raymond Bauer, *The Soviet Citizen* (New York: Athenaeum, 1968), pp. 233-34.

14. Over one-third said they had been imprisoned or "repressed" in the USSR, and 28 percent had a parent who had been imprisoned. Another clue to their alienation is provided by their newspaper reading habits. They much preferred nonparty newspapers to *Pravda*. For details on Soviet readers' preferences, see Zvi Gitelman, "Recent Emigrés and the Soviet Political System: A Pilot Study in Detroit," *Slavic and Soviet Series* 2, no. 2 (Fall 1977): 52-54.

15. G. Beijer, N. H. Frijda, B. P. Hofstede, and R. Wenholt, *Characteristics of Overseas Migrants* (The Hague: 1961), quoted in Arnold Rose, *Migrants in Europe* (Minneapolis: University of Minnesota Press, 1969), p. 9. For another discussion of immigrants' motivations, see S. N. Eisenstadt, *The Absorption of Immigrants* (London: Routledge and Kegan Paul, 1954), pp. 3-4.

16. Judith Shuval, Elliot Markus, and Judith Dotan, *Patterns of Integration over Time: Soviet Immigrants in Israel* (Jerusalem: Israel Institute of Applied Social Research, August 1975), p. 36.

17. "Why Did They Come to Israel," in *Abraham David Katz: Jew, Man and Sociologist*, ed. Aaron Antonovsky (Jerusalem, 1975), p. 22. Of the respondents, 15 percent had made no independent decision to come on aliyah, as they were simply following spouses.

18. Commission on Security and Cooperation in Europe, Report to the Congress of the United States on Implementation of the Final Act of the Conference on Security and Cooperation in Europe, *Findings and Recommendations Two Years After Helsinki*, mimeographed (Washington, D.C., August 1, 1977), p. B-2.

19. Zvi Gitelman, "Soviet Jewish Emigrants: Why Are They Choosing America?" *Soviet Jewish Affairs* 7, no. 1 (1977): 39-40.

20. The government survey of 1969-70 immigrants found that only 36 percent of the American immigrants had not visited Israel previously; 18 percent had visited Israel at least three times. Central Bureau of Statistics, *Immigrants Arrived in 1969/70: The First Three Years in Israel* (Jerusalem, 1975), p. 31.

21. In 1967, Wladyslaw Gomulka, then first secretary of the Polish United Workers party, said that those Polish Jews who sympathized with Israel, to whatever degree, should be encouraged to leave Poland. In 1967-68 there was a mass exodus of Polish Jews, though most did not go to Israel. It has been suggested that Gomulka's speech, reprinted in Soviet newspapers, played a role in convincing the Soviet authorities to allow — even encourage — Jewish emigration.

22. Immigrants from Odessa have a bad reputation among resettlement workers in the United States, the country to which more than 90 percent of Odessa emigrés have come in the last five years or so. Odessans have the reputation of being wheelers and dealers, materialistic, and difficult to please. Whether myth or reality, this image has wide currency among other Soviet immigrants.

23. Taft, p. 71.

24. A perceptive journalist, discussing Soviet immigrant expectations, at least those in the first wave of mass immigration, notes that the Israeli standard of living is a pleasant surprise. However, the immigrants are disappointed that they are not given "recognition and respect," including a special pin for those who were imprisoned for Zionist activity. (Anyone who visits the USSR, especially on a national holiday, will be struck by the number of pins, medals, and other insignia so many Soviet citizens wear.) "Among all the beautiful things [the Soviet immigrant] includes in his picture of Israel is the assumption that here a man is a man, and not a file or a number." For this reason, the immigrants are disappointed in the Israeli bureaucracy. See Eliahu Salpeter, "Hitnagshut hakhalom bamtsiut," *Haaretz*, March 21, 1971.

25. An American who left Israel wrote to the Jerusalem *Post* (March 5, 1978): "We are former immigrants who left Israel, not because of economic reasons, but solely because the general behavior got us down, especially the effect it was having on our three children in school in a good neighborhood of Jerusalem."

26. Eisenstadt, p. 116.

27. Ibid.

28. Taft, p. 57.

29. For an excellent survey and analysis of Russian-language publications, see Edith Rogovin Frankel, "The Russian Press in Israel," *Soviet Jewish Affairs* 7, no. 1 (1977). See also Zvi Gitelman, "Russian Publications in Israel," *Jewish Book Annual* 38 (New York: Jewish Book Council, 1980).

30. Frankel, p. 54.

31. We were able to construct an index of political information for the Israeli election study, based on eight items. On this index, Zapadniki scored higher than heartlanders, who scored considerably higher than Georgians. This may imply that the better explanation for the lower scores of the Zapadniki in the 1972-75 study is that their educational level is lower.

32. In her study of post-World War II immigrants (*Immigrants on the Threshold*), Shuval found that "with a given exposure, immigrants with a prior Zionist commitment absorbed more information about Israel . . . than those without a Zionist frame of reference" (p. 55). Perhaps our heartlanders' rapid assimilation of information is due to their highly conscious Zionist commitment.

33. Yehudit Shuval and Yehuda Markus, *Dfusai histaglut shel olai Brihm* (Jerusalem: Israel Institute of Applied Social Research, 1973), Part 1, pp. iiiff.

34. Shuval, Markus, and Dotan, p. 6.

35. Ibid., p. 26.

36. Haviva Bar-Shimerling and Eliahu Louis Guttmann, "Hashnatayim harishonot beyisrael: tmurot behistaglut olim khadashim," mimeographed

(Jerusalem: Israel Institute of Applied Social Research and The Hebrew University, Faculty of Social Sciences, September 1975), passim.

37. Gad Nakhshon, "Darkonim kekhulim, kartisim yerukim," *Maariv*, September 17, 1976.

38. A study of people who returned to Britain after immigrating to Canada concludes that "the most distinctive feature of those remaining in Britain was their low level of social integration in Canada." Anthony H. Richmond, "Return Migration from Canada to Britain," *Population Studies* 22, no. 2 (July 1968): 269.

7

IMMIGRANT POLITICAL SOCIALIZATION AND POLITICAL INVOLVEMENT

An immigrant from Georgia. Courtesy The Jewish Agency.

How the Israeli political system attempts to resocialize immigrants from the USSR and the United States and the results of such attempts constitute the major themes of this chapter. We will examine some of the more visible agents of immigrant political socialization and the political interests and activities of the immigrants, which may be at least partially the outcomes of socialization efforts.

Although political participation has been a favorite subject for study by political scientists,[1] few have studied immigrant participation. Those who have make little effort to link resocialization efforts with participation. Paul Wilson's study of British and Italian immigrants in Australia observes less political participation by both immigrant groups than by native Australians, with British immigrants generally participating more extensively than Italians. Wilson does not pay much attention to agents of resocialization but he does find that high-status occupation is the most powerful determinant of intensive political participation. For those who are neither intensively involved in politics nor totally apathetic, the longer they stay in Australia and the more "assimilated" they become, the greater their political interest and active participation. Those who are of "medium" socioeconomic status start out in Australia with levels of political participation below those they had exhibited in their countries of origin. In their first years they are concerned mainly with achieving economic security. Later on they have the time to devote to political pursuits and their levels of interest and activity rise. It is this intermediate group that does experience political resocialization, whereas the behavior of the perpetually politically active and the perpetually apathetic is perhaps better explained by concepts of socialization that stress the decisive nature of formative years and that pay little attention to continuing resocialization.[2]

Since the Soviet and American immigrants we interviewed were more or less of the same social and economic status, we cannot determine whether the same relationship between status and political involvement Wilson found in Australia holds also in Israel. Data from the Israeli election study of immigrants (1973) suggest that the lower socioeconomic groups do, in fact, exhibit less political interest than the higher ones, and this jibes with findings among nonimmigrants in many countries.

In Australia, political parties make no great effort to court the immigrants.[3] As we have seen, historically this has not been true of Israel. In the *yishuv* period, many immigrants were politically socialized in their countries of origin because they were members of movements there that were affiliated with parties in Palestine. Even today movements that parallel Israeli parties are quite active in some West European and Latin American Jewish communities. One study of Latin American immigrants to Israel found that those who had belonged to a Jewish youth movement were much more likely to vote and join a political party than those who had not been so affiliated.[4] For obvious reasons, there are no formal Jewish movements in the USSR (though about half of our respondents claim to have been involved with a group concerned with emigration). Zionist political movements now play only a minor role in the American Jewish community. Whereas three-quarters of our American interviewees had been members of a Jewish organization in the United States, only 11 were members of a Zionist organization and not all of these had a partisan ideology. Thus, among our group, only a few Americans experienced partisan socialization before their arrival in Israel.

Once having arrived in Israel, the immigrants are most likely to come in contact with three kinds of organizations that have the potential for acting as socialization agents: immigrant associations, the Histadrut (General Confederation of Labor), and political parties.

IMMIGRANT ASSOCIATIONS

In many countries immigrants form their own associations, whose aims are generally self-help, social contact, and, sometimes, the preservation of the immigrants' culture. There are many such associations in Israel, with considerable variation in their size and importance for the immigrants and in public affairs. These associations used to get a substantial portion of their budgets from the Jewish Agency. It has been said that funds were sometimes distributed on the basis of partisan political calculations, as the potential of the associations for political recruitment was recognized. The Ministry for Immigrant Absorption assumed responsibility for funding the associations after 1968 and it attempted to establish objective criteria by which allocations would be determined (for example, size of the association, numbers of immigrants expected from the country represented by the association). MIA officials charged that the Agency continued to "supplement" MIA funds to the associations, perpetuating their politicization.[5]

Perhaps the least politicized of these immigrant organizations is the Association of Americans and Canadians in Israel. Founded in 1951, the AACI has consciously sought to avoid political coloration, reflecting its cultural bias against the involvement of political parties in what are seen as "purely" economic, social, and cultural functions. Nevertheless, the AACI does receive financial help from the authorities in addition to collecting dues. It claims to enroll — and hence to represent — well over half the North American immigrants in Israel, and it has established affiliates in North America whose aim is to encourage aliyah and to prepare potential olim for living in Israel. The AACI sponsors Hebrew language courses, social and cultural events, English publications, and a wide range of ombudsman-type services for its clientele. It acts, often together with other immigrant associations, as a lobby, pressing for more favorable mortgages and tax breaks for immigrants, improvement of absorption procedures, and new techniques for promoting aliyah. AACI has frequently complained that, despite its knowledge of the North American immigrant "mentality," and its experience in dealing with American newcomers, it has been ignored by government decision makers and agencies dealing with immigration.

> It is an historic omission on the part of the authorities not to recognize that the immigrant associations are one of the most positive − if not the main factor − for this trend [increased American immigration]. Instead of realizing that the authorities and immigrants can be full partners in working for the common goal of successful absorption, with a resultant increase in *aliyah*, the authorities prefer to make decisions and plans without prior consultation.[6]

The AACI has been careful to limit its political activities to lobbying on behalf of immigrant concerns over which there are no partisan differences. When it sponsors lectures or symposia on political issues, one notices that opposing points of view are represented, and the AACI itself does not take policy positions. Nor is there any other evidence to suggest involvement with a political grouping.

The Union of Soviet Immigrants presents an entirely different picture. In late 1970, with an increasing awareness of the potential for a mass Soviet immigration, efforts were made by members of the then ruling Labor party (Avodah) to locate immigrants from the USSR, irrespective of the date of their arrival. Some 16,000 members were registered, 9,000 having come to Israel between 1957 and 1970, and the rest before 1957. The first congress of the Union was held in early 1971, and Yonah Kesse, a Labor party activist who had left the USSR in the 1920s, was elected chairman. In his report to the second congress, held in July 1973, Kesse stated that a basic principle of the Union was that it was to be "an organization, not for immigrants, but of immigrants. We must involve veteran settlers in the activities of the Union in order to benefit from their knowledge and experience."[7] Indeed, there were many members of the Union's leading organs who had left the USSR as far back as the 1920s, though there were also representatives of the most recent waves. Not only was Kesse prominently identified as a Labor party activist, but the executive director of the Union, Eli Ronen, was a native-born Israeli, a member of a kibbutz, who does not speak Russian. Ronen, in his mid-thirties, began as the head of the Labor party's absorption department, and then doubled in brass as the Union's executive director between 1971 and 1974. He said that "98 percent of my time" was spent with the Union,[8] which made sense since the Soviets made up the bulk of immigrants to Israel at that time. Moreover, Ronen's dual position was facilitated by the physical location of the Union's headquarters: directly across the street from the Labor party's national headquarters in Tel Aviv. How did Ronen justify the fact that a native Israeli, nonspeaker of Russian, served as executive director of the Soviet immigrant association? He told one journalist: "I have experience — I worked for four years on absorption matters [in the Labor party] and on organizational problems linked to them. I admit that, in this post, knowledge of Russian could only help, and if there were someone with my qualifications who spoke Russian perhaps he would be more suitable."[9] On another occasion Ronen explained the seeming anomaly of his position as follows: "These people come from a dictatorship. They don't know how to operate in a democracy, and my job is to teach them that."[10] He also justified the presence in the leadership of long-time settlers on similar grounds: The newcomers simply did not know how to operate in the Israeli system. Nevertheless, because of pressure from the recent arrivals, 72 of the most recent arrivals were coopted in late 1971 to the 130 original members of the governing council, over half of whom had arrived after 1957.

By the second congress, held in July 1973, 65 local branches of the Union had been established, encompassing a total membership of some 25,000. Since at the beginning of 1971 there were already 16,000 members, and in 1971-72 and the first half of 1973 about 58,500 Soviet immigrants had arrived in Israel, membership growth was not very great, even assuming that only heads of households would join. Of course, it may be that as the more recent arrivals came to dominate the Union, the veteran settlers, who presumably had less need of its services, dropped out. On the other hand, of the Soviet immigrants surveyed by the MIA in 1974, 20 percent did not even know of the Union's existence and only another 20 percent had any connection with it, mostly in order to obtain loans or to have documents translated.[11]

In 1973 the Union reported that it had disseminated about 30,000 dictionaries, maps of Israel, and other materials designed for the new immigrant; it held seminars in Russian, Georgian, and Yiddish; and organized libraries and excursions. Of the over 2,000 immigrants who turned to the Union's absorption department in 1972, the greatest number did so in connection with housing, employment being the second most frequent concern.[12] Other major activities of the Union are the translation of Soviet documents into Hebrew, assistance in drawing up invitations (*vyzovy*) to Soviet citizens who wish to emigrate, and providing personal and business loans to the immigrants.[13]

The tension between older and more recent immigrants, and also between Labor party supporters and others, reached a climax at the second congress of the Union, held in Beersheba at the end of July 1973. "The convention was tumultous and bitter almost throughout. Speakers were heckled and shouted down, tempers flared and heated disputes erupted in various parts of the auditorium."[14] Even the presence of Prime Minister Golda Meir did not exert a calming influence. An oppositionist group charged that of the 400 delegates, 42 had never set foot on Soviet territory and another 95 were kibbutz members, all veteran settlers, who were sent without being elected by any of the local branches. This group walked out and formed its own organization (which subsequently disappeared), whose membership would be restricted to those who came from the USSR after June 1967. Yonah Kesse rejected the charges of Labor party manipulation and pointed out that the elections committee had a majority of Herut (Likud) sympathizers.[15] The issue of delegate credentials actually reached the courts. The legal outcome was not as important as the fact that the Union had become an arena for combat between supporters of Labor and Herut (Gahal, Likud) with most of the immigrants apparently disgusted by, or uninterested in, the partisan disputes. Having overplayed their hand, the Labor leaders drew back, and by the summer of 1974, Kesse and Ronen had both been replaced by recent immigrants.

The new executive director, who had come from Lithuania in 1971, claimed to be nonpartisan. However, he explained, since the Union was dependent for its annual budget of about $100,000 on the Jewish Agency and the MIA, both controlled by the ruling governmental coalition, "we have to behave ourselves." He admitted that when Ronen was in office "it was a bit easier to get money," but it was still better to have removed the obvious Labor party presence. He agreed with Ronen that the immigrants were not adept at the Israeli "political game" and expressed disappointment at their inactivity. The Union found it hard to act as a lobby for the immigrants because the "establishment" was intent on limiting its role to service and cultural matters "and we ourselves are incapable of acting as advocates of the immigrants because of the conflicts among us – on the basis of geography and ethnic background, mainly."[16] By 1975 separate organizations of Baltic and Georgian immigrants had been formed, and the Union's attempts to act as a "roof organization" for all the groups were not always successful. The parties continued to try to control the associations. For example, a second-generation Israeli of Georgian origin, a Labor party activist named Rafi Bar-Lavi, changed his name back to Balvashvili and headed one of several Georgian associations. In 1977 he was an unsuccessful Labor party candidate in the national elections.

By late 1975 the Union's claimed membership had reached 44,000 (the executive director admitted that most did not pay dues) out of a total of about 110,000 post-1967 individual Soviet immigrants. The Union claimed that some 38,000 members participated in its national election of December 1975. Once again, political parties were involved in the election, though the extent of their involvement was disputed.[17] This time, the rival election lists were made up exclusively of post-1967 immigrants.

Nevertheless, most of the immigrants seem to be put off by the involvement, or "interference," of the parties in Union matters. There is no doubt that the Union has not been a very effective agent of partisan socialization, nor perhaps even of general socialization into the political system. Some of the smaller Soviet immigrant associations may have been more effective as partisan socializers. It is possible that experience with Union politics may have been instructive in the ways of democracy, though not in the way Eli Ronen had envisaged it.

THE HISTADRUT

Historically, the Histadrut, or General Confederation of Labor, played a major role in the integration of immigrants. It was active in providing jobs, housing, health care, and social and cultural services to newcomers. Organized along partisan lines, and dominated by the Labor party and its predecessors, the Histadrut also introduced many immigrants to the Israeli political world. In the 1960s and 1970s the arrival of less dependent immigrants and the assumption by the MIA of many of the tasks of immigration reduced the Histadrut's importance in resettlement and resocialization. Whereas in the 1950s, 90 percent and more of the immigrants were enrolled immediately in the Histadrut, in 1971 only 38 percent enrolled — and this at a time when 87 percent of all employees in the country, and 62 percent of the total population, were Histadrut members.[18] It could be expected that as the immigrants joined the labor force, a higher proportion would enroll in the Histadrut — for most employees this is not a matter of choice. Even earlier, a connection with the Histadrut would be established through its health care system, *Kupat kholim*, by far the largest such system in Israel. The MIA automatically enrolls newcomers in the Histadrut *Kupat kholim*, unless an immigrant would explicitly ask to be enrolled in another plan. Of course, most immigrants, especially from the USSR, have no knowledge of the other plans, and so they are enrolled in the Histadrut organization. However, this seems to have little consequence for their political outlook or affiliation, as the health plan is seen as nothing more than that.

The Histadrut has an immigrant absorption department that, according to its former director, tries to fill in the gaps left by the Agency and the MIA, especially in the area of employment. Working through its local labor councils, the Histadrut seeks to obtain employment for those with particular difficulties in this area — the old, the handicapped, people with exotic skills, and those with no skills at all. Sometimes loans are given to enterprises to enable them to employ immigrants, at least temporarily, and the Histadrut has endorsed retraining programs for immigrants who need new skills. It also sponsors numerous seminars on both practical and theoretical subjects and has tried to promote "social integration" through sponsorship of social gatherings, holiday celebrations, and the like.[19] In all this the political element seems to be absent or very much muted. So while the immigrant may be introduced to the general values and outlook of the labor movement, it is unlikely that the Histadrut is a major instrument of political, and especially partisan, resocialization.[20]

POLITICAL PARTIES

Despite the drastic decline in their functions as settlers of immigrants, most of the political parties in Israel retain the perhaps vestigial organ of an "absorption (*klitah*) department." Interviews with the heads of such departments of nine parties revealed that they shared the same view of their function: to serve the immigrant, running interference for him in his dealings with official agencies, and (thereby) to win the immigrants' support for their respective parties. Most of the parties are able to extend small loans to immigrants, recognizing that they would not always be repaid. Parties identified with the Histadrut try to place jobless immigrants in Histadrut enterprises, whereas the religious parties and those connected with private enterprise appeal to their members, apparently with considerable success, to employ immigrants who have come to the party for assistance. Those parties with ministers in the cabinet, or other highly placed officials, ask them to intervene in individual cases, especially in connection with housing and employment, in order to cut through red tape. However, the parties expend most of their efforts on what they call "social integration." Reasoning that official agencies can hardly be expected to create Israeli friends and social circles for the immigrants, the parties see this as a gap they can fill. A leader of the Independent Liberal party remarked wistfully that "in the old days, before television, we could provide entertainment for the immigrant and we could get people to come out to meetings. Today, people stay home in front of the TV set and don't look for social activity outside the home, so we try to set up parlor meetings [*khugai bayit*] with immigrants and veteran settlers."[21] Excursions, holiday celebrations, and cultural events are used to bring immigrants together with Israeli members of the party sponsoring the event. A memorandum of the Liberal party (allied with Herut in what was then Gahal and is now the Likud) urged the formation of "friendship groups" of three to five families that were to meet at least every two weeks "with an Israeli family of the party. The latter will maintain regular contact with the group and help the immigrants with advice and instruction, with small gestures and in all the thousand small problems which in the final analysis determine the absorption of the family in Israel."[22] However, of 300 party activists polled, only a dozen or so were willing to work with such "friendship groups."[23]

The religious parties operate differently, more in conformity with the life styles of their constituents and the institutional structure of their communities. A spokesman for Agudat Yisrael explained that "our work in social integration is done through the synagogue and the schools and our warm-hearted people who don't need to be pushed and prodded into making friends with newcomers — they understand that they have a religious obligation to do this."[24] The Labor party, too, operates somewhat differently, since local labor councils, the Histadrut, and other organizations under its influence can promote social contacts with immigrants, with the party presence less visible.

Some of the parties are able to reach the immigrants very soon after their arrival because temporary housing and Hebrew language courses are provided in kibbutzim and other rural settlements. For example, in 1972 the Kibbutz Artzi, a network of kibbutzim affiliated with Mapam, housed 26 *ulpanim* (accelerated language courses) and two full-scale immigrant absorption centers. The Herut party bemoaned the fact that no *ulpanim* were located in its settlements, very few in number in any case, but it does have immigrant children in its youth villages. The Independent Liberals sponsor five educational institutions with dormitories specifically for immigrant children. Their spokesman said that the party tried to reach the parents of its students and draw them closer to the party, with indifferent success. The religious parties enroll children in their schools, many of which have dormitories, and there is sometimes a struggle between the school systems for the children of immigrants.

The parties vary considerably in the extent to which they publish materials for the immigrants. The Independent Liberals concentrate on the Romanian immigration, and so a disproportionate amount of their publications are in that language. Labor, the National Religious party, and Herut (Likud) publish more in English than the other parties, and Labor, Mapam, and Herut have the most extensive Russian-language publications. In the early 1970s Herut was publishing a mimeographed monthly, *Doma* (At Home), which called itself a "review of political, economic, and social problems of Israel." Herut spokesmen claimed that this was a continuation of an underground periodical in the USSR, *Domoi* (Homeward), which it had promoted. Later the party stood behind the popular weekly, *Nedelia*. The Mapam party also began with a mimeographed publication, *My* (We), but by 1975 it was appearing twice a month in a large newspaper format of eight pages. The Russian-language daily, *Nasha strana*, is perceived as reflecting the Labor party's views. Religious parties sponsor translations of classic Jewish texts and liturgical works. Of course, there is considerable political material in the nonparty Russian-language publications that have emerged in Israel in the last decade.

In the 1970s the parties concentrated their efforts on the Soviet immigrants, for obvious reasons. Despite a significant immigration from English-speaking countries, most of the parties did not pay much attention to the "Anglo-Saxons." Americans, explained the head of the Labor party's absorption department, come from a society with no real parties "and our East European-type system is strange to them. We concentrate on ideologies and programs, not just personalities. We debate issues, not personalities."[25] The Mapam spokesman was equally unenthusiastic about Americans, explaining that "they don't like to turn to anyone for help, they like to take care of themselves, and no one seems to know how they integrate into Israeli society."[26] Even the religious parties, which should be attractive to the American immigration because of its high proportion of religious people, view the Americans as pretty much of a lost cause because the parties can do little for them: "They don't need material assistance, the intelligentsia among them find their own social circles, and they don't like to be organized."[27] There seems to be a mutual incomprehension between the party organizers and the Americans, each believing that the other operates in a "peculiar" political culture. The high social and material status of the Americans makes them unlikely to turn to parties for material or social needs, and the seeming resistance of Americans to being openly partisan puts off the party recruiters. Highly educated, middle class Americans seem to pride themselves on their nonpartisan "independence" in the United States. These attitudes carry over to Israel, where the large number of parties and their "bickering" put off many Americans.

The attitude of the parties to the Soviet immigration is quite different. We have seen how the Labor party in effect abandoned its efforts toward other immigrants by transferring the head of its absorption department almost full time to the Union of Soviet Immigrants. Despite the Soviet immigrants' hostility to the kibbutz, which they associate with collectivized agriculture, the Mapam party, whose strength is overwhelmingly in the kibbutzim, was paying considerable attention to them. A Mapam spokesman explained this with the hypothesis that Soviet conditions had made the Jews very nationalistic and at the same time hostile to socialism. But having achieved "national self-determination," the immigrant would come to see the welfare aspects of the Soviet system in a more favorable light, as he realized that the Israeli economy was not providing him with the free health and educational services he had enjoyed in the USSR. "We then try to show them that we combine national rights with the positive aspects of the Soviet system. . . . In the longer run, we think they will come to us."[28] The hypothesis is logical, but there is no evidence that it has been proved. With a Mapam minister heading the MIA and kibbutz members drafted or volunteering to help in immigrant absorption, the other parties feared that Mapam would recruit a substantial proportion of the Soviet newcomers. This fear turned out to be groundless. In fact, Mapam suffered a general decline in the late 1970s, losing half its Knesset seats in the 1977 election.

In contrast to Mapam's hopes, the common perception in Israel was that the Soviet immigrants would support the right-wing Likud. In 1973 the New York *Times* reported that "Israel's 30,000 recent immigrants from the Soviet Union appear to be leaning politically to a new grouping of nationalist parties [the Likud] that will attempt to unseat the Government in the parliamentary election. . . . It appears that many of the newcomers favor Likud."[29] Menachem Begin confidently predicted that Soviet immigrants would support his party and ideology, citing what was to become a conventional wisdom explaining the reasons for their outlook: They were influenced by the Russian writings of Vladimir (Zeev) Zhabotinsky, the ideologist of Herut; there were among their leaders former members of the right-wing Revisionist movement, especially in the Baltic area; Soviet conditions had made them highly nationalistic, as well as antisocialist.[30] Indeed, some who had been refused permission to emigrate had declared themselves adherents of Herut already in the Soviet Union, and Herut created the impression that it was more militant on behalf of Soviet Jews and their right to emigrate than the ruling parties. Among the first arrivals in the mass emigration were people — Dov Sperling, Leah Slovina, Boris Kochubievsky — whose struggle for emigration had been well publicized and who now proclaimed their allegiance to Herut, which even employed a few of them. Later arrivals and those from the Slavic republics and

Georgia did not identify so prominently with Herut, but the first impression lingered. In the absence of hard data, it is impossible to tell to what extent Soviet immigrants voted disproportionately for the Likud in 1973, 1977, or 1981, but ecological inferences alone indicate that they did not lopsidedly support Likud compared to the rest of the electorate. Nevertheless, Likud leaders made sure to be photographed with well-known Soviet activists, attended their weddings and other family celebrations, and lauded them in the press. Likud sympathizers struggled to wrest control of the Union of Soviet Immigrants, with some success, and dominated the Organization of Prisoners of Zion, whose membership consisted largely of Soviet and East European immigrants who had been imprisoned for Zionist activities.[31]

If Mapam and Herut perceived logical reasons for Soviet immigrants to support them, the religious parties could not. The head of Agudat Yisrael's absorption department called the Jews from the European USSR "partners of the regime, spoiled by its ideology," and his counterpart in the National Religious party saw them as "innocents taken into heathen captivity [*tinokot shenishbu bain hagoyim*]." The religious parties placed their hopes with the immigrants from Georgia and Central Asia. They were used to living apart from the mainstream of society, as they would have to do in Israel if they were to preserve their familial and religious traditions. Moreover, their needs were not only material, but also religious, and it was not the MIA or a secular party that would supply them with the Talmud, phylacteries, or religious education for their children.

These perceptions led to a struggle among three religious parties, the Labor party, and the Habad (Lubavitch) Hassidic movement. The Union of Georgian Immigrants was organized first and presided over by the native-born Israeli Labor activist Rafi Balvashvili (Bar-Lavi). It was recognized by the MIA as the representative of the Georgian immigrants and received some funds from it. When a competing organization, the Organization of Georgian Immigrants, was formed, the MIA refused to recognize and fund it and urged that it merge with the older group.[32] The moving force behind the second organization was the Agudat Yisrael, and its secretary was a Rabbi Lifschitz — who did not bother to attach a "shvili" to his name. The Poalai Agudat Yisrael (PAY) also reached out to the Georgians, with its Member of Knesset (M.K.) Abraham Werdiger intervening on behalf of Georgian stevedores and fighting for their right not to work on the Sabbath.[33] The PAY claims to have enrolled "hundreds of Georgian families," though whether their affiliation goes beyond a one-time payment of dues is hard to tell.[34]

Joining the fray were the Habad Hassidim, part of whose ideology is "reaching out" to nonreligious Jews and those whose religious needs are not being met otherwise. The NRP charged that the MIA was assigning religious activities among Georgian and Central Asian newcomers to Habad, for the latter is a nonpolitical movement and is preferable, from the MIA point of view, to political movements. Indeed, several hundred Georgian families were housed in a Habad project in Kiryat Malakhi, special classes for Georgian and Central Asian children were established in Habad schools, and leaders of the immigrant communities were accorded the high honor of being invited to spend religious holidays with the "Rebbe," the leader of the movement, Rabbi Menachem Mendel Schneerson, at his headquarters in Brooklyn.[35]

When Georgian stevedores in the ports and the international airport complained that they had to work on the Sabbath as a condition of their employment, Agudat Yisrael and Poalai Agudat Yisrael were quick to seize upon the issue and broaden it, charging that the government was forcing immigrants to abandon their religion. The issue was brought to the Knesset floor in February 1972 in the form of a resolution of no confidence in the government, sponsored by Agudat Yisrael. Invoking the memory of European refugee children and Yemenite children who had been taken from religious environments and raised in secular ones, M.K. Lorincz of Agudat Yisrael charged that the Mapam-dominated MIA was seeking to do the same with the religious immigrants from the USSR. Religious M.K.s demanded to know why the MIA had no religious employees (in private conversation, one religious party official characterized the MIA as *judenrein*). They charged that religious immigrants were being assigned housing in scattered localities so that they could be more easily influenced by secular environments, that they were being discouraged from sending their children to religious schools, and that synagogues were not being built in their neighborhoods. Speaking on behalf of the government, Prime Minister Meir charged that

> there is an unholy competition for the souls of the Georgian Jews.
> . . . We are all members of parties, let's call a spade a spade, and not

dignify it with religion. . . . It is a commandment [*mitzvah*] to capture members for a party, it's a secular commandment, very secular. This has nothing to do with religious observance.[36]

Indeed, it is hard to resist the notion that the two religious parties were seeking to make political capital of a genuine religious issue, though in the Israeli system it is often impossible to separate the two. Though the motion of no confidence was decisively rejected, the religious parties succeeded in publicizing the issue and themselves, but it is doubtful whether they won any members or voters from among those whose interests they were representing. The Israeli election study (1973) and other evidence show that the Georgians are not very attentive to the media and display little knowledge of, or interest in, politics. As one Georgian activist put it, they appreciate the help of parties and politicians, but their loyalty remains to the ethnic group. They have no commitment to a specific variant of Zionist ideology, and their religious convictions are also not easily translated into allegiance to a particular religious party. Their approach to the politicians is therefore completely pragmatic: Whoever can do most to serve their needs at a particular moment will win their allegiance. – for that moment.

For all their professed interest in the Soviet immigrants, the parties have not given them leading positions on electoral lists or within the party apparatus. Neither in the eighth Knesset, elected in 1973, nor in the ninth, elected in 1977, was there a post-1967 immigrant from the USSR. This is not surprising in light of the general slowness of political mobility in Israel, where people are expected to work their way up the party hierarchy. With the exception of army officers after the 1967 War, few are ever coopted into leadership positions or move laterally from nonpolitical elite positions into political leadership. Herut did include eight Soviet immigrants among the 270 members of its central committee (1974-75), but even by 1976 there was no Soviet immigrant in the Labor party's central organs. Some of the smaller parties included Soviet immigrants on their electoral lists in 1977 and 1981, but so far down the list that they had no realistic chance of being elected. There is no reason to believe that the parties were singling out the Soviet immigrants and keeping them from rising to leadership positions. The general reluctance of the immigrants to identify with parties and Israel's slow political mobility combined to delay the emergence of prominent politicians who came to Israel from the USSR after 1967. No doubt, their day will come in the not-too-distant future.

AGENTS OF POLITICAL RESOCIALIZATION AND THEIR EFFECTIVENESS

We cannot determine how effective the organizations and parties are in resocializing the immigrants politically. However, only if immigrants affiliate in some way with these organizations can they be potential resocializers. One reanalysis of the data gathered by Gabriel Almond and Sidney Verba in their five-nation study of the "civic culture" concluded that in all the countries studied, organizational involvement is the most powerful predictor of political participation. Even people who are not very well informed about politics, who do not feel politically efficacious and who are not very attentive to political matters, will participate in politics if they are organizationally involved.[37] Even if Israeli organizations do not directly resocialize immigrants, those who affiliate with them are more likely to be politically involved, if the conclusion above holds also for Israel.

The immigrants in our group were asked whether they belonged to any organization at all in Israel. In both 1972 and 1975 only about one-third of the Soviet immigrants said they belonged to some organization — and this was equally true for Zapadniki and heartlanders — while two-thirds of the Americans claimed such affiliation. It should be noted that when the data are analyzed by individual cases, it turns out that the same number of Soviet olim who joined an organization between 1972 and 1975 *dis*affiliated from one in that period. In other words, while the group as a whole did not change its pattern of organizational affiliation over the three years, individuals within it did. In both the American and Soviet groups the proportion of 1972-only respondents who belonged to organizations was somewhat lower (in 1972) than among those who were reinterviewed in 1975. That a higher proportion of Americans should be organizationally involved is reasonable, as Americans are widely reputed to be "joiners," whereas in the Soviet Union all organizations are connected to the state in some way, and to "voluntarily" join an organization means either to be compelled to do so or to do so for some ulterior motive, in the great majority of cases. No doubt, many Soviet immigrants have acquired an aversion to organizational membership. In any case, this is not a "natural impulse" for them, as it is likely to be for Americans. The fact that as many disaffiliated as joined in 1972-75 may be due to the fact that some of the 1972 memberships were free or "automatic," that is, achieved without conscious action on the part of the immigrants, and that these then lapsed. At the same time, other Soviet immigrants were abandoning their prejudice against organizational affiliation.

The organizations immigrants are most likely to join are the immigrant associations and the Histadrut. In 1972, 43 of the 54 American immigrants said they were members of the Association of Americans and Canadians in Israel, but only 32 of the 148 Soviets (22 percent) were members of the Union of Soviet Immigrants. This is in line with the findings of the MIA study that showed relatively little Soviet affiliation with the immigrant association. Five Americans who had been members in 1972 dropped out by 1975, and two who had not been members joined by 1975, so that there was little net change among them. Among the Soviets, only seven people dropped out between 1972 and 1975, but 29 joined up, so that over half the group in 1975 were Union-affiliated, whereas less than one-quarter had been in 1972. For some Americans the services provided by the AACI, including its social functions, may be no longer needed after three years in the country. On the other hand, it seems to take the Soviet newcomers longer to learn about the existence of the Union and to be formally enrolled. We have noted the growth in the Union's membership from 25,000 in 1973 to 44,000 in 1975, the year our informants were reinterviewed, and their higher affiliation rate may reflect the more general success of the Union in enrolling its potential membership. Formal membership, of course, does not tell the whole story. In fact, both the Americans and the Soviets who were members of their respective associations reported that they were becoming less active as time went on. They had less objective need for the services provided by the association and their identities were changing away from that of *olim khadashim* (new immigrants). The situation is slightly different in regard to members of the *Asirai tsion*, or Prisoners of Zion organization. In 1972, 23 Soviet informants who had been imprisoned for Zionist beliefs or activities had membership in this organization; 17 of them were reinterviewed in 1975, all of them still members of the organization. This group defines its mission as continuing the struggle for Jews in the USSR, not so much for immigrants, and therefore it made just as much sense to belong in 1975 as in 1972.

Histadrut officials expressed anxiety over the fact that new immigrants were not joining the organization in the same proportions as the population as a whole. There are several indications that this is true only for the first year or so of the immigrants' stay in the country, or for immigrants from certain countries. Both our data and those from the Israeli election study (1973) show that the proportion of immigrants affiliated with the Histadrut is only slightly lower than that for the entire population. It is true that in 1972 only about 60 percent of our Soviet informants were members, but by 1975, 73 percent were members (17 individuals who had not been members in 1972 joined by 1975, while only eight who had been members dropped out). However, only about one-third of the Americans were Histadrut members in either 1972 or 1975 (four Americans affiliated in the interval, but two dropped their membership). There is a greater proportion of self-employed among the Americans, who are also less enthusiastic about the Histadrut's *Kupat kholim* than the Soviets. The latter are more familiar with the polyclinic system and are less able to afford the services of a private doctor or are less aware of the other health plans available to them. The Zapadniki affiliate earlier with the Histadrut than heartlanders, probably because there is a greater proportion of Zapadniki among the earlier waves, and hence they were employed somewhat earlier. Zapadniki were more favorably impressed than the others with "the job the Histadrut is doing," and Americans were least impressed by it.

As with the Israeli public generally, those who are not members of the Histadrut, or those who take a dim view of its activities, are more likely to identify with right-wing parties, those opposed to Labor. This does not mean that the Histadrut is an effective recruiting device for the Labor party and its allies, because there are too many intervening variables — for example, income, class affiliation, occupation — that may determine both Histadrut affiliation or non-affiliation as well as political outlook. Nevertheless, if one bears in mind the findings of Nie, Powell, and Prewitt on the importance of organizational membership for political participation, the very fact of Histadrut membership might be highly influential in an individual's general political behavior, whether or not it is conducive specifically to sympathy for the Labor party, independent of other factors.

Before turning to the immigrants' partisan sympathies, we should consider two other potential elements in their political resocialization, or lack of it. These are the "political referents" or "role models" of the immigrants – to whom they turn for information and advice on political matters – and major events occurring in Israel that might reasonably be expected to influence their thinking about politics.

Many of the immigrants of the yishuv period and those who came in the 1940s and 1950s had acknowledged guides to whom they could turn for political advice. Whether it was the party leader to whom the immigrant was referred back in his country of origin, the instructor on the moshav, or the *politruk* in the youth movement or military organization, there was an authority who could provide political guidance. There is no such figure for contemporary immigrants who are, after all, less in need of such guidance and for whom the parties play less of a role than they did for earlier immigrants. When our informants were asked whether they had someone to whom they could turn for advice on Israeli politics, about half the Soviet immigrants questioned in both the Israeli study and our own said they knew such a person, though only one-third of the Georgians did so. However, no clear profile of such referents emerged, as they included friends and relatives, newcomers and veterans, party and nonparty people. So we can make no judgment as to the role of such people in the overall process of resocialization. It is likely, however, that, in contrast to earlier periods, most such people are located by the immigrant, rather than the other way around. This increases the randomness and fluidity of possible interaction between immigrants and Israelis who could act as direct political socializers.[38]

The major national event between 1972 and 1975 was the war in October 1973, when Israel suffered considerable losses before reversing its initial military setbacks, and, in the opinion of many, suffered irreversible political losses. National elections had been scheduled for the month when the war broke out and they had to be postponed to the end of December, thus taking place in the shadow of what was seen as a national catastrophe. The Labor government, caught unaware by the Egyptian offensive, was blamed for the *mekhdal*, or foul-up, and it was thought that it would be turned out of power for the first time in Israeli history. However, the Labor Alignment managed to win 51 Knesset seats (down from

56 in 1969) and formed the government coalition that was to hold together, more or less, until 1977. The Likud, uniting Gahal with smaller oppositionist parties at the urging of one of the few Israeli military heroes of the 1973 War, General Arik Sharon, went from 26 seats to 39. This foreshadowed the election of 1977, when the Likud got 43 seats and Labor declined drastically to 32.[39] While the 1973 election was not a "critical election" in the sense V. O. Key used the term, the October War had made a great impact and it was felt in the political arena as well. Its impact on immigrants was no less than on others. Nearly all our informants acknowledged that the war had affected them personally in one way or another. Some spoke of its spiritual or psychological impact. One American said that "it gave me a much stronger connection to Israel — I felt that I belonged, that I had something to do here." But another said that as a result of the war "I believed less in my ability to control my life. I had no say in this war, I couldn't change it, though I didn't believe in it." Several Americans and Soviets, for whom this was their first experience in the army, commented on the disorganization they had found. Others, however, found the experience "inspiring" and "uplifting." Reflecting the sentiments of many Israelis, two-thirds of the Americans said the war had turned them against the government at the time, and a smaller proportion of the Soviets also mentioned this effect. One Soviet immigrant commented that the war had left him "an unbeliever in the government which says one thing and then something else happens." As we shall see, between 1972 and 1975 there was a shift in political sympathy among the American and Soviet informants from Labor to the Likud, and while we cannot attribute this definitely to the 1973 War, it must have played no less a role among the immigrants than among the rest of the population. In fact, since the immigrants' shift was visible already in 1975, before the scandals in the Labor party had been exposed — scandals that did a great deal to erode Labor's strength — we can attribute more of the shift in the immigrants' political sympathies to the war than to any other political events.

Whatever and whoever politically socializes the immigrants, what are the outcomes? To what extent are the immigrants interested in politics and knowledgeable about it? How do they act in the political arena? What are their partisan sympathies and activities and what motivates them?

POLITICAL INTEREST AND POLITICIZATION

An index of political interest was constructed from five variables using our 1975 data. A similar index was constructed from the Israeli election study, based on seven variables, four of which were identical to those from our own study. (These two indexes are detailed in Appendixes F and G.) The first index, from our study, is summarized in Table 7.1.

Not a single American scored "low" on his interest in politics, though both Soviets and Americans were fairly evenly split between the "medium" and "high" categories. Data from the other study allow for comparisons among three groups of Soviet immigrants (see Table 7.2). Again, the respondents are quite evenly split between the "medium" and "high" categories. The Georgians, as might be expected, score lower than the other two groups, and the Balts, who have been in Israel somewhat longer than the heartlanders, score somewhat higher. On measures of knowledge of Israeli politics, the Balts scored much higher than the others, and the heartlanders were decisively ahead of the Georgians. Taking only the single question of professed interest in politics — the same question was posed in both studies — our own group professes a higher interest. Not a single person in our group claimed to have no interest at all in politics, whereas 71 in the Israeli election study, 38 of them Georgians, made this claim. When we recall that 40 percent of those surveyed in 1973 had less than a complete high school education — among Georgians the figure is 52 percent — and that all of our own interviewees had at least a high school education, the difference in political interest between the two groups is understandable. The better-educated immigrant group even displays considerably higher

TABLE 7.1
Index of Interest in Politics — 1972/75 Study
(1975 data, in percentages)

	Heartlanders	*Zapadniki*	*Soviets*	*Americans*
Low	12	4	8	0
Medium	38	52	46	40
High	50	44	46	60

TABLE 7.2
Index of Interest in Politics — Israel Election Study
(1973, in percentages)

	Balts	Georgians	Heartlanders	Total
Low	3	18	13	11
Medium	44	47	53	48
High	53	35	34	41

political interest than did a national sample of Israelis (1973), while the immigrants in the other study, interviewed at the same time as the national sample, exhibited somewhat less.[40]

The Americans thought it very important to understand Israel's political problems, and the Soviets, especially the heartlanders, were somewhat less convinced of this. On the other hand, Soviet immigrants were more interested in the platforms and programs of the parties than the Americans, perhaps because, as one of the party functionaries cited earlier had noted, Americans are not terribly interested in ideologies and platforms and may view democratic politics somewhat as a spectator sport, whereas Soviets view it more seriously, at least at an early stage. Whereas four out of five of the Americans felt it important to give their children a "political education," only half the Soviets thought so, perhaps because of the connotations "political education" has in the Soviet context. In fact, 40 percent of the Soviets were quite definitely opposed to giving their children any political education.

To what extent does professed interest in politics translate into political action? It is quite possible for people to be passionately interested in politics as spectators without themselves becoming gladiators in the arena. It is reasonable to think that this is even more characteristic of immigrants. Even those immigrants who are intensely interested in politics may not be active politically in their first few years in the country, as they would first want to "learn the ropes." Our group was asked about their participation in political meetings, signing of political petitions, and participation in public debates. They were also asked whether they had ever written to a Knesset member. The Soviets have a greater propensity for signing petitions, understandable in light of appeals circulated on behalf of Jews in the USSR, while the Americans are more likely to attend political meetings. There are no differences between Zapadniki and heartlanders on these modes of participation, and not much difference between the claimed participation of Soviets and Americans. In both groups no more than 10 percent claim to be active "often" in each of the four activities.

The immigrants were asked a more concrete question: whether or not they had voted in the 1973 election. All the Soviets were eligible to vote in that election, but 14 of the Americans were not, as they were still "temporary residents." Only seven of the Soviets and three of the eligible Americans said they had not voted, so that their claimed turnout was no lower than the usual overall turnout in Israel, which runs above 80 percent. In the Israeli election study, conducted shortly before the election, only three-quarters of those questioned about their intention to vote said they would do so. As in other cases, the Baltic respondents showed the greatest interest and the Georgians the least (only 61 percent of the latter intended to vote). Again, differences in education are the likely explanation both for the variation within the 1973 sample as well as for the difference between our group and that sample. It might be noted that in the Israeli national sample surveyed in 1973, 89 percent declared their intention to vote.

For most of the Soviet interviewees, the 1973 election was their first outside the USSR. Questioned about the significance of their voting, most attributed what might be called a "reflexive" rather than "transitive" significance to it. That is, they did not speak in terms of the effect their vote had on the alignment of political power but rather of the effect it had on them. More than half said it made them feel "part of Israel." It is precisely the parallel sentiment about the USSR that participation in Soviet elections, which have no "transitive" value whatsoever, is supposed to evoke. We should not make too much of this because a similar proportion of the Americans expressed the same sentiments. Most of the other Soviets were evenly divided between those who said their participation simply meant that they had done their civic duty, and those who said it meant "nothing." (In 1973, half the Israeli sample said they voted because it made them "feel part of the people" [19 percent], or to "fulfill my duty to the country" [31 percent].) Again, these would be expected responses to inquiries about the significance of Soviet elections, but almost all the Soviets said that

Israeli and Soviet elections were significantly different and the Israeli one is far preferable.[41] The Americans, by contrast, prefer the American system. Voting "would mean in the States working and fighting for a certain personality I believe in and therefore, as an independent, I could choose the person I wanted. Whereas here, not voting for a personality, just for a party, I feel no identification with any party and therefore no desire to vote."

Trying to see what might characterize those who participate least in political life in Israel, we discover that, among the Soviets, it is people who have low incomes, who are in the youngest group, and who do not have strong Jewish backgrounds. Americans with a strong Jewish background are likely participants as are those who prefer to have Israeli friends and neighbors rather than people from their own countries. In other words, those who see themselves as Israelis, rather than as "Americans living in Israel," are more likely to act as Israelis in the political, as well as in other, realms.

PARTY IDENTIFICATION AND PARTISAN ACTIVITY

The extent to which people identify themselves as supporters of a particular political party varies considerably across democratic systems, and within them over time. In the 1960s in several West European countries about three-quarters of the population surveyed identified with a party, though the proportion in France was higher and that in Great Britain lower. In India and in Britain a substantial majority were classified as "strong" identifiers, whereas in the United States or Norway identification with parties was far less intense.[42] In India and elsewhere it has been noted that partisan identification is unevenly distributed among different strata of the population. In India, for example, illiterates and those with only a minimal education are more strongly committed to parties than others, and in at least three societies those with college educations were found to be less inclined to identification with a party.[43] In Israel, studies conducted between 1969 and 1973, based on national samples, disclosed that between 34 and 41 percent identified themselves as supporters of a party, and between 12 and 25 percent said they were members of a party.[44] In Israel, too, it is the less educated who tend to identify more consistently with a single party.

Immigrants might generally be less inclined to a partisan identification than others, except under unusual circumstances, such as those in pre-1948 Palestine. After all, studies have shown that party identification is often formed very early in life, almost in "hereditary" fashion, or is shaped by some decisive experience of an individual or an entire society. Immigrants' early experiences are usually irrelevant to the political system to which they migrate,[45] and they have not grown up in a "Democratic household" or a "Conservative family." They may not have shared in the events that led to secular shifts in partisan affiliations, and their unfamiliarity with the political system and the more urgent need to establish themselves economically, culturally, and socially may lead them to postpone interest in a political party. As one of our American informants said, "I'm not interested . . . I have too many problems right now to worry about Labor, Histadrut, Mapai." The little evidence there is indicates that immigrants elsewhere are, indeed, slow to develop partisan identities. The seeming rapidity with which Israeli immigrants appear to have developed identifications with parties is exceptional and can be explained by the unusual role played by parties in the very process of immigrant resettlement.[46]

As we shall see shortly, even in the present period, when the role of parties in resettlement has been considerably reduced, levels of party identification and even membership among Soviet immigrants are not dramatically lower than those for the population as a whole. Is this because the immigrants have been actively sought out by partisan recruiters? The parties are active among the Soviet immigrants, but only the larger ones attempt to reach the broad mass of newcomers, and the more narrowly based parties limit their appeals to a carefully circumscribed constituency, as they have done traditionally. Among our group of immigrants, about 40 percent of the Soviets and 60 percent of the Americans report that at some point someone had asked them to join a party. These recruiters were party members themselves, but, according to the immigrants, their efforts were largely in vain. Almost all the Soviets and most of the Americans who recalled being asked to join a party asserted that they reacted either negatively or with indifference to the recruiters' efforts. Those who did end up joining parties, or identifying with one of them, did not mention successful recruiting efforts, nor did they identify people who brought them into the party or to sympathy with it. If we are to credit their recollections, we must conclude that this highly educated, relatively affluent group of immigrants was either unaffected by individual recruitment efforts or, at the least, these immigrants were reluctant to admit that they were won over by a recruiter for a party.

Of the 202 immigrants questioned in 1972, 107 (53 percent) identified a party to which they felt "closest." By 1975, of the 108 immigrants reinterviewed, 68 (63 percent) identified such a party. The phrasing of the question — "Of all the parties in Israel, which one do you feel closest to?" — may have elicited a more affirmative response than had the question been whether they felt close to any party at all. On the basis of pre-tests, however, it was felt that the latter question also contained a "cue" to the respondent to deny any "closeness" to a party. The seriousness with which our question was taken, the opportunity to say that the respondent did not feel close to *any* party, and responses to follow-up questions wherein reasons for the identification were given, all gave us confidence that "non-attitudes" were generally not elicited.

Beginning with an examination of the information obtained in 1972, we found 86 Soviet immigrants (58 percent) identifying with a party. Among the 54 Americans, 21 (39 percent) did so. Table 7.3 shows with which parties the immigrants identified. The relative support that each party enjoyed among the immigrants

TABLE 7.3
Immigrants' Party Identification, 1972
(absolute numbers)

	Heartlanders	Zapadniki	Soviets	Americans
Rakah*	1	—	1	—
Avneri†	—	—	—	1
Mapam	—	5	5	3
Labor	11	22	33	4
Independent Liberals	5	2	7	—
National Religious Party	1	2	3	4
Agudat Yisrael	—	—	—	1
Gahal	18	19	37	8
None	35	27	62	33

*The Communist party, officially recognized by the Soviet Union.

†Uri Avneri, editor of a sensational magazine, formed his own party, but in 1977 joined leaders of other parties to form the Sheli party.

in 1972 can be seen more clearly in Figure 7.1. It can be seen readily that the Americans, a smaller proportion of whom identified with parties, were more scattered across the parties, whereas the sympathies of the Soviets were directed largely to the two main parties. As one Soviet informant commented, "what you need in a democracy is a realistic opposition party, not all of these small groups who have no chance of getting power." The Soviets' clustering around the two major parties (81 percent identified with them) may also have stemmed from their lesser familiarity with the other parties and their outlooks, as compared to the Americans who, even in the United States, had far greater opportunity to familiarize themselves with Israel's party spectrum. Of course, 5 of the 21 American identifiers associated themselves with religious parties and this accounted for

FIGURE 7.1
Party Identification, 1972, Soviet and American Immigrants

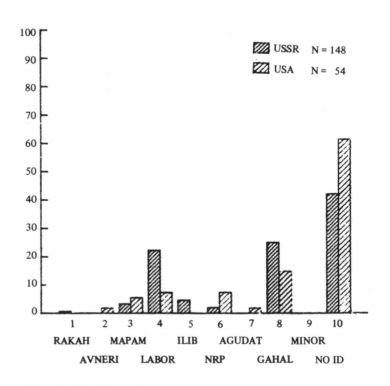

Source: Compiled by the author.

much of the minor party identification. Their identification with those parties can be attributed to their concern for religious matters − schooling, public observance of the Sabbath, and the like − so it is somewhat misleading to see this in terms of conventional Western political ideology.

It is true that Gahal (later the Likud) was favored by a few more Soviet immigrants than Labor, but not nearly to the extent one would have expected from the mythology about the right-wing sentiments of the antisocialist Soviet immigrants. Of course, our group was not a representative one, but we shall see the same phenomenon in the Israeli election study. In the absence of any other empirical evidence, we must reserve judgment about the conventional belief in the right-wing inclinations of the Soviet immigrants, at least before the general swing to the right following the 1973 War and culminating in the national election four years later. Separating the Soviets into Zapadniki and heartlanders allows one to observe that the Gahal advantage over Labor is created by the heartlanders, and that among the Zapadniki, Labor does slightly better than Gahal. If one thinks of the "alignment," that is, Labor and Mapam, then Labor's advantage among the Zapadniki increases. Again, it is worth noting that in the Israeli election study as well we shall see that identification with Labor is strongest among the Zapadniki (or Balts). In both studies a somewhat higher proportion of Zapadniki than heartlanders express their identification with a party. The most likely explanation is their longer time in Israel, and perhaps their more extensive knowledge of Jewish culture and history, including contemporary political history.

How stable is the immigrants' identification with parties? Are they "shopping around" for a party that suits their tastes or have they developed the kind of party identification often found in Western democracies, an identification that remains stable, sometimes transcending personal development and change in the outer world? Does party identification increase or decrease with time − do the immigrants have an initial fascination with the parties that is then dulled by familiarity with them, or do they acquire interest in parties as they become more familiar with the Israeli system and, presumably, liberated from some of the immediate worries connected with resettlement? As noted, there is evidence from other countries that the longer the immigrant is in the country, the more likely he is to be interested and participate in politics. Our group appeared to identify with a party slightly more in 1975 than it did in 1972, as already observed. Among the Soviets in 1975 there were 48 men identifying with a party, representing 62 percent of the group (compare 58 percent in 1972). The Americans showed a clearer increase: 20 of the 30 Americans reinterviewed in 1975 identify with a party (compare 39 percent in 1972).

With whom did the 1975 interviewees identify? Table 7.4 and Figure 7.2 show that there have been some apparent shifts from 1972. Comparing the 1972 and 1975 responses, it appears that the major shift was among the Soviets, away from the Labor party and toward Gahal. Gahal had outranked Labor by 18 to 11 among heartlanders in 1972, but in 1972 its advantage was increased to 14-3; whereas Labor had a slight edge over Gahal in 1972 among the Zapadniki, three years later it was Gahal that had 20 identifiers and Labor had only 8. Among the Americans, Labor actually fared a bit better in 1975 than it did in 1972, though so few Americans were involved that it is difficult to interpret the results.

How much actual change do these figures represent? First of all, the increase between 1972 and 1975 in the proportion of both Soviets and Americans who have any party identity at all is not as great as it first seemed, because the 1972/75 group — those 1972 immigrants who were reinterviewed in 1975 — were more likely than the 1972-only group to have had a party identity when first interviewed.

TABLE 7.4
Immigrants' Party Identification, 1975
(absolute numbers)

		Heartlanders	*Zapadniki*	*Soviets*	*Americans*
Mapam		—	1	1	—
Labor		3	8	11	6
Independent Liberals		1	—	1	2
National Religious Party		—	—	—	3
Agudat Yisrael		—	—	—	—
Gahal		14	20	34	6
Other*		—	1	1	3
None	14	14	16	30	10

*Citizens' Rights Movement, Shinui, and so on. Avneri's party had disappeared, and the Rakah party was not mentioned by anyone.

FIGURE 7.2

Party Identification, 1975, Soviet and American Immigrants

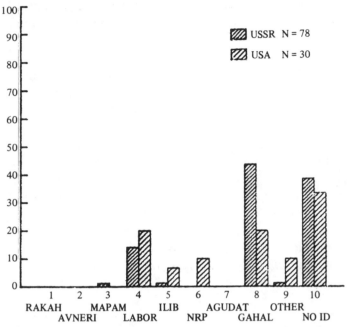

Source: Compiled by the author.

Among the Soviets, for example, 69 percent of the 1972/75 group (54 people) had a party identity, while only 47 percent (32 people) of the others did. Among the Americans, 18 of the 30 who reappeared in 1975 had a partisan identity, but only 3 of the 24 in the 1972-only group had such an identity. (Those who stayed in Israel had a higher propensity for party identification in 1972, so perhaps this would be one indicator of their "integration.") It turns out, therefore, that there is really a very slight *decline* in the proportion of Soviet partisan identifiers (from 69 percent of the 1972/75 group to 62 percent among them in 1975). Among the Americans there is an increase, but it, too, is very slight (from 60 to 67 percent).

Second, the Soviets' shift in identification away from Labor and to Gahal is *not* illusory. Of the 37 Gahal identifiers in 1972, 13 were not reinterviewed in 1975; but of the 24 who were, 19 still identified with them in 1975. In sharp contrast, out of 22 Labor identifiers (11 were not reinterviewed), only 7 stuck with the party over the three years. An equal number defected to Gahal and yet another 7 dropped any partisan identity, with one going to a minor party.

There is not a single person who switched from Gahal to Labor among the Soviets. These shifts can be seen in Table 7.5. Of the four Americans who identified with Labor in 1972, two stayed with Labor in 1975, and one each went to the Independent Liberals and to Gahal; but Labor picked up one person previously identifying with Gahal and three who had no party identification at all in 1972. Of the eight 1972 Gahal identifiers, two remained with the party, one each went to Labor and the NRP, two no longer had a party identification in 1975, and two were not reinterviewed.

Taking the entire group of immigrants into consideration, we see that of the 37 people who had identified with Labor in 1972, only 9 remained so identified in 1975. Eleven were not reinterviewed, but even had all remained in the country and with Labor, the party's loss of support would have been considerable. Gahal identifiers were more loyal, with 21 of 45 remaining with the party — and even if all 15 not reinterviewed had defected, Gahal would still have retained a higher proportion of its followers than Labor. It is striking that *all* shifts that did occur were toward the right side of the political spectrum: from Mapam to Labor, from Labor to Gahal, and so on, except for those who dropped all identification. Finally, we note that while there was substantial shifting among party identifications, there was a marked tendency for those who had *some* partisan identity in 1972 to have one in 1975 (the correlation between some party identification in 1972 and 1975 is .40). At least among this group of immigrants, therefore, identification with a political party, if it was to occur at all, came about relatively *early* in an immigrant's stay in Israel. Identification with a party does *not* increase monotonically nor does the strength of that identification, as reported by our group. Perhaps there is a certain formative period in the immigrant's life history when party loyalty can be "imprinted," though, as we have seen, *which* party will be identified with may change markedly in a short period of time. Neither do we have a large enough group of respondents nor were we able to follow this question over a long enough period of time to make this any more than a suggestion.

Of the 86 Soviet party identifiers, only 29 said they felt "very close" to that party, and only 2 of the 21 American identifiers said so in 1972. We can therefore understand why among the Soviets there were only 15 people who claimed party *membership* in 1972, and only two Americans — the same two who said they felt "very

TABLE 7.5
Individual Soviets' Party Identification, 1972 and 1975
(absolute numbers)

1975 Party Identification	1972 Party Identification					
	Mapam (5)	Labor (33)	Independent Liberals (7)	National Religious Party (3)	Gahal (37)	No Identification (62)
Mapam	1	—	—	—	—	—
Labor	1	7	—	—	—	—
Independent Liberals	—	—	1	—	—	—
National Religious Party	—	—	—	1	—	—
Gahal	—	7	1	1	19	6
No identification	—	7	1	2	5	15
Not reinterviewed	3	11	4	—	13	38

close" to a party. This puts the immigrants below the national norm for party membership. As expected, 12 of the 17 party members were in the 1972/75 group. Three of the Soviets dropped party membership and only one person joined in the three-year interval (three Americans did so).[47] Among those reinterviewed in 1975, 14 percent were party members, not very different from what had been found in the Israeli population as a whole. In 1972 and 1975 the proportion of party members in our group was higher than that in the group surveyed by the Israeli election study, where only three Balts, three heartlanders, and eight Georgians said they were members of political parties (6 percent of the sample). In our group, better educated and with a higher proportion of people who had been leaders of the aliyah movement in the USSR, partisan commitment was higher than in the group surveyed in 1973, and came fairly close to that of the Israeli population.

The Israeli election study was conducted seven months before the election, which had been postponed more than two months. Soviet immigrants in the study were asked for whom they intended to vote, but only one-third, or 81 of the 243, named a party for whom they would vote (see Table 7.6). Among those with more than 12 years of schooling, and hence with educational levels roughly similar to those of our own group, the proportion of those saying they did not know for whom they would vote and the distribution of their intended votes is about the same as among the others. We see that Labor was decisively preferred among the Balts, as was the case with the Zapadniki in our group in 1972, but its margin narrowed

TABLE 7.6
Intention to Vote in 1973, Israeli Election Study
(in percent)

	Labor	*Gahal*	*National Religious Party*	*Agudat Yisrael*
Balts	79 (26)	15 (5)	6 (2)	—
Georgians	44 (11)	40 (10)	12 (3)	4 (1)
Heartlanders	52 (12)	44 (10)	—	4 (1)

Notes: Percentage is of those saying for whom they would vote in each of the geographic groups. Absolute numbers are in parentheses.

among the heartlanders and Georgians. Aside from the two major parties, only the religious parties were even mentioned by the respondents. Questioned about three major issues — the occupied territories, immigrant absorption, and the "social gap" (poverty) — a majority of Balts agreed with Labor's positions on all three, a majority of Georgians supported Labor on two of the three, and a majority of heartlanders identified with Labor's position on only one of the issues. It is on the issue of occupied territories that Gahal gained most support among all three groups.

Those interviewed in 1975 from our group were asked to recall how they had voted in 1973. Bearing in mind that recollection of acts performed two years before may be inaccurate, we note that 71 of the 78 Soviets said they voted in 1973, but only 13 Americans did (14 were ineligible as "temporary residents" and 3 eligibles did not vote). The recollected votes were strikingly different both from the party identifications given in 1972, a year and a half before the election, as well as from the intended votes of the respondents in the Israeli election study. For the Soviets, however, recollected votes were quite similar to the party identifications they gave in 1975, a year and a half *after* the election, and these, we recall, differed considerably from the 1972 identifications. In the election itself, if the memories of the respondents are to be credited, the Likud got twice as many votes as Labor, whereas it was Labor that got twice as many intended "votes" in the Israeli election study. Moreover, according to responses given in 1975, the Likud would have done even better among the Soviets and the Americans in 1975 than it had in the actual election of 1973. Asked for whom they would vote "today" (1975), the Soviets gave the Likud a 42-10 margin over the Labor party (9 people mentioned other parties or "no one"). The Americans gave it a 10-5 margin, with 4 sticking with the National Religious Party and 4 others naming Shinui or the Citizens' Rights Movement. Thus, by 1975 a definite shift away from Labor and toward the Likud had taken place, foreshadowing what was to happen in the national election two years later and, again, in 1981. As in the 1977 election, the losses of Labor were greater than the gains for the Likud. So while the image of Soviet immigrants as enthusiastic supporters of Gahal-Likud was certainly exaggerated and perhaps even completely distorted before the 1973 War and election, at least among our group there was a shift to Likud in the post-1973 period and probably even by the election in that year.

When we try to understand why the immigrants were changing their minds about the parties, we should remember the weaknesses of the leadership revealed in the 1973 War, Golda Meir's resignation in 1974, and the involvement of some of Labor's leaders in financial scandals that were revealed in 1976-77. Both Soviets and Americans did credit Labor at least in part with the accomplishments of Israel during its brief history; but Americans, especially, talked about Labor and its leaders having "outlived their usefulness." Some of the Soviets thought that Labor had been in power "too long," and this idea was expressed rather sharply by a few who spoke of a "party dictatorship" or a "Bolshevik-type elite, very similar to the USSR." Others objected to Labor's "socialism" or its "combination of the worst features of socialism and capitalism."

Despite Labor's historic dominance, nearly one-half the Soviets and one-quarter of the Americans could not correctly identify the leaders — any leaders — of the Labor party in 1972. By 1975, however, the great majority of both groups was able to do so, though even in 1972 the group that was to be reinterviewed in 1975 displayed somewhat better knowledge than the others. Zapadniki were substantially more knowledgeable than heartlanders in 1972, but the latter had "caught up" by 1975, as is the case in many other areas. The same was true of Likud leaders — considerable ignorance of the party's leaders in 1972 was replaced with impressive knowledge in 1975, and the initial edge of the Zapadniki was wiped out.

Curiously, more respondents in 1972 were able to discuss what they saw as the features of Gahal (Likud) than were prepared to discuss Labor. Gahal seems to have had a sharper image than the ruling party. In 1972, those Soviets who admired Gahal mentioned with approval its "foreign policy" (almost always meaning its stance on the occupied territories and toward the Arabs generally), its nationalism, and its "principled, uncompromising stand." These evaluations echoed traditional absolutist values so characteristic of the political cultures of Eastern Europe. The Americans, also reflecting their political culture, admired Gahal as an underdog, for being in the opposition, and for its sympathy to religious concerns without being a "religious party." One wealthy businessman admired their free enterprise philosophy but also added that "I would like to separate religion from politics, and that means I have to find a party that, while it isn't religious, it has sympathy with my religious convictions — and they do. Their leader, for example, will not ride on the *shabbat*, and so on." Like some of the Soviets, some Americans are attracted to Gahal by its nationalism. A rabbi who no longer identified with the party recalled that "many years ago . . . I felt close to it because they represented the Jew in a different light — one who was capable of defending himself. Because Israel has already proven that point, I don't feel close to Herut but I'd choose Begin as a political leader I feel close to." By the same token, Gahal was criticized by some for its "fanatic nationalism" or for "being an opposition just for the sake of opposition." A few of the Soviets objected to Gahal's sympathy for the religious.

By 1975, commentary on the Likud is focused largely on its position on the territories, an issue that had been made more salient by the 1973 War. By that time the Likud had carved out for itself a distinct position on the territories and it was attacking the government on this issue. In 1972 only 40 of the 202 immigrants identified the territories as an issue on which Labor and Likud differed, but by 1975, 54 of 108 did so. In 1972, but especially in 1975 when Golda Meir was no longer prime minister, the immigrants talked a good deal about Gahal's leader, Menachem Begin. For some, the government leaders they identified did not stand out in their minds as leaders of the Labor party as well. In 1975 every single immigrant was able to name at least one Likud leader, while six were unable to do so for Labor. Thus, recognition of Likud's position on the territories and of its leader was high, but its much-publicized campaign on behalf of Soviet Jewry was mentioned by only five Soviet immigrants. Moreover, despite all the talk about the militant Zapadniki who had been attached to the Revisionist movement even before 1939 and the influence the movement had in the Soviet Baltic, neither in our own group nor in the Israeli election study did the immigrants from these areas support the Likud more than the others. In fact, in 1972 and 1973 it is Labor that did better among the Baltic immigrants than among the heartlanders.

Those who identified with smaller parties were, of course, acutely aware of the programs and leaders of those parties since they had to be more than casually interested in order to even mention these parties. The Americans who identified with Mapam approved of its "very positive social policy," of its socialism, of its idealism. One singled out its "policies regarding relationships between Arabs and Jews" for approval. Supporters of the religious parties explained their position on the basis of their vision of a

Jewish state as one in which Judaism would be widely observed. Those who identified themselves with Avneri's party or the protest parties formed after 1973 spoke mostly in terms of the need to adopt a more peaceful posture toward the Arabs. All these people had a realistic view of their parties' constituencies, realizing that they were narrow and very specifically defined.

Soviet interviewees were less inclined to identify with any of the smaller parties. One supporter of the Independent Liberals said he preferred it to the major parties because it was "more principled" and less self-interested than the others. He admired its "higher intellectual level," but was made uncomfortable by the "caste system in the party, a party that consists of intellectuals of Central European origin." Some of the Soviets were confused or disgusted by the parties. "They are always combining and breaking up," complained one, reflecting a wider sentiment that there were too many parties squabbling over petty issues and constantly reorganizing. "All Israeli parties are abominable" was the exasperated judgment of another. "Perhaps at an earlier period when there were other needs, the parties were all right, but I think they have lost their raison d'être." The Americans, with their greater familiarity with the Israeli system prior to immigrating, and, in some cases, with some connection to affiliates of Israeli parties in the United States (religious and youth movements), were more likely to take the smaller parties seriously, but the Soviets clustered around the two major parties. After all, in comparison with the system from which Soviets had come, there was a 100 percent increase in the number of parties one has to take into account.

THE CORRELATES OF PARTY IDENTIFICATION

After living in Israel between six months and three years, about half the immigrants interviewed identified with one of the political parties. Three years later a somewhat higher proportion was willing to identify a party that they felt "close to." Personality, age, previous interest in politics, specific experiences in Israel, or their overall experience in resettlement are among the many factors determining why some immigrants identify with a party and others do not. We shall try to determine what kinds of characteristics are associated with party identification and nonidentification and whether it is the background characteristics or organizational affil-iations of some immigrants that contribute to partisan identification. Perhaps partisan identification grows out of their experiences in Israel and the degree to which they have involved themselves in its society. Or perhaps it is influenced most by the immigrants' general political outlooks and their positions on some of the major issues agitating Israeli society.

In many countries with multiparty systems, class and party affiliations are nearly congruent: workers identify with a labor party, property owners vote for a bourgeois party, and so on. There are, of course, notable exceptions, such as "working class Conserva-tives" in England or nonpeasants who identified with the Slovak People's party or the Serbian and Croatian Peasant parties in the interwar period because those parties spoke for the ethnic group as a whole. One of the Israeli Labor party's major achievements was that it broadened its base far beyond its original urban and rural working class constituency to include, as our respondents put it, the "average Israeli," be he or she worker or boss, Sefardi or Ashkenazi, rich or poor. Some would argue that this success was eventually vitiated by the price paid for it, the erosion of Labor's original values and its decline into an *interessengemeinschaft*, a kind of holding company for political favors. There is no denying, however, that for nearly three decades Labor was truly a national party, transcending ethnic, educational, and class lines. The end of Labor dominance in 1977 may have seen "the crystallizing of a tendency toward class politics in Israel,"[48] but the 1981 elections seemed more about ethnic than about class politics, and it is still not possible to identify *a* class with *a* party.

Within our group of immigrants there is no clear distinction between the social and economic status of those who identified with Gahal and those who identified with Labor, though, taking educa-tion alone, Gahal supporters had slightly higher educational levels. Among the Soviet men, professionals and artists were more inclined to the right-wing parties than industrial workers: In 1972 and 1975, four of five Soviets who identified with the right-wing parties, almost always Gahal, were professionals, whereas only half of those who identified with Labor or left-of-center parties were professionals. Among those who identified with Labor and the left there were three times as many workers as among those who identified with Gahal and the right. Religious people, whether Soviet or American, were more inclined to the right-wing parties, excluding the religious ones, than were others. People who were consciously antireligious associated themselves with Mapam or the Independent Liberals. This was true also of the Israeli electorate generally.

The unchanging distribution of power among the parties throughout Israel's pre-1977 history has often been remarked upon. It is all the more impressive not only because of the great influx of people from different political cultures, but also because there were so many dramatic events and rapid changes in Israeli society that one might have expected different waves of immigrants to be "imprinted" by them, and perhaps with different political results. If such imprinting did occur, it was apparently largely to Labor's benefit. The Soviet and American immigrants studied here did come in two different waves, though they were very close in time (1968 to June 1970; 1971 to May 1972). There is only a slightly higher proportion of first-wave immigrants with a party identification, though some had been in Israel as much as three years longer than some in the second wave. This difference held also in 1975, so that the second wave had not "caught up" by then. The partisan sympathies of the first and second waves were not very different; both Soviet waves gave Gahal a slight edge in 1972. The one difference was that the party identification of the first wave was more stable. By 1975, Gahal's advantage in the second wave had increased from 29-26 to 27-8, whereas in the first wave it changed only from 16-11 to 13-9. Minor party identification was also more stable in the first wave. These differences were not due to the contrast between the 1972/75 and 1972-only groups. Perhaps they arose because by 1972 the first wave had settled on their partisan identities, whereas those who came later were still "looking around," especially after the October War. Then, too, the first wave had a higher proportion of Zapadniki, and they displayed a greater and more stable attachment to Labor.

Are those who are organizationally involved more likely to have a party identification, and vice versa? After all, membership in some types of organizations might make people more aware of the issues of the day and more inclined to involve themselves in them. Conversely, identification with a party is perhaps an indicator of concern about issues, and to do something actively about them might necessitate organizational activity or, at least, membership. It turns out that there was only a very slight tendency for organization members to identify with a political party.[49] There was also no relation between identifying with a party and the type of organization one belonged to, or the frequency of participation in that organization.

The only exception to this generalization was membership in the Soviet immigrant association. (Members of the AACI were no different from nonmembers as far as identification with a party was concerned.) In 1972 and 1975 nearly 70 percent of the Soviets who belonged to the Union identified with a party, while less than half of the nonmembers did so. Moreover, among the Soviets there was a positive relationship between the strength of one's identification with a party and membership in the immigrant association (gamma = .43; tau b = .25; signif. = .01). The few party members were almost all members of the Union. It may be that the politically minded, including the politically ambitious, see the immigrant association as the natural locus of their political expression, especially since, as we have seen, the Union had been politicized and its leadership was to a large extent identified with several of the parties. Perhaps the relationship can work in reverse as well: Those who join the Union are exposed to politics within it and become aware of linkages to politics outside it, absorbing knowledge of and commitment to national parties. Which of these causal relationships, if either, is actually operative cannot be determined with the information at hand.

The other connection between membership in an organization and identification with a party is the Histadrut. As with other Israelis, Histadrut membership is associated with Labor party identification among the olim. In 1972, of the 37 who "feel closest to Labor," 27 were Histadrut members, but only 20 of the 45 Gahal sympathizers belonged to the union. For the Soviets alone, 26 of 33 Labor sympathizers, but only 18 of 37 Gahal sympathizers, were Histadrut members. In 1975 every Labor supporter was a Histadrut member, but 13 of the 33 Gahal identifiers were not. Only one of the seven immigrants identifying with the National Religious Party was a member. There is a strong positive association between Histadrut membership and identifying with the Labor party, even though, as we have seen, the Histadrut does not seem to resocialize the immigrants politically in a direct way. It should be borne in mind that for many, Histadrut membership is not a matter of choice, since those employed in Histadrut and government enterprises are in effect obliged to join a Histadrut union. This might be especially germane to those Gahal sympathizers who are nevertheless members of the Histadrut. Since nearly all Soviet immigrants who were employed in commerce and industry were employed in the public and Histadrut sectors, it is very likely that Gahal sympathizers among them, even those with explicit reservations about the trade union, would be Histadrut members.

Thinking about the possible relationship of identifying with a political party and overall adjustment to Israeli life, alternative hypotheses suggest themselves: either integration into the new society and satisfaction with life in it lead one to take an interest in the society's politics and to identify with a party, or it is alienation and dissatisfaction that lead one to try to change things or protest against the situation by sympathizing with a party in opposition. A third possibility is political disinterest, which may also be the outcome of two opposing outlooks: satisfaction with things as they are may breed political apathy and quiescence, or dissatisfaction may be the cause of this same apathy, but it is an expression of resignation and hopelessness. Are Soviet and American immigrants who identified with parties "better integrated," using our "index of integration," than those who did not? The answer is a rather unambiguous "yes." In 1972, not one of the people who did not identify with a party scored "high" on integration, and three-quarters of the nonidentifiers scored "low." Even within the 1972/75 group, whose integration scores in 1972 were higher than the others, the nonpartisan identifiers scored lower than the others. Within the group of partisan identifiers, those who identified with Labor scored a bit higher on integration than those who identified with Gahal.[50] So nonidentifiers scored lowest on integration, Labor identifiers highest, and Gahal identifiers were in between. By 1975, however, while the nonidentifiers continued to score lower than the others, those who identified with Gahal scored higher on integration than those identified with Labor (15 Gahal identifiers scored "high" and only 2 Labor sympathizers did). In 1972 it was more the "thing to do" to identify with the dominant party, as yet undisturbed by the events of 1973, whereas by 1975 the country had swung to the right, and some of the immigrants with it. Those who, by other measures, were in the "mainstream of society" could identify with Gahal as reasonably as they could with Labor.

The positive relationship between integration and partisan identification is supported by the finding that a similar relationship exists between the *strength* of identification — how close one feels to the party — and integration. Of the 31 men who felt "very close" to a party, 13 scored "high" on integration, but only 1 of the

28 with "some" closeness to the party scored "high." To put it another way, less than 25 percent of those with strong party identification scored "low" on integration, but 60 percent of those with no identification scored in this category. There is thus a strong correlation between the strength of partisan identity and integration (gamma = .57; tau b = .38; signif. = .0001; n = 102). As could be expected by now, party *members* scored high on integration: Of 17 party members in 1972, 11 scored "high." In 1975 members continued to score much higher on integration than nonmembers.

PARTY IDENTIFICATION AND
FULFILLMENT OF EXPECTATIONS

Trying to explain the supposed leaning of the Soviet immigrants toward Gahal, some suggested that this was a "protest vote," an expression of the frustrations and dissatisfactions of being a Soviet immigrant in Israel. Since we questioned our informants about the extent to which their expectations of Israel, and those of other immigrants, had been fulfilled, we can examine the relationship between party identification and fulfillment of expectations. It turns out that the more satisfied Soviet immigrants were more likely to identify with Labor in 1972, but it was *not* true that Gahal supporters were highly dissatisfied. They were less satisfied than Labor sympathizers, but they were not the least satisfied. The latter identified either with the smaller parties or, in the great majority of cases, with no party at all. Table 7.7 shows that 58 percent of the Labor identifiers and 43 percent of the Gahal identifiers saw their expectations as having been completely fulfilled (excluding those who did not answer the question or were not sure about the fulfillment of their expectations). Only 28 percent of those without partisan identity felt the same about their expectations, and the same was true of 23 percent of those affiliated with the minor parties.

The strength of one's partisan identification and party membership also correlates positively with the fulfillment of expectations. For example, in 1972 none of the party members, but one-fifth of the nonmembers, said their expectations "were not at all fulfilled," and more than half of the party members had their expectations "completely" fulfilled. The same relationship held in 1975. All these findings point in the same direction: The Soviet immigrant

TABLE 7.7
**Number of Soviet Immigrant Party Identifiers
within Satisfaction Groups**

Party Identification (number in parentheses)	Expectations				
	Completely Fulfilled	Mostly Fulfilled	Somewhat Fulfilled	Not Fulfilled	No Answer or Don't Know
Labor (33)	18	1	9	3	2
Gahal (37)	15	3	12	5	2
Other (16)	3	3	5	2	3
None (32)	9	1	11	6	5
Overall (percent)	42	9	33	16	

whose expectations have been fulfilled identifies with the major parties, including Gahal; the discontented are more likely to identify with no party at all. Partisan politics is apparently seen, not as a way of protesting against or changing the system, but as an affirmation of it. Except for a few who identify themselves with one of the smaller parties, it is largely the satisfied immigrants who become partisan Israelis. Perhaps this is partly a carryover from the immigrants' earlier political culture. In the Soviet Union political passivity is a common mode of expressing dissatisfaction. Refusal to join the Communist party when invited to do so is often taken to be a protest against it. On the other hand, those satisfied with Soviet life affirm this by active participation in the many forms sanctioned and encouraged by the state. For the Soviet newcomer to claim "close-ness" to an Israeli party is to assert his agreement and satisfaction with the system.[51]

POLITICAL OUTLOOKS AND PARTISAN IDENTIFICATION

Whether or not a person will identify with a party may be influenced by his general political values, his feelings about his place in the political world, and his positions on specific issues. From several questions we asked about how important political matters are to the respondent, we learned, not surprisingly, that politics is more important to those who expressed some partisan loyalties than to those who did not. Labor identifiers were a bit less concerned about politics, as befits those whose favorite party is in power and merely has to swim along with the mainstream, whereas supporters of the opposition, almost by definition more agitated by politics, are more concerned. Of course, politics is most salient to party members. They are the most eager to understand positions taken by different parties, to give their children a political education, and to express opinions on the issues of the day. In 1972 the party members were also the most attentive to the Israeli media,[52] and this was true also within the 1972/75 group, but three years later there was no difference in attention to the media between party members and the others. Perhaps the party members are those who have been resocialized politically early in their stay in Israel — and very effectively — but in the course of three years the others come to resemble them more in the way they interact with Israeli society. It is as if the party members of 1972 plunged head first into the society, adopting many of the characteristics of what they considered the "average Israeli." The others tested the waters and entered them more gradually. After three years both groups were swimming with roughly equal skill.

As regards political efficacy — the perception that the person can influence the political world — in our American group one's sense of efficacy is *not* associated with one's partisan identification. Those who identified with parties did not have significantly higher scores on our index of efficacy than the others. In the Soviet group, on the other hand, those who identified with parties did display slightly higher efficacy than the others in both years they were questioned.[53] The same holds for party members. From our conversations with the Americans it became obvious that many were contemptuous of the Israeli parties, and few saw them as potential agents for the kinds of changes the Americans would like to see in Israel. The Soviets take a more charitable view of the parties; though, as we have seen, some of them share the Americans' disdain for them. The Soviet immigrant who feels that he would like to — or can — affect the political world he inhabits is more apt to develop a partisan loyalty than either the American immigrant or his fellow Soviet immigrant who has a less optimistic view of his prospects for affecting politicians and political life.

On specific policy issues the partisans of Labor and Gahal differed between themselves more than they did, taken together, from the nonpartisan immigrants. All immigrants agreed that security was the major problem confronting Israel; but there were sharp differences on the role of the occupied territories in providing security. On no other issues were the differences between supporters of Labor and of Gahal so visible. In 1972 nearly twice as great a proportion of Gahal sympathizers wanted to "keep all" the territories. The nonpartisans were also less inclined than the Gahal supporters to "keep all." In 1975, when enthusiasm for keeping the territories had waned, half the Gahal identifiers still wanted to "keep all" when only one person among the Labor sympathizers (and one-third of the nonpartisans) agreed. This indicates full awareness by the immigrants of the positions taken on this volatile issue by the Labor and Gahal parties.

There are other differences, also reflecting their party's positions, between the pro-Labor and pro-Gahal elements. Gahal identifiers would like the Israeli government to be more restrained, withdrawing to some undefined extent from the areas of commerce, religion, and personal life (mainly marriage and divorce as regulated by state-sanctioned religious authorities). Labor identifiers wished to see less of a government role only in personal life. They were more in favor than the Gahal supporters of a strong and active government, and those that stayed with Labor maintained this posture over the three years. Not surprisingly, they had a more charitable view of Israeli government officials than Gahal supporters. More of them thought that the government generally took decisions with the benefit of the people in mind. Two-thirds of Gahal supporters thought that government officials served their own interests primarily, a view held by more than half of all respondents, but only by slightly more than one-third of the Labor identifiers. All of this is consistent with the respective party identification of the immigrants in the group. Those immigrants who identified with parties did not do so haphazardly; they were aware of the positions taken by the parties, and their own views conformed to those positions. It might well be that the immigrants chose their party affiliations more "rationally," with more attention to issues, than other Israelis, whose party loyalties may have been more influenced by family tradition, or by their having been "assigned" to a party when they came as immigrants, or by loyalty to a choice made years ago on grounds that are no longer relevant. The newcomer, unburdened by history or sentiment, was more free to look over the rather wide field presented by the Israeli party system and make his choices on the basis of his interests and his outlook.

SUMMARY AND CONCLUSION

This chapter has taken up two questions: How does the Israeli political system attempt to resocialize immigrants? and To what extent have the immigrants we have studied become involved in that system? Unfortunately, it has not been possible to solve the problem of how the first and second question are linked, that is, to describe and analyze the extent to which immigrants' political behavior is the "result" of conscious and direct efforts at socialization.[54]

Examining how the contemporary Israeli system resocializes immigrants politically, we have focused on immigrant associations, the Histadrut, and political parties. It is clear that some of the Americans were already socialized to some outlooks directly relevant to Israeli politics and even to some partisan loyalties while they were still in America, but this is less the case for the Soviet immigrants who come from a country where Zionist activity is not permitted. On the other hand, the American immigrant association in Israel seemed to play no role in political resocialization, though perhaps it helped to sustain values of that American political subculture from which most of the immigrants came. Values such as participation and citizen organization, advocacy of a cause such as consumer protection, and avoidance of partisan sponsorship for such causes typified the well-educated, middle class, urban society in which most of the Americans lived before they set out to become Israelis. The Union of Soviet Immigrants, on the other hand, was more politicized, though probably no more effective as an advocate of immigrants' interests. Despite its politicization, the Union was not an agent of partisan resocialization, though the major parties certainly tried to make it such. Labor seemed to be in an excellent position to do so until its heavy-handed ways were rejected by those active in Union affairs. In a broader sense the Union may have functioned as a resocialization agency because it was an arena for the play of immigrant politics. It was a microcosmic simulation of the larger Israeli political world, though not a perfect replication of it. At the same time, it was different from some immigrant associations in other countries because its politics were not isolated from the larger society's but were linked to it through individuals who were active in Israeli politics. The Union of Soviet Immigrants was not concerned with "old world politics," unlike other groups of Soviet (and earlier Russian) emigrés in other countries. The issues debated in the

Union were Israeli ones, even if they were sometimes specific to the immigrants. No doubt the Israeli parties hoped their "representatives" and sympathizers in the Union would swing immigrant votes their ways, as in the "good old days" immigrant elites might have delivered a clan or larger group. Since the immigrants did not have the same loyalty to the Union that earlier ones had to their clan or to their spiritual and lay leaders, the association did not mobilize political loyalties or votes. The "Union label," to borrow a term, is not given to any candidate, nor would it help him very much; but the Union might have been the place where some of the immigrants did, after all, learn how to operate in the democratic system.

The Histadrut also did not play a major or direct role in resocializing the Soviet and American newcomers. However, we did see a replication among its membership of the pattern found in the Israeli population as a whole: Histadrut members were more likely to associate themselves with the Labor party than were the others. The Histadrut did bring the immigrants into an institutional network whose wide range encompassed health care, education, and social encounters in addition to more conventional trade union activities, and in a very real sense introduced them to the "labor movement."

As the state had taken over many of their former functions, the importance of political parties in the resocialization process had diminished. Nowadays the parties try to play the role of ombudsmen, mediating between the immigrant and the government. They did this in the past, too, but then they did directly what the government does now — provide housing, jobs, social life, and even education for the immigrants. The parties also try to do what the government cannot, namely, to bring the newcomers into social contact with the veteran population and try to eradicate the social distinction between olim and vatikim.

The parties were not very interested in the American immigrants, seen as too independent, too distant from the European-type system that Israel is, and too few or unstable in their residence to be worth a major recruitment effort. The Soviets were another matter. They were the most numerous, best publicized immigrants of the last decade and they did not wander back home or to other countries. Only the religious parties (and the Communists) remained unenthusiastic about the Soviet immigrants as potential recruits. The religious parties concentrated their efforts on a well-defined segment, the Georgians and Central Asians. With all the publicity given to competition among parties for the votes of the Soviet olim, none of the latter had yet been elected to the Knesset or to any mayoralty, and only a few had been included in the central organs of a political party, none in the "inner circles." Neither American nor Soviet immigrants had achieved spectacular political mobility, despite their educational and experiential assets.

Our investigation does not show that Israeli organizations or political "role models" have been effective agents of socialization. In fact, the 1973 War had a strong impact on the political perception of the immigrants we studied. For some, it strengthened their solidarity with the country; for others, it disillusioned them about the army and the government. The 1973 War was the most likely cause of the shift to the political right we observed among the Soviets.

If we cannot be sure of the effects on the immigrants of some of the attempts at resocialization, we can at least observe the involvement of the immigrants in politics, some of which may be the consequence of those efforts. The olim in our group exhibited considerable interest in politics, and our data and that of the Israeli election study show that the more educated immigrants were the most interested in politics. If the immigrants' intentions to vote and recollections of having done so can be credited, their participation in the 1973 national election was not less than that of the general population. International studies have concluded, however, that voting is the minimal form of participation, requiring minimal effort and producing direct results. Were the immigrants willing to engage in more demanding, less immediately rewarding forms of political participation?

In 1972 slightly more than half of them identified a party they said they felt "close" to, and in the 1972/75 group the proportion was higher. A few more Soviets identified with Gahal than with Labor, though among the Zapadniki, Labor had a narrow edge. A smaller proportion of the Americans identified with a party, and those who did were more widely scattered across the political map, whereas the Soviets clustered around the two major parties. However, the party identities asserted in 1972 were not very stable. Between 1972 and 1975 the Soviet olim individually and collectively shifted from Labor to Gahal, but then so did the Israeli electorate. There was continuity in that those who identified with some party in 1972 were the most likely to identify with one in 1975.

Few of the immigrants had joined parties, but the proportion of party members among them was not much lower than among the general population. These party members were people who seemed genuinely interested in politics, as they were the most attentive to the media and the most knowledgeable about politics. They were not men whose names had been merely entered on party rolls, but people with definite political views who were willing to engage in political activity.

With time the immigrants gained in political knowledge. Their ability to answer questions about parties and politicians was significantly better in 1975 than in 1972, even when the responses of the 1972/75 group in both years were compared. Political learning *did* occur. Our informants were able to discourse on the strengths and weaknesses of the parties, as they saw them. In the minds of most, Labor's outstanding asset was its leadership, and this made it vulnerable after the losses of the 1973 War. The characteristic of Gahal most salient to the informants was its position on the occupied territories and generally tough stance toward the Arab countries. Still, Gahal's leaders, especially Menachem Begin, were even better known to the immigrants than Labor's.

If we cannot isolate the determinants of identification with parties, we can discuss the correlates of it. Neither in the general population nor among the immigrants was there a congruence between class and partisan identity. However, the workers in the Soviet group did tend quite markedly to identify with the Labor party. Most of these people were Zapadniki, but the causal link between their geographic-cultural origin and their party preference was more obscure than the link between their employment, and consequent Histadrut membership, and their Labor sympathies. There was not much difference between immigrants who came earlier and those arriving later in the proportion who identified with parties or on the distribution of that identification, though the party identity of the earlier arrivals was considerably more stable. In general, organizations did not act as the conduit bringing the immigrants to identification with parties, but those who were members of the Union of Soviet Immigrants were very likely to identify also with a party. Perhaps this was because the politically minded and ambitious immigrants saw the Union as the logical place in which first to try out political life in Israel.

There was a strong positive relationship between personal satisfaction, integration into Israel, and partisanship. The Labor party identifiers were most satisfied and the best integrated, those who identified with a minor party or with none at all the least satisfied and integrated. Gahal supporters were not embittered or disappointed people who had failed to integrate, as some have speculated, but almost as highly satisfied and integrated as the Labor identifiers. In general, the stronger one's identification with a party, the more one's expectations have been fulfilled and the more integrated one is. Moreover, those whose expectations of Israel had been most fulfilled were also the most partisan. Partisan politics among the Soviet immigrants was not a protest against the system but an affirmation of it.

Identification with parties was also related to one's feelings of political efficacy. Those with a strong sense of their efficacy were the ones who came to "feel close" to a party. This did not hold for the Americans, probably because they did not see the parties themselves as efficacious, that is, as effective change agents. It is as if the Americans and the party functionaries viewed each other with mutual disdain, each convinced that the other was not a force for the kind of politics Israel should have. Identification with *specific* parties by both Americans and Soviets was related consistently and logically to the positions taken by the parties on salient issues. Those who favored less government involvement in the economy and in social life, but who wanted Israel to retain the occupied territories, were those who identified with the party, Gahal, that supported those positions. Labor supporters were equally articulate and consistent in setting out their policy preferences, which were precisely those of the party with which they identified.

By 1975, three to six years after coming to Israel, the immigrants were in the political arena to the same extent as the general population. They made different entries, but in their diversity they were fairly similar to veteran Israelis. Our group, an educated and sophisticated one, did know the issues and where the parties stood on them, and it made its choice of parties in close conformity with its opinions on the issues. This raises a nagging doubt: Perhaps we are overly concerned with how the system got them where they were. We have been asking who brought them to where they are politically, and we have examined a variety of possible socialization agents. More than any other it seems to be the 1973 Arab-Israeli War that affected the partisan disposition of the immigrants, and perhaps broader outlooks and commitments as well. Thus, it was not a component of the Israeli system, but an event, that just might have had the greatest direct impact on the immigrants. Have we been misled by an "oversocialized conception of man," in this case of immigrants?[55] Perhaps our group was not dragged in or seduced by parties or by the larger political system, but made deliberate, rational choices about the extent and content of its political involvement. Unquestionably these choices were influenced by the larger experience the immigrants had in Israel, their satisfactions and disappointments in the country. Undoubtedly, too, that experience had been shaped in part by antecedent factors; but it may be that these individuals steered their own routes in politics. There were pilots to light their way but they remained captains of their own fates. Some remained and others became free men, and both assumed the responsibilities and made the choices that democratic societies give their citizens, even the very new ones. To what extent and how the immigrants actually changed in their political orientations is the subject of the next chapter.

NOTES

1. Among the better-known works in the literature are Lester Milbrath, *Political Participation* (Chicago: Rand McNally, 1970); Guiseppe di Palma, *Apathy and Participation* (New York: The Free Press, 1970); Sidney Verba and Norman Nie, *Participation in America* (New York: Harper and Row, 1972); Alex Inkeles, "Participant Citizenship in Six Developing Countries," *American Political Science Review* 63 (December 1969).

2. Paul R. Wilson, *Immigrants and Politics* (Canberra: Australian National University Press, 1973), pp. 43-70, 86-136. Another commentator on immigrants in Australia concludes that, except within the immigrant organizations, politics is of little interest to them. "Migrants are people whom politics has already failed: their apathy runs deep." Alan Davies, "Migrants in Politics," in *New Faces: Immigration and Family Life in Australia*, ed. Alan Stoller (Melbourne: F. W. Cheshire, 1966), p. 114. A study of Jewish immigrants in Melbourne found that they were less interested in politics than native-born Jews, but that their interest increased with time. The explanation given is that immigrants are "first concerned with building themselves economically." Ronald Taft and John Goldlust, "The Current Status of Former Jewish Refugees in Melbourne," *The Australian and New Zealand Journal of Sociology* 6, no. 1 (April 1970): 37.

3. Wilson, p. 109.

4. Fernando Peñalosa, "Pre-Migration Background and Assimilation of Latin-American Immigrants in Israel," *Jewish Social Studies* 34, no. 2 (April 1972).

5. A. Geva, "Mi yeargen et haaliya," *Lamerkhav*, November 10, 1970. For the complaints of the Latin American Association against the MIA, see Y. Ben-Amir, "Taanot olai drom-Amerika al mekhdalim vesirbul," *Davar*, July 30, 1969. See also Uzi Benziman, "Misradim meyutarim," *Haaretz*, May 5, 1974.

6. Moshe Goldberg, "American 'Olim' Want State to Consult Them," Jerusalem *Post*, March 10, 1972.

7. Hitakhdut olai Brih"m, *Hav'eida hashniya* (Tel Aviv, 1973), p. 3.

8. Interview with Eli Ronen, February 10, 1972.

9. Adar Kesari, "Tsabar yotsai kibbutz mazkir hitakhdut olai Brih"m," *Haaretz*, June 16, 1972.

10. Interview with Eli Ronen.

11. MIA, "Klitat olai Brih"m betashlag betom hashana harishona lealiyatam," internal report, November 1974, p. 3.

12. *Hav'eida hashniya*, p. 5.

13. The activities of the Union are reported in its Hebrew and Russian newsletters (*Igeret lekhaver, Nashe slovo*, and so on).

14. George Leonof, "Rebels and Veterans in Fierce Clash at Soviet Immigrant Convention," Jerusalem *Post*, August 7, 1973.

15. Interview with George Leonof, Jerusalem *Post*, August 24, 1973.

16. Interview with Daniel Bludz, July 10, 1975.

17. See Jerusalem *Post*, January 1, 1976, and the exchange between Daniel Bludz and Sarah Honig in the Jerusalem *Post*, February 29, 1976.

18. S. Katznel'son, "Rol' Gistadtrut v integratsii alii," *Sion*, no. 2-3 (1972), p. 145.

19. Interview with Hillel Zeidel, then director of the Histadrut's absorption department, January 12, 1972. Zeidel was then a leader of the Independent Liberals, with whom he later broke while serving as a member of the Knesset.

20. On Histadrut seminars for immigrants, see *Davar*, January 13, 1972. On its activities among Soviet immigrants, see *Nasha strana*, January 28, February 9, and February 11, 1972.

21. Interview with Yitzkhak Artzi, February 23, 1972.

22. Memorandum of the Liberal party's absorption department, undated, p. 1.

23. Interview with Roberto Aron, head of the Liberal party's absorption department, January 9, 1972.

24. Interview with Rabbi Mintz, head of Agudat Yisrael's Department for Russian and Georgian Immigrants, February 6, 1972.

25. Interview with Eli Ronen.

26. Interview with Asher Yizrael, head of the absorption department of Mapam, February 7, 1972.

27. Interviews with Rabbi Mintz of Agudat Yisrael, and Yitzhak Kadmon, head of the National Religious Party's absorption department, January 13, 1972.

28. Interview with Asher Yizrael.

29. "Soviet Migrants to Vote in Israel," New York *Times*, September 30, 1973.

30. Menachem Begin, "Olim miBrit Hamoetsot," *Maariv*, March 3, 1972.

31. Interview with Lifsha Jameson, head of the absorption department of Gahal (Likud), January 31, 1972.

32. See the interview with MIA Minister Peled, *Maariv*, May 12, 1972. See also *Yediot akhronot*, January 6, 1972. On Rafi Balvashvili, see Uzi Benziman, "Kokhah shel hasiyomet shvili," *Haaretz*, December 10, 1971.

33. See Yair Kotler, "Hamanhig Avraham Sepiashvili," *Haaretz*, July 20, 1973.

34. Interview with Yaakov Yisraeli, head of the absorption department of Poalai Agudat Yisrael, February 7, 1972.

35. See Uzi Benziman, "Imperiya ushma Habad," *Haaretz*, January 7, 1972; *Yediot Akhronot*, December 30, 1972; and *Nasha strana*, April 4, 1972.

36. From my notes on her speech, February 8, 1972. For an account of the debate and preceding it, see *Maariv*, January 13 and February 9, 1972.

37. Norman H. Nie, G. Bingham Powell, Jr., and Kenneth Prewitt, "Social Structure and Political Participation: Developmental Relationships," *American Political Science Review* 68, nos. 2 (June) and 3 (September 1969).

38. In Shuval's study of immigrants of the 1950s, she found that two-thirds preferred to rely on veteran Israelis "as their major source of advice and information," and not on other new immigrants. Judith T. Shuval, *Immigrants on the Threshold* (New York: Atherton, 1963), p. 206.

39. On the 1973 election, see Asher Arian, "Were the 1973 Elections in Israel Critical?" *Comparative Politics* 8, no. 1 (October 1975). On the 1977 elections, see Howard R. Penniman, ed., *Israel at the Polls* (Washington, D.C.: American Enterprise Institute, 1979).

40. About 44 percent of the Israelis said they discussed politics "sometimes" or "often," while 67 percent of our Soviet informants and 75 percent of the Americans placed themselves in these categories. On the other hand, only 33 percent of the Zapadniki and heartlanders (and only 21 percent of the Georgians) in the 1973 study were in these categories. Data from the Israeli samples were furnished by Professor Asher Arian.

41. One person, however, argued against the view that Soviet elections are "a joke. No, it's showing your solidarity with the general line of the party." Another said that Soviet and Israeli elections are not very different: "The candidates make noise, they show themselves off, and then they do whatever they want." An embittered cinematographer, who came to Israel from Moscow but left Israel after a few years, charges that "in Hertzliya, all the houses on Brenner Street are occupied by recent immigrants from the USSR. Only a handful of denizens of this street, those who had immediately sensed where the power lay and . . . had rushed demonstratively into the camp of the ruling party, received the invitation to vote. The rest never even found out where the elections were held." Ephraim Sevela, *Farewell, Israel!* (South Bend, Ind.: Gateway Editions, 1977), p. 87.

My own observation of the 1977 election leads me to believe that this charge is absurd. No "invitation to vote" is needed and the location of polling places is very well publicized. Under the conditions Sevela describes, one could hardly account for the 85 percent turnouts characteristic of Israeli national elections. Sevela's general outlook can be seen in his statement that "there is a complete blanket of purely totalitarian power exercised by one, or, at the very best, a group of related socialist parties. . . . Whenever one attempts to do anything in Israel, one feels the deathly chill of this dictatorship on the back of one's neck. . . . Israel is doomed and is unlikely to survive a decade" (pp. 80-81, 293).

42. Samuel J. Eldersveld, "Party Identification in India in Comparative Perspective," *Comparative Political Studies* 6, no. 3 (October 1973): 276.

43. Ibid., p. 289.

44. See Eva Etzioni-Halevy and Rina Shapiro, *Political Culture in Israel: Cleavage and Integration Among Israeli Jews* (New York: Praeger, 1977), p. 73. The studies cited are those by Asher Arian in 1969 and the spring and fall of 1973, and by the Israel Institute of Applied Social Research in 1970 and December 1973.

45. British immigrants in Australia are one exception, some of whom are reported to maintain partisan affiliations they developed in Britain. See Wilson, p. 118.

46. See ibid. Wilson notes that Australian parties "do not court the immigrants." A study of North African Jewish immigrants in France also showed that partisan identification was weak and that the immigrants were much more likely to participate in professional, labor, and sports organizations. Doris Bensimon-Donath, *L'integration des Juifs Nord-Africains en France* (Paris: Mouton, 1971), pp. 182-83.

47. Information on two other Soviet immigrants who were members in 1972 is missing for 1975.

48. Asher Arian, "The Electorate: Israel 1977," in Penniman, p. 85.

49. Of the organization members, 43 identified with a party and 32 did not; of the nonmembers, 62 identified and 60 did not.

50. Six of 37 (16 percent) Labor identifiers scored "high," 17 (46 percent) scored "medium," and 14 (38 percent) scored "low." Of the 45 Gahal identifiers, 6 (13 percent) scored "high," 15 (33 percent) scored "medium," and 24 (53 percent) scored "low."

51. The numbers involved are too small to allow any conclusions to be drawn, but among the Americans the reverse is true: The satisfied Americans have no party identification, whereas the dissatisfied do. Again, perhaps this reflects a former political culture wherein political activism, not passivity, is a form of protest.

52. Of the 17 party members, 14 scored "high" on an index of media exposure constructed from items dealing with the frequency of newspaper reading, radio listening, TV watching, and what kinds of articles and programs were paid the most attention. Of the nonparty members, 59 percent received "high" scores.

53. Thus, 58 percent of Labor identifiers and 49 percent of Gahal identifiers scored "high," while 40 percent of the nonidentifiers did.

54. A survey of studies of adult socialization points out that while socialization is described as a process, it is studied as a product. "That is to say, scholars have neither observed how young people come to acquire the values they profess to, [sic] nor have they tried to ascertain observationally or experimentally

whether these statements really constitute values for the respondents." Roberta S. Sigel and Marilyn Brookes Haskin, "Perspectives on Adult Political Social-ization — Areas of Research," in *Handbook of Political Socialization*, ed. Stanley Renshon (New York: The Free Press, 1977), p. 291.

55. See Dennis H. Wrong, "The Oversocialized Conception of Man in Modern Sociology," *American Sociological Review* 26 (1961).

8
CHANGING POLITICAL ORIENTATIONS AND ATTITUDES

Cellist Mikhail Maisky, formerly of Leningrad. Courtesy The Jewish Agency.

After all the research that has been done on political attitudes and political behavior, the relationship between them remains somewhat obscure. Political attitudes do not necessarily predict political behavior, for the latter is influenced also by social, situational, and institutional pressures. The determinants of political behavior are many, complex, and shifting. This study examines both attitudes and actions, since the central question is that of continuity and change, of the degree to which both outlooks and behavior change, irrespective of the linkage between them.

In this chapter we are concerned with three types of attitudes: basic orientations concerning human nature and the proper role of the individual in relation to others; attitudes on general and abstract political concepts; and attitudes toward specific political issues in Israel. It has been suggested that fundamental beliefs about human nature and the ways of the world are so deeply imbedded in an individual, that even a change in physical and social environment will not alter them. The "primacy principle," which we have discussed, is assumed to be so powerful as to cancel the effects of situational and personal change in later life. Thus, the person who, for example, develops a cynical and suspicious outlook early in life is unlikely to alter it, even if his later experiences do not reinforce his outlook. On the other hand, perhaps specifically political notions will be significantly affected and altered by changes in the political environment. Regarding attitudes toward specific political issues, we would like to know in what ways they are influenced by either the fundamental dispositions or general political attitudes, or by the social environment. We would like to know how the immigrants compare on these issues with each other and with mass public opinion in Israel.

FUNDAMENTAL ORIENTATIONS:
ATTITUDES TOWARD AUTHORITY

Three fundamental orientations were probed: attitudes toward authority, political efficacy, and trust in others. Five questions were asked relating to authority. Specifically, the respondents were asked whether some power ought to be obeyed without question, whether a few leaders could do more for the country than "all the discussions and the laws," whether "the people" or leaders know what is best for the country, whether people could generally be divided into the weak and the strong. Respondents were also asked to choose between a system that involved few people in decision making but made decisions rapidly, and one in which many were involved but decisions emerged slowly. Using the responses to these questions, a measure of attitudes toward authority was constructed, with respondents rated from most deferential to authority to least deferential. A comparison of the measure is in Table 8.1.

Americans, trained in a political culture that encourages questioning of authority and self-assertion of the ordinary individual, are less deferential to authority than Soviet immigrants. Attitudes toward authority vary more among heartlanders than among Zapadniki,

TABLE 8.1
Summary Measure of Attitudes toward Authority
(in percent)

	Heartlanders		Zapadniki		Americans	
	1972	1975	1972	1975	1972	1975
Most deferential	14.3	18.5	8.8	7.3	2.1	0.0
Somewhat deferential	49.2	40.7	63.2	61.0	39.6	60.7
Least deferential	36.5	40.7	27.9	31.7	58.3	39.3

the great majority of the latter falling into the middle category. More importantly, the results for both Soviet groups are quite similar in the two years. Comparing individuals' responses in 1972 and 1975 shows that two-thirds remained in the same category. This indicates that attitudes toward authority do not change easily and that they are, in this group at least, a kind of "primitive belief" that is not much altered even when there is a change in the authorities with whom one interacts. Among the Americans, however, one does notice a shift between 1972 and 1975, with a movement from the "least deferential" to the intermediate category. This is because seven Americans gave more deferential responses than they had given in 1972, and only three gave less deferential ones.

Disaggregating the measure reveals that the Americans did not change their attitudes, except that on one question – whether leaders can do more for the country than discussions and laws – there is a shift in a more authoritarian direction. This was sufficient to change the distribution of results on the overall measure. It may well be that Americans were reacting to the specifics of the Israeli situation in 1975: Disappointed in the weak leadership of Yitzhak Rabin and his government, Israelis and American immigrants among them were looking for a "stronger hand" to guide the country, and in the 1977 elections they turned to Menachem Begin, regarded as a "strong man" both within his party and vis-a-vis the outside world. As we shall see, the Soviet immigrants also increased their preference for strong leadership, but they had a greater preference for it than the Americans in 1972, and so their change was not as sharp.

In the USSR one will often hear the opinion that while Stalin may have erred – and worse – he was a "strong leader," and without such a leader the war against the Nazis might have been lost, the USSR might not have been modernized, and it might not have become a superpower. "The Russian people need a strong hand to guide them" is a common expression. Therefore, it is not surprising to find Soviet immigrants favoring strong leadership more than the Americans. In this regard the Soviet immigrants are closer to the views expressed by the Israeli population as a whole. This can be discerned in Table 8.2, which includes data from our own study and from the 1969 Israeli electoral study that posed the same question. Moreover, when the question was repeated in the 1973 Israeli electoral study, which included a sample of Soviet immigrants, the results for the immigrants were almost identical to those for the Israeli sample, half of each group agreeing with the statement.

There was no difference in the responses of the 1972/75 and 1972-only groups, and the only change from 1972 to 1975 is the one already mentioned, the increase in American agreement with the proposition. There is a consistent and striking relationship between education and response to this question. The more educated the respondent is, the less likely he is to agree with the statement. In the 1973 study, the Georgians agreed with the statement more than the Balts, and the Balts more than the heartlanders. In our study, too, the Zapadniki were more inclined to favor the leaders

TABLE 8.2
"There are those who think that a few strong leaders can do more for the state (*mogut sdelat' bol'she dlia gosudarstva*) than all the discussions and the laws. Do you agree with this opinion?"
(1972, in percent)

	Soviets	Americans	Israelis (1969)*
Completely agree	21.8	9.8	35.3
Agree	45.1	39.2	27.2
Neither agree nor disagree	5.9	4.2	3.3
Disagree	22.3	35.3	15.4
Disagree completely	6.3	9.8	18.8

*It should be noted that the immigrant groups are being compared with the total Israeli sample, not with the subgroup of Israelis who resemble them in education, sex, income, and occupation.

Source: Data provided by Prof. Asher Arian, Tel Aviv University.

than the heartlanders were. Analysis of the data by level of education shows that, irrespective of regional origin, less education is associated with greater deference to leaders. Perhaps this is because the sense of political efficacy of less educated people is lower and they are more willing to defer to their "betters." When asked whether political leaders or "the people" know what is best for the country, two-thirds of all respondents, irrespective of country or area of origin, asserted that leaders know better. Americans explained their responses by citing the greater amount of information the leaders have and also pointed to the fact that the government had a mandate from the people and so it should be assumed that it "knows best." Most Americans believed this held true equally for the American and Israeli governments, but nearly half the Soviets said that while Israeli leaders know what is best for the country, Soviet leaders do not.

Confidence in our summary measure of attitudes toward authority is increased by the strong consistency among the answers given. Thus, those who gave answers deferential toward authority to one question were very likely to do so on another, with the (tau b) correlations among answers ranging from .26 to .42. It is the younger Soviets and Americans — and they were the best educated — who were less deferential. The less deferential were the most efficacious; that is, those who did not prefer the "strong leader" or who preferred decision making involving many people, or who did not believe in blind obedience to "some power," were also more likely to feel that voters can change public policy, that the ordinary man has a say in government.

On the other hand, Soviet immigrants who were consistently deferential to authority were most likely to desire a strong role by the government in the provision of welfare services, and when asked whether these services ought to be provided even at the cost of government interference in their personal lives, they were more likely than the others to respond affirmatively. These people fit the picture of "welfare state authoritarians," which some have painted of Soviet citizens and of some Soviet emigrés.

From the perspective of resocialization, the most important finding is the stability of attitudes toward authority in the transition from the Soviet Union and the United Sates to Israel and over the three years in Israel. Apparently, a change in authorities and in their relation to the citizen is not sufficient to bring about basic reorientation in attitudes.

POLITICAL EFFICACY

Does a change in political system lead to a change in one's sense of efficacy, that is, the feelings one has about his ability to influence the political world around him? Is efficacy a personality character-istic that is little influenced by objective circumstances and changes in the realistic possibility of the individual having an impact on the political system, or does one's sense of political efficacy change when one's political circumstances are altered?

We asked four questions tapping the sense of political efficacy of the respondents. This enabled us to construct a summary measure of the sense of efficacy (explained in Appendix E), presented in Table 8.3.

Americans were more efficacious than the Soviets in 1972, and Zapadniki were somewhat more efficacious than heartlanders. In the course of three years the Zapadniki became even more effica-cious, and the heartlanders also increased their sense of efficacy, but the Americans seemed to move in the opposite direction. However, when we compared the 1972 results for Soviets who reappeared in 1975 and for those who did not, we found that the 1972/75 group was more efficacious, but that there was still an increase of effica-cious feelings within the group between 1972 and 1975 (see Table 8.4). So while there was a gain in feelings of efficacy among the Soviets, it was less dramatic than might appear, since the 1972/75 group was already more efficacious than the others. From this we might conclude that efficacy, as measured here, is influenced by the political environment. As the Soviet immigrants spend more time in

TABLE 8.3
Sense of Political Efficacy, Summary Measure
(in percent)

	Heartlanders		Zapadniki		Americans	
	1972	*1975*	*1972*	*1975*	*1972*	*1975*
Low	12.7	6.3	11.7	2.2	3.7	0.0
Medium	42.3	40.6	37.7	23.9	22.2	40.0
High	45.1	53.1	50.6	73.9	74.1	60.0
1972 mean	3.352		3.351		3.778	
1972 median	3.383		3.513		3.882	

TABLE 8.4
Sense of Political Efficacy, Soviet Groups
(in percent)

	Soviets 1972-only	*Soviets 1972/75*	*Heartlanders 1975*	*Zapadniki 1975*
Low	12.8	11.6	6.3	2.2
Medium	44.3	35.9	40.6	23.9
High	42.9	52.6	53.1	73.9

a democratic system, they become more convinced of the possibility of ordinary people influencing political life. Second, those who have made a good general adjustment in Israel have a more optimistic outlook, and are more likely to have a stronger sense of their political efficacy. The higher level of efficacy shown by the Zapadniki may also be testimony to the importance of environment; for historical and situational reasons, they may have retained a greater faith in their ability to influence the political world than the heartlanders.

The American case also points to environmental determinants of the sense of efficacy. In Table 8.3 we notice that the Americans' sense of efficacy grows a bit weaker over time. This slight shift is statistically insignificant but there is a possible explanation for it. Americans come from a political system that teaches them to believe in the political worth and power of the "common man." For educated, middle class, urban Americans, this teaching is probably reinforced by political experience (recall how many expressed the belief that the American people could do something to solve the country's problems, how many had been politically aware and active). Their experience in Israel, however, a new and "peculiar" system, dampens their feelings of efficacy. One immigrant argued that in Israel there were really no elected leaders. "They're all appointed by the party. And the people are blinded by the great Israeli myth." He explained that in the United States he had not only voted, but had worked for "individuals I believed in. Here I doubt I would ever help in a campaign because I don't believe in straight party voting . . . and I could never find it in my conscience to work for a list of hacks." Another immigrant explained that in

Israel, "not voting for a personality, just a party, I feel no identification, no influence." Convinced that political decisions are made by a small clique of older Labor leaders of East European background and political style, some Americans felt that they and their ways were alien to the system and could have little influence on it.

Our findings support the idea that political efficacy is not an immutable personality characteristic but is influenced by the specific political environment in which a person operates. Changes in the environment, or changes *of* environment, will influence the sense of efficacy. This does not mean that the environment will produce the same feelings of efficacy in all citizens. As Coleman and Davis point out, there is both "external" and "internal" efficacy, with the former referring to the regime and the latter to the individual. External efficacy refers to regime responsiveness and internal efficacy refers to personal competence. "In pluralist regimes external efficacy might be seen as a facilitating but not sufficient condition for the existence of internal efficacy."[1] In their move to Israel, Soviet immigrants exchange a regime with relatively low external efficacy for one with higher external efficacy, and so there is a general rise in the sense of political efficacy among them, although, since efficacy also involves subjective political competence, "the belief in system responsiveness [and not all Soviet immigrants believe the Israeli system is responsive] does not guarantee the belief in personal efficacy."[2] Some of the Americans, on the other hand, feel that they are moving from a more responsive system to a less responsive one, so there is a decline in the belief in personal efficacy.

How do the immigrants compare with the Israeli population as a whole in their sense of political efficacy? One might think that, being new to the political system, immigrants would be unsure of their political competence, even if they thought the system were responsive. On the other hand, it could be that as newcomers they are more likely to accept at face value the myths of the system and its claims to responsiveness and the efficaciousness of the individual. The question cannot be resolved definitively here, but we can compare the results obtained from two questions asked of an Israeli national sample and of our respondents, as well as of Soviet immigrants in the 1973 electoral study (see Table 8.5). The Israeli sample was more inclined to believe in the influence of the "man in the street" than the Americans or any of the Soviet groups. The immigrants seemed to take a more cynical view of politicians than the

TABLE 8.5
"Some people say that politicians tend not to consider the opinion of the man in the street."
(in percent)

	Soviets			Americans		Israelis
	1973	1972	1975	1972	1975	1969
Do not consider it	45	58.4	66.2	40.0	58.6	37
Perhaps consider it	28	41.7	32.5	54.0	37.9	33
Definitely consider it	15	–	1.3	6.0	3.4	25
No opinion	11					6

Source: The source for the 1969 Israeli data, based on a national sample of 1,314, is *Elections Study, 1969: Findings* (Tel Aviv: Political Science Department, Tel Aviv University, 1971).

Israelis. When the 1973 Soviet sample is broken down by region of origin, almost no difference at all appears in the responses of Baltic, Georgian, and heartlander immigrants. There were two other questions in the study that related to efficacy and a composite "efficacy score" showed no great differences among the three groups, but the Balts, as might be expected, ranked ahead of the heartlanders, who, in turn, outscored the Georgians. In our own study, there were no meaningful differences observed between Zapadniki and heartlanders on questions relating to efficacy.

While they may not express as much personal efficacy as the Israelis, the immigrants perceive the system as quite responsive, though some Americans compare it unfavorably with the United States. Those who have a high sense of efficacy are inclined more to the view that decision making should involve as many people as possible, even at the cost of efficiency, and are less willing to defer to authority. They are also the ones most likely to report that their expectations of Israel have been met, again suggesting a link between the perception of the system generally and one's sense of political efficacy. Tentatively we may suggest that the sense of efficacy is more sensitive to the specific political system, whereas attitudes toward authority are more immune to changes in the political environment. Perhaps that is because attitudes toward authority are formed outside the political arena — in the home, school, among peers — to a greater extent than they are shaped within it, whereas the sense of political efficacy is more exclusively related to the political system itself.[3]

TRUST

How much trust there is among the citizens of a country is crucial to the nature of its political system. It is only because of a fundamental trust that citizens have in each other that one party can replace another in power in a democratic system. In a totalitarian system, on the other hand, the level of trust is very low, since, as Nazism and Stalinism demonstrated, misplaced trust can cost a person his life. Americans are said to come from an open society where the level of trust is fairly high, whereas those from the Soviet Union have come from a system where for a long time it was assumed that in any crowd of three, at least one person was a police informer. If this is at all accurate, then there should be significant differences between Soviets and Americans in the degree of trust they have in others. What happens when they come to Israel, a democratic but highly competitive and heterogeneous society? It has been suggested that in multiparty systems, such as Israel's, there are low levels of trust, because each party holds firmly to its ideology and platform, unwilling to trust others and enter into an American-type "umbrella" party with them. Moreover, in recently formed states, or in those with a great deal of ethnic and regional diversity, there is a tendency to proliferate parties because citizens are unfamiliar with each other and each other's ways and find it difficult to compromise their own ways and build broader groupings. Israel is a heterogeneous and relatively young country. Its political tradition derives largely from Eastern Europe, where levels of trust are often low. So Israel seems to have all the characteristics associated with low levels of trust and conducive to multiple parties. On the other hand, their struggle for survival and their common identity as Jews may have made Jewish Israelis more trustful than might be expected. How do the immigrants compare their new and old societies on the question of trust?

Shuval and Markus, having asked their Soviet immigrant respondents three questions relating to trust, find that 44 percent feel that one can be more trusting in Israel, but, they point out, taking into account the kind of system that exists in the USSR, the fact that 17 percent feel that one cannot be more trusting in Israel is "worrisome." Moreover, there is no increase at all in the trust of others by Soviet immigrants as they spend more time in Israel. That is, those who have been in Israel for ten years exhibit the same levels of trust as those who arrived recently, so one cannot argue that only the newcomers, uncertain about their new environment and fearful that they will be taken advantage of, are less trusting.[4] Shuval, Markus, and Dotan, commenting on the stability in trust observed among immigrants who came in different years, note that "on the one hand it points to the deeply-rooted tenacious quality of this basic inter-personal orientation; however, it also raises some questions as to the nature of social interaction between Soviet immigrants and representatives of the host society which apparently does not serve to diffuse this orientation over time."[5]

We found rather similar results among our own respondents. There was no great change in the immigrants' feelings of trust over three years, so this orientation seems to be quite stable. However, we did find that the 1972-only immigrants were less trusting than those who were still around in 1975. We also observed that, consistently, Americans were more sanguine, more trusting than the Soviets, and that the heartlanders were more trusting than the Zapadniki. When asked whether people deal fairly with each other or exploit each other, in both Israel and their countries of origin, Americans were most inclined to the view that people deal fairly, and Zapadniki most inclined to believe that they exploit each other. The same configuration was observed in responses to the question of whether people generally help each other or tend to think of themselves. Over 60 percent of all respondents thought that these human characteristics obtained in the United States, in the Soviet Union, and in Israel. Most of the rest expressed the view that one could be more trusting in the United States or in the USSR than in Israel. An American explained that "in general I always felt that . . . you trust people in America, anyone is innocent until proven guilty. In Israel I've found that people do not trust each other. As a matter of fact, they have the attitude toward their neighbor that he has to prove himself innocent." Some Americans claimed that they were systematically cheated by storekeepers who assumed that as "greenhorns" they could be overcharged and short-weighted. Others were appalled by the fact that to rent an apartment one needed a contract, the services of a lawyer, bank guarantees, and letters of reference, all of which indicated to them how little Israelis trusted each other. Coming from a society where one can check into a hotel, stay for several days, and pay only upon leaving – and with a personal check at that – one can understand the Americans' chagrin. Some Soviets also expressed the feeling that Israelis were to be trusted less than the people among whom they had lived. One insight offered was that "there they didn't try to fool you personally, they just lied generally [*global'no*]. Here they cheat you every day – personally." The same kind of distinction was drawn by the person who noted that while the Israeli government was not taking advantage of people, the citizens themselves were doing so. "In the USSR the system was set up to exploit people, but there were better relations among people. Everyone pulls his load there [*tianut liamku*]." Of course, Soviet immigrants, confronting for the first time different prices for the same goods in different stores, were quick to conclude that somehow they were "being taken," as did American immigrants who had been warned of "sharp practices," but these feelings did not seem to diminish with time and they were not erased by experience in the system.

We see that fundamental orientations relevant to politics do not change very much over the first years in Israel, and we suspect that they have not changed greatly from what they had been in the Soviet Union and the United States. These may be so firmly embedded, as the result of socialization, or of "imprinting" at critical stages of life, that they function like personality characteristics, not easily shaped by changing environments. Of the three orientations discussed, political efficacy, the one most directly related to a specific political environment, appears most malleable and dependent on a specific political system. Attitudes toward authority and trust, however, appear to be more firmly implanted. A possible implication is that basic and general outlooks on political life – those involving the nature of authority and of the relations of human beings to each other – will be transferred from one political culture to another and will not be altered easily. While the immigrants' outward behavior and even specific political attitudes may change, fundamental orientations may remain in place and eventually influence critical choices by the individual.

POLITICAL CONCEPTS

Moving from fundamental orientations related to politics, we inquired about attitudes toward specific concepts that we thought would be both salient to the immigrants, considering the political cultures from which they had come, and also decisive in shaping their political allegiances and behavior. These concepts are socialism, social class, freedom, and ethnic relations. Expecting to find sharp contrasts between Soviets and Americans, we were curious about changes that might occur in these attitudes as a result of presumed resocialization in Israel.

We expected the concepts of socialism and social class to be very familiar to our Soviet informants, especially. We thought they would give pat, "textbook" definitions or, alternatively, definitions that would reject Soviet conceptions.[6] This expectation was not fulfilled, as the immigrants gave a very wide range of definitions of socialism, and a surprisingly high proportion could not or would not give any definition at all. Thus, 15 respondents stated explicitly that they did not know what socialism was, and another 43 did not answer the request for a definition. This seemed to reflect not ignorance but confusion and uncertainty about what socialism really is. One possible explanation is that the official Soviet conception had been rejected, probably because it was contradicted by the individual's experience and perception of Soviet reality, but no alternative notion of socialism had yet been formed. In order to test this hypothesis, a definition of socialism was again asked for in 1975, on the supposition that in the course of three years some fairly definite conception would have been formed. In 1975 only 17 percent could not give a definition of socialism (compare 39 percent in 1972), but the range of answers was as wide as it had been three years earlier. Apparently, in 1972 the immigrants had been confused by the *multiple* contradictions between "socialism" (Soviet and Israeli versions) and reality (Soviet and Israeli). Over three years this confusion diminished, but perceptions of what socialism is remained highly individual.

It should be emphasized that, despite the wide range of answers, about 40 percent of the Soviet immigrants included economic equality and social justice in their definitions of socialism, whereas about 35 percent of the Americans mentioned government involvement in the economy in both 1972 and 1975. Both Americans and Soviets took pains to differentiate between socialism in theory and in practice, with the Soviets commenting that Soviet reality fell short of the socialist ideal, and the Americans frequently pointing out that *Israeli* reality did not seem to coincide with their abstract conception of socialism. An American who eventually left the country remarked that

> at one time I considered myself leaning toward socialism, but after seeing it in practice I'm against it. . . . Socialism has left the working class without incentive, without satisfaction from work, and without drive, and so they are vegetables working day to day. . . . Incentives are stymied or short-circuited by the bureaucratic workings of socialism in Israel — that's the only socialism I know.

Some Soviet immigrants admitted that there was probably a difference between the Soviet and Israeli versions of socialism, but they had developed an almost visceral repugnance for anything identified as socialist and therefore could not evaluate Israeli socialism objectively. "I know that here the socialism is different from the kind I learned about in school and which I came to hate. Still, when I hear the word 'socialism' I place myself on guard immediately."

In discussing the concept of social class in 1972, the immigrants again offered a wide variety of definitions, including such Soviet-type ones as "the relations of a group of people to the means of production" as well as less orthodox definitions. While Americans in 1972 overwhelmingly defined social class in terms of education and income, the Soviets were much less comfortable with the concept in 1972, and nearly 10 percent said that they did not like the "formulation of the question." Only one-third defined social class in economic terms and a good number explicitly rejected the Soviet conception. Since there is relatively little private property in the USSR, Marxist definitions of class are irrelevant and people must develop non-Marxist conceptions of class.[7] As one put it: "I don't agree with the Soviet definition, and have not managed to become familiar with Western definitions." Some mentioned different social classes and included not only workers, peasants, and intelligentsia, but also such groups as "the bureaucrats" or "party workers" as distinct classes. By 1975, however, nearly *two*-thirds of the Soviets defined class in economic terms, as did the Americans.

Both groups seem to have concluded from their observation of Israeli society that class is largely a matter of economic status.

As expected, when asked to define their own social class in 1972, over 75 percent of the Americans placed themselves in the "middle class." Surprisingly, 60 percent of the Soviets placed themselves in the same class, and 84 percent said they had belonged to the same class in the USSR as they did in Israel. In other words, a high proportion of the Soviet emigrés saw themselves as "middle class" even in the USSR, where such a class theoretically does not exist. Only 9 percent defined themselves spontaneously as "intelligentsia," though all the Soviet respondents had at least secondary education and 78 percent had some form of higher education. (It may be that, despite the official Soviet definition, "intelligentsia" is understood by most Soviet citizens to mean "creative intelligentsia," writers, artists, composers, and this may explain why more respondents did not identify themselves as *intelligenty*.) This suggests that there is an unofficial conception of class in the Soviet Union that does include some sort of "middle class" and that the Soviet immigrants were more inclined to use this term than "intelligentsia." It would seem that Soviet socialization has failed to convince at least these people of the accuracy and aptness of the official view of social class structure. Similarly, Machonin's nationwide study of Czechoslovakia in 1967 revealed that only one-tenth of the respondents saw society as stratified into a working class, peasantry, and intelligentsia. Social status was determined by type of work, education, and the way in which leisure time was spent, or, more generally, "life style."[8] Thus, official views of class structure in socialist countries may not be very widely accepted.

FREEDOM OR ANARCHY?

It has often been remarked that the Russian political tradition is one that emphasizes authority and strong rule, not valuing individual or collective freedom to the same degree as some Western political cultures. A recent reminder that some Russians, as well as foreigners, hold to this view has been provided by the writings and speeches of Aleksander Solzhenitsyn. An earlier observer of Russia noted that "every form of government is more or less the result of the cultural and social standard of the country. Would not red Tsarism seem to historians sociologically a more natural successor to Tsarist absolutism in illiterate Russia than the democratic republic which the Mensheviks and Social Revolutionaries set up during the March revolution?"[9] Whether or not a dictatorial government is "inevitable" or "natural" in Russia cannot be debated here, but we are curious about the views of former Soviet citizens, presumably in disagreement with the present form of Soviet government, regarding freedom and the rights of the individual to self-expression.

In the 1940s, when interviewing refugees from the USSR, the social scientists of the Harvard Project discovered that "the freedom of dissident groups in America to criticize the government disturbed many of them" and that "they were disturbed that the American government does not do more to direct the activities of its citizens *for their own good*. They objected to the laxity of American authorities in not exercising more control over the routine behavior of the public."[10] Nearly 30 years later, when interviewing Soviet immigrants in Detroit, we found that while a substantial proportion complained about the lack of *political* freedom in the Soviet Union, a similar proportion objected to what they saw as the excessive *social* freedom in America, arguing that crime, disrespect to elders, and improper behavior in public (lewd dress, loud talking, and so on) resulted from it.[11]

The emigrés in Israel expressed similar feelings. They complained about the public behavior of Israelis, especially youth, and wondered why the government did nothing to curb it. They remarked on the dirty streets, and when asked to speculate on the reasons for this, they spoke most often of "Levantine, backward culture" or of the "lack of public order and discipline." They criticized a seeming lack of governmental decisiveness and willingness to discipline the population. Several times we heard recommendations that "the government take these hooligans in hand and deal with them firmly." One respondent commented that the government itself sets a poor example for public behavior because "I often see what goes on in the Knesset . . . we should not have to see that disorder." (One wonders whether unconsciously he is thinking of the orchestrated unanimity of the Supreme Soviet as his model of what a parliament should be.) Another immigrant objected to caricatures of former Premier Golda Meir (a cartoonist's delight) as being disrespectful, and some objected to the picture of Anwar Sadat appearing on the front page of the newspaper. "In the Soviet Union they would never publish the enemy's picture on the front page!" Like the emigrés of the 1940s, the Soviet immigrants in Israel complained about pornography and "too broad" freedom of the press. One suggested that the government regulate art and the cinema more closely because "they show too much American pornography." Another's opinion was that while freedom was desirable, it should be limited in Israel because "the population is not ready for it." "Democracy needs freedom, not anarchy," remarked another. Several times it was pointed out that the amount of freedom given to a people should depend on its "cultural level," and the higher the level attained, the more freedom could be given. While most suggested that there be tighter controls of public behavior, quite a few argued for greater freedom in religious matters, feeling that the absence of recognized civil marriage in Israel and the unavailability of public transportation on the Sabbath restricted individual freedom.

Americans, by contrast, generally found that there was too *little* freedom in Israel. Some pointed to the fact that civil liberties could be easily suspended in Israel, a country legally in a state of emergency since 1948, and others found some laws unduly restrictive. A student remarked that there was not enough individual participation in government, that there was not enough "freedom to change one's place of residence. I don't think people's religion should be written in their identity card . . . I think there should be more freedom to dissent here. It's hard to be a nonconformist in Israel."

The differences between the American and Soviet immigrants emerged most clearly in the answers to one of our questions about freedom (see Table 8.6). More than half of the Americans thought there should be more freedom, whereas about one-third of the

TABLE 8.6
"Some people think there should be more freedom than we have now; others think there should be less; what is your opinion?"
(in percent)

	Americans		Soviets	
	1972	*1975*	*1972*	*1975*
More freedom	50.0	56.6	16.3	24.0
Less freedom	9.1	3.3	36.4	32.0
Just about the right amount	40.9	40.1	47.3	44.0

Soviets in both 1972 and 1975 found that freedom was already excessive. These attitudes remained quite stable over the three years, and there was no difference between the 1972/75 and 1972-only groups. We conclude that attitudes on the question of freedom are deeply ingrained, that they are culturally dependent, and that, having been formed in the immigrants' previous political culture, they are not easily changed.

Like earlier Soviet emigrés, our group was prepared to allow the government a good deal of latitude, on the question of freedom as well, though here the contrast with the Americans was not so sharp. Nearly half the Soviets, but less than one-fifth of the Americans, said that the government "should decide how much freedom there should be." The others felt that "the people" or individuals should establish the degree of freedom in a society. There was stability over time in the attitudes expressed, and there was no difference in 1972 between immigrants who were reinterviewed and those who were not. However, in both years heartlanders tended to favor restrictions on freedom and the government's right to limit it more than Zapadniki did, perhaps as a result of longer exposure to Soviet political socialization.

In order to probe the Soviet immigrants in particular, and see whether they really fit the stereotype of "welfare state authoritarians," we asked the immigrants to choose between a system of government that gave people freedom "to do what they like" but did not provide housing, employment, and health care, and a system where the government did provide these services but could "mix into people's lives." Here we found less stability of attitude than on the other questions. In 1972 about 33 percent of the Soviets preferred the system providing welfare, but with government control, and over 40 percent preferred the system where the government neither provided those services nor did it "mix into people's lives." Surprisingly, the American responses were not that different, though more rejected the very idea of such a dichotomy and argued for a "mixed" system in which welfare and freedom are combined. In 1975, however, two-thirds of the immigrants from the USSR said they would choose a system where the government does not "mix in," even though it would not provide welfare services. This shift is impressive, especially considering the fact that the 1972/75 group had been somewhat more inclined to the control-cum-welfare system in 1972 than had the others. Thus, the Soviet respondents seem to have moved away from what might be seen as a Soviet model. Perhaps they have been able to do so because Israel *is* a welfare state, and they have not really experienced a situation of freedom-without-welfare, though they have now experienced freedom-with-welfare. The Americans moved in the same direction as the Soviets, though not as forcefully. Also, the Americans rejected even more the dichotomy we presented to them, and they stressed the advantages of the "mixed" system, presumably the kind of system that exists in Israel. The American willingness to accept government welfare services is due, perhaps, to their urban, liberal Democratic background in the United States and their status as immigrants, dependent on government services, in Israel. By 1975, well established in Israel and no longer considered immigrants by the government, they were less concerned with government welfare services.

We found a significant positive correlation between the desire for welfare services, at the expense of personal autonomy, and the notions that freedom in Israel is excessive and that the government has the right to determine its limits. In addition, those who felt that freedom was excessive were also the most likely to be deferential to authority and to see the Israeli government as a beneficient one. There was an interesting contrast in the political tendencies of Americans and Soviets who thought there was not enough freedom in Israel. Among the Soviets, this feeling was correlated with nonmembership in the Labor-dominated Histadrut and with identification with right-wing political parties. Among the Americans, on the other hand, those who identified with the right wing tended to think there was too much freedom in Israel and believed that the government has the right to determine how much freedom there should be.

IMAGES OF ETHNIC GROUPS

The United States, the USSR, and Israel are multiethnic societies, and in each of them ethnic relations are an important political issue, though in very different ways. The Soviet Union's federal structure gives more explicit recognition to the existence of ethnic cultures than do the institutional arrangements in the United States and Israel, and the latter two have only recently moved away from a "melting pot" ideology to greater recognition of the legitimacy and even desirability of ethnic-cultural pluralism. On the other hand, ethnic groups in the USSR have complained of Russian domination, the suppression of their own cultures, and discrimination against members of their groups. Thus, all three countries have grappled with the problem of achieving political integration in a multiethnic setting. Obviously, the attitudes toward ethnicity and ethnic groups that are held by individual citizens are important in defining the nature and scope of the problem and affect its solution, even in the USSR where the input of citizens in the political process is less than in the other two countries. If we are to understand better the political cultures that shaped the immigrants, and if we are to gain greater insight into their perceptions of and interactions with the Israeli social and political systems, we should inquire into the attitudes of the immigrants toward ethnic groups.

Our inquiry focused on ethnic groups in the Soviet Union and in Israel (American immigrants were questioned only about Israeli ethnic groups). One of the techniques used for both sets of ethnic groups was a modified ethnic distance scale wherein the immigrants were asked to indicate whether they would want members of specific interest groups as close relatives by marriage, close personal friends, neighbors, or fellow workers.[12] The data were then aggregated to determine what proportion of the Soviet immigrants had positive, ambivalent, or negative feelings toward specific Soviet ethnic groups. The latter included Russians, Ukrainians, and Belorussians, the three major, Slavic nationalities among whom the heartlanders lived (and with whom the Zapadniki were likely to have had considerable contact); Latvians, Lithuanians, and Moldavians, borderland nationalities among whom the Zapadniki had lived; the Uzbeks, chosen as "representative" of Soviet Asian (and Muslim) nationalities; and Georgian Jews, included because we wanted to see how the respondents would feel about a group so different culturally and socially, but Jewish nevertheless. By calculating mean scores for each nationality, it is possible to rank order the nationalities in terms of the attitudes of the immigrants toward them (see Table 8.7). These data must be treated with caution, for several reasons. First, a low ranking does not necessarily imply actively hostile feelings toward a nationality. From the comments of the respondents, it became clear that few had hostile attitudes toward Uzbeks, but that they considered the latter so remote — geographically, culturally, and socially — that it was not realistic to think of them as marriage partners or even

TABLE 8.7
Ranking of Soviet Ethnic Groups by Soviet Immigrants
(from positive[10] to negative [0])

Heartlanders	*Zapadniki*
1. Russians (7.0)	1. Russians (5.5)
2. Georgian Jews (4.9)	2. Georgian Jews (4.8)
3. Belorussians (4.7)	3. Lithuanians (4.1)
4. Latvians (4.7)	4. Belorussians (3.4)
5. Lithuanians (4.3)	5. Moldavians (3.3)
6. Moldavians (4.1)	6. Latvians (2.8)
7. Ukrainians (4.0)	7. Ukrainians (2.8)
8. Uzbeks (3.3)	8. Uzbeks (2.8)

neighbors and friends. Second, about 20 respondents consistently refused to answer the questions about nationalities, stressing that ethnicity was of no importance in social relations and that therefore the question was meaningless and irrelevant to them. Most of those refusing to answer the questions were highly educated. Finally, only 17 people answered the questions pertaining to Latvians, so this datum must be treated with even more than the usual caution.

Bearing these caveats in mind, we can analyze the results. The heartlanders felt more positively toward the Soviet peoples than did the Zapadniki. Culturally and socially more assimilated, the heartlanders may have found it more "natural" to associate closely with members of other ethnic groups than did the Zapadniki who, for the most part, did not have such relations with non-Jewish populations before the Soviet period. Both Jewish groups placed Russians at the top of their scales, and Georgian Jews in second place. Over 33 percent of the respondents displayed positive feelings toward the Russians, and only 15 percent showed negative feelings, with half categorized as "ambivalent." There is much less ambivalence regarding the controversial Georgian Jews, and there is a greater polarization of attitudes toward them. This is the only instance in which a higher proportion of heartlanders than Zapadniki expressed negative feelings. In general, it appears that Zapadniki were more ethnocentric than heartlanders, that they retained a stronger "ingroup" feeling and saw themselves as more distant from non-Jewish groups. From among the non-Jewish groups, however, Russians, the dominant group numerically, politically, and culturally, were ranked highest by the Zapadniki, higher even than Georgian Jews.

Ukrainians, often thought of as the "second nationality" of the USSR, ranked quite low for both heartlanders and Zapadniki. This may be due to the historic tensions between Jews and Ukrainians, tensions that still exist today.[13] The other major Slavic nationality, Belorussians, were ranked ahead of the Ukrainians, despite the fact that the former are generally less prominent in Soviet science, politics, and culture. Though the Zapadniki lived among Lithuanians, Latvians, and Moldavians, they did not rank them very differently from the heartlanders.[14]

A second measure of ethnic attitudes, or, more precisely, images, was employed. Immigrants were asked to rate ethnic groups on a seven-point scale, using seven paired adjectives for each group. Thus, immigrants were asked to say how philo-Semitic/anti-Semitic, cultured/uncultured, good-hearted/mean, tough/soft, kind/cruel, powerful/weak, and trustworthy/untrustworthy each of the groups were. Without detailing the ratings for each group, we note that, again, the Zapadniki took a less favorable view of the Soviet nationalities than did the heartlanders, but their rank ordering was not much different. Again, Ukrainians came out on the bottom of the scale, and Russians toward the top. However, in contrast to the findings from the first scale, Uzbeks were judged favorably by both Zapadniki — among whom they ranked ahead of all others — and heartlanders — among whom they ranked second. The explanation we offer for this is that while Uzbeks are seen as most "different" from Soviet Jews — they are Muslim, Asiatic, rural — they are not seen as hostile or "bad." Perhaps their very remoteness allows the respondents to maintain a more charitable stereotype of this group than of the other peoples, with whom they lived in closer proximity.

In addition to Soviet nationalities, respondents were questioned about Americans, Soviet citizens, and "Arabs." Arabs were rated least favorably by all groups, including American immigrant respondents, and the distance between them and the next group was substantial. The Americans rated Israelis a bit more favorably than they rated Americans, and they placed Soviet citizens ahead of Arabs, but distinctly less favorably than Americans. The Soviet immigrants also rated the Israelis more favorably but did not display great affection or admiration for Americans. In fact, Americans were rated more favorably than Arabs only, and "Soviet citizens" and

Ukrainians were regarded more positively than Americans. Moreover, both Zapadniki and heartlanders displayed greater admiration for Russians, Balts, and Uzbeks than for Israelis. Again, it should be emphasized that the two measures we employed may have tapped different sentiments: The first measured emotional and psychological affinity, while the second asked for a more "objective" description of traits. One may feel closer to a less admirable person if one is related to that person or even just familiar with him, while one may well admire — from afar — those who are perceived as very different and far removed from one's own life. While Russians are both admired and seen as fairly desirable relatives, neighbors, and coworkers, Uzbeks may be thought of as having admirable traits, but they are not seen as potential friends and colleagues, let alone relatives.

More educated Soviet respondents tended to place less distance between themselves and Soviet nationalities. It is also the case that those who have completed higher education have a more favorable image of other nationalities, including Arabs, Israelis, and Americans.

Turning to Jewish ethnic groups in Israel (defined by country of origin), we asked our immigrant groups to respond to the same ethnic distance measures described earlier. The groups inquired about included Israelis, Persians, Moroccans, and American, Soviet, English, and Polish immigrants. Israelis were chosen in order to see how desirous the respondent might be to "become Israeli" and whether Israelis are a positive model. Persians and Moroccans are considered "Oriental" Jews, or Sefardim, with Moroccans generally ranked lowest on the ethnic totem pole in Israel. We wanted to see how the two immigrant groups — Soviets and Americans — regarded each other, and how they regarded groups presumed to be closest to them, Englishmen and Poles. Finally, we added a nonethnic paired group, religious and nonreligious people, since religion is, with ethnicity, the major social cleavage in Israeli society. The ranking of these groups, done by aggregating the answers to several questions about them, is presented in Table 8.8.

The first thing that strikes us is the decline in the position of Israelis between 1972 and 1975. Newly arrived immigrants held up the Israelis as an ideal group to associate with, as friends, neighbors, relatives. After all, this would mean "integration" into Israeli society, or at least acceptance by it. (Over 90 percent of a sample of Soviet immigrant students said their close friends were also Soviet immigrants;

TABLE 8.8
Ranking of Israeli Groups by Soviet and American Immigrants
(ranked from positive to negative)

1972		1975	
Americans	*Soviets*	*Americans*	*Soviets*
Israelis	Israelis	English olim	Soviet olim
American olim	Soviet olim	American olim	Nonreligious
English olim	American olim	Israelis	Israelis
Soviet olim	Nonreligious	Religious	American olim
Persians	Polish olim	Nonreligious	Polish olim
Nonreligious	Persians	Soviet olim	Persians
Religious	Moroccans	Persians	Religious
Moroccans	Religious	Moroccans	Moroccans

and over 90 percent said it's very important for them to make friends with Israelis.)[15] By 1975 Israelis have slipped to third place among both Americans and Soviets, and, strikingly, they have been replaced by immigrants from their own countries. In other words, our respondents may be more interested in being with "their own" in 1975, and may have become less enthusiastic about "melting" into the Israeli population and associating with "real Israelis." In fact, the Shuval-Markus study shows that Soviet immigrants tend to remain in their own social circles for many years.[16]

The immigrants did not need three years to learn that Persians and Moroccans rank low in Israeli society, and their ranking does not change significantly. In both years, most immigrants were positive toward newcomers from their own countries. Americans were enthusiastic about English olim, fellow "Anglo-Saxons," but Soviet immigrants were less enthusiastic about Polish newcomers (Zapadniki, culturally closer to these East European Jews, were more interested in associating with Polish Jews). Soviet immigrants were warmer toward American newcomers than the Americans were toward the Soviets.

In 1972 neither Americans nor, especially, Soviets desired close associations with religious people, though Americans ranked nonreligious just above the religious and the Soviets ranked them considerably higher. However, in 1975 the religious move up in the Americans' scale (though the nonreligious remain close to them), while staying near the bottom of the Soviet scale. Why? It turns out that, as noted earlier, in the 1972/75 American group, 40 percent defined themselves as religious, whereas only 27 percent of the 1972-only group did so. Religious Americans preferred religious people as neighbors or relatives, but they showed no preference in regard to friends or coworkers. This might also explain why the Soviets fell in the American rankings — the religious Americans found the Soviets, who were generally nonreligious, less attractive as neighbors and associates. Soviet immigrants, on the other hand, found living among religious people restrictive, as they felt that they were not as free to enjoy their Saturday leisure in the way they wish. They also associated religiosity with the Oriental communities, and so attitudes toward religious people were highly correlated with those toward Persians and Moroccans. Zapadniki were more inclined to live among Israelis, less interested in people from the USSR, and also somewhat more hostile toward both the religious and the Orientals than were the immigrants from the heartland. They were closer to typical Israeli preferences than the heartlanders. Americans, perhaps because of their antecedent socialization, were more willing to associate with Oriental Jews than were the Soviets. The latter, coming from a society where they were discriminated against because of their ethnicity, nevertheless did not hesitate to express their contempt for the Orientals and one-third said they did not wish to live with Moroccans, nor would they want to have them as relatives.

These findings are, of course, misleading in some ways. First, they show only *relative* preferences. Second, as mentioned earlier, they probably measure perceived distance from groups rather than indicate evaluation of them, though the line between these is quite blurred, no doubt. Third, these are aggregated results and they conceal as much as they reveal. For example, there was great variance of opinion among both Americans and Soviets regarding Moroccans and Persians, and the low ranking of the two Oriental groups reflects the fact that negative attitudes toward them were strongly held, not that *all* the American and Soviet respondents saw them in a negative light. Finally, there was some variation by education, though not as much as might have been supposed. Among the Soviet respondents, those with higher education were more positive than the others toward the religious and Moroccan groups, though only two or three of the highly educated Soviets were themselves religious.

Although the Soviet immigrants were themselves victims of a system that did not easily tolerate cultural (and certainly political) pluralism, they seemed to have assimilated prevalent Soviet attitudes in discriminating among ethnic groups. Like many people in the USSR, they had little patience for ethnic pluralism, at least insofar as Israel is concerned, and quite a few of our informants displayed attitudes that would be characterized in Soviet jargon as "great-power chauvinist." After much difficulty in conveying the notion of cultural pluralism to Soviet participants in our pretest, we managed to formulate the following question, apparently understood by the great majority: "Some people believe that Israeli society should aim at being homogeneous. Others feel that Israel should preserve the different characteristics of the different ethnic groups in the State. How do you feel?" While about 60 percent of the American respondents favored the ethnic pluralist option, less than 10 percent of the Soviet immigrants did so. Americans, reflecting an ethos emerging among their social peers in the United States, were reluctant to endorse a policy of active and deliberate homogenization, though some favored such a process as long as it was "spontaneous." As one said, "I think the little mafia of Hungarian, Romanian, North African, and other immigrants has to be eliminated if this is going to be a successful society. But the answer is not putting anything through a blender or letting it come out as one homogeneous pap." Another pointed out that "Jews were always diverse, there were always differences, but ultimately it is essential to get rid of the differences to have a viable state, but it should be a slow, passive process."

A few Soviet immigrants discussed ethnicity in terms reminiscent of the Soviet distinction between *sblizhenie*, or the drawing closer of peoples, and the later and "higher" stage of *sliianie*, or fusion of peoples into an amalgam where ethnic differences will be melted down. Most prescribed an effort to homogenize Israeli society, and the sooner the better. One suggested using "the methods of Peter the Great" to eliminate the "undesirable" features of society and preserve the "good" in it. Another suggested that "in ethnic relations there should be homogeneity [*odnorodnost'*], while in political relations there should be diversity." Several pointed out that the society should be built to conform to "European" values and that it should avoid "Levantization." The very notion that there could be cultural-ethnic diversity in the Jewish state struck some as a contradiction in terms. ". . . There can be no talk of any preservation [of ethnic characteristics]. We are not immigrants, we are not Russian immigrants in France or Polish immigrants in America. . . . We are Jews in Israel, and we didn't come here in order to preserve our immigrant mentality." This kind of sentiment was especially strong among Zapadniki, who never developed the attachments to "Mother Russia" that some heartlanders displayed. Among the latter, one does find a "nostalgia for birch trees," a desire to educate their children in classical Russian culture, and lingering sentimental attachments to various forms of Russian culture, usually accompanied by explicit rejection of *Soviet* values. So while part of the Soviet immigration may be rabid "assimilationists" in Israel, others see positive value in preserving part of their former culture – though this does not necessarily mean that they are willing to grant the legitimacy of preserving *other* cultures brought to Israel. Americans pay lip service to the notion of cultural diversity, though they rank some cultures ahead of others and are probably no less anxious than the Soviets to see European culture prevail over Middle Eastern. In fact, it is easier for Americans than for Soviets to support the notion of preserving ethnic characteristics in Israel because the American "characteristics" (real or imagined) – efficiency, modernity, technological capability, English culture – are much admired in Israel, whereas Soviet Russian culture does not enjoy high status. Still, there is a marked contrast in the views of Americans and Soviets on ethnic preservation policies and they reflect their previous socialization.

THE IMMIGRANTS AND THE ISSUES

Anyone even vaguely familiar with Israeli history will not be surprised to learn that security is widely perceived as the most important issue facing the state. For more than 30 years Israelis have lived with the question of whether they would survive physically to greet the next day, and they have attempted to fashion a "normal" daily existence nevertheless. Immigrants are quick to perceive security as the major issue, and it is so identified by our Soviet and American respondents as well as by the Soviet respondents in the 1973 election study. Immigrant absorption, the economy, and the maintenance and strengthening of Zionist ideology are the other major problems of Israeli society identified by the immigrants. While economics is the vital concern of most Israelis, the immigration and Zionist issues are much more salient to the immigrants than to the population at large, though our American respondents did not identify immigrant absorption as frequently as did the Soviets. The immigrants were concerned about Zionism because so many of them came to Israel out of ideological motivations, only to find that most Israelis seemed uninterested in that ideology and, indeed, sometimes referred to "Zionism" with a good deal of irony.

In 1972 the Soviet immigrants, especially, tended to the opinion that all that could be done to "solve" the security problem would be to "stand fast," maintaining both Israel's military position as well as its ideals and principles. By 1975, having experienced the Yom Kippur War and its political consequences, these immigrants were less unwilling to compromise on a political solution and more willing to criticize the government, as were the Americans.

The 1972/75 group was generally more sanguine about the possibility of solving Israel's problems and the efficacy of the citizenry in doing this. Between 1972 and 1975, however, the ardor and enthusiasm of the Americans for organization and political activism cooled somewhat, while that of the Soviets increased. As both groups "learned the ropes," they moved in opposite directions: The Americans, having come full of ideas and a naive belief that they could "change things," learned that Israelis were not terribly eager to accept the Americans' prescriptions; the Soviets, on the other hand, became more familiar with the workings of a society considerably more open than their country of origin, and began to see the possibilities of organization and activism.

Soviet immigrants took great pride in Israel's military exploits, and cited these as giving them great satisfaction, while Americans tended to pay more attention to social and economic achievements, though by no means were they indifferent to military successes. What disturbed the Soviet newcomers most were sentiments expressed against immigrant "privileges." The Soviets were the most visible of the immigrants and the most frequent target of those who resented Israel's policies toward newcomers. Americans, enjoying a higher social status, were less sensitive to anti-immigrant sentiments and pointed more to discrimination against Israeli Arabs and Oriental Jews as sources of dissatisfaction.

ATTITUDES TOWARD ARABS

We have examined immigrants' attitudes toward ethnic groups in the USSR and Israel. Attitudes toward Arabs involve more than ethnicity, for they touch on foreign policy issues, the question of Israel's nature as a Jewish, yet nonsectarian, state, and majority-minority relations in a country where national and political integration are crucial to its existence.

In 1972 over three-quarters of the respondents felt there would be a war with the Arabs within the following decade. The war of 1973 proved them right and strengthened their conviction that there would be Arab-Israeli wars in the future, for in 1975 there was even stronger agreement with the proposition that another war would come. Americans, however, were slightly more optimistic than the Soviets in both 1972 and 1975, 30 percent thinking in 1972 there would be no war, and 11 percent maintaining this opinion in 1975.

In all the Arab-Israeli wars, Israeli Arabs have remained generally loyal to Israel, though few have been called upon to fight for Israel against their fellow Arabs. Nevertheless, there is considerable prejudice against the Arabs and suspicion of their ultimate loyalties and intentions, and Arab-Jewish relations remain an important domestic issue, though overshadowed by the conflict between Israel and the Arab states. In order to compare attitudes toward Israeli Arabs held by the immigrants with those held by Israelis generally, in a way measuring the extent to which the immigrants might have been socialized to Israeli attitudes, we asked the same question that had been posed to Israeli national samples, and the results are displayed in Table 8.9. It would appear that before the Yom Kippur War only the Zapadniki were as skeptical of the Arabs in Israel as were the Israelis. After the war, however, when the non-Israeli Arabs showed that they could inflict serious damage upon the Jews, even the Zapadniki took a less skeptical view. Unfortunately, we do not have data that would show changes, if any, in Israeli perceptions after 1973. The heartlanders and Americans did not change their opinions very much, and they may not have made a connection between the situation of the Israeli Arabs and the capabilities of the external ones. In any case, by 1975 all groups were split fairly evenly in their assessment of the chances that Israeli Arabs "will reach the level of the Jews."

TABLE 8.9
"Some people say that even if the Israeli Arabs make great progress, they will not reach the level of the Jews. What's your opinion?"
(in percent)

	Heartlanders		Zapadniki		Americans		Israelis
	1972	1975	1972	1975	1972	1975	1969
Completely agree	15	10	14	13	12	7	43
Agree	33	43	54	31	36	52	18
Disagree	43	37	27	52	46	35	23
Completely disagree	8	10	6	4	6	7	13
No answer							3

Source: The Israeli data are from the 1969 electoral survey conducted by Professor Alan Arian and reported in *Elections Study 1969: Findings* (Tel Aviv: Political Science Department, Tel Aviv University, 1971).

Having been asked to make what looked like an empirical judgment of Israeli Arabs, the respondents were then asked for their responses to a normative statement regarding them. They were asked to indicate their agreement or disagreement with the statement that "Israeli Arabs should have equal rights with Jews." We have noted that both Soviets and Americans have come from multiethnic states that espouse equality for all, but where that has not been achieved. Here we found that in both 1972 and 1975 over 90 percent of the Americans agreed with the statement, but the percentage agreeing among the Soviets was around 75, with the Zapadniki agreeing to a somewhat lesser extent than the heartlanders. Apparently, the 1973 War did not cause any real alterations in the immigrants' feelings that equal rights are due the Israeli Arabs, as the distribution of opinions in 1975 was very much the same as it had been three years earlier.

Since there was a nearly even split on the question of whether or not Arabs will "reach the level of the Jews," we supposed that education might be the key variable explaining different attitudes. There are no differences between the 1972 and 1972/75 groups, and there is little variance on this question by education. On the other question, there is only a slight tendency for those with higher education to be more in favor of equal rights for the Arabs.

THE OCCUPIED TERRITORIES

No other issue has aroused as much controversy in Israel during the last 15 years as what should be done with territories occupied after the 1967 War. Even the description of these territories — "occupied," "administered," or "liberated" — is a matter of fierce debate. This issue — and it is related to the question of attitudes toward Arabs — is a major item in party platforms and media discussions, and the immigrants, like most of the rest of the population, have some very definite opinions on it. It is also one of the most important issues in determining one's general political stance and party affiliation, and it may be so for the immigrants as well.

Since considerable information is available on the attitudes of the general population on the occupied territories, we can see how the immigrants compare on this issue. The great majority of Israelis favored keeping most of the occupied territories, at least until President Sadat's visit to Jerusalem in November 1977. However, after the 1973 War the proportion willing to "return some" rose considerably and the proportion of those wishing to hold on to the territories declined.

In the survey of Soviet immigrants taken in May 1973, the results shown in Table 8.10 were obtained. The distribution of opinions among the Soviet immigrants was quite similar to that among the Israeli population, though the Soviets were somewhat more adamant about returning "nothing." However, considerably more immigrants had no opinion on this matter, as might be expected

TABLE 8.10
Soviet Immigrant and Israeli Opinions Regarding the Occupied Territories

(in percent)

	Balts	Heartlanders	Georgians	Soviets	Israelis
Return nothing	42	52	53	49	31
Return a small part	43	28	19	30	52
Return some	5	6	4	5	10
Return all or almost all	3	0	4	2	2
No answer	8	14	21	14	5

from newcomers. Among the Georgians, those with the least education and the least exposure to the Israeli media (because of linguistic
limitations), over one-fifth of the respondents had no opinion or
did not answer the question, though the opinions of the others
were very much the same as those of the other immigrants and
of the Israelis.

Among our own Soviet respondents we found a distribution of
opinions strikingly similar to that observed in the 1973 election
study, even though our group had considerably more education.
Like the Israelis, our Soviet informants changed their views following
the 1973 War and were more willing to entertain thoughts of giving
back some of the occupied territory. However, the Soviet immigrants
remained less willing to do so than the Americans, who were not as
enthusiastic about keeping the territories as either the Soviets or
the Israelis. The Soviet informants, in explaining their positions,
frequently made reference to the USSR's behavior in international
affairs, and their views seemed to be influenced to some extent by
ideas assimilated in the Soviet Union, just as the Americans may have
been influenced by the Vietnam experience. "That which is taken
with blood should not be returned; this is what all nations do and
what we should do — we should take an example from the Soviet
Union." A few mentioned the fact that they had come from a huge
country to a tiny one and the occupied territories would give them
at least some feeling of *prostor*, of "wide open spaces."

A comparison of the opinion distribution among the immigrant
groups and over three years can be seen in Table 8.11. The movement — by both Soviets and Americans — to the idea of returning

TABLE 8.11
Soviet and American Immigrants' Opinions
on the Occupied Territories
(in percent)

	Heartlanders		Zapadniki		Soviets		Americans	
	1972	*1975*	*1972*	*1975*	*1972*	*1975*	*1972*	*1975*
Return nothing	53	39	43	32	48	35	28	23
Return some	41	54	51	61	46	58	52	63
Return all	6	7	7	7	6	7	20	13

some of the territories parallels the movement in the opinions of the Israeli mass public, though a majority of Americans held this view already in 1972. Those Americans who wanted Israel to hold on to all the territories were disproportionately religious, had been in Israel longer, and tended not to belong to the Histadrut (which was dominated by the Labor party, whose views on the territories were more compromising than those of the Likud). These people felt less at home in the United States than the others and they may have been less trusting of non-Jews, including Arabs, than the others. There was a positive correlation between wishing to keep the territories and maintaining that Arabs in Israel should *not* enjoy equal rights, as there was with belief that there will be a war with the Arabs in the next decade. These positions are logically related, of course. Moreover, in recent years it has become apparent that majority sentiment among religious Israelis is for retaining the territories, not using them as bargaining chips in negotiations with the Arabs.

POLITICAL ATTITUDES: CONTINUITY
OR RESOCIALIZATION?

The Soviet and American immigrants included in our study had political orientations that clearly reflected their earlier socialization in their countries of origin. Attitudes toward authority and feelings of efficacy and trust bore the stamps "made in U.S.A." and "made in U.S.S.R." Attitudes toward authority, developed and reinforced outside as well as inside the political arena, changed least over the three years. Feelings of trust seemed to change only a bit, though there may have been more situational influence on feelings of trust than we have been able to show. The sense of political efficacy changed more than the other orientations we have labeled as "basic." The experience of the immigrants lends support to the notion that efficacy is only partially a personal, psychological trait, and that it is affected — but not determined — by the realistic possibility of exerting personal or group political influence in a particular system.

In retrospect, the choice of the term "basic" to describe the political orientations discussed seems apt, for they changed less than the other political attitudes examined. There was noticeable change in conceptions of socialism, though there was no resocialization to a single — or even a few — conception(s) of it. Immigrants also changed their ideas of social class, perceiving that there were different determinants of class in Israeli and Soviet/American socie- ties. They also discerned changes in their own class status and were able, for the most part, to explain those changes. Attitudes toward freedom, perhaps more abstract, seemed to be less malleable and more culturally specific. What is freedom to most American immi- grants is anarchy to their Soviet counterparts. The stability mani- fested on this issue does not arise out of indifference to it and lack of thought about it, but rather from deep concern about liberty or license, an issue the immigrants see as being played out every day in Israeli political and, especially, social life.

Attitudes toward ethnic groups seem more changeable than those toward freedom, but they change less rapidly than those relating to socialism and social class. In fact, images of other groups may not change very much at all, with the one exception of images of Israelis, whom the immigrants tend to idealize and set up as models in their first period in the country, later moving to a stated social preference for their own ethnic group. On this question it is impossible to sort out the degrees of continuity and change in attitude from the USA/ USSR to Israel. Despite the fact that Soviet Jews had not seen Israeli Arabs or Moroccan Jews in the USSR, it is entirely possible that they formed images of these peoples in the USSR, generalizing from stereotypes of Arab students in the USSR or from rumor and infor- mation about Israel gotten from official Soviet and other sources. Americans also may have formed images from their own tourism, from reading and hearing about Israel, and from analogizing from what they thought were parallel ethnic groups and situations in the United States. If the images were, indeed, formed in Israel, we cannot determine by what means: Who were the socializing agents forming these images; what was the role of direct personal experi- ence; to what extent is conformity to perceived Israeli norms involved here?

It is on specific political issues — Israeli Arabs, the disposition of the occupied territories — that we find most flexibility and change, though even here the influence of antecedent socialization — whether middle class American liberalism or Soviet authoritarian- ism — is definitely felt. By comparing immigrant attitudes with those displayed by national representative samples of Israelis, we determined that the distribution of immigrant opinion on current issues was not very different, though, again, we do not know how the immigrants acquired these attitudes and why exactly a particular person holds to this or that opinion. Immigrant opinion did shift in the same direction as Israeli mass opinion after the 1973 War, though both Americans and Soviets retained distinctive distributions of opinion.

In sum, the general picture is one showing a good deal of both continuity and stability in political orientations, considerable stability in attitudes toward certain general political concepts, but substantial change on specific political issues. It might be argued that external events — notably the Yom Kippur War of 1973 — caused the observed change on issues, and without it we might have seen the same stability as on the other issues. This may well have been, though so many changes took place in the immigrants' individual lives in their three or five years in Israel, and the Israeli system was so different from the ones they knew, that change even in basic orientations might have been expected. One should also add that immigrants were interviewed at only two points in time. Were they to be reinterviewed, say, five years after arrival, we might observe more change. However, for whatever reason, three years is generally accepted in Israel as the period of resettlement, and the fifth-year data from the MIA panel study do not indicate any need to change this. There is an Israeli anecdote that explains why three years are required for resettlement. Resettlement is described as stages of resentment and hatred. In the first year after his arrival the immigrant hates the Jewish Agency for having brought him to Israel. In the second year, he resents the Ministry for Immigrant Absorption for trying to resettle him in the country. By the third year, the immigrant has been successfully absorbed, and he now hates new immigrants.

NOTES

1. Kenneth M. Coleman and Charles L. Davis, "The Structural Context of Politics and Dimensions of Regime Performance," *Comparative Political Studies* 9, no. 2 (July 1976): 191.

2. Ibid., p. 193. Our findings agree with Langton's contention that "political efficacy responds to life cycle changes and is not generalizable across situations. . . . There is a real question whether we can continue to treat political efficacy as a global psychological disposition or personality attribute. Its variation across situations leads us to think otherwise." Kenneth P. Langton, *Political*

Participation and Learning (North Quincy, Mass.: Christopher Publishing House, 1980), p. 128.

3. Tamar Horowitz concluded, on the basis of a psychological test, that the Soviet immigrant is much more alienated "from both his fellow man and the government" than the English-speaking immigrant. The Soviet immigrant "feels powerless in the face of the government and incapable of influencing it." Tamar Horowitz and Khava Frankel, *Olim bemerkazai klitah* (Jerusalem: Henrietta Szold Institute, 1975), Research Report No. 185, Publication No. 538, p. 220.

4. Yehudit Shuval and Yehuda Markus, *Dfusai histaglut shel olai Brithamoetsot* (Jerusalem: Israel Institute of Applied Social Research, 1973), p. 12. See also Part 2, p. 66.

5. Judith Shuval, Elliot Markus, and Judith Dotan, *Patterns of Integration Over Time: Soviet Immigrants in Israel* (Jerusalem: Israel Institute of Applied Social Research, 1975), p. 30.

6. The following section draws from Zvi Gitelman, "Soviet Political Culture: Insights from Jewish Emigrés," *Soviet Studies* 29, no. 4 (October 1977): 556-57.

7. I am indebted to Professor Wesley Fisher of Columbia University for this point.

8. Pavel Machonin, *Československa společnost* (Bratislava: Epocha, 1969), pp. 86ff.

9. Jan Slavik in the final chapter of Thomas Garrigue Masaryk, *The Spirit of Russia* (London: George Allen and Unwin, 1961), Vol. II, p. 619.

10. Alex Inkeles and Raymond Bauer, *The Soviet Citizen* (New York: Atheneum, 1968), pp. 248-49.

11. For details, see Zvi Gitelman, "Soviet Immigrants and American Absorption Efforts: A Case Study in Detroit," *Journal of Jewish Communal Service* 55, no. 1 (September 1978).

12. For the application of ethnic distance scales to Soviet emigré respondents — 30 Balts and 66 Soviet Germans — see Juozas A. Kazlas, "Social Distance Among Ethnic Groups," in *Nationality Group Survival in Multi-Ethnic States*, ed. Edward Allworth (New York: Praeger Publishers, 1977).

13. For details, see Zvi Gitelman, "The Social and Political Role of the Jews in the Ukraine," in *Ukraine in the 1970's*, ed. Peter Potichnyj (Oakville, Ont.: Mosaic Press, 1975), pp. 167-86.

14. On attitudes of the Lithuanian and German emigrés toward Jews, see Kazlas, p. 245.

15. *Klitat studentim olim miBrih"m* (Jerusalem: Ministry for Immigrant Absorption, December 1975), p. 12.

16. Language is more important than length of residence in Israel in determining the composition of one's circle of friends. One-third of those interviewed were not happy with their neighbors. Shuval and Markus, Part 2, pp. 82 and 90.

9
CONCLUSION

Homecoming.

Immigration is more important to Israel than to any other country. The reestablishment of a Jewish state in Palestine was possible only with a massive "return" by the Jewish people to the area. That return has occurred, and the new Jewish state has existed for more than 30 years. Because its existence is still not secure, and because the Zionist ideal is to have a maximum number of Jews living in the Jewish state, immigration continues to be of vital importance to Israel. Jews are so widely scattered that those who settle in Israel bring with them an astounding variety of cultures, including political cultures. Attention has most often been focused on Israel's largely successful attempts at economic, cultural, and social resettlement

341

of immigrants; but there is little doubt that the state would not have been viable had it not succeeded in *politically* integrating the successive waves of immigrants, absorbing them into a modern, Western democracy, the kind of system from which only a tiny fraction had come. In the last decade most of the immigrants have come from the USSR and developed Western countries, in contrast to earlier waves of immigrants, many of whom came as refugees from East European and Afro-Asian countries.

The Israeli political system has proved flexible in adapting to qualitatively and quantitatively different immigrations. In the prestate period it was dominated by political parties that were deeply involved in recruiting and selecting immigrants abroad, bringing them to Palestine, and resettling them. The parties' involvement meant that the distribution of political power remained quite stable, despite tremendous changes in the population. It also meant the politicization of the processes of resettlement and integration. The British Mandatory authorities were not interested in Jewish immigration, to say the least, and the parties were the only organizations capable of organizing immigration and resettlement.

After 1948 the new Israeli government began to assume many of the tasks connected with immigration, but it was not until 20 years later that a ministry for immigration was established. The role of the parties faded, but has not disappeared. They have changed their tactics of political recruitment and seem to have adapted gracefully to the changing times. On the other hand, the nongovernmental Jewish Agency, long the instrument of the parties, has fought very hard and quite successfully to keep its role in immigrant affairs and has not reconciled itself to a division of labor with the Ministry for Immigrant Absorption, whose very existence it opposes. This bureaucratic struggle has not redounded to the immigrants' benefit, but there is probably no other country in the world that gives the immigrant more special considerations than Israel. Though one hears many complaints about the ways in which immigrants are treated by the resettlement bureaucracy, complaints that to the outsider often seem justified, the fact remains that this resource-poor country whose security is constantly in doubt has managed to attract millions of immigrants. True, many had no other place to go and many others came to Israel only because it is a Jewish state, not because life is easier than elsewhere, but the absorption of so many different kinds of people under conditions of constant stress must be ranked as one of the contry's outstanding achievements.

Our concern has been generally with Israel's migration and resettlement system and policies, and specifically with a particular group of immigrants. Because we believe that the ultimate outcome of an immigration process is the resultant of interaction between the sending society, the immigrants, and the host society, we have described in some detail the evolution and current operation of Israeli resettlement procedures, particularly as regards political absorption, which we see as a process of political resocialization. For the same reason, we analyzed the circumstances surrounding the decisions made by the subjects of the study to leave the United States and the USSR in the 1960s and 1970s, especially those that are likely to affect the immigrants' political outlooks generally, and in their new homes in particular. In the Soviet case, this meant an examination of the struggle between potential emigrés and a reluctant government that has been forced to evolve emigration policies, as yet not made explicit. Thus we have touched on all three areas identified by Tomas Hammar as the major ones for political analysis of migration: migration policies, the political outlooks and behavior of the migrants themselves, and the process of political resocialization of immigrants.

The last has been treated as an open question: Are immigrants, in fact, resocialized politically, or do they remain outside the political arena? If they are resocialized, is it only on the level of outward behavior, while the fundamental political *weltanschauung* remains unchanged, a product of the political culture of the "old country?" What remains, if anything, of their former political cultures if they are resocialized into a new one? If there is, indeed, a process of resocialization going on, who are its "agents"? These questions are part of a larger one that should be of interest to all students of socialization and of political change: Are political values, beliefs, and behavior patterns established in childhood once and for all, or do the environment and events make such an impact on adults that what has been learned early in political life can be "unlearned" later on? Although immigration is a special case of adult resocialization, not experienced by most people, there are important lessons to be learned from it. There are, after all, millions of immigrants all over the world, let alone internal migrants, so that physical movement is a common adult experience that may affect political life. Moreover, it can be argued that the study of immigration can at least provide a partial answer to the question of the "primary principle's" validity. It can indicate whether under certain not altogether unusual circumstances this principle obtains, or whether the political cultures of adults are more malleable than might be supposed.

The group of immigrants to Israel that we have studied are Soviet and American males who resemble each other on several important dimensions, so that differences that appear between them on political matters could more legitimately be ascribed to variables on which the two groups differ. In 1972, 202 immigrants were interviewed personally, and 108 of them were reinterviewed three years later. Thus we could trace changes in outlook and behavior during the first few years of the immigrants' residence in Israel. As much information as possible was gathered about those who had left the country, and their 1972 responses to our questions were compared to those of the people who were reinterviewed. In addition, a thorough search was made of other studies of immigrant political resocialization, immigrant resocialization in Israel, and, especially, of Soviet and American immigrants in Israel. We were fortunate to have access to a political survey of Soviet immigrants conducted before the 1973 election, and since some of the questions in that study were the same as ours, the results of each could be compared. The differences between our more highly educated and ethnically homogeneous group and the group studied in 1973 point to the importance of education and regional political cultures in determining how an immigrant will perceive the political world and act in it.

The major conclusion of this book is that immigrants do undergo a process of political resocialization. However, this process affects attitudes toward specific issues most, abstract political ideas less, and fundamental orientations to politics least. Second, for relatively educated, economically self-sufficient immigrants there is no single agent of political resocialization. To no less a degree than veteran settlers, and in contrast to earlier immigrants, the Soviet and American immigrants of the 1970s make thoughtful and deliberate political choices. Third, to the extent that immigrants involve themselves in Israeli social, cultural, and economic life, so too do they enter the political arena, though they are slow to attain positions of leadership.

Our group of informants had, indeed, experienced political resocialization. Between 1973 and 1975 they had changed some of their political outlooks and behavior. Those reinterviewed in 1975 displayed a greater interest in and knowledge of Israeli politics already in 1972 than those who could not be located in 1975. The group reinterviewed in 1975 also scored significantly higher on our measure of general integration into Israeli society. Over the course of three years the immigrants increased their knowledge of Israeli politics considerably, especially those who came to Israel with a weak Jewish background and little knowledge of the Israeli system. Their lag behind the others was wiped out almost completely by 1975. In other respects, however, the background the immigrants acquired in their home countries continued to influence their political perceptions and behavior, even three to seven years after their resettlement in Israel.

Specifically, in our group fundamental orientations to politics changed least over three years, some abstract political concepts changed more, and attitudes on specific issues and policies were most changeable. The fundamental orientations we inquired about were attitudes toward authority, political efficacy, and trust. Attitudes toward authority appear to be the most stable of the three, and there are sharp contrasts here, as there are on most other orientations and concepts, between the American and Soviet immigrants. In light of their antecedent political cultures, we were not surprised to find Soviet immigrants more favorably disposed to governmental authority and involvement than the Americans. There was greater variation in the immigrants' feelings of political efficacy. The efficacy of the Soviets rose in the course of three years, as they became more familiar with the new system, but the Americans, explicitly expressing their feeling that "the system" was hard to influence, did not move in the same direction. There is strong evidence that feelings of efficacy are a function of both the immediate political environment and of personality alone. Two people in the very same political environment, and with similar socioeconomic and cultural characteristics, may well display different levels of efficacy, indicating that this is partially a matter of personality. Our evidence supports the idea that efficacy has a second component, one that comes as a rational response to a specific political environment. As the Soviet immigrant learns the language, understands the system, and begins to see its possibilities, his sense of efficacy rises. In fact, already in 1972 those who had made a better overall adjustment to the system felt more efficacious. The American immigrant, on the other hand, felt less efficacious over the first few years in Israel and seemed frustrated by the proportional representation system. Feelings of trust among both groups of immigrants did not change much over the years, but it was difficult to separate out the impact of outlooks acquired in the United States or the USSR from that made by experience in Israel. In this case, Israeli experiences may be simply reinforcing previously acquired beliefs about how much one can trust another, but some immigrants did distinguish between the two societies with which they were familiar.

Socialism, social class, and freedom were the political concepts discussed with the newcomers. The Soviets were quite befuddled regarding the meaning of socialism, despite the fact that it is a word they had grown up with. Their puzzlement decreased over three years when they apparently sorted out the multiple contradictions between the Soviet and Israeli views of socialism and Soviet and Israeli realities. There was still a very wide range of opinion on what socialism meant. There was more similarity between Soviets and Americans on social class than on the other subjects. It is evident that even in the USSR our informants had conceptions of the class structure of society that were at considerable variance from the official, widely known conception. This gap between official and popular perceptions of class structure has been observed in other Marxist-Leninist systems as well. By 1975 the components that made up social class were seen rather similarly by Soviet and American informants.

On conceptions of freedom, however, Soviet and American interviewees differed sharply, reflecting the dominant values of their previous political cultures. In many cases, what is "freedom" to Americans is "anarchy" to people from the USSR. As on most other issues, the differences between those who had come from the Western peripheries of the USSR (the Zapadniki) and those who came from the three Slavic republics (heartlanders) were not very great, or were narrowed between 1972 and 1975. There were very distinct differences between the two groups in Jewish background, education, and occupation, and these were reflected, especially in 1972, in matters pertaining to Israeli politics and society. The initial advantage enjoyed by the more knowledgeable Zapadniki, many of whom had been in the country somewhat longer than the others, were eliminated by 1975. However, the Zapadniki, who included almost all the workers in the group, showed greater sympathy for the then-ruling Labor party than the heartlanders, mostly professionals, whose sentiments were for Gahal (Likud). This difference may be explained not only by class, occupational, and organizational dissimilarities among the two groups, but also by the different expectations each has of Israel. The Zapadniki, coming from areas that 40 years ago had large and flourishing Jewish communities, saw Israel as the re-creation of the Jewish life obliterated by the Nazis. The heartlanders, who had not known a free Jewish culture for three and four generations, tended more to abstract, highly ideological conceptions of Zionism, and hence of Israel, and the more ideological and militant program of the Likud was closer to the conceptions they had formed while still in the USSR.

One observes the most change in the immigrants' preferences on the salient issues of policy toward Arabs and toward territories occupied after the 1967 War. Our group was well informed on these issues. Positions taken on them are consistent with those taken on other issues, as well as with the partisan sympathies that many of the immigrants profess. The 1973 War decisively influenced attitudes on these issues, with the general trend being toward greater willingness to give up *some* of the territories in return for some peace agreements. At the same time, like the Israeli population in general, the immigrants were influenced by the war to turn away from Labor and toward Gahal (Likud). Although Gahal was less willing to negotiate territories, it did turn out to be the party in power in 1979 when the Israeli government agreed to return the Sinai to Egypt in return for a peace agreement.

The respondents in the Israeli electoral study, especially the Georgians among them, were less politically interested and aware than those in our group, and education seemed to be the major variable explaining the differences. On the issues of Arabs and the occupied territories the respondents in the electoral study had less interest and less clear cut positions, although they, too, may have changed their outlooks after the October War.

The common assumption is that the kinds of changes we have observed are the product of "resocialization," and if such a process is going on there must be agents of resocialization. Our survey of the political resocialization process in Israeli history identified such agents in the past: party functionaries, youth leaders, agricultural instructors, military officers, teachers, and so on. Who are the agents of resocialization for today's adult immigrants? We examined the roles of the media, organizations, and individuals, but did not succeed in uncovering the detailed steps by which the immigrant is inducted into the new political culture and, specifically, to partisan loyalties. As intelligent, educated people, our informants have a critical and selective attitude toward the media, though after some time in the country they are quite attentive to it. Our impression is that for this group of immigrants, individuals playing explicit resocializing roles were not effective agents. That is, though individuals may have been instrumental in reshaping immigrants' outlooks on political matters, these were probably not official representatives of parties or movements, but rather chance acquaintances. Unlike earlier decades, there is now no role or office that could be identified as the one linking the immigrant to the system or recruiting the immigrant to it. Neither could organizations be said to play this role. True, those involved in the Soviet immigrant association tended to higher political consciousness than the others and were more likely to identify with a party. The association may serve as a kind of school for political involvement, though it is equally plausible to suppose that those who are already politically inclined will join and become active in the association, for this is the most natural first framework for their activities. The Histadrut, while not a major instrument of political recruitment or activation, does seem to have the effect it has in the Israeli population generally: Its members are more likely than others to sympathize with the Labor party. Since all workers are members of the Histadrut, it is hard to know how much of a role the trade union actually has in developing Labor loyalty. The parties, their role in immigration greatly diminished, still maintain departments whose latent function is immigrant recruitment, but only the largest have attempted to reach out to the Soviet and American immigrants generally. The parties do not see the Americans as promising recruits, and the Americans are suspicious of the European-style parties they find in Israel, preferring the American type of party and its political style. As the largest immigrant group, the Soviets are the most tempting target for the parties, but the smaller parties see only narrowly defined segments of the Soviet immigration as potential recruits. The two largest parties compete intensely for the loyalty of the immigrants, but neither has promoted a Soviet immigrant to a high party position nor nominated one to a realistic place on their electoral lists.

In our group, identification with and membership in parties reached the same proportions it does among the Israeli population generally. Curiously, it did not increase with time. Those who were partisans became so within a short time after their arrival, and relatively few moved to identify with a party as the years went on. Political interest and knowledge did increase with time, but in our group between 1972 and 1975 there was no appreciable increase in partisanship. In the same period those who did express their support of a party shifted to the political right, joining a trend discernible among the general electorate since 1969. The popular notion that Soviet immigrants are disproportionately Gahal supporters did not hold true in 1972 among our group, nor among those surveyed shortly before the 1973 elections. Their recollection of their votes in 1973, as well as their stated preferences in 1975, showed that our group had moved decisively from Labor to the Likud (formerly Gahal) after the Yom Kippur War. The national elections of 1973 and 1977 showed that in this respect they were in tune with the rest of the country, though by 1981 Likud's appeal had been diminished after its four years in power.

Partisan identification cannot be explained easily on class grounds, nor on the basis of organizational involvement, though both factors appear to have some influence. It is quite clear that there is a positive relationship between overall integration into Israeli society and partisan identification. Partisanship is not an expression of discontent and of protest, but is associated with satisfaction and involvement with life in the new country. Even those who supported what was in 1972-75 the main opposition party, Gahal (Likud), were not the alienated or the disappointed. True, Labor identifiers scored highest on integration, but Gahal supporters were not far behind. It was those who identified with the minor parties, or, especially, with no party at all, who were the least contented, the most likely to leave Israel.

The group we followed over three years did, then, enter the Israeli political system to the same degree that it became involved with Israeli society generally. Political resocialization, while it might appear lower on the priority list of both host society and immigrant, is part of the process of general desocialization/resocialization. The immigrant who is not much touched by the general process, who remains an outsider, an alien in his adopted land, remains outside the political system as well, and does not appear even to use it in order to express his frustrations. The Soviet and American immigrants who remained in the country in 1975 became more like most other Jewish Israelis in their language, cultural habits, and social contacts, and they came to resemble the general population in politics as well. This was not because they were manipulable dependents, but as thinking, independent individuals they considered the issues of the day, issues that affected them directly, and selected parties whose positions matched their own, learning an impressive amount about the political life of the country. For the Soviets it was a country that none had seen before they arrived as immigrants, who had almost no possibility of turning back, and one whose political ideology and system had been reviled and ridiculed in the Soviet media. They came to Israel not knowing the language, let alone the workings of the political system, but after three to seven years they were able to discuss the major issues and personalities, and some of them took an active part in the political process. Some groups, such as the Georgians, chose to remain enclosed in their ethnic circle and to participate less in the political life of the country. This was not a function of education alone, but of preferences. After all, highly educated Americans who were quite knowledgeable about the system were less inclined to take an active part in it than European Soviets with similar demographic characteristics. The Americans tended to cling more to the system that formed them, a system that few of them renounced and in whose fate most remained deeply interested. They assumed that their way was the better one, and if this put them apart from the mainstream of Israeli society, so much the worse for the latter. Secure in their material status and in the knowledge that they could "go back," they could afford to stay on the margins of the political system and to regard it with detached interest, or even amusement or disgust.

Since not even the Georgians seemed to have been manipulated by the system, we wonder whether the picture we presented of the early state period might not have been overdrawn. Not having observed immigrant resocialization at the time, and drawing on the literature by those who had, may have distorted the picture somewhat. After all, it is always tempting to highlight the amusing situations, the slightly crooked and crafty characters who inhabit any political system, and to downplay the less dramatic, but perhaps more typical, routine processes whereby citizens are made. Unquestionably, the Israeli system of immigrant resocialization, like those elsewhere, involved complementary relationships of dependence and manipulation, "going along" and paternalism. However, one must ask, in Leninist fashion, *kto-kogo*? Who was manipulating whom? In fact, is manipulation the correct term? What was going on was an exchange. The immigrants were trading their meager resources, in this case a vote, for things they needed — licenses, permits, housing, jobs, favors. Even on this level the process of political resocialization is not one in which the newcomer is simply an object to be manipulated, but one in which resources are exchanged between rational actors. Moreover, it is not only possible, but entirely likely, that even some impoverished newcomers made their political choices in conformity with ideas and ideals, not simply material or other needs of the moment. Certainly our group, still dependent on the state no matter their economic and educational standing, seems to be making its political choices in this way. In Israel, at least, immigrants do not have to sit on the sidelines watching the political fray and hoping that at least their children will be allowed to play the game. It is a society of immigrants that exists for immigrants. Sometimes this is forgotten, not only by the ordinary citizen, but even by the official whose responsibility it is to deal directly with the newcomers. It is a country, however, where Jews become citizens in a few months, if they wish to, unlike other countries where most newcomers can either never become citizens or must wait several years before doing so. This is not a meaningless formality, because, as this study has concluded, the immigrant who so wishes can become a politically active citizen in a very short time.

This is not to say that the immigrant easily becomes the political equal of the veteran Israeli. Political leadership in Israel is usually attained by a slow climb up the political ladder from the lowest rungs of local politics. Lateral movement into leadership positions is rare, the exceptional case being the victorious generals and colonels of the 1967 War. None of the leaders of the Jewish aliyah movement in the USSR has become a political leader in Israel. Some did not aspire to political leadership and turned to their original vocations as soon as they could. Others' aspirations were stymied by their complete unfamiliarity with the workings of Western political systems, the traditions of the Israeli one, and the natural reluctance of those who themselves are trying to find room at the top to yield their hard-won gains to newcomers. Soviet immigrants, like their Middle Eastern and North African predecessors, will undoubtedly work their way up the ladder, and probably more rapidly than the others did, but their ascent will be measured in years. American immigrants are unlikely to even try to climb the ladder. Those who are politically active tend toward reformism and fall back on American patterns of group mobilization and public campaigns, eschewing the less public and more painstaking methods of working from within the parties of the establishment. A few Americans have become active in the smaller parties that lie outside the establishment, and these are unlikely vehicles to power.

In recent years there have been a few gestures in the direction of cultural pluralism, including changes in school curricula to bring out the cultural heritage of Sefardim, ethnic festivals, and attempts to revive authentic folk dances and music; but the dominant ethos remains the melting pot. In their eagerness to fix permanently Israel's character as a Hebrew-speaking, Western state with a modern economy and a European-oriented culture, the founding fathers tried to obliterate other languages, denigrated the Afro-Asian cultures brought in by thousands of immigrants, and discouraged the pursuit of some traditional occupations. In this they succeeded, perhaps all too well. Hebrew is by far the dominant language of the Jewish population, Israel belongs culturally more to Europe than to the Levant, and the great majority have been absorbed into modern industry and agriculture. Afro-Asian and European Jewish traditions have been the objects of derision or benign neglect, but residential segregation and the insistence by minorities on preserving their traditions have produced a cultural pattern in Israel that resembles a mosaic rather than a surface of uniform coloration. There is an overall unity, but it is made up of many identifiable components. Dress and language have become nearly uniform and there is a steady increase in marriages between people of different origins and cultures, but cultural tastes and styles remain distinguishable. Both the Soviet Union and the United States have found that the melting pot, even when it is a pressure cooker, does not easily reduce its ingredients to a uniform mass. Immigrants from those countries, people who did not lose their special identities in their birthplaces, are now firmly embedded in the mosaic of Israeli society and politics.

APPENDIXES

APPENDIX A

INDEX OF JEWISH BACKGROUND

This is composed from three variables, measuring the respondent's assessment of the Jewish atmosphere in his parents' home, his parents' native language, and his own native language. The responses were arranged to give scores ranging from "low" to "high".

APPENDIX B

LEVELS OF POLITICAL INFORMATION

The index of political information includes questions about the decision-making mechanisms of the Israeli government, how many national leaders were named and correctly identified with their parties, how many Israeli parties the respondent could name, who are the leaders of the Labor and Likud parties, and on what issues the two parties differ. Scores were given for each answer, and a total score was computed for each respondent and categorized from "low" to "high."

APPENDIX C

INDEX OF INTEGRATION — 1972/75 STUDY

Shuval and Markus argue that the process of integration into a new society is multidimensional, that there are many ways by which an immigrant can enter a new social system. Hence, one should not seek a single overall concept or measure of integration. While accepting this premise, we have constructed a summary score that includes many possible dimensions of integration. Thus, if an immigrant scores poorly on one measure — say, social contact with Israelis — he may score very well on another — say, attentiveness to Hebrew-language media. Making the assumption that there is no single "key" to integration, we feel that success in one sphere may compensate for failure (perhaps temporary) in another. Therefore, we feel justified in adding up the scores on all the measures we use to give a composite picture of "integration," which really means involvement with Israeli people, institutions, the media, culture, the economy, and the political system, as well as the immigrants' own evaluation of their satisfaction with life in Israel. The fact that the index worked so well in predicting whether or not the 1972 interviewees would stay in Israel gives us confidence in the measure.

Variables in the measure focusing on "subjective" integration include whether one feels Russian/American or Israeli, whether one feels himself a new immigrant, whether expectations have been fulfilled, where one sees oneself living in five years, whether Israelis or immigrants are preferred as friends, whether immigrants should adopt Israeli ways. Variables of an "objective" nature include whether or not one is politically and organizationally aware and involved (voting, joining, and participating) the extent of exposure to mass media, whether that exposure is primarily in Hebrew or not, whether one is employed, and whether or not one is an Israeli citizen.

Answers were scored from "high" to "low," with each "high," "medium," and "low" answer being assigned the same numerical value. The sum of all the values is the "integration score" of the individual.

APPENDIX D

INDEX OF INTEGRATION, ISRAELI ELECTION STUDY

The index was composed in the same way as the one for the 1972/75 study. It consists of 12 variables: feeling oneself Israeli, language of radio listening, language of TV viewing, frequency of newspaper reading, membership in the Histadrut, interest in Knesset elections, knowledge of ministers of defense, education, foreign affairs, and police, intention to vote in elections, and general satisfaction in Israel. Each answer was scored for each respondent and a total score was arrived at for each respondent. Scores were then grouped in categories, from "low" to "high."

APPENDIX E

INDEX OF POLITICAL EFFICACY

This index was constructed from four statements with which the respondent was asked to agree or disagree: "Some people say that people's votes don't really change public policy"; "People like you and me have no say about what the government does"; "Some say that politicians tend not to consider the opinion of the man in the street"; "Sometimes government and politics seem so complicated that a person like me can't really understand what's going on." Answers ranged from "completely agree" to "completely disagree." Strong agreement was taken as an indication of low political efficacy. The responses to each question were scored from "low" to "high" and each person's responses were cumulated to give a total "efficacy score."

APPENDIX F

INDEX OF INTEREST IN POLITICS – 1972/75 STUDY

This summary measure is composed of five questions: "To what degree is it important to you to understand political problems in Israel?" "To what degree is it important to you to understand the position of the various parties on political problems?" "To what degree is it important to you to give your children a political education?"

357

"To what degree is it important to you to express your opinion on political matters?" [These four questions were coded as follows: (1) to a considerable degree, (2) to some degree, (3) to a small degree, (4) not at all, (5) don't know, no answer.] "What interests you most in the newspapers or on radio/TV?" (1) economic news; (2) sports; (3) foreign news; (4) Israeli politics; (7) other; (9) don't know; no answer. Code 1 of the first four questions was given the "high" value of 3, code 2 was given a value of 2, code 3 a value of 1, and codes 4 and 5 a value of 0. For the fifth question, code 4 was given a value of 4, code 1 of 3, code 3 of 2, code 2 of 1, and codes 7 and 9 of 0. The scores of each respondent were then added, so that the highest score of political interest would be 16. Scores of 1-5 were classified as "low interest," 6-10 as "medium," and 11-16 as "high."

APPENDIX G

INDEX OF INTEREST IN POLITICS – ISRAELI ELECTION STUDY

This summary measure is composed of seven variables, four of them identical to questions from the 1972/75 study. The other three were: (A) "Do you generally discuss political matters with your family?" (1) a great deal; (2) some; (3) a bit; (4) not at all; (9) don't know, no answer. (B) "Do you intend to participate in the forthcoming national election?" (1) yes; (2) no; (3) don't know, no answer. (C) "Would you like to get explanations of elections and parties in Israel?" (1) yes; (2) no; (3) don't know, no answer. Each variable's codes were grouped into "low, medium, high" categories, since some were dichotomous and others not. All "high" scores were then given a value of 5, all medium of 3, and all low of 1. Scores were then calculated for individuals and the total scores were arranged in "low, medium, high" categories, with "low" encompassing total scores up to 12, "medium" from 13-24, and "high" from 25-35.

INDEX

ABOUT THE AUTHOR

ZVI GITELMAN is Professor of Political Science and Director of the Center for Russian and East European Studies at The University of Michigan, Ann Arbor. He has written widely on the subject of Soviet and East European politics and Israeli politics. He is the author of *Jewish Nationality and Soviet Politics* and coauthor of *Public Opinion in European Socialist Systems* (with Walter Connor, Praeger, 1977) and of *East-West Relations and the Future of Eastern Europe* (with Morris Bornstein and William Zimmerman). His articles and reviews have appeared in *Problems of Communism*, *Journal of Politics*, *Comparative Politics*, *Studies in Comparative Communism*, *Soviet Studies*, and other journals.

Educated at Columbia University, where he received his B.A., M.A., and Ph.D. degrees, Dr. Gitelman also holds a B.H.L. from The Jewish Theological Seminary. He has taught at Columbia College and has been a visiting professor at Tel Aviv University, The City College, and the YIVO Institute for Jewish Research.